THE PICADOR BOOK OF

Latin American Stories

CARLOS FUENTES was born in Mexico in 1928. He is the author of more than a dozen novels, as well as numerous short stories, plays, literary and political essays and articles. Among the prizes he has been awarded are Mexico's National Prize for Literature in 1984 and the 1987 Miguel de Cervantes Prize for Literature from Spain – the highest award bestowed on a Spanish language writer. He served as Mexico's ambassador to France from 1974 to 1977. In 1986–7 he was the Robert F. Kennedy Professor of Latin American Studies at Harvard University and in 1988 he held the Simón Bolívar Chair at Cambridge University. Carlos Fuentes divides his time between Mexico City and London.

JULIO ORTEGA was born in Peru in 1942. He is the author of several works of literary criticism including *Poetics of Change, The New Spanish-American Narrative* (1984), *Gabriel García Márquez and the Powers of Fiction* (1988) and *El principio radical de lo nuevo* (1997). He has held the Simón Bolívar Chair at Cambridge University and is currently professor and chairman of Hispanic Studies at Brown University.

THE PICADOR BOOK OF

Latin American Stories

Edited by Carlos Fuentes and Julio Ortega

PICADOR

First published 1998 by Picador

This edition published 1999 by Picador
an imprint of Macmillan Publishers Ltd
25 Eccleston Place, London SW1W 9NF
Basingstoke and Oxford
Associated companies throughout the world
www.macmillan.co.uk

ISBN 0 330 33955 0

College 752
Nov 99
£8.99

Contents

Contents

Acknowledgements

We are grateful to the authors or their families for their help in compiling this book. In many cases we were able to discuss with the authors themselves our choices and their translations. As this book emphasizes the innovative quality of the Latin American short story, we focused less on national or standard criteria and more on the new and more imaginative trends in literature. We would like to thank those many colleagues and friends from Latin America who provided suggestions and texts.

Special thanks are for Mary Mount for her dedicated help with the manuscript.

JO *and* CF

The Storyteller

Carlos Fuentes

The novel is an ocean liner. The short story, a sailboat hugging the coast. An Olympic team is required to write a novel. Singular as he or she may seem, the novelist is a team of painters, city planners, gossip columnists, fashion experts, architects and set designers; a justice of the peace, a real estate agent, midwife, undertaker; a witch and a high priest, all in one.

The short-story writer on the contrary is a lonely navigator. Why this fidelity to solitude? Why this need to be in sight of the coast? Perhaps because the storytellers know that if they do not tell the tale this very night, near the shore, with no time to cross the ocean, there might be no tomorrow. Every storyteller is a child of Scheherazade, in a hurry to tell the tale so that death may be postponed one more time.

As in the Arabian nights, urgency and brevity embrace in the short story. But brevity does not exclude depth or impose certifiable measures. The short story is not a pigmy novel. It is an object with its own totality, integrity and beauty. It has its own epiphany, but not the revelation to be found in the exceptional instants of Proust or Joyce. The short story has to reveal its beauty, its meaning, its intensity, almost instantaneously; visible, as Sean O'Faolain says, like a child's kite in the sky, 'a small wonder, a brief, bright moment'.

Yet the response to the short story as a postponement of death can be as varied as Gogol's, from whose humble *Overcoat*'s pockets came the million and one pages of the Russian novel; as Poe's, for whom the preconceived 'effect' or 'design' was the principle of composition, or Chekhov's, for whom a short story was a rush of satellite figures rapidly displaced by the one central character, the 'sun' of the story.

The Latin American short story is not alien to any of these preoccupations. All of the major currents of the Latin American novel have been reflected or even forecast in its short stories. Cosmopolitanism, surrealism, naturalism, regionalism, the Indian, peasant and urban worlds, have all made their appearance in our short stories. Yet these are not hermetically sealed-off styles. Each one is constantly invading the other. One of the sires of the modern Latin American short story, the Uruguayan Horacio Quiroga (1878–1937), sets his tales in the jungle territories of Misiones, but his characters fall prey less to an overwhelming, inhuman nature, as in the realistic novels of the Colombian José Eustasio Rivera (1889–1928) or the Venezuelan Rómulo Gallegos (1884–1969), but more to quite recognizable modern and urban ailments: fear, derangement, alienation, loneliness, suicide … Conversely, a city-writer such as the Argentinian Roberto Arlt (1900–1942) convincingly depicts Buenos Aires as a savage jungle where people are as senselessly cruel as a boa, a panther or a piranha.

The new Latin American society, present in the Picador anthology as a dying or nascent, yet always actual, community, continues as it can not fail to do (even when breaking with them) these opposing yet complementary traditions of our past fictions. And with good reason: the former separation between town and village, city mouse and country mouse, has been quickly deteriorating as the majority of Latin Americans now live in large metropolitan areas. Rio de Janeiro, Mexico City, Lima, Caracas, or Bogotá are sprawling capitals receiving thousands of peasants each day, torn from their villages by civil war, terrorism, hunger, fallow lands or brittle illusions about city life. They end up, very often, living in garbage dumps, sewers, or the gigantic shanty-towns known as *favelas* in Brazil, *cayampas* in Chile, *ranchos* in Venezuela, or, literally, lost cities, *ciudades perdidas*, in Mexico.

The sheer weight of social problems and quickened change in Latin America have effected and will affect our writing, but will not absolve us from the demand of shaping, giving form, giving speech and imagination, *to* our societies. The political urge manifest in many Latin American writers is explainable: we are citizens and legitimately act as such. But as writers, our contribution to society lies less in political action or thematic 'correctness' than in the two social needs that a writer is best prepared to fulfil: language and imagination. Deprive a society of its words or its memory, of its speech or its desires, and you are easy prey to false illusions, providential leaderships and other traditional ills of the Latin American polity.

Which is one of the reasons why writing and publishing and reading literature are so important in a world such as Latin America. In the midst of our turmoils we yearn for the epiphany, Joyce's sudden spiritual manifestation born from the most ordinary of speeches and gestures; we must dunk our madeleine in tea. But whereas in Joyce or Proust the epiphany – the fugitive moments of authentic self-knowledge – appears suddenly and exceptionally, immersed, as it were, in a vast ocean of narration, in the short story the epiphany must coincide with the very time of the tale; it must be simultaneous, in other words, with the tale itself. The Mexican Juan Rulfo, the Colombian Gabriel García Márquez, or the Brazilian Clarice

Lispector, perfectly exemplify this coincidence of the epiphany, the exceptional spiritual or anecedotal moment, that occurs alongside the story itself.

Yet whatever the stress we wish to put on a Latin American – or, for that matter, North American, European, Asian or Asiatic – short story as it addresses society or the soul, both the community and the individual's tales require a form, a valid aesthetic approach, a fidelity to the tradition from which the story springs and to which it contributes, a vessel so that its shape can both contain itself and sail forth, hugging the shore and postponing the Caliph's sentence of death.

The responses to the short story as a postponement of death can, indeed, be as varied as Gogol's, Poe's or Chekhov's. But when it comes to Latin America, I like to keep in mind the lessons of two great masters, the Argentineans Julio Cortázar and Jorge Luis Borges.

Cortázar translated the complete works of Poe into Spanish and was keenly aware of the American's mandate for immediate effect in the tale. Cortázar excelled in giving his stories a sense of immediate sensation. The visitor to an aquarium discovers his own face in that of an axolotl, the swimming dark salamander in a perpetual larval state but with an eerily human face. An Aztec being sacrificed in a pyramid dreams that he is being operated on in a modern hospital where a man being operated on dreams that he is being sacrificed on top of a pyramid. A house is taken over, inch by inch, by invisible forces.

In Cortázar, the stories are discreet units, closed in on themselves.

Borges, on the contrary, conceives stories that open into other stories, creating interrelated narrative constellations. His whole work is, as he titled an emblematic story, 'a garden of forking paths'. His literature is made of great themes that disguise one another, like the mythical cities of 'Tlon, Uqbar and Orbis Tertius', hidden behind the screens of time, sustained by memory and created only by language. The story of 'Pierre Menard, the Author of Don Quixote', is the greatest example we have of this art of prolonging through concealment.

Menard, a minor notary in the French provinces, decides to rewrite Cervantes's novel. But all he does is copy it, word for word. Yet the work is new because, in rewriting *Don Quixote*, Menard has taught us to read *Don Quixote* in a new way, with everything that happened between the publication of the novel in 1605 and the present-day reading creating a wholly new context for the narrative. Borges reveals, through this technique, that the past has its own novelty and that the next reader of *Don Quixote* will also be its newest reader.

Granted the formal and thematic variety of the short-story writers in

The Storyteller

this volume, I think it is difficult to write in this genre in Latin America without remembering Borges and Cortázar. One writes, like Cortázar, discreetly, each story a self-contained unity, or indiscreetly, each story harking back and forth to other tales, told or untold. But whether you belong to the family of Cortázar or to that of Borges you are, at the same time, expected to construct your stories in one of two ways: in either a 'realistic' or a 'fantastic' mode. I, for one, have always tried to avoid this stark choice by recalling the lesson of Balzac and particularly *The Wild Ass's Skin*. The novelist who wished to be the public notary of French social classes 'carried a whole society' in his head, but also carried ghosts, myths, fears, unexplainable occurrences and a wild ass's skin that fulfils your desires but shrinks every time it gives, until, at the end, it takes life from the hapless owner and disappears.

All stories have, explicitly or implicitly, a fantastic dimension. They try to recapture, or reveal, or anticipate, time. They finally borrow, as Walter Benjamin said, their authority from death. They broaden the field of social behaviour to admit new desires, new demands of both the individual and the collective being. They see human beings as both transparent and enigmatic. They make each one of us – because of our fears because of our violence, because of our love, because of our death – indispensable, unique beings. That is also why so much of our literature is angry. Also, why it is tender and merciful.

Yet, tender, angry or merciful, 'realistic' or 'fantastic', at the end of each story a question must hang over it, a perfume must linger, permitting the story to be complete, but to remain open. After all, if a story is a declaration against death, its author is nothing but a perpetual convalescent.

November 1998

Introduction

Julio Ortega

1999 is the centenary of the birth of Jorge Luis Borges (1899–1986), the great pioneer of the new Latin American short story. Although the short story originated in these countries as a modern form (critical, secular and urban), it was with Borges in the 1940s that it acquired its characteristic fluidity, its inclination to transgress the usual boundaries.

Right from the first sentence a Latin American story distinguishes itself from others by its creative ambition: it presents itself as a brief essay on the radical reorganization of the world. This transformative tendency is poetic rather than prescriptive, wrought with irony, taking pleasure in both structure and storytelling: even catastrophe is depicted as a grandiose spectacle, injustice as boundless absurdity.

One reason for the worldwide impact of Latin American fiction (Borges, Cortázar, García Márquez, Carlos Fuentes, Nélida Piñón) is the diverse, insubordinate and imaginative response it gives to all-encompassing world-views, social overcodification, and norms and regulations.

Two overriding debates about Latin American literature converge in Borges's short stories; firstly, its free interaction with the European cultural tradition and, secondly, the quest for an individual identity within marginal cultures.

Borges was a modernist from a peripheral country who intimated himself with Western knowledge (or at least the *Encyclopaedia Britannica*) and in the process reordered the conventions of literature. He was a great sub-verter of the notion of authority and one of the first to question the dictum of universal truth. He declared that metaphysics was a branch of 'fantastic literature' and that, as Carlos Fuentes has explained, anyone who reads *Don Quixote* rewrites the book himself, transforming it into a completely separate work by his own reading. Borges seems to have held the opinion that peripheral experience leads to a more fragmented and less enclosed national identity, one less fettered and doctrinaire. He once wrote that the European writer exists as a consequence of his national literary tradition, whereas the Latin American writer moves about amongst all traditions, as he likes, with a larger appetite.

The first Latin American short story, 'The Slaughterhouse' by Esteban Echeverría (Argentina, 1805–1851), was already a hybrid form. Written as a political pamphlet against the Rosas dictatorship, the story begins as an account of contemporary customs, continues as a sociological study in marginal city life, carries on as an essay in public morality before finishing as a national allegory representing the ultimate impossibility of a democratic community.

So from its birth the Latin American short story is doubly modern: it is a critical form that questions the social order, but above all it is a new cultural form, made from a dynamic mixture of current voices and events. Effectively urban (often featured in newspapers) the short story sets itself in the present, disputing the sense of future – hence its political nature. 'The Slaughterhouse' wasn't published in the author's lifetime: as, according to its editor, Rosas would have had him killed.

This facet of national parable and tale of the promised modernity is one of the dominant traits of the Latin American short story at the beginning of the twentieth century. Ricardo Palma (Peru, 1833–1919) mixed together history and fiction for his 'traditions', seeing his new form as a true story, part of popular legend and an example of conflicting nationalities. He was also the first to democratize the relationship with the colonial past, transforming it into a familiar, antiheroic and anecdotic narrative. If Echeverría's view of history is one of political tragedy then Palma's is domestic comedy. Borges, in contrast, goes on to represent history as fable: a dream that man relives over and over again in search of his own self. Ultimately the traitor and the hero are one and the same, since it is the roles people play rather than the individuals themselves that account for history. Anyone could have been the traitor, and anyone the hero; they could even be the same person caught between two roles. But this in turn means that, if man is universal and causal, every wicked deed denigrates all of us as much as a good deed redeems us. We are the historical consequence of others. When Borges had to give a literary response to the Perón dictatorship, having been shifted from his job in a library to a post as a municipal poultry inspector, he followed the example of 'The Slaughterhouse' in his sarcastic parody of the prevailing brutality. The story was called 'The Monster's Siesta' and was signed, judiciously, under a pseudonym.

Two great latter-day writers, Julio Cortázar and Gabriel García Márquez, pick up the Borgesian legacy. Cortázar explored the subjective aspect of the fantastic in his tales, tackling the question of an individual's indeterminancy, his unsettled and often unreadable psyche. *One Hundred Years of Solitude* would not have been possible without Borges's 'fictions'. The circular times, the larger role of the reader, and the symmetrical plotting of the fable are all elements of García Márquez's delight in the storytelling.

Cortázar and García Márquez are indeed two of the great practitioners and new masters of the art of the short story in Spanish, but between the two stands a quiet Mexican: Juan Rulfo, the author of a brief volume of stories, *Burning Plain* (1953), and of a single novel, *Pedro Paramo* (1957). Rulfo's world is a moonscape: bare and desolate. Like in one of Beckett's scenes, his characters are either emaciated wretches or eloquent ghosts perpetuating their penury.

Rulfo writes at the end of modern Mexico's history, when the revolution's promises have remained unfulfilled for the majority and poverty and lack of democratic process contradicts the state's rhetoric. Unlike earlier literature there is no longer talk of a new Mexico, reborn and regenerated for 'los de abajo' (the underdogs), but nor indeed does it offer any sort of allegory for Mexico's future. Rather, in Rulfo's work Mexico becomes a linguistic spectre: murmurs from ghosts of the national discourse who wander about telling the stories of their broken narratives and looking somehow for an explanation.

Cortázar approaches the new Latin American short story identifying the pitfalls and cracks in daily life; García Márquez influences the genre with his creative freedom, as if Latin America's future was still a project under construction. Rulfo, in an altogether different way, seems to say that Latin America has ended up in a state of desperate and wholesale destitution, which contradicts the many representations of it as a land of plenty. Any change in that reality is possible only through a rigorous critical eye that can give names to those who have been killed, and bring the guilty to justice through the strength of a language capable of restoring truth and restitution.

In the works of these three major authors who dominated the unbridled innovation in Latin American writing in the 1960s, metaphorical allusions to their countries are substituted for politics of difference (in genre, social cast and 'otherness'). Following on from these and other writers (such as Guimarães Rosa, José María Arguedas, José Lezama Lima), so determined on raising up a sort of cultural map as a source of belonging and futurity, a state of nomadic identity beyond borders is uncovered by recent writers, expanding lines of cultural resistance, openness and reappropriation. Faced with traditional state authoritarianism and more recently with market fundamentalism, which when combined has further fragmented an already divided society, these new writers talk about a life in which joy and endurance are possible, defying all evidence to the contrary. This accounts for a cultural citizenship that has proved able to survive many manners of violence and marginalization. Already in the work of García Márquez legend is the ultimate truth, because communities invent themselves as a collective telling.

Just as the Borgesian dialogue is continued in stories by Alejandro Rossi, Luis Loayza and José Emilio Pacheco, Cortázar's introspection is further developed by Antonio Benítez Rojo, Luisa Valenzuela, José Balza and Alfredo Bryce Echenique. There are also echoes of García Márquez in Salvador Garmendia, Antonio Skármeta and Angeles Mastretta. This is not just an obvious stylistic influence as seen in their paradoxical games, or the exploratory quality of their writing, or indeed magical realism itself, but is a rather more demanding legacy, involving the rich evolution of a radical way of writing, now rooted in the colloquial and with an earthly humour, but always exploring a free open-form.

The history of the contemporary Brazilian short story is no less illustrious. Nélida Piñón and Moacyr Scliar inherit different gifts from Guimarães Rosa's work. Scliar recalls Rosas's spirit of adventure and wandering narrative whereas Nélida Piñón echoes the writer's versatility. These narrators are as much preoccupied with their locality as they are with the universal, and while Guimarães tries to bestow some sort of lucidity in his exploration of a labyrinthine world, Nélida Piñón confronts the feminine experience through myth and Scliar redeems mundane life with poetry. Perhaps it is no coincidence that these three extraordinary storytellers have, in different ways, explored the experience of migration, the legendary realm of the journey and the evolving epic stories of the backlands.

Today the short story is the most popular genre in Latin America, not simply because of its versatility and variety, and the writer's inner vitality, but also due to its place in the modern tradition. It is not just an appealing and engaging saga but also a form of cultural self-reflection. The exceptional deeds of each story draw the reader into the fractures of daily life with humour and blurs its margins, offering a fresh perspective against codified social contexts. The Latin American short story has a unique characteristic of its own, heralded in Borges's 'El Aleph'; one which asks us to look at things always in a new, different order.

Among the most recent authors (Ampuero, Villoro, Fresán) one senses a more acute perception of an uncertain present, a fluid time in which people blindly search for each other in the context of general breakdown, recreating their histories out of dialogue. Before, the story tended towards the need to interpret and analyse, to look at things in a lucid light. Now it seems to call into question the very powers of reading, suggesting that the spaces between the words are as important as the words themselves. The most recent form of the Latin American short story renews its radical tradition of rewriting and questioning; it strives for pertinence. Most recently the short story has been mapping the poetry of daily life, trying not only the exceptional but also the beauty and texture of immediacy.

This anthology is intended to be faithful to this very distinctive form. It is not just meant as an illustration of the historic evolution of a genre; that would be the equivalent of confining it to some museum of literature from which it would escape as some sort of hybrid force. Instead the idea is just the opposite: to convey the dynamic nature of a remarkable body of stories moving both forward into the future and outwards to the reader, engaging and transforming the forum of reading. Unlike other cultural forms, Latin American literature cannot be explained only in historical terms, since it expands and unfolds in the ever changing reinvention of the present moment, expressing an underlying poetry of fluidity and change.

November 1998

Translated by Matt Jameson Evans

Jorge Luis Borges

The Aleph

O God! I could be bounded in a nutshell, and count myself a King
of infinite space . . .

– Hamlet, II, 2

But they will teach us that Eternity is the Standing still of the
Present Time, a *Nunc-stans* (as the Schools call it); which neither
they, nor any else understand, no more than they would a *Hic-stans* for an Infinite greatness of Place.

– Leviathan, IV, 46

On the burning February morning Beatriz Viterbo died, after braving an
agony that never for a single moment gave way to self-pity or fear, I noticed
that the sidewalk billboards around Constitution Plaza were advertising
some new brand or other of American cigarettes. The fact pained me, for I
realized that the wide and ceaseless universe was already slipping away
from her and that this slight change was the first of an endless series. The
universe may change but not me, I thought with a certain sad vanity. I
knew that at times my fruitless devotion had annoyed her; now that she
was dead, I could devote myself to her memory, without hope but also
without humiliation. I recalled that the thirtieth of April was her birthday;
on that day to visit her house on Garay Street and pay my respects to her
father and to Carlos Argentino Daneri, her first cousin, would be an
irreproachable and perhaps unavoidable act of politeness. Once again I
would wait in the twilight of the small, cluttered drawing room, once again
I would study the details of her many photographs: Beatriz Viterbo in
profile and in full colour; Beatriz wearing a mask, during the Carnival of
1921; Beatriz at her First Communion; Beatriz on the day of her wedding to
Roberto Alessandri; Beatriz soon after her divorce, at a luncheon at the Turf
Club; Beatriz at a seaside resort in Quilmes with Delia San Marco Porcel
and Carlos Argentino; Beatriz with the Pekinese lapdog given her by
Villegas Haedo; Beatriz, front and three-quarter views, smiling, hand on her
chin . . . I would not be forced, as in the past, to justify my presence with

modest offerings of books – books whose pages I finally learned to cut beforehand, so as not to find out, months later, that they lay around unopened.

Beatriz Viterbo died in 1929. From that time on, I never let a thirtieth of April go by without a visit to her house. I used to make my appearance at seven-fifteen sharp and stay on for some twenty-five minutes. Each year, I arrived a little later and stayed a little longer. In 1933, a torrential downpour coming to my aid, they were obliged to ask me to dinner. Naturally, I took advantage of that lucky precedent. In 1934, I arrived, just after eight, with one of those large Santa Fe sugared cakes, and quite matter-of-factly I stayed to dinner. It was in this way, on these melancholy and vainly erotic anniversaries, that I came into the gradual confidences of Carlos Argentino Daneri.

Beatriz had been tall, frail, slightly stooped; in her walk there was (if the oxymoron may be allowed) a kind of uncertain grace, a hint of expectancy. Carlos Argentino was pink-faced, overweight, grey-haired, fine-featured. He held a minor position in an unreadable library out on the edge of the Southside of Buenos Aires. He was authoritarian but also unimpressive. Until only recently, he took advantage of his nights and holidays to stay at home. At a remove of two generations, the Italian 'S' and demonstrative Italian gestures still survived in him. His mental activity was continuous, deeply felt, far-ranging, and – all in all – meaningless. He dealt in pointless analogies and in trivial scruples. He had (as did Beatriz) large, beautiful, finely shaped hands. For several months he seemed to be obsessed with Paul Fort – less with his ballads than with the idea of a towering reputation. 'He is the Prince of poets,' Daneri would repeat fatuously. 'You will belittle him in vain – but no, not even the most venomous of your shafts will graze him.'

On the thirtieth of April, 1941, along with the sugared cake I allowed myself to add a bottle of Argentine cognac. Carlos Argentino tasted it, pronounced it 'interesting', and, after a few drinks, launched into a glorification of modern man.

'I view him,' he said with a certain unaccountable excitement, 'in his inner sanctum, as though in his castle tower, supplied with telephones, telegraphs, phonographs, wireless sets, motion-picture screens, slide projectors, glossaries, timetables, handbooks, bulletins . . .'

He remarked that for a man so equipped, actual travel was superfluous. Our twentieth century had inverted the story of Mohammed and the mountain; nowadays, the mountain came to the modern Mohammed.

So foolish did his ideas seem to me, so pompous and so drawn out his exposition, that I linked them at once to literature and asked him why he didn't write them down. As might be foreseen, he answered that he had already done so – that these ideas, and others no less striking, had found their place in the Proem, or Augural Canto, or, more simply, the Prologue Canto of the poem on which he had been working for many years now, alone, without publicity, without fanfare, supported only by those twin staffs universally known as work and solitude. First, he said, he opened the floodgates of his fancy; then, taking up hand tools, he resorted to the file. The poem was entitled *The Earth*; it consisted of a description of the planet, and, of course, lacked no amount of picturesque digressions and bold apostrophes.

I asked him to read me a passage, if only a short one. He opened a drawer of his writing table, drew out a thick stack of papers – sheets of a large pad imprinted with the letterhead of the Juan Crisóstomo Lafinur Library – and, with ringing satisfaction, declaimed:

> Mine eyes, as did the Greek's, have known men's towns and fame,
> The works, the days in light that fades to amber;
> I do not change a fact or falsify a name—
> The *voyage* I set down is . . . *autour de ma chambre*.

'From any angle, a greatly interesting stanza,' he said, giving his verdict. 'The opening line wins the applause of the professor, the academician, and the Hellenist – to say nothing of the would-be scholar, a considerable sector of the public. The second flows from Homer to Hesiod (generous homage, at the very outset, to the father of didactic poetry), not without rejuvenating a process whose roots go back to Scripture – enumeration, congeries, conglomeration. The third – baroque? decadent? example of the cult of pure form? – consists of two equal hemistichs. The fourth, frankly bilingual, assures me the unstinted backing of all minds sensitive to the pleasures of sheer fun. I should, in all fairness, speak of the novel rhyme in lines two and four, and of the erudition that allows me – without a hint of pedantry! – to cram into four lines three learned allusions covering thirty centuries packed with literature – first to the *Odyssey*, second to *Works and Days*, and third to the immortal bagatelle bequeathed us by the frolicking pen of the Savoyard, Xavier de Maistre. Once more I've come to realize that modern art demands the balm of laughter, the scherzo. Decidedly, Goldoni holds the stage!'

He read me many other stanzas, each of which also won his own approval and elicited his lengthy explications. There was nothing remarkable about them. I did not even find them any worse than the first one.

Application, resignation, and chance had gone into the writing; I saw, however, that Daneri's real work lay not in the poetry but in his invention of reasons why the poetry should be admired. Of course, this second phase of his effort modified the writing in his eyes, though not in the eyes of others. Daneri's style of delivery was extravagant, but the deadly drone of his metric regularity tended to tone down and to dull that extravagance.*

Only once in my life have I had occasion to look into the fifteen thousand alexandrines of the *Polyolbion*, that topographical epic in which Michael Drayton recorded the flora, fauna, hydrography, orography, military and monastic history of England. I am sure, however, that this limited but bulky production is less boring than Carlos Argentino's similar vast undertaking. Daneri had in mind to set to verse the entire face of the planet, and, by 1941, had already dispatched a number of acres of the State of Queensland, nearly a mile of the course run by the River Ob, a gasworks to the north of Veracruz, the leading shops in the Buenos Aires parish of Concepción, the villa of Mariana Cambaceres de Alvear in the Belgrano section of the Argentine capital, and a Turkish baths establishment not far from the well-known Brighton Aquarium. He read me certain long-winded passages from his Australian section, and at one point praised a word of his own coining, the colour 'celestewhite', which he felt 'actually *suggests* the sky, an element of utmost importance in the landscape of the continent Down Under'. But these sprawling, lifeless hexameters lacked even the relative excitement of the so-called Augural Canto. Around about midnight, I left.

Two Sundays later, Daneri rang me up – perhaps for the first time in his life. He suggested we get together at four o'clock 'for cocktails in the salon-bar next door, which the forward-looking Zunino and Zungri – my land-lords, as you doubtless recall – are throwing open to the public. It's a place you'll really want to get to know.'

More in resignation than in pleasure, I accepted. Once there, it was hard to find a table. The 'salon-bar', ruthlessly modern, was only barely less ugly than what I had expected; at the nearby tables, the excited customers spoke breathlessly of the sums Zunino and Zungri had invested in furnishings

---

* Among my memories are also some lines of a satire in which he lashed out unsparingly at bad poets. After accusing them of dressing their poems in the warlike armour of erudition, and of flapping in vain their unavailing wings, he concluded with this verse:

But they forget, alas, one foremost fact – BEAUTY!

Only the fear of creating an army of implacable and powerful enemies dissuaded him (he told me) from fearlessly publishing this poem.

without a second thought to cost. Carlos Argentino pretended to be astonished by some feature or other of the lighting arrangement (with which, I felt, he was already familiar), and he said to me with a certain severity, 'Grudgingly, you'll have to admit to the fact that these premises hold their own with many others far more in the public eye.'

He then reread me four or five different fragments of the poem. He had revised them following his pet principle of verbal ostentation: where at first 'blue' had been good enough, he now wallowed in 'azures', 'ceruleans', and 'ultramarines'. The word 'milky' was too easy for him; in the course of an impassioned description of a shed where wool was washed, he chose such words as 'lacteal', 'lactescent', and even made one up – 'lactinacious'. After that, straight out, he condemned our modern mania for having books prefaced, 'a practice already held up to scorn by the Prince of Wits in his own graceful preface to the *Quixote*. He admitted, however, that for the opening of his new work an attention-getting foreword might prove valuable – 'an accolade signed by a literary hand of renown'. He next went on to say that he considered publishing the initial cantos of his poem. I then began to understand the unexpected telephone call; Daneri was going to ask me to contribute a foreword to his pedantic hodgepodge. My fear turned out unfounded; Carlos Argentino remarked, with admiration and envy, that surely he could not be far wrong in qualifying with the epithet 'solid' the prestige enjoyed in every circle by Álvaro Melián Lafinur, a man of letters, who would, if I insisted on it, be only too glad to dash off some charming opening words to the poem. In order to avoid ignominy and failure, he suggested I make myself spokesman for two of the book's undeniable virtues – formal perfection and scientific rigour – 'inasmuch as this wide garden of metaphors, of figures of speech, of elegances, is inhospitable to the least detail not strictly upholding of truth'. He added that Beatriz had always been taken with Álvaro.

I agreed – agreed profusely – and explained for the sake of credibility that I would not speak to Álvaro the next day, Monday, but would wait until Thursday, when we got together for the informal dinner that follows every meeting of the Writers' Club. (No such dinners are ever held, but it is an established fact that the meetings do take place on Thursdays, a point which Carlos Argentino Daneri could verify in the daily papers, and which lent a certain reality to my promise.) Half in prophecy, half in cunning, I said that before taking up the question of a preface I would outline the unusual plan of the work. We then said goodbye.

Turning the corner of Bernardo de Irigoyen, I reviewed as impartially as possible the alternatives before me. They were: *a*) to speak to Álvaro, telling him this first cousin of Beatriz' (the explanatory euphemism would allow me to mention her name) had concocted a poem that seemed to draw out into infinity the possibilities of cacophony and chaos; *b*) not to say a word to Álvaro. I clearly foresaw that my indolence would opt for *b*.

But first thing Friday morning, I began worrying about the telephone. It offended me that that device, which had once produced the irrecoverable voice of Beatriz, could now sink so low as to become a mere receptacle for the futile and perhaps angry remonstrances of that deluded Carlos Argentino Daneri. Luckily, nothing happened – except the inevitable spite touched off in me by this man, who had asked me to fulfil a delicate mission for him and then had let me drop.

Gradually, the phone came to lose its terrors, but one day towards the end of October it rang, and Carlos Argentino was on the line. He was deeply disturbed, so much so that at the outset I did not recognize his voice. Sadly but angrily he stammered that the now unrestrainable Zunino and Zungri, under the pretext of enlarging their already outsized 'salon-bar', were about to take over and tear down his house.

'My home, my ancestral home, my old and inveterate Garay Street home!' he kept repeating, seeming to forget his woe in the music of his words.

It was not hard for me to share his distress. After the age of fifty, all change becomes a hateful symbol of the passing of time. Besides, the scheme concerned a house that for me would always stand for Beatriz. I tried explaining this delicate scruple of regret, but Daneri seemed not to hear me. He said that if Zunino and Zungri persisted in this outrage, Doctor Zunni, his lawyer, would sue *ipso facto* and make them pay some fifty thousand dollars in damages.

Zunni's name impressed me; his firm, although at the unlikely address of Caseros and Tacuarí, was nonetheless known as an old and reliable one. I asked him whether Zunni had already been hired for the case. Daneri said he would phone him that very afternoon. He hesitated, then with that level, impersonal voice we reserve for confiding something intimate, he said that to finish the poem he could not get along without the house because down in the cellar there was an Aleph. He explained that an Aleph is one of the points in space that contains all other points.

'It's in the cellar under the dining room,' he went on, so overcome by his worries now that he forgot to be pompous. 'It's mine – mine. I discovered it when I was a child, all by myself. The cellar stairway is so steep that my aunt and uncle forbade my using it, but I'd heard someone say there was a world down there. I found out later they meant an old-fashioned globe of the world, but at the time I thought they were referring to the world itself. One day when no one was home I started down in secret, but I stumbled and fell. When I opened my eyes, I saw the Aleph.'

'The Aleph?' I repeated.

'Yes, the only place on earth where all places are – seen from every angle, each standing clear, without any confusion or blending. I kept the discovery to myself and went back every chance I got. As a child, I did not foresee that this privilege was granted me so that later I could write the poem. Zunino and Zungri will not strip me of what's mine – no, and a thousand times no! Legal code in hand, Doctor Zunni will prove that my Aleph is inalienable.'

I tried to reason with him. 'But isn't the cellar very dark?' I said.

'Truth cannot penetrate a closed mind. If all places in the universe are in the Aleph, then all stars, all lamps, all sources of light are in it, too.'

'You wait there. I'll be right over to see it.'

I hung up before he could say no. The full knowledge of a fact sometimes enables you to see all at once many supporting but previously unsuspected things. It amazed me not to have suspected until that moment that Carlos Argentino was a madman. As were all the Viterbos, when you came down to it. Beatriz (I myself often say it) was a woman, a child, with almost uncanny powers of clairvoyance, but forgetfulness, distractions, contempt, and a streak of cruelty were also in her, and perhaps these called for a pathological explanation. Carlos Argentino's madness filled me with spiteful elation. Deep down, we had always detested each other.

On Garay Street, the maid asked me kindly to wait. The master was, as usual, in the cellar developing pictures. On the unplayed piano, beside a large vase that held no flowers, smiled (more timeless than belonging to the past) the large photograph of Beatriz, in gaudy colours. Nobody could see us; in a seizure of tenderness, I drew close to the portrait and said to it, 'Beatriz, Beatriz Elena, Beatriz Elena Viterbo, darling Beatriz, Beatriz now gone forever, it's me, it's Borges.'

Moments later, Carlos came in. He spoke drily. I could see he was thinking of nothing else but the loss of the Aleph.

'First a glass of pseudo-cognac,' he ordered, 'and then down you dive into the cellar. Let me warn you, you'll have to lie flat on your back. Total darkness, total immobility, and a certain ocular adjustment will also be necessary. From the floor, you must focus your eyes on the nineteenth step. Once I leave you, I'll lower the trapdoor and you'll be quite alone. You needn't fear the rodents very much – though I know you will. In a moment or two, you'll see the Aleph – the microcosm of the alchemists and Kabbalists, our true proverbial friend, the *multum in parvo!*'

Once we were in the dining room, he added, 'Of course, if you don't see it, your incapacity will not invalidate what I have experienced. Now, down you go. In a short while you can babble with *all* of Beatriz' images.'

Tired of his inane words, I quickly made my way. The cellar, barely wider than the stairway itself, was something of a pit. My eyes searched the dark, looking in vain for the globe Carlos Argentino had spoken of. Some cases of empty bottles and some canvas sacks cluttered one corner. Carlos picked up a sack, folded it in two, and at a fixed spot spread it out.

'As a pillow,' he said, 'this is quite threadbare, but if it's padded even a half-inch higher, you won't see a thing, and there you'll lie, feeling ashamed and ridiculous. All right now, sprawl that hulk of yours there on the floor and count off nineteen steps.'

I went through with his absurd requirements, and at last he went away. The trapdoor was carefully shut. The blackness, in spite of a chink that I later made out, seemed to me absolute. For the first time, I realized the danger I was in: I'd let myself be locked in a cellar by a lunatic, after gulping down a glassful of poison! I knew that behind Carlos's transparent boasting lay a deep fear that I might not see the promised wonder. To keep his madness undetected, to keep from admitting that he was mad, *Carlos had to kill me.* I felt a shock of panic, which I tried to pin to my uncomfortable position and not to the effect of a drug. I shut my eyes – I opened them. Then I saw the Aleph.

I arrived now at the ineffable core of my story. And here begins my despair as a writer. All language is a set of symbols whose use among its speakers assumes a shared past. How, then, can I translate into words the limitless Aleph, which my floundering mind can scarcely encompass? Mystics, faced with the same problem, fall back on symbols: to signify the godhead, one Persian speaks of a bird that somehow is all birds; Alanus de Insulis, of a sphere whose centre is everywhere and circumference is nowhere; Ezekiel, of a four-faced angel who at one and the same time moves east and west, north and south. (Not in vain do I recall these inconceivable analogies; they bear some relation to the Aleph.) Perhaps the gods might grant me a similar metaphor, but then this account would become contaminated by literature, by fiction. Really, what I want to do is impossible, for any listing of an endless series is doomed to be infinitesimal. In that single gigantic instant I saw millions of acts both delightful and awful; not one of them amazed me more than the fact that all of them occupied the same point in space, without overlapping or transparency. What my eyes beheld was simultaneous, but what I shall now write down will be successive, because language is successive. Nonetheless, I'll try to recollect what I can.

On the back part of the step, towards the right, I saw a small iridescent sphere of almost unbearable brilliance. At first I thought it was revolving; then I realized that this movement was an illusion created by the dizzying world it bounded. The Aleph's diameter was probably little more than an inch, but all space was there, actual and undiminished. Each thing (a mirror's face, let us say) was infinite things, since I distinctly saw it from every angle of the universe. I saw the teeming sea; I saw daybreak and nightfall; I saw the multitudes of America; I saw a silvery cobweb in the centre of a black pyramid; I saw a splintered labyrinth (it was London); I saw, close up, unending eyes watching themselves in me as in a mirror; I saw all the mirrors on earth and none of them reflected me; I saw in a backyard of Soler Street the same tiles that thirty years before I'd seen in the entrance of a house in Fray Bentos; I saw bunches of grapes, snow, tobacco, lodes of metal, steam; I saw convex equatorial deserts and each one of their grains of sand; I saw a woman in Inverness whom I shall never forget; I saw her tangled hair, her tall figure, I saw the cancer in her breast; I saw a ring of baked mud in a sidewalk, where before there had been a tree; I saw a summer house in Adrogué and a copy of the first English translation of Pliny – Philemon Holland's – and all at the same time saw each letter on each page (as a boy, I used to marvel that the letters in a closed book did not get scrambled and lost overnight); I saw a sunset in Querétaro that seemed to reflect the colour of a rose in Bengal; I saw my empty bedroom; I saw in a closet in Alkmaar a terrestrial globe between two mirrors that multiplied it endlessly; I saw horses with flowing manes on a shore of the Caspian Sea at dawn; I saw the delicate bone structure of a hand; I saw the survivors of a battle sending out picture postcards; I saw in a showcase in Mirzapur a pack of Spanish playing cards; I saw the slanting shadows of ferns on a greenhouse floor; I saw tigers, pistons, bison, tides, and armies; I saw all the ants on the planet; I saw a Persian astrolabe; I saw in the drawer of a writing table (and the handwriting made me tremble) unbelievable, obscene, detailed letters, which Beatriz had written to Carlos Argentino; I saw a monument I worshipped in the Chacarita cemetery; I saw the rotted dust and bones that had once deliciously been Beatriz Viterbo; I saw the circulation of my own dark blood; I saw the coupling of love and the modification of death; I saw the Aleph from every point and angle, and in the Aleph I saw the earth and in the earth the

Aleph and in the Aleph the earth; I saw my own face and my own bowels; I saw your face; and I felt dizzy and wept, for my eyes had seen that secret and conjectured object whose name is common to all men but which no man has looked upon – the unimaginable universe.

I felt infinite wonder, infinite pity.

'Feeling pretty cockeyed, are you, after so much spying into places where you have no business?' said a hated and jovial voice. 'Even if you were to rack your brains, you couldn't pay me back in a hundred years for this revelation. One hell of an observatory, eh, Borges?'

Carlos Argentino's feet were planted on the topmost step. In the sudden dim light, I managed to pick myself up and utter, 'One hell of a – yes, one hell of a.'

The matter-of-factness of my voice surprised me. Anxiously, Carlos Argentino went on.

'Did you see everything – really clear, in colours?'

At that very moment I found my revenge. Kindly, openly pitying him, distraught, evasive, I thanked Carlos Argentino Daneri for the hospitality of his cellar and urged him to make the most of the demolition to get away from the pernicious metropolis, which spares no one – believe me, I told him, no one! Quietly and forcefully, I refused to discuss the Aleph. On saying goodbye, I embraced him and repeated that the country, that fresh air and quiet were the great physicians.

Out on the street, going down the stairways inside Constitution Station, riding the subway, every one of the faces seemed familiar to me. I was afraid that not a single thing on earth would ever again surprise me; I was afraid I would never again be free of all I had seen. Happily, after a few sleepless nights, I was visited once more by oblivion.

*

Postscript of March first, 1943 – Some six months after the pulling down of a certain building on Garay Street, Procrustes & Co, the publishers, not put off by the considerable length of Daneri's poem, brought out a selection of its 'Argentine sections'. It is redundant now to repeat what happened. Carlos Argentino Daneri won the Second National Prize for Literature.† First Prize went to Dr Aita; Third Prize, to Dr Mario Bonfanti. Unbelievably, my own book *The Sharper's Cards* did not get a single vote. Once again

---

* 'I received your pained congratulations,' he wrote me. 'You rage, my poor friend, with envy, but you must confess – even if it chokes you! – that this time I have crowned my cap with the reddest of feathers; my turban with the most *caliph* of rubies.'

dullness and envy had their triumph! It's been some time now that I've been trying to see Daneri; the gossip is that a second selection of the poem is about to be published. His felicitous pen (no longer cluttered by the Aleph) has now set itself the task of writing an epic on our national hero, General San Martín.

I want to add two final observations: one, on the nature of the Aleph; the other, on its name. As is well known, the Aleph is the first letter of the Hebrew alphabet. Its use for the strange sphere in my story may not be accidental. For the Kabbala, that letter stands for the *En Soph*, the pure and boundless godhead; it is also said that it takes the shape of a man pointing to both heaven and earth, in order to show that the lower world is the map and mirror of the higher; for Cantor's *Mengenlehre*, it is the symbol of transfinite numbers, of which any part is as great as the whole. I would like to know whether Carlos Argentino chose that name or whether he read it – applied to another point where all points converge – in one of the numberless texts that the Aleph in his cellar revealed to him. Incredible as it may seem, I believe that the Aleph of Garay Street was a false Aleph.

Here are my reasons. Around 1867, Captain Burton held the post of British Consul in Brazil. In July, 1942, Pedro Henríquez Ureña came across a manuscript of Burton's, in a library at Santos, dealing with the mirror which the Oriental world attributes to Iskander Zu al-Karnayn, or Alexander Bicornis of Macedonia. In its crystal the whole world was reflected. Burton mentions other similar devices – the sevenfold cup of Kai Kosru; the mirror that Tariq ibn-Ziyad found in a tower (*Thousand and One Nights*, 272); the mirror that Lucian of Samosata examined on the moon (*True History*, I, 26); the mirrorlike spear that the first book of Capella's *Satyricon* attributes to Jupiter; Merlin's universal mirror, which was 'round and hollow ... and seem'd a world of glas' (*The Faerie Queene*, III, 2, 19) – and adds this curious statement: 'But the aforesaid objects (besides the disadvantage of not existing) are mere optical instruments. The Faithful who gather at the mosque of Amr, in Cairo, are acquainted with the fact that the entire universe lies inside one of the stone pillars that ring its central court ... No one, of course, can actually see it, but those who lay an ear against the surface tell that after some short while they perceive its busy hum ... The mosque dates from the seventh century; the pillars come from other temples of pre-Islamic religions, since, as ibn-Khaldun has written: "In nations founded by nomads, the aid of foreigners is essential in all concerning masonry."'

Does this Aleph exist in the heart of a stone? Did I see it there in the cellar when I saw all things, and have I now forgotten it? Our minds are porous and forgetfulness seeps in; I myself am distorting and losing, under the wearing away of the years, the face of Beatriz.

Translated by Thomas di Giovanni and the author

Felisberto Hernández

The Balcony

I liked to visit this town in summer. A certain neighbourhood emptied at that time of the year when almost everyone left for a nearby resort. One of the empty houses was very old; it had been turned into a hotel, and as soon as summer came it looked sad and started to lose its best families, until only the servants remained. If I had hidden behind it and let out a shout, the moss would have swallowed it up.

The theatre where I was giving my concerts was also half empty and invaded by silence: I could see it growing on the big black top of the piano. The silence liked to listen to the music, slowly taking it in and thinking it over before venturing an opinion. But once it felt at home it took part in the music. Then it was like a cat with a long black tail slipping in between the notes, leaving them full of intentions.

After one of those concerts, a timid old man came up to shake my hand. The bags under his blue eyes looked sore and swollen. He had a huge lower lip that bulged out like the rim of a theatre box. He barely opened his mouth to speak, in a slow, dull voice, wheezing before and after each word.

After a long pause he said:

'I'm sorry my daughter can't hear your music.'

I don't know why I imagined his daughter was blind, although I realized at once that that would not have prevented her from hearing me, so that she was more likely deaf or perhaps out of town – which suddenly led to the idea that she might be dead. Yet I was happy that night: everything in that town was quiet and slow as the old man and I waded through leafy shadows and reflections.

Suddenly bending towards him, as if sheltering some frail charge, I caught myself asking:

'Your daughter couldn't come?'

He gasped in apparent surprise, stooped to search my face and finally managed to say:

'Yes, that's it. You've understood. She can't go out. Sometimes she can't sleep nights thinking she has to go out the next day. She's up early in the morning preparing for it, getting all excited. But after a while it wears off, she just drops into a chair, and she can't do it.'

The people leaving the concert soon disappeared into the surrounding streets and we went into the theatre café. He signalled the waiter, who brought him a dark drink in a small glass. I could only spend a few minutes with him: I was expected elsewhere for dinner. So I said:

'It's a shame she can't go out. We all need a bit of entertainment.'

He had raised the glass to his big lip but interrupted the motion to explain:

'She has her own way of keeping entertained. I bought an old house, too big for just the two of us, but it's in good shape. It has a garden with a fountain and in her bedroom there's a door that opens on to a winter balcony. It's a corner room, facing the street, and you could almost say she lives in that balcony. Or sometimes she goes for a walk in the garden and on some nights she plays the piano. You can come and have dinner with us whenever you want and I'll be grateful to you.'

I understood at once. So we agreed on a day when I would go for dinner and play the piano.

He called for me at the hotel one afternoon when the sun was still high. From a distance, he showed me the corner with the winter balcony. It was on a second floor. The entrance to the house was through a large gate on one side. It opened on to a garden with a fountain and some statuettes hidden in the weeds. Around the garden ran a high wall. The top of the wall was all splintered glass stuck in mortar. A flight of steps led up into the house, through a glassed-in corridor from which one could look out at the garden. I was surprised to see a large number of open parasols in the long corridor. They were different colours and looked like huge hothouse plants. The old man hastened to explain:

'I gave her most of the parasols. She likes to keep them open to see the colours. When there's nice weather she picks one and goes for a short walk in the garden. On windy days you can't open this door because the parasols blow away, we have to use the other entrance.'

We reached the far end of the corridor by going along the space left between the wall and the parasols. We came to a door and the old man rapped on the glass. A muffled voice answered from inside. The old man showed me in, and there was his daughter standing in the centre of the winter balcony, facing us, with her back to the coloured panes. We were halfway across the room before she left the balcony and came forward to meet us. Reaching out through space she offered me her hand and thanked me for my visit. Backed against the darkest wall of the room was a small open piano. Its big yellowish smile looked innocent.

She apologized for not being able to leave the house and, pointing to the balcony, said:

'He's my only friend.'

I indicated the piano and asked:

'How about this sweet soul? Isn't he your friend, too?'

We were lowering ourselves into chairs at the foot of her bed. I had time to notice many small paintings of flowers, all hung at the same height, along the four walls, as though parts of a frieze. The smile she had abandoned in the middle of her face was as innocent as the piano's, but her faded blonde hair and wispy figure also seemed to have been abandoned long ago. She was starting to explain why the piano wasn't as close a friend as the balcony when the old man left the room almost on tiptoes. She went on saying:

'The piano was a great friend of my mother's.'

I made as if to go over and look at it, but she raised a hand and opened her eyes wide to stop me.

'I'm sorry but I'd rather you tried the piano after dinner, when the lights are on. Since I was a little girl I've been used to hearing the piano only at night. That was when my mother played it. She used to light the four candles in the candlesticks and play each separate note so slowly in the silence, it was as if she were also lighting up the sounds, one by one.'

A minute later she rose and, excusing herself, went out on the balcony, where she leaned her bare arms on the panes as if she were resting them on someone's breast. But she came right back and said:

'When I see the same man go by several times through the red pane, he usually turns out to be violent or hot-tempered.'

I couldn't help asking her:

'Which pane did you see me through?'

'The green one. It usually means someone who lives alone in the country.'

'I happen to like being alone among plants,' I said.

The door opened and the old man came in followed by a maid who was so short that I couldn't tell whether she was a child or a dwarf. Her ruddy face shone over the little table she was carrying in her stubby arms. The old man asked me:

'What will you have?'

I was about to say 'nothing', but I thought that would offend him, so I named the first drink that came to mind. He had the maid bring him a small glass with the same dark drink I'd seen him take after the concert.

As night fell we started for the dining room. We had to go through the corridor of the parasols. The girl rearranged a few of them and glowed when I praised them.

The dining room was below street level. Through the small barred windows one could see the feet and legs of the people going by on the pavement. A lamp with a green shade poured its light straight on to the white tablecloth, where old family treasures had gathered as if to celebrate happy memories. We sat down, without a word, and for a moment each object seemed like a precious form of silence. When our pairs of hands started to appear on the tablecloth it seemed as natural as if they'd always lived there. I couldn't stop thinking of the life in hands. Years back, hands had moulded these objects on the table into certain shapes. After changing hands many times, the plates, glasses, and other small beings had found their home in a sideboard. Over the years they'd had to serve all sorts of hands. Any one of those hands could pile food on the plates' smooth bright faces, make the pitchers fill and empty their hips and the knives and forks sink into the meat, cut it up and bring the pieces to the mouth – after which the small beings were scrubbed, dried, and led back to their small dwellings in the sideboard. Some of these beings could outlive many pairs of hands, some of which would treat them lovingly and be long remembered, but they would have to go on serving in silence.

A while back, when we were in the girl's bedroom and she had not yet turned on the light – she wanted to enjoy every last bit of the evening glow coming from the balcony – we had spoken about the objects. As the light faded we could feel them nestling in the shadows as if they had feathers and were preparing for sleep. She said they developed souls as they came in touch with people. Some had once been something else and had another soul (the ones with legs had once had branches, the piano keys had been tusks). But her balcony had first gained a soul when she started to live in it.

Suddenly the ruddy face of the dwarf maid appeared over the edge of the tablecloth. Although she reached out confidently to grasp things in her tiny hands, the old man and his daughter slid their plates towards her. But when she handled them, the objects on the table lost their dignity. The old man also had a hasty, tactless way of grabbing the pitcher by the neck and wringing the wine out of it.

At first, conversation was difficult. Then a grandfather clock made its presence felt by pounding out the time. It had been ticking against the wall behind the old man, but I had forgotten it was there. When we started up again the girl asked me:

'Aren't you fond of old clothes?'

'Sure I am. And going back to what you were saying about objects, clothes are the ones that have been in closest touch with us' – here I laughed but she remained serious – 'and I wouldn't be surprised if they kept something more of us than just the shapes of our bodies and a whiff of our skin.'

But she wasn't listening. Instead, she had been trying to interrupt, like someone watching others play jump-rope, waiting for her chance to cut in. No doubt she had asked the question thinking of what she would have answered. Finally she said:

'I make up my poems in bed' – she had already mentioned those poems in the afternoon – 'and I have a white nightgown that has been with me ever since my first poems. Some summer nights I wear it in my balcony. Last year I wrote a poem for it.'

She had stopped eating and did not seem to notice the dwarf's arms coming and going. Staring as in a vision she began to recite:

'To my white nightgown.'

I braced myself to listen, at the same time observing the dwarf's hands. Her tiny stubby fingers were clenched as they approached things. They unbent only at the last moment, to clasp them.

At first I looked for different ways to show attention, but then I just nodded in time with the swinging motion of the clock's pendulum. This bothered me, adding to the agony I was already in, trying to think of something to say before the girl finished. Besides, the old man had a bit of chard dangling from his lower lip near the corner of his mouth.

The poem was corny, but she seemed to have kept count of her syllables. She'd found an unexpected rhyme for 'nightgown': I would tell her it was fresh. Watching the old man, I had passed my tongue over my lower lip – but he was listening to his daughter. Now I began to feel the poem would never end. And then suddenly she rhymed 'night' with 'white' and it was over.

I sat there in serene contemplation, listening to myself, hoping to convey the impression that I was about to come up with something.

'I'm struck by the childish quality of the poem,' I began. 'It's very fresh and . . .'

The word 'fresh' wasn't out of my mouth when she started to say:

'I have another one . . .'

I felt miserable . . . and treacherously concerned only with my own selfish needs. The dwarf was back with the next platter and I made a show of helping myself to a generous amount. All the glamour was gone from the objects on the table, the poem, the house overhead, even the parasols in the corridor and the ivy that grew up one whole side of the house. Wrapped up in myself, I gorged on the food, shamelessly. There wasn't a time the old man clutched the neck of the pitcher when my glass wasn't empty.

When she had finished her second poem I said:

'If this weren't so tasty' – and I nodded at my plate – 'I'd ask to hear more.'

The old man said at once:

'She ought to eat first. There'll be time for that later.'

I was starting to feel cynical and at that moment I wouldn't have minded growing a huge paunch. But then something made me want to cling to the poor old man and be kind to him. So, pointing to the wine, I said I'd recently heard a funny story about a drunkard. I told the story and when it ended they both laughed desperately, so I told them some more stories. There was sorrow in the girl's laughter, but she begged me to go on telling my stories. Her mouth had stretched at the edges, into a painful gash. Her eyes, caught in their web of 'crow's feet', were full of tears, and she was pressing her clasped hands between her knees. The old man was coughing so hard he had to put down the pitcher before filling his glass. The dwarf laughed, bending over as if to bow.

We had all been miraculously united and I felt not the least regret.

That night I did not play the piano. They begged me to stay and showed me to a bedroom on the side of the house where the ivy grew. As I started up the stairs I noticed a cord that ran from the grandfather clock all the way up the winding staircase. I followed it into the bedroom, up to the canopied bed, where it ended, tied to one of the slender bedposts. The room had ancient, paunchy furniture that shone yellowish in the lamplight. I put my hands on my stomach and eyed the old man's stomach. His last instructions that night were:

'If you can't sleep and want to know what time it is, pull on the cord. You'll hear the dining room clock from here. First it will give you the hour, then, after a pause, the minutes.'

Suddenly he began to laugh and went out, waving goodnight. He was probably remembering one of the stories, the one about the drunkard who talked to a clock.

He was still making the wooden stairs creak with his heavy steps when I started to feel alone with my body: it had absorbed all that food and drink like an animal swallowing other animals, and now it would have to struggle with it all night long. I stripped it naked and made it go barefoot around the room.

Later, in bed, I tried to figure out what I was doing with my life those days. I fished a few recent events out of my memory and thought of some people who were very far away. By then I was sinking into something like the bowels of silence, feeling sad and a bit lewd.

The next morning I looked back over my life with a smile, almost happily. It was very early. I dressed slowly and went out into a corridor built over the edge of the garden. On this side, too, there were weeds and tall, shady trees. I heard the old man and his daughter talking and realized they were on a bench right beneath me. I caught her words first:

'Ursula is unhappier now. She not only loves her husband less, but loves someone else more.'

The old man asked:

'Can't she get a divorce?'

'No, because she loves her children and the children love her husband and not the other man.'

Then the old man said timidly:

'She could tell the children that her husband has several mistresses.'

She got up angrily:

'Just like you to say that! When will you understand Ursula? She would never say such a thing!'

I was very much intrigued. They couldn't be talking about the dwarf: her name was Tamarinda. Yet the old man had told me they lived completely alone. So where did this news come from? Could it have reached them during the night? After her burst of anger the girl had gone into the dining room. In a while she came back out into the garden carrying a salmon-coloured parasol with white gauze ruffles. She did not come to the table for lunch. The old man and I ate and drank little. Afterwards I went out to buy a book suitable for reading in an abandoned house among weeds, on a still night and a full stomach.

On my way back, just ahead of me, I saw a poor old black man limp past the balcony. He wore a green hat with a wide brim, like a Mexican. Just then a patch of white skin appeared in the balcony, behind the green pane.

That night, as soon as we sat down to eat, I started to tell my stories, and she did not recite her poems.

The belly laughs the old man and I let out covered up for the brutal amounts of food and drink we were putting away.

There was a moment when we fell silent. Then the daughter said:

'I want some music tonight. I'll go in ahead of you and light the candles on the piano. It's been a long time since they were lit. The piano will be happy, poor thing: it will think Mother is back.'

Neither the old man nor I said another word. After a while Tamarinda
came in to say the young lady was waiting for us.

When I was about to strike the first chord, the silence was like a heavy
animal with a paw raised. The chord broke into rippling sounds like the
wavering candlelight. I tried another chord, as if advancing one more step
– and almost at once, before I could move on, a string snapped. The girl
cried out. The old man and I leaped up. He bent over his daughter, who
had her face in her hands, and tried to calm her, telling her the strings were
old and rusted. But she would not take her hands off her face or stop
shaking her head. I didn't know what to do: I had never snapped a string
before. I asked to be excused, and on the way to my room I was afraid of
stepping on the parasols in the corridor.

The next morning I slept late and missed part of the conversation on the
garden bench, but I was in time to hear the girl say:

'Ursula's love came wearing a big green hat with a wide brim.'

I couldn't believe she meant the old black man I had seen limping by
the previous afternoon, nor could I imagine who might have brought the
news during the night.

At noon the old man and I had lunch alone again. It was my chance to
say:

'There's a lovely view from my corridor. I was there earlier but didn't
stay because you were discussing a certain Ursula and I was afraid to
intrude.'

The old man stopped eating and whispered:

'You heard us?'

I realized he wanted to confide in me, so I answered:

'Yes, I heard everything. But I don't see how Ursula can find that old
black man handsome with his limp and that wide green hat.'

Oh, but you haven't understood,' he said. 'Since my daughter was knee-
high she's been making me listen to her stories and take part in the lives of
the characters she invents. And since then we've been keeping track of
them as if they really existed and we kept hearing from them. She imagines
them wearing and doing things she sees from the balcony. If yesterday she
saw a man in a green hat go by, it's not surprising the hat turned up today
on one of her characters. I'm too slow to keep up with her and she gets
angry with me. Why don't you help her? If you want I'll . . .'

I didn't let him finish.

'I wouldn't think of it. I'd only invent things that would hurt her.'

That evening, too, she was absent from the table. The old man and I ate,
drank, and chatted until well into the night.

In bed, afterwards, I heard a board creak; it wasn't the furniture. It took me a while to realize someone was coming up the stairs. The next moment there was a soft rap on my door. I asked who it was and the girl's voice answered:

'It's me. I want to talk to you.'

I switched on the lamp and opened the door a crack, and she said:

'It's no use hiding behind the door. I can see you in the mirror, standing there without a stitch on.'

So I shut the door and asked her to wait.

When I invited her in she walked straight across the room to another door I had not been able to open. She opened it with the greatest ease and groped her way into the darkness of some other room. She came back out with a chair that she placed by my bed. She reached into a blue cape she was wearing, took out a notebook, and started to read poems from it. I had to make a great effort not to fall asleep. I tried to force my eyes open but all I could do was roll them back, so that I must have looked like I was dying. Suddenly she cried out, as she had done when the piano string snapped, and I jumped up in bed. In the middle of the room was a huge spider. By the time I saw it it was no longer walking: it had gathered up three of its hairy legs as if ready to pounce. I threw my shoes at it and missed. I got out of bed, but she told me to stay away or it would jump at me. So I took my lamp and edged along the walls of the room to the washbasin, from where I threw a brush, a cake of soap, and the lid of the soap dish. The soap dish finally hit it and it rolled up into a dark woolly ball. She asked me not to tell her father, who didn't like her to be up working or reading so late. When she had left I squashed the spider with the heel of my shoe and went back to bed without turning out the light. As I was about to fall asleep I felt my toes curl. I thought the spider was in bed with me and I jumped up again.

In the morning the old man came in to apologize for the spider. His daughter had told him everything. I said it was nothing to worry about, and, to change the subject, I spoke of a concert I was about to give in a nearby town. He thought it was a pretext for leaving and I had to promise to return after the concert.

As we parted, I couldn't stop the girl from kissing my hand. I didn't know what to do. The old man hugged me and suddenly I felt him kiss me near my ear.

I never got to my concert. A couple of days later I received a phone call from the old man. After the first few words he said:

'Your presence is needed here.'

'Has something serious happened?'

'I'd say a real tragedy.'

'To your daughter?'

'No.'

'To Tamarinda?'

'No, no. I can't tell you now. If you can postpone the concert, catch the four o'clock train and I'll meet you at the theatre café.'

'But your daughter is well?'

'She's in bed. Not ill, but she refuses to get up or face the light of day. She can only stand lamplight and has had all the parasols folded.'

'All right, I'll be there.'

The theatre café was too noisy, so we moved elsewhere. The old man was depressed but eager to clutch at any hope I might offer him. He ordered his dark drink in the usual small glass and said:

'The day before yesterday there was a storm. We were sitting in the dining room in the evening when we heard a loud clatter. We realized at once it wasn't the storm. My daughter ran up to her room and I followed her. When I got there she had already opened the door to the balcony and all she saw was the sky and the light of the storm. She covered her eyes and fainted.'

'You mean the light hurt her?'

'But, my dear friend! Don't you understand?'

'What?'

'That we've lost the balcony! It fell out! It wasn't the balcony light she saw.'

'But a balcony ...'

It was better to say nothing. He made me promise not to mention the subject to the girl. So what was I to do? The poor old man was counting on me. I remembered the orgies we'd had together and decided to simply wait and hope I'd be able to think of something when I met her.

It was distressing to see the corridor without the parasols.

That night we ate and drank little. Then the old man took me to his daughter's bedside and immediately left the room. She had not said a word, but as soon as he was gone she turned towards the door that opened into space and said:

'You see how he left us?'

'But I can't ... Balconies don't fall out ...'

'He didn't fall. He jumped.'

'All right, but ...'

'He loved me – as much as I loved him. I know because he'd already proved it.'

I hung my head. I felt involved in an act of responsibility for which I was not prepared. She had started to pour her soul out and I didn't know how to receive it or what to do with it.

Now the poor girl was saying:

'It was all my fault. He got jealous the night I went to your room.'

'You don't mean . . . ?'

'Who do you think I mean? The balcony, my balcony.'

'Now, isn't that making too much of it? Remember how old he was. There are things that fall of their own weight.'

She wasn't listening. She went on:

'That same night I understood the warning and the threat.'

'Come on, now. You're not suggesting . . .'

'Don't you remember who threatened me? Who stared and stared at me, twitching those three hairy legs?'

'Yes, of course! The spider!'

'It's him all over.'

She looked up at me. Then she threw off the covers and got out of bed in her nightgown. She headed for the balcony door and I thought she was going to jump out. I started to reach for her – but she was in her nightgown. While I hesitated she changed her course. Now she was going towards a small table next to the door that opened into space. On the small table, just before she reached it, I saw the notebook with the black oilcloth cover from which she read her poems.

She sat in a chair, opened the notebook and started to recite:

> 'To a balcony
> from his widow . . .'

Translated by Luis Harss

João Guimarães Rosa

The Third Bank of the River

My father was a dutiful, orderly, straightforward man. And according to several reliable people of whom I enquired, he had had these qualities since adolescence or even childhood. By my own recollection, he was neither jollier nor more melancholy than the other men we knew. Maybe a little quieter. It was Mother, not Father, who ruled the house. She scolded us daily – my sister, my brother, and me. But it happened one day that Father ordered a boat.

He was very serious about it. It was to be made specially for him, of mimosa wood. It was to be sturdy enough to last twenty or thirty years and just large enough for one person. Mother carried on plenty about it. Was her husband going to become a fisherman all of a sudden? Or a hunter? Father said nothing. Our house was less than a mile from the river, which around there was deep, quiet, and so wide you couldn't see across it.

I can never forget the day the rowboat was delivered. Father showed no joy or other emotion. He just put on his hat as he always did and said goodbye to us. He took along no food or bundle of any sort. We expected Mother to rant and rave, but she didn't. She looked very pale and bit her lip, but all she said was: 'If you go away, stay away. Don't ever come back!'

Father made no reply. He looked gently at me and motioned me to walk along with him. I feared Mother's wrath, yet I eagerly obeyed. We headed towards the river together. I felt bold and exhilarated, so much so that I said: 'Father, will you take me with you in your boat?'

He just looked at me, gave me his blessing, and, by a gesture, told me to go back. I made as if to do so but, when his back was turned, I ducked behind some bushes to watch him. Father got into the boat and rowed away. Its shadow slid across the water like a crocodile, long and quiet.

Father did not come back. Nor did he go anywhere, really. He just rowed and floated across and around, out there in the river. Everyone was appalled. What had never happened, what could not possibly happen, was happening. Our relatives, neighbours, and friends came over to discuss the phenomenon.

Mother was ashamed. She said little and conducted herself with great composure. As a consequence, almost everyone thought (though no one said it) that Father had gone insane. A few, however, suggested that Father might be fulfilling a promise he had made to God or to a saint, or that he might have some horrible disease, maybe leprosy, and that he left for the sake of the family, at the same time wishing to remain fairly near them.

Travellers along the river and people living near the bank on one side or the other reported that Father never put foot on land, by day or night. He just moved about on the river, solitary, aimless, like a derelict. Mother and our relatives agreed that the food which he had doubtless hidden in the boat would soon give out and that then he would either leave the river and travel off somewhere (which would be at least a little more respectable) or he would repent and come home.

How far from the truth they were! Father had a secret source of provisions: me. Every day I stole food and brought it to him. The first night after he left, we all lit fires on the shore and prayed and called to him. I was deeply distressed and felt a need to do something more. The following day I went down to the river with a loaf of corn bread, a bunch of bananas, and some bricks of raw brown sugar. I waited impatiently a long, long hour. Then I saw the boat, far off, alone, gliding almost imperceptibly on the smoothness of the river. Father was sitting in the bottom of the boat. He saw me but he did not row towards me or make any gesture. I showed him the food and then I placed it in a hollow rock on the river bank; it was safe there from animals, rain, and dew. I did this day after day, on and on and on. Later I learned, to my surprise, that Mother knew what I was doing and left food around where I could easily steal it. She had a lot of feelings she didn't show.

Mother sent for her brother to come and help on the farm and in business matters. She had the schoolteacher come and tutor us children at home because of the time we had lost. One day, at her request, the priest put on his vestments, went down to the shore, and tried to exorcise the devils that had got into my father. He shouted that Father had a duty to cease his unholy obstinacy. Another day she arranged to have two soldiers come and try to frighten him. All to no avail. My father went by in the distance, sometimes so far away he could barely be seen. He never replied to anyone and no one ever got close to him. When some newspapermen came in a launch to take his picture, Father headed his boat to the other side of the river and into the marshes, which he knew like the palm of his hand but in which other people quickly got lost. There in his private maze, which extended for miles, with heavy foliage overhead and rushes on all sides, he was safe.

We had to get accustomed to the idea of Father's being out on the river.

We had to but we couldn't, we never could. I think I was the only one who understood to some degree what our father wanted and what he did not want. The thing I could not understand at all was how he stood the hardship. Day and night, in sun and rain, in heat and in terrible mid-year cold spells, with his old hat on his head and very little other clothing, week after week, month after month, year after year, unheedful of the waste and emptiness in which his life was slipping by. He never set foot on earth or grass, on isle or mainland shore. No doubt he sometimes tied up the boat at a secret place, perhaps at the tip of some island, to get a little sleep. He never lit a fire or even struck a match and he had no flashlight. He took only a small part of the food that I left in the hollow rock – not enough, it seemed to me, for survival. What could his state of health have been? How about the continual drain on his energy, pulling and pushing the oars to control the boat? And how did he survive the annual floods, when the river rose and swept along with it all sorts of dangerous objects – branches of trees, dead bodies of animals – that might suddenly crash against his little boat?

He never talked to a living soul. And we never talked about him. We just thought. No, we could never put our father out of mind. If for a short time we seemed to, it was just a lull from which we would be sharply awakened by the realization of his frightening situation.

My sister got married, but Mother didn't want a wedding party. It would have been a sad affair, for we thought of him every time we ate some especially tasty food. Just as we thought of him in our cosy beds on a cold, stormy night – out there, alone and unprotected, trying to bail out the boat with only his hands and a gourd. Now and then someone would say that I was getting to look more and more like my father. But I knew that by then his hair and beard must have been shaggy and his nails long. I pictured him thin and sickly, black with hair and sunburn, and almost naked despite the articles of clothing I occasionally left for him.

He didn't seem to care about us at all. But I felt affection and respect for him, and, whenever they praised me because I had done something good, I said: 'My father taught me to act that way.'

It wasn't exactly accurate but it was a truthful sort of lie. As I said, Father didn't seem to care about us. But then why did he stay around there? Why didn't he go up the river or down the river, beyond the possibility of seeing us or being seen by us? He alone knew the answer.

My sister had a baby boy. She insisted on showing Father his grandson. One beautiful day we all went down to the riverbank, my sister in her white wedding dress, and she lifted the baby high. Her husband held a parasol above them. We shouted to Father and waited. He did not appear. My sister cried; we all cried in each other's arms.

My sister and her husband moved far away. My brother went to live in a city. Times changed, with their usual imperceptible rapidity. Mother finally moved too; she was old and went to live with her daughter. I remained behind, a leftover. I could never think of marrying. I just stayed there with the impedimenta of my life. Father, wandering alone and forlorn on the river, needed me. I knew he needed me, although he never even told me why he was doing it. When I put the question to people bluntly and insistently, all they told me was that they heard that Father had explained it to the man who made the boat. But now this man was dead and nobody knew or remembered anything. There was just some foolish talk, when the rains were especially severe and persistent, that my father was wise like Noah and had the boat built in anticipation of a new flood; I dimly remember people saying this. In any case, I would not condemn my father for what he was doing. My hair was beginning to turn grey.

I have only sad things to say. What bad had I done, what was my great guilt? My father always away and his absence always with me. And the river, always the river, perpetually renewing itself. The river, always. I was beginning to suffer from old age, in which life is just a sort of lingering. I had attacks of illness and of anxiety. I had a nagging rheumatism. And he? Why, why was he doing it? He must have been suffering terribly. He was so old. One day, in his failing strength, he might let the boat capsize; or he might let the current carry it downstream, on and on, until it plunged over the waterfall to the boiling turmoil below. It pressed upon my heart. He was out there and I was forever robbed of my peace. I am guilty of I know not what, and my pain is an open wound inside me. Perhaps I would know – if things were different. I began to guess what was wrong.

Out with it! Had I gone crazy? No, in our house that word was never spoken, never through all the years. No one called anybody crazy, for nobody is crazy. Or maybe everybody. All I did was go there and wave a handkerchief so he would be more likely to see me. I was in complete command of myself. I waited. Finally he appeared in the distance, there, then over there, a vague shape sitting in the back of the boat. I called to him several times. And I said what I was so eager to say, to state formally and under oath. I said it as loud as I could:

'Father, you have been out there long enough. You are old ... Come back, you don't have to do it anymore ... Come back and I'll go instead. Right now, if you want. Any time. I'll get into the boat. I'll take your place.'

And when I had said this my heart beat more firmly.

He heard me. He stood up. He manoeuvred with his oars and headed the boat towards me. He had accepted my offer. And suddenly I trembled, down deep. For he had raised his arm and waved – the first time in so many, so many years. And I couldn't ... In terror, my hair on end, I ran, I fled madly. For he seemed to come from another world. And I'm begging forgiveness, begging, begging.

I experienced the dreadful sense of cold that comes from deadly fear, and I became ill. Nobody ever saw or heard about him again. Am I a man, after such a failure? I am what never should have been. I am what must be silent. I know it is too late. I must stay in the deserts and unmarked plains of my life, and I fear I shall shorten it. But when death comes I want them to take me and put me in a little boat in this perpetual water between the long shores; and I, down the river, lost in the river, inside the river ... the river ...

Translated by William L. Grossman

Virgilio Piñera

The One Who Came to Save Me

I always had one great fear: not knowing when I would die. My wife claimed it was my father's fault; my mother was dying, he set me in front of her and made me kiss her. I was ten years old at the time and we all know the business about how the spectre of death leaves a profound impression on children ... I'm not saying the assertion is wrong, but my case is different. What my wife doesn't know is that I saw a man executed, and saw it purely by accident. Unusual justice: two men tied a noose around another man's neck in the bathroom of a movie theatre and slit his throat. How did I see? I was in a stall taking a shit, and they couldn't see me; they were at the urinals. I was calmly taking a shit and all of a sudden I heard: 'But you're not going to kill me ...' I looked through the grating and saw a knife slitting a throat, torrents of blood; I heard a scream, and feet running away at full speed. When the police arrived at the scene of the crime, they found me unconscious, nearly dead, in what they call 'a state of shock.' For a month, I hung between life and death.

Now don't think that thereafter I would be afraid of having my throat slit. Well, think that if you want, it's your prerogative. If someone sees a man's throat being slit, it's logical he would think the same thing could happen to him too, but it's also logical to think it highly unlikely that the damned coincidence of fate – or whatever – would assign him the same luck as the man whose throat they slit in the bathroom of the movie theatre.

No, that was not my fear. The fear I felt at the very moment they slit the guy's throat could be expressed in these words: When will it happen? Imagine an eighty-year-old man, quite ready to face death; I think the single thought in his mind can only be to wonder: Will this be the night ...? Will it be tomorrow ...? Will it be three in the morning the day after ...? Will it be right now, while I'm thinking it will be the day after at three in the morning ...? Knowing and feeling that his remaining time is quite short, he figures his calculations of the 'fatal hour' are precise enough, but at the same time, the impotence he experiences as he tries to determine 'the moment' reduces his calculations to nothing. On the other hand, the guy murdered in the bathroom knew at once when his time would come.

The moment he uttered the words 'But you're not going to kill me...' he knew his time had come. Between his desperate exclamation and the hand that guided the knife to slit his throat, he knew the exact moment of his death. That is, if, for example, the exclamation was uttered at four minutes and five seconds past nine in the evening, and his throat was slit at four minutes eight seconds past nine, he knew the time of his death precisely three seconds beforehand.

On the other hand, lying here on the bed alone (my wife died last year and anyway, I don't know how that poor woman would be able to help me with this business about the moment of my death), I am racking what little brains I have left. It's well known that when one is ninety years old as I am, like the traveller, one is dependent on the clock, with the difference that the traveller knows what time it is and the ninety-year-old does not. But let's not get ahead of ourselves.

When the guy had his throat slit in the bathroom, I was only twenty years old. Being 'full of life' in those days and, moreover, seeing life stretch ahead of me almost like an eternity, that bloody picture and that distressing question were soon erased. When you're full of life, you only have time to live and be alive. You feel alive and say: 'How healthy I am. I exude health from all my pores, I could eat an ox, copulate five times a day, work twenty hours straight without tiring...' and at that moment one can't conceive of what it means to die and to be dying. When I got married at twenty-two, my wife, observing my passion, said to me one night: 'Will you be the same with me when you're an old man?' And I replied: 'What's an old man? You think you know?'

Of course, she didn't know either. And since neither she nor I could, at the time, imagine an old man, well, we started laughing, and then we made love like crazy.

But soon after turning fifty, I began to see a glimmering of what it meant to be an old man and I also began to think about this business of the moment of death ... Of course I kept on living, but at the same time, I was beginning to die, and a sickly, ravenous curiosity was forcing me to face the fatal moment. Since I had to die, at least knowing at what moment my death would occur, the way I know, for example, the precise moment I brush my teeth...

And as I grew older, this thought became more and more obsessive until it was what we call a fixation. When I was in my early seventies, I – unexpectedly – took my first plane trip. I received a cablegram from the wife of my only brother informing me that he was dying. So I took the plane. Two hours into the flight we encountered bad weather. The plane was a feather in the storm; it was everything they say about planes in the middle of a tempest: passengers filled with terror, the comings and goings of the stewardesses, objects falling to the floor, screams of women and children mixed with the Lord's Prayer and Hail Marys – in short, that *memento mori* that is all the more *memento* at an altitude of forty thousand feet.

'Thank God,' I said to myself. 'Thank God that for the first time I'm approaching a certain precision concerning the moment of my death. At least on this plane in danger of being dashed to pieces, I can already start calculating the moment. Ten, fifteen, thirty-eight minutes . . . ? It doesn't matter. I'm close and you, death, will not be able to surprise me.'

I confess that I rejoiced wildly. Not for an instant did it occur to me to pray, review my life, make an act of contrition, or (that simple physiological function) vomit. No, I was only attentive to the imminent crash of the plane so I might know, as we were dashed to pieces, that this was the moment of my death.

Once the danger had passed, a passenger said to me: 'Listen, I was watching you while we were falling, and you looked as if nothing was wrong.' I smiled, didn't answer her; she, anguish still showing on her face, was unaware of 'my anguish', which for once in my life had been transformed at forty thousand feet into a state of grace comparable to that of the most illustrious saints of the Church.

But it isn't every day one finds oneself at an altitude of forty thousand feet in a plane whipped by storm winds – the only paradise glimpsed during my long life. On the contrary, we each inhabit the hell we ourselves create: its walls are of thought, its roof terrors, and its windows abysses . . . And within, one freezes over a low flame, that is, one's life seeps out amidst flames that adopt unusual forms: 'at what hour', 'a Tuesday or a Saturday', 'in the fall or in the spring . . .'

'And I freeze myself and burn myself more and more. I've become a worn-out exhibit from a museum of teratology and at the same time, the very picture of malnutrition. I'm sure it's not blood but pus that runs through my veins; my scabs – festering, purplish – and my bones seem to have conferred a very different anatomy on my body. My hip bones, like a river, have overflown their banks; my collarbone (as I lose my flesh) is like an anchor hanging over the side of a ship; the occipital bone makes my head look like a coconut bashed in with a sledgehammer.

In spite of this, the stuff in my head continues thinking, and thinking its *idée fixe*; right now, at this very instant, stretched out on the bed in my bedroom, with death hovering overhead, with death, who might be that photograph of my dead father, who looks at me and says: 'I'm going to surprise you, you'll never know, you're watching me but you don't know when I'll deal you the blow...'

In response, I looked more intently at the photograph of my father and said to him: 'You won't have your way. I'll know the moment you make a move, and before you do, I'll shout: "Now's the time!" and you'll have to admit defeat.' And just at that moment, that moment that shares reality and anomaly, I heard footsteps that were also part of that same reality and unreality. I turned my eyes from the photograph and unconsciously focused them on the closet mirror facing my bed. In it, I saw reflected the face of a young man – only his face, since the rest of his body was hidden from my sight by a folding screen placed between the foot of the bed and the mirror. But I didn't pay much attention to him – something that would have been unthinkable had I been a younger man; I mean, at the age when you're truly alive and the unexpected presence of a stranger in your bedroom would elicit anything from surprise to terror. But at my age, and in the state of languor in which I found myself, a stranger and his face were just a part of the reality-unreality you must tolerate. That is, the stranger and his face were either another among the many objects that populate my bedroom, or among the many ghosts that populate my head. So I turned my eyes again to the photograph of my father, and when I looked back at the mirror, the stranger's face had disappeared. I looked once more at the photograph and thought I noticed that my father's face was angry; that is, my father's face inasmuch as it was his, but with a face that was also not his, but rather, looked as if it were made up like a character out of a tragedy. Who knows ... On this boundary between reality and unreality, everything is possible, and, more importantly, everything occurs and doesn't occur. At that point, I closed my eyes and began to say aloud: now, now ... Suddenly I heard the sound of footsteps very near the head of my bed. I opened my eyes and there in front of me was the stranger, his body a mile high. I thought: 'Bah, the same as the one in the mirror...' and I looked again at the photograph of my father. But something told me to look again at the stranger. I didn't disobey my inner voice and looked at him. Now he wielded a knife and was slowly bending over as I watched him intently. Then I understood that this stranger was the one who was coming to save me. I knew several seconds beforehand the exact moment of my death. When the knife sank into my jugular vein, I looked at my saviour and said to him, through torrents of blood: 'Thank you for coming.'

Translated by Mark Schafer

Juan Carlos Onetti

Hell Most Feared

The first letter – the first photograph – was delivered to him at the newspaper office between midnight and press time. He was pounding on his typewriter, a bit hungry, a bit sick from all the coffee and tobacco, surrendered with a kind of familiar happiness to the flow of the phrase and the orderly arrival of the words. He was writing: 'It is worth noting that the officials saw nothing suspicious or even out of the ordinary about the decisive victory of Play Boy, who was able to take advantage of the wintry field and shoot off like an arrow at the decisive moment,' when he saw the red and ink-stained hand of Politics come between his face and the typewriter, offering him the letter.

'This is for you. They always get our mail mixed up. Not even one damn invitation to the clubs, and later they come crying when election time grows near and the space they are granted never seems like enough to them. And it's already midnight and *you* tell me how I'm supposed to fill up my column.'

On the envelope were his name, Racing Department, *El Liberal.* The only odd things were the pair of green stamps and the Bahia postmark. He finished the article just as they came up from the typesetter to ask him for it. He was tired and happy, almost alone in the huge space of the city desk, thinking about his last sentence: 'We insist again, with the objectivity which for years has marked our statements: we owe our existence to the fans.' At the back of the room, the black clerk was looking through the envelopes in the archives, and the older woman from the Society Page was slowly taking off her gloves in her glass booth, when Risso carelessly opened the envelope.

It contained a three-by-five photograph: a dark picture, taken in insufficient light, hate and sordidness filling the dark edges, forming uneven wide borders like a relief, like drops of sweat around an anguished face. He looked with surprise, not fully understanding, discovering that he would give anything to forget what he had seen.

He stuffed the photograph in his pocket and was putting on his overcoat when Society Page came out, cigarette in hand, from her glass booth, a sheaf of papers in her hand.

'Hi,' she said, 'look at me, at this hour, and the party just ended.'

Risso looked at her from above. Her light-coloured dyed hair, the wrinkles on her neck, the double chin that sank round and pointy like a little belly, the small, rather exaggerated, touches of colour that decorated her clothing. 'She's a woman, even she is. Only now am I noticing the red scarf around her neck; the purple nails on her old, tobacco-stained hands; the rings and bracelets; the dress she was given in exchange by a designer, not a lover; the endless, perhaps somewhat twisted, heels; the sad curve of her mouth; the almost frantic enthusiasm she thrusts on her smiles. Everything will be easier if I can convince myself that she too is a woman.'

'It seems like something thought of and planned for a lark. When I come in you are on your way out, almost as if you were running away from me. It's cold as hell outside. They leave me the material they promised, but without even a name or a note. Guess, make a mistake, publish some fantastic rubbish. I don't know the names of anyone but the lucky couple, thank God at least for that. Excess and bad taste, that's what there was. They entertained their friends with a glittering reception at the home of the bride's parents. But nobody gets married on Saturday anymore. Get ready, the wind is cold as hell out on the street.'

*

When Risso married Gracia Cesar, we all gathered in silence, ignoring pessimistic predictions. At that time, she contemplated the inhabitants of Santa Maria from the tall signs of the Sotano, the Repertory Theatre, from walls that looked old because it was the end of autumn. Sometimes intact, sometimes with a moustache drawn in or scratched at by vengeful finger-nails or by the first rain, she had her head half-turned to watch the street, alert, a bit defiant, a bit excited by the hope of convincing and being understood. Revealed by the shininess of the retouched eyes of the enlargements from Orloff Studios, you could read in her face that she gave her whole life over to the farce of love, to the determined and single-minded quest for pleasure.

All of which was fine (he must have thought), desirable and necessary, and coincided with the result of multiplying the number of months that Risso had been a widower by the sum total of the countless Saturday afternoons he had discreetly repeated the polite gestures of waiting and familiarity in the brothel by the shore. A glow, that of the eyes in the poster, was linked with the frustrated skill he showed, tying yet another sad, new, black tie before the portable oval mirror in the brothel bedroom.

They got married and Risso thought it sufficient to keep on living the way he always had but devoting himself to her, without thinking about it, almost without thinking about her, the fury of her body, the mad search for absolutes that possessed him during the long nights.

She thought of Risso as a bridge, an escape, a beginning. She had kept her virginity intact through two engagements (one with a director, one with an actor), perhaps because for her the theatre was a craft as well as a game and she thought that love should be born and grow separate from it, uncontaminated by what one does to earn money and oblivion. With one, then with the other, during their dates in the town squares, on the promenade or in the café, she was condemned to feel the tedium of rehearsals, the effort to get into the part, the attention to her voice and hands. She always saw her own face a moment before making any expression, as if she could look at it or touch it. She acted brave and sceptical, taking stock constantly of her face and of the other's, the sweat and the theatrical make-up that covered them, inseparable, signs of the age.

*

When the second photograph arrived, from Asuncion and with a man who was obviously not the same one, Risso was afraid, above all, of not being able to stand an unknown feeling that was neither hate nor pain, that would die with him without ever having a name, that was linked to injustice and fate, to the primal fears of the first man on earth, to nihilism and the beginning of faith.

The second photograph was delivered to him by Police Desk one Wednesday night. Thursday was the day he always spent with his daughter, from ten in the morning until ten at night. He decided to tear up the envelope without opening it and put it away, and it was only on Thursday morning, while his daughter was waiting for him in the boarding house living room, that he permitted himself a quick glance at the photograph before tearing it up and flushing it down the toilet: in this one, too, the man was facing the other way.

But he had looked at the photograph from Brazil many times. He kept it for almost a whole day; in the early morning he imagined that it must be a joke, a mistake, some passing silliness. Already, many times, he had woken up from a nightmare, smiling abjectly and gratefully at the flowers on the wallpaper of his room.

He was lying in bed when he took the envelope out of his jacket and took the photograph out of the envelope.

'Well,' he said aloud, 'that's right, that's all right, that's the way it is. It isn't important; even if I didn't see it, I'd know what's going on.'

(When she took the picture with the self-timer, when she developed it in the darkened room, beneath the encouraging red glow of the lamp, she probably anticipated this reaction by Risso, this challenge, this refusal to give himself over to anger. She also anticipated, or barely desired, with slight, ill-recognized hopes, that he would discover a message of love in the obvious offence and the astonishing humiliation.)

He sheltered himself again before looking: 'I am alone and freezing to death in a boarding house on Piedras Street, in Santa Maria, in the wee hours, alone, regretting my solitude as if I had sought it out, proud as if I deserved it.'

In the photograph the headless woman was ostentatiously digging her heels into the edge of the sofa, waiting impatiently for the dark man, made enormous by the unavoidable foreshortening; she was sure that she had no need to show her face to be recognized. On the back the neat hand-writing read: 'Greetings from Bahia.'

In the night that followed the second photograph, he thought he could understand the whole evil and even accept it. But he knew that there, beyond his reach, lurked an act of will, persistence, the organized frenzy with which the revenge was being carried out. He measured its excess, felt himself unworthy of so much hatred, of so much love, of such a desire to cause pain.

When Gracia met Risso she could guess many things about the present and the future. She glimpsed his solitude when she looked at his chin and at a button of his jacket; she guessed that he was embittered but not beaten and that he needed a release but could not admit it. Sunday after Sunday she watched him in the square, before the show, carefully observing his sad, impassioned expression, the greasy hat he had forgotten on his head, the large, lazy body he was letting go to fat. She thought of love the first time they were alone together, or of desire, or of a hope of lessening the sadness in the man's cheeks and temples with the touch of her hand. She also thought of the town, in which the only possible and prudent course was giving up in time. She was twenty and Risso was forty. She set herself the task of believing in him, discovered intensity in his curiosity, told herself that you really are alive only when each day brings some surprise.

During the first few weeks, she shut herself in to laugh alone, devoted herself to fetishistic worship, learned to distinguish moods by their smell. She learned to discover what was behind the voice, the silences, the tastes, and attitudes of the man's body. She loved Risso's daughter and modified her face, praising her resemblance to her father. She did not leave the theatre because the city government had just begun to help support it and the Sotano now provided her with a reliable salary, a world apart from her home, from her bedroom, from the frantic and indestructible man. She did not seek to distance herself from lust; she wanted to rest and forget it, to let lust rest and forget. She made plans and followed them, confident of the infinity of the universe of love, sure that each night would give them a different, freshly created surprise.

'Anything,' Risso insisted, 'absolutely anything can happen to us, and we will always be happy and in love. Anything: be it created by God or by ourselves.'

Actually, he had never had a woman before and thought he was creating what was in fact being imposed on him. But it wasn't she who was imposing anything on him. She, Gracia Cesar, Risso's creation, was separated from him so as to complement him, like air from a lung, like a winter from the wheat.

*

The third photograph took three weeks to arrive. Also, it came from Paraguay and did not arrive at his house but instead at the boarding house, and the maid brought it to him at the end of the afternoon. He was waking up from a dream in which he had been advised to defend himself from fear and madness by keeping any future photograph in his wallet and turning it into an incident of his life, something impersonal and inoffensive, by means of a hundred absentminded glances a day.

The maid knocked on his door, and he saw the envelope hanging from one of the slats of the blinds; he began to feel its vile qualities, its pulsating threat, filtering into the twilight, filling the dirty air. He was watching it from his bed as if it were a poisonous insect squashed while awaiting a brief distraction, some propitious mistake.

In the third photograph she was alone, pushing back the shadows of a badly lit room with her whiteness, her head thrust painfully back towards the camera, her shoulders half-covered by her loose, full, manelike hair. She was now as unmistakable as if she had had her picture taken in some studio, posing with the most tender, meaningful, and oblique of smiles.

Now he, Risso, felt only a powerless pity for her, for himself, for all those who ever loved in the world, for the truth and error in their beliefs, for the simple absurdity of love, for the complex absurdity of love created by men.

But he tore up this picture also and discovered that it would be impossible for him to look at another one and stay alive. Yet, in the magic sphere where they had begun to understand one another and to converse, Gracia no doubt realized that he would tear up the photographs as soon as they arrived, each time with less curiosity, with less remorse.

In that magic realm, all of the urgent men, whether vulgar or shy, were no more than obstacles, inevitable steps in the ritual act of choosing the most gullible and inexperienced man in the street, restaurant, or café who would lend himself to her designs without suspecting anything, with a comic sort of pride during the exposure, facing the camera and the shutter release, the least unpleasant of those who would buy a memorized spiel worthy of a travelling salesman.

'It's just that I never had a man like you, so unique, so different. And, thanks to my life in the theatre, I never know where I will be tomorrow, whether I will ever see you again. I want at least to look at you in a photograph when we are far apart, when I miss you.'

And after this conversation, which usually went smoothly, she thought about Risso or deferred her thoughts for the next day, carrying out the task she had set herself, arranging the lights, preparing the camera, and turning on the man. If she was thinking about Risso, she evoked some remote event, reproaching him again for not having hit her, for having sent her off forever with a clumsy insult, an intelligent smile, a comment that lumped her together with all other women. And without understanding – showing that he had never understood, despite all the nights and conversations.

Without getting her hopes up, she bustled sweatily around the inevitable sordid and muggy hotel room, measuring distances and lights, correcting the position of the man's numb body. Using any excuse, lure, drunken lie, she forced the man of the hour to turn his cynical, suspicious face towards her. She tried to smile and to tempt him, aping the affectionate clucking noises you make to newborn infants, calculating the passage of the seconds, at the same time calculating the intensity with which the picture would allude to her love for Risso.

But since she was never able to discover this, since she didn't even know whether the photographs reached Risso's hands, she began to intensify the testimony of the pictures and turn them into documents that had little to do with them, Risso and Gracia.

She even went so far as to allow and require that the faces drawn by desire, dulled by the old masculine dream of possession, confront the camera aperture with a hard smile, a shamefaced insolence. She found it necessary to slip down on her back and sink herself deeper into the picture, allowing her head, her short nose, her huge, unflinching eyes to descend from the void beyond the photograph and form part of the filthiness of the world, the crude and deceptive photographic vision, the satires on the love she had sworn to send regularly to Santa Maria. But her real mistake was changing the addresses on the envelopes.

*

The first separation, six months after the wedding, was welcome and overly distressing. The Sotano – now the Santa Maria Municipal Theatre – went on tour to Rosario. There she fell once again into the old hallucinatory game of being an actress among actors, of believing what was happening on stage. The audience was moved, applauded or resisted being won over. The programmes and reviews appeared on time, and people accepted the game and helped it go on until the end of the evening, speaking of what they had seen and heard, of what they had paid to see and hear, conversing with a certain desperation, with a sort of earnest enthusiasm, about the acting, the sets, the speeches, and the plots.

So the game, the remedy, alternately moody and exhilarating, initiated when she slowly approached the window looking out on the fjord and, trembling, whispered to the whole theatre: 'Perhaps . . . but I too have a life full of memories that remain closed to others,' a line also accepted in Rosario. Cards were always laid on the table in response to those she put down, the game was structured, and soon it was impossible for her to distance herself and look at it from the outside.

The first separation lasted exactly fifty-two days, and during them Risso tried to continue exactly the same life that he had had with Gracia Cesar during the six months of married life. Always going to the same café at the same hour, to the same restaurant, seeing the same friends, rehearsing moments of silence and solitude on the promenade, walking back to the boarding house, obediently suffering through the anticipation of their meeting, brow and mouth stirring with the excessive images born of idealized memories or of ambitions impossible to realize.

He went ten or twelve blocks, alone and slower now, through nights fanned by warm and chilly winds, along the uneasy edge that separated spring from winter. They gave him a chance to measure his need and his helplessness, to know that the madness he was part of at least had the grandeur of being without a future, of not being the means to anything.

As for her, she had believed that Risso gave a theme to their common love when he whispered, prostrate with a fresh feeling of surprise, dazed: 'Anything can happen and we will still be happy and in love.'

The phrase was no longer a judgement, an opinion; it expressed no desire. It was dedicated and imposed on them, it was a verification, an ancient truth. Nothing that they did or thought could lessen the madness, the inescapable and changeless love. All human possibilities could be made use of and everything was destined to nourish it.

She believed that beyond them, outside the room, lay a world bereft of all meaning, inhabited by beings who did not matter, filled with events without value.

So she only thought about Risso, about the two of them, when the man began waiting for her at the stage door, when he invited her and took her along, when she began taking off her clothes.

It was the last week in Rosario, and she saw no need to mention it in her letters to Risso, for the event was not separated from them and at the time had nothing to do with them, because she had acted like a curious, alert animal, with a certain degree of pity for the man, with some scorn for what she was adding to her love for Risso. And when she returned to Santa Maria, she preferred to wait until Wednesday evening – because Risso didn't go to the paper on Thursday – until a timeless night, until an early morning exactly like the twenty-five they had lived through together.

She began telling about it before taking off her clothes, with the simple pride and tenderness of having invented a new caress. Leaning on the table, in shirtsleeves, he closed his eyes and smiled. Afterwards he made her undress and asked her to repeat the story, now standing up, walking barefoot on the carpet and almost without moving forward or sideways, her back to him, her body rocking as she stood on one foot, then on the other. At times she saw Risso's long sweaty face, his heavy body leaning on the table, his shoulders shielding his glass of wine, and at times she only imagined them, absent-minded, in her zeal for fidelity in the tale, for the joy of reliving that odd intensity of love she had felt for Risso in Rosario, next to the man whose face she had forgotten, next to nobody, next to Risso.

'Good, now you can get dressed again,' he said, with the same astonished, hoarse voice that had said over and over that anything was possible, that everything would belong to them.

She examined his smile and put her clothes back on. For a while the two of them sat looking at the designs on the tablecloth, the stains, the bird-shaped ashtray with a broken beak. Then he finished dressing and went out, devoting his Thursday, his day off, to conversations with Dr Guiñazu, to convincing him of the urgent need to approve divorce laws, to block all talk of reconciliation in advance.

Afterwards there was a long unhealthy period during which Risso wanted to have her back and at the same time hated the pain and loathing

Hell Most Feared 41

of every imaginable new encounter. Later he decided that he needed Gracia, and now a bit more than before. That reconciliation was necessary and that he was inclined to pay any price for it so long as his will was not involved, so long as it was possible to have her again at night without saying yes to her even with his silence.

He started spending his Thursdays once more going out with his daughter and listening to the list of predictions that had come true which the grandmother always made to enliven the after-dinner conversations. He had vague, cautious news of Gracia, began imagining her as if she were an unknown woman whose gestures and reactions had to be guessed or deduced, as if she were a woman who remained intact and alone amid people and places, destined to be his and be loved by him, perhaps at first sight.

Almost a month after the start of the separation, Gracia gave out differing addresses and left Santa Maria.

'Don't worry,' Guiñazu said. 'I know women well and was expecting something like this. This confirms the abandonment of the home and simplifies our course of action, now made easier by an obvious delaying manoeuvre, further evidence of the defendant's folly.'

It was a damp start of spring, and often Risso came home at night from the newspaper or the café on foot, calling the rain names, reviving his suffering as if blowing on a coal, pushing it farther away to see it better and still not believe it, imagining acts of love he had never experienced so as to be able instantly to set himself the task of remembering them with a desperate greed.

Risso had destroyed the last three messages without looking at them. Now, both at the paper and at the boarding house, he constantly felt like a rat in its hole, like an animal that hears the hunters' shots echoing at the door of its lair. He could only save himself from death and from the idea of death by forcing himself into stillness and ignorance. Curled up, his whiskers, snout, paws were twitching; he could only hope for the other's fury to be used up. Without allowing himself words or thoughts, he felt forced to begin to understand, to confuse the Gracia who sought out and chose men and poses for the photographs with the girl who, many months before, had planned dresses, conversations, make-up, gestures of affection for his daughter to win over the widower devoted to grief, a man who earned a small salary and who could only offer women an astonished but loyal lack of understanding.

He had begun to believe that the girl who had written long and over-stated letters during the brief separations the summer of their courtship was the same one who sought his despair and annihilation when sending him the photographs. And he thought too that the lover who, in the hopeless stubbornness in bed, always manages to breathe the dark smell of death is condemned (for his own sake and for hers) to seek annihilation, the final peace of nothingness.

He thought about the girl who used to walk on the promenade hand in hand with two girfriends in the afternoon, dressed in the ample inlaid dresses of stiff cloth that his memory invented and imposed, and who glanced across the overture of the *Barber of Seville* that capped the Sunday band concert to look at him for a moment. He thought of that bolt of lightning by which she turned her furious expression into a proposal and a challenge, showing him directly the almost virile beauty of a pensive and capable face, in which she chose him, dazed by bereavement. And, little by little, he came to admit to himself that the same woman – naked, a little heavier now, with a certain expression of aplomb and self-knowledge – was the one sending him photographs from Lima, Santiago, and Buenos Aires.

He even thought, why not, why not accept that the photographs, elaborately prepared and promptly mailed, were all born of the same love, the same capacity for looking back, the same inborn loyalty.

*

The next photograph arrived from Montevideo; it was not sent to the paper or the boarding house. And he was never to see it. He was leaving *El Liberal* one night when he heard the hobbling of old Lanza chasing after him down the steps, the trembling cough behind him, the innocent and deceitful phrase of the prologue. They went to eat at the Bavaria. And Risso could have sworn afterwards that he knew that the unkempt, bearded, sick man, who during the after-dinner conversation puffed again and again on a cigarette moistened by his sunken mouth, who did not want to look him in the eye, who recited obvious comments about the news that UP had sent the paper that day, was impregnated with Gracia, with the frantic absurd perfume prepared by love.

'From one man to another,' Lanza said with resignation. 'Or from an old man who has no happiness left in life except the uncertain one of staying alive. From an old man to you, and I don't know, because one never knows, who you are. I know some facts and have heard comments. But I no longer have any interest in wasting time believing or doubting. It's all the same to me. Each morning I verify that I'm alive, with no bitterness and no feeling of gratitude. I drag a sick leg and my arteriosclerosis through Santa Maria and around the newspaper office; I remember Spain, correct the proofs, write, and sometimes talk too much. Like tonight. I received a dirty photograph, and there's no doubt about who sent it. I can't guess why I was chosen. On the back it reads: "To be donated to the Risso collection," or something like that. It reached me on Saturday, and for two days I wondered whether to give it to you or not. I decided that the best thing was to tell you about it, because sending that picture to me is an act of madness without extenuating circumstances and perhaps it would do you good to know that she is crazy. Now you know. I want only to ask your permission to tear up the picture without showing it to you.'

Risso told him to do so; that night, while watching the light of the streetlamp on the ceiling of his room until daybreak, he understood that the second misfortune, the revenge, was essentially less serious than the first one, the act of infidelity, but at the same time much harder to stand. He felt his long body exposed like a nerve to the pain of the air, helpless, beyond hope of finding rest.

The fourth photograph that was not addressed to him was thrown on the table by his daughter's grandmother the following Thursday. The girl had gone to take a nap, and the picture had been put back inside its envelope. It fell between the seltzer bottle and the candy bowl, long, traversed and coloured by the reflection of a bottle, displaying eager letters in blue ink.

'I'm sure you understand that after this—' the grandmother stuttered. She was stirring her coffee and looking at Risso's face, searching his profile for the secret of universal filth, the cause of her daughter's death, the explanation for so many things she had suspected without having the nerve to believe them. 'You understand,' she repeated with fury, her voice comic and aged.

But she didn't know what he needed to understand, and Risso didn't understand either, no matter how hard he tried, staring at the envelope that had stopped in front of him, one edge resting on his plate.

Outside the night was heavy, and the open windows of the city mixed the mysteries of the lives of men, their desires and habits with the milky mystery of the sky. Rolling over in bed, Risso believed he was starting to understand, that understanding, like some sickness, like a feeling of well-being, was taking place within him, free of his intellect and will. It was simply taking place, from the contact of his feet with his shoes up to the tears that reached his cheeks and neck. Understanding was taking place within him, and he was not interested in knowing what it was that he understood; he remembered or saw weeping and stillness, the stretched passivity of the body in the bed, the bulging clouds in the window, past and future scenes. He saw death and friendship with death, the proud scorn for rules all men had agreed to live by, the true surprise of freedom. He tore the photograph to pieces on his chest, never taking his eyes from the whiteness in the window, slowly and carefully, afraid of making noise or interrupting something. Afterwards he felt a new air stirring, perhaps one breathed in his childhood, filling the room and extending with a clumsy slowness through the streets and the buildings, all unprepared for it, an air awaiting him, offering him refuge for the following day and those after.

Since early that morning, he had made the acquaintance of indifference, of motiveless happiness, of the acceptance of solitude, as if of cities that had seemed inaccessible to him. And when he woke up at noon, as he loosened his tie and belt and wristwatch, as he walked sweating to the window, towards the putrid smell of a storm, he was invaded for the first time by a paternal fondness for men and for everything that men had done and built. He had resolved to discover Gracia's address, to call her or to go live with her.

That night at the paper he was a slow, happy man, acting with the clumsiness of a newborn infant, filling his quota of pages with the absent-mindedness and the mistakes that one is accustomed to forgive in a newcomer. The big piece of news was Ribereña's inability to run at San Isidro, because we are in a position to inform our readers that the good fortune which the stud Gorrion has enjoyed heretofore has become uncertain today due to pain in his hindquarters, evidence of an inflammation of the tendon the name of which clearly expresses the origin of the disease that troubles him.

*

'When you recall that he covered racing,' Lanza recounted, 'you try to explain that feeling of bewilderment, comparing it to that of the man who gambled his whole pay-cheque on a tip he had been given, confirmed in turn by the trainer, the jockey, the owner, and even the horse. Because even though, as we all know, he had the strongest possible motives for feeling pain and taking all of the capsules of sleeping pills in all of the drugstores in Santa Maria all at once, what he showed me no more than a half hour earlier was nothing but the reasoning and the attitude of someone who has been swindled. A man who had been safe, out of danger, but is no longer, and who cannot explain to himself how it could happen, what mistake of reckoning produced the failure. But at no moment did he call the bitch who was scattering the filthy pictures all over the city the bitch that she was, and he did not even accept the way out I offered him, insinuating, without quite believing it myself, that the bitch – in heat and naked, as she preferred to let it be known, or on stage observing the ovarian problems of other bitches made famous by world drama – might very possibly be completely out of her mind. Nothing. He had made a mistake, not in marrying her but at some other moment he refused to mention. The fault was his alone. Our conversation was unbelievable and frightening because he had already told me that he was going to kill himself and he had already convinced me that it was useless, even grotesque and useless all over again, to try and argue with him to save him. And he spoke to me coldly, without accepting my requests that he get drunk. He had been mistaken, he insisted; he, not that damned slut who had sent the picture to the little girl, there in the convent school. Perhaps thinking that the mother superior would open the envelope, perhaps desiring that it reach the hands of Risso's daughter intact, sure this time of finding the one place where Risso was truly vulnerable.'

Translated by Daniel Balderston

Juan Rulfo

Luvina

Of the mountains in the south Luvina is the highest and the rockiest. It's infested with that grey stone they make lime from, but in Luvina they don't make lime from it or get any good out of it. They call it crude stone there, and the hill that climbs up towards Luvina they call the Crude Stone Hill. The sun and the air have taken it on themselves to make it crumble away, so that the earth around there is always white and brilliant, as if it were always sparkling with the morning dew, though this is just pure talk, because in Luvina the days are cold as the nights and the dew thickens in the sky before it can fall to the earth.

And the ground is steep and slashed on all sides by deep barrancas, so deep you can't make out the bottom. They say in Luvina that one's dreams come up from those barrancas; but the only thing I've seen come up out of them was the wind, whistling as if down below they had squeezed it into reed pipes. A wind that doesn't even let the dulcamaras grow: those sad little plants that can live with just a bit of earth, clutching with all their hands at the mountain cliffsides. Only once in a while, where there's a little shade, hidden among the rocks, the chicalote blossoms with its white poppies. But the chicalote soon withers. Then you hear it scratching the air with its spiny branches, making a noise like a knife on a whetstone.

'You'll be seeing that wind that blows over Luvina. It's dark. They say because it's full of volcano sand; anyway, it's a black air. You'll see it. It takes hold of things in Luvina as if it was going to bite them. And there are lots of days when it takes the roofs off the houses as if they were hats, leaving the bare walls uncovered. Then it scratches like it had nails: you hear it morning and night, hour after hour without stopping, scraping the walls, tearing off strips of earth, digging with its sharp shovel under the doors, until you feel it boiling inside of you as if it was going to remove the hinges of your very bones. You'll see.'

The man speaking was quiet for a bit, while he looked outside.

The noise of the river reached them, passing its swollen waters through the fig-tree branches, the noise of the air gently rustling the leaves of the almond trees, and the shouts of the children playing in the small space illumined by the light that came from the store.

The flying ants entered and collided with the oil lamp, falling to the ground with scorched wings. And outside night kept on advancing.

'Hey, Camilo, two more beers!' the man said again. Then he added, 'There's another thing, mister. You'll never see a blue sky in Luvina. The whole horizon there is always a dingy colour, always clouded over by a dark stain that never goes away. All the hills are bare and treeless, without one green thing to rest your eyes on; everything is wrapped in an ashy smog. You'll see what it's like – those hills silent as if they were dead and Luvina crowning the highest hill with its white houses like a crown of the dead–'

The children's shouts came closer until they penetrated the store. That made the man get up, go to the door and yell at them, 'Go away! Don't bother us! Keep on playing, but without so much racket.'

Then, coming back to the table, he sat down and said, 'Well, as I was saying, it doesn't rain much there. In the middle of the year they get a few storms that whip the earth and tear it away, just leaving nothing but the rocks floating above the stony crust. It's good to see then how the clouds crawl heavily about, how they march from one hill to another jumping as if they were inflated bladders, crashing and thundering just as if they were breaking on the edge of the barrancas. But after ten or twelve days they go away and don't come back until the next year, and sometimes they don't come back for several years – No, it doesn't rain much. Hardly at all, so that the earth, besides being all dried up and shrivelled like old leather, gets filled with cracks and hard clods of earth like sharp stones, that prick your feet as you walk along, as if the earth itself had grown thorns there. That's what it's like.'

He downed his beer until only bubbles of foam remained in the bottle, then he went on: 'Wherever you look in Luvina, it's a very sad place. You're going there, so you'll find out. I would say it's the place where sadness nests. Where smiles are unknown as if people's faces had been frozen. And, if you like, you can see that sadness just any time. The breeze that blows there moves it around but never takes it away. It seems like it was born there. And you can almost taste and feel it, because it's always over you, against you, and because it's heavy like a large plaster weighing on the living flesh of the heart.

'The people from there say that when the moon is full they clearly see the figure of the wind sweeping about Luvina's streets, bearing behind it a black blanket; but what I always managed to see when there was a moon in Luvina was the image of despair – always.

'But drink up your beer. I see you haven't even tasted it. Go ahead and

drink. Or maybe you don't like it warm like that. But that's the only kind
we have here. I know it tastes bad, something like donkey's piss. Here you
get used to it. I swear that there you won't even get this. When you go to
Luvina you'll miss it. There all you can drink is a liquor they make from a
plant called hojasé, and after the first swallows your head'll be whirling
around like crazy, feeling like you had banged it against something. So
better drink your beer. I know what I'm talking about.'

You could still hear the struggle of the river from outside. The noise of
the air. The children playing. It seemed to be still early in the evening.

The man had gone once more to the door and then returned, saying:
'It's easy to see things, brought back by memory, from here where there's
nothing like it. But when it's about Luvina I don't have any trouble going
right on talking to you about what I know. I lived there. I left my life there
– I went to that place full of illusions and returned old and worn out. And
now you're going there – All right. I seem to remember the beginning. I'll
put myself in your place and think – Look, when I got to Luvina the first
time – But will you let me have a drink of your beer first? I see you aren't
paying any attention to it. And it helps me a lot. It relieves me, makes me
feel like my head had been rubbed with camphor oil – Well, I was telling
you that when I reached Luvina the first time, the mule driver who took us
didn't even want to let his animals rest. As soon as he let us off, he turned
half around. "I'm going back," he said.

'"Wait, aren't you going to let your animals take a rest? They are all
worn out."

'"They'd be in worse shape here," he said. "I'd better go back."

'And away he went, rushing down Crude Stone Hill, spurring his animals
on as if he was leaving some place haunted by the devil.

'My wife, my three children, and I stayed there, standing in the middle
of the plaza, with all our belongings in our arms. In the middle of that place
where all you could hear was the wind ...

'Just a plaza, without a single plant to hold back the wind. There we
were.

'Then I asked my wife, "What country are we in, Agripina?"

'And she shrugged her shoulders.

'"Well, if you don't care, go look for a place where we can eat and spend
the night. We'll wait for you here," I told her.

'She took the youngest child by the hand and left. But she didn't come
back.

'At nightfall, when the sun was lighting up just the tops of the mountains, we went to look for her. We walked along Luvina's narrow streets,

until we found her in the church, seated right in the middle of that lonely church, with the child asleep between her legs.

'"What are you doing here, Agripina?"

'"I came to pray," she told us.

'"Why?" I asked her.

'She shrugged her shoulders.

'Nobody was there to pray to. It was a vacant old shack without any doors, just some open galleries and a roof full of cracks where the air came through like a sieve.

'"Where's the restaurant?"

'"There isn't any restaurant."

'"And the inn?"

'"There isn't any inn."

'"Did you see anybody? Does anybody live here?" I asked her.

'"Yes, there across the street – Some women – I can still see them. Look, there behind the cracks in that door I see some eyes shining, watching us – They have been looking over here – Look at them. I see the shining balls of their eyes – But they don't have anything to give us to eat. They told me without sticking out their heads that there was nothing to eat in this town – Then I came in here to pray, to ask God to help us."

'"Why didn't you go back to the plaza? We were waiting for you."

'"I came in here to pray. I haven't finished yet."

'"What country is this, Agripina?"

'And she shrugged her shoulders again.

'That night we settled down to sleep in a corner of the church behind the dismantled altar. Even there the wind reached, but it wasn't quite as strong. We listened to it passing over us with long howls, we listened to it come in and out of the hollow caves of the doors whipping the crosses of the stations of the cross with its hands full of air – large rough crosses of mesquite wood hanging from the walls the length of the church, tied together with wires that twanged with each gust of wind like the gnashing of teeth.

'The children cried because they were too scared to sleep. And my wife, trying to hold all of them in her arms. Embracing her handful of children. And me, I didn't know what to do.

'A little before dawn the wind calmed down. Then it returned. But there was a moment during that morning when everything was still, as if the sky had joined the earth, crushing all noise with its weight – You could hear the breathing of the children, who now were resting. I listened to my wife's heavy breath there at my side.

'"What is it?" she said to me.

'"What's what?" I asked her.

'"That, that noise."

'"It's the silence. Go to sleep. Rest a little bit anyway, because it's going to be day soon."

'But soon I heard it too. It was like bats flitting through the darkness very close to us. Bats with big wings that grazed against the ground. I got up and the beating of wings was stronger, as if the flock of bats had been frightened and were flying towards the holes of the doors. Then I walked on tiptoes over there, feeling that dull murmur in front of me. I stopped at the door and saw them. I saw all the women of Luvina with their water jugs on their shoulders, their shawls hanging from their heads and their black figures in the black background of the night.

'"What do you want?" I asked them. "What are you looking for at this time of night?"

'One of them answered, "We're going for water."

'I saw them standing in front of me, looking at me. Then, as if they were shadows, they started walking down the street with their black water jugs.

'No, I'll never forget that first night I spent in Luvina.

'Don't you think this deserves another drink? Even if it's just to take away the bad taste of my memories.'

*

'It seems to me you asked me how many years I was in Luvina, didn't you? The truth is, I don't know. I lost the notion of time since the fevers got it all mixed up for me, but it must have been an eternity – Time is very long there. Nobody counts the hours and nobody cares how the years go mounting up. The days begin and end. Then night comes. Just day and night until the day of death, which for them is a hope.

'You must think I'm harping on the same idea. And I am, yes, mister – To be sitting at the threshold of the door, watching the rising and the setting of the sun, raising and lowering your head, until the springs go slack and then everything gets still, timeless, as if you had always lived in eternity. That's what the old folks do there.

'Because only real old folks and those who aren't born yet, as they say, live in Luvina – And weak women, so thin they are just skin and bones. The children born there have all gone away – They hardly see the light of day and they're already grown up. As they say, they jump from their mothers' breasts to the hoe and disappear from Luvina. That's the way it is in Luvina.

'There are just old folks left there and lone women, or with a husband who is off God knows where – They appear every now and then when the storms come I was telling you about; you hear a rustling all through the town when they return and something like a grumbling when they go away again – They leave a sack of provisions for the old folk and plant another child in the bellies of their women, and nobody knows anything more of them until the next year, and sometimes never – It's the custom. There they think that's the way the law is, but it's all the same. The children spend their lives working for their parents as their parents worked for theirs and who knows how many generations back performed this obligation . . .

'Meanwhile, the old people wait for them and for death, seated in their doorways, their arms hanging slack, moved only by the gratitude of their children – Alone, in that lonely Luvina.

'One day I tried to convince them they should go to another place where the land was good. "Let's leave here!" I said to them. "We'll manage somehow to settle somewhere. The government will help us."

'They listened to me without batting an eyelash, gazing at me from the depths of their eyes from which only a little light came.

'"You say the government will help us, teacher? Do you know the government?"

'I told them I did.

'"We know it too. It just happens. But we don't know anything about the government's mother."

'I told them it was their country. They shook their heads saying no. And they laughed. it was the only time I saw the people of Luvina laugh. They grinned with their toothless mouths and told me no, that the government didn't have a mother.

'And they're right, you know? That lord only remembers them when one of his boys has done something wrong down here. Then he sends to Luvina for him and they kill him. Aside from that, they don't know if the people exist.

'"You're trying to tell us that we should leave Luvina because you think we've had enough of going hungry without reason," they said to me. "But if we leave, who'll bring along our dead ones? They live here and we can't leave them alone."

'So they're still there. You'll see them now that you're going. Munching on dry mesquite pulp and swallowing their own saliva to keep hunger away. You'll see them pass by like shadows, hugging to the walls of the houses, almost dragged along by the wind.

'"Don't you hear that wind?" I finally said to them. "It will finish you off."

'"It keeps on blowing as long as it ought to. It's God's will," they answered me. "It's bad when it stops blowing. When that happens the sun pours into Luvina and sucks our blood and the little bit of moisture we have in our skin. The wind keeps the sun up above. It's better that way."

'So I didn't say anything else to them. I left Luvina and I haven't gone back and I don't intend to.

'—But look at the way the world keeps turning. You're going there now in a few hours. Maybe it's been fifteen years since they said the same thing to me: "You're going to San Juan Luvina."

'In those days I was strong. I was full of ideas — You know how we're all full of ideas. And one goes with the idea of making something of them everywhere. But it didn't work out in Luvina. I made the experiment and it failed . . .

'San Juan Luvina. That name sounded to me like a name in the heavens. But it's purgatory. A dying place where even the dogs have died off, so there's not a creature to bark at the silence; for as soon as you get used to the strong wind that blows there all you hear is the silence that reigns in these lonely parts. And that gets you down. Just look at me. What it did to me. You're going there, so you'll soon understand what I mean . . .

'What do you say we ask this fellow to pour a little mescal? With this beer you have to get up and go all the time and that interrupts our talk a lot. Hey, Camilo, let's have two mescals this time!

'Well, now, as I was telling you . . .

But he didn't say anything. He kept staring at a fixed point on the table where the flying ants, now wingless, circled about like naked worms.

Outside you could hear the night advancing. The lap of the water against the fig-tree trunks. The children's shouting, now far away. The stars peering through the small hole of the door.

The man who was staring at the flying ants slumped over the table and fell asleep.

Translated by George Schade

Julio Cortázar

Blow-up

It'll never be known how this has to be told, in the first person or in the second, using the third person plural or continually inventing modes that will serve for nothing. If one might say: I will see the moon rose, or: we hurt me at the back of my eyes, and especially: you the blonde woman was the clouds that race before my your his our yours their faces. What the hell.

Seated ready to tell it, if one might go to drink a bock over there, and the typewriter continue by itself (because I use the machine), that would be perfection. And that's not just a manner of speaking. Perfection, yes, because here is the aperture that must be counted also as a machine (of another sort, a Contax 1.1.2) and it is possible that one machine may know more about another machine than I, you, she – the blonde – and the clouds. But I have the dumb luck to know that if I go this Remington will sit turned to stone on top of the table with the air of being twice as quiet that mobile things have when they are not moving. So, I have to write. One of us all has to write, if this is going to get told. Better that it be me who am dead, for I'm less compromised than the rest; I who see only the clouds and can think without being distracted, write without being distracted (there goes another, with a grey edge) and remember without being distracted, I who am dead (and I'm alive, I'm not trying to fool anybody, you'll see when we get to the moment, because I have to begin some way and I've begun with this period, the last one back, the one at the beginning, which in the end is the best of the periods when you want to tell something).

All of a sudden I wonder why I have to tell this, but if one begins to wonder why he does all he does do, if one wonders why he accepts an invitation to lunch (now a pigeon's flying by and it seems to me a sparrow), or why when someone has told us a good joke immediately there starts up something like a tickling in the stomach and we are not at peace until we've gone into the office across the hall and told the joke over again; then it feels good immediately, one is fine, happy, and can get back to work. For I imagine that no one has explained this, that really the best thing is to put aside all decorum and tell it, because, after all's done, nobody is ashamed of breathing or of putting on his shoes; they're things that you do, and when something weird happens, when you find a spider in your shoe or if you take a breath and feel like a broken window, then you have to tell what's happening, tell it to the guys at the office or to the doctor. Oh, doctor, every time I take a breath ... Always tell it, always get rid of that tickle in the stomach that bothers you.

And now that we're finally going to tell it, let's put things a little bit in order, we'd be walking down the staircase in this house as far as Sunday, 7 November, just a month back. One goes down five floors and stands then in the Sunday in the sun one would not have suspected of Paris in November, with a large appetite to walk around, to see things, to take photos (because we were photographers, I'm a photographer). I know that the most difficult thing is going to be finding a way to tell it, and I'm not afraid of repeating myself. It's going to be difficult because nobody really knows who it is telling it, if I am I or what actually occurred or what I'm seeing (clouds, and once in a while a pigeon) or if, simply, I'm telling a truth which is only my truth, and then is the truth only for my stomach, for this impulse to go running out and to finish up in some manner with, this, whatever it is.

We're going to tell it slowly, what happens in the middle of what I'm writing is coming already. If they replace me, if, so soon, I don't know what to say, if the clouds stop coming and something else starts (because it's impossible that this keep coming, clouds passing continually and occasionally a pigeon), if something out of all this ... And after the 'if' what am I going to put if I'm going to close the sentence structure correctly? But if I begin to ask questions, I'll never tell anything, maybe to tell would be like an answer, at least for someone who's reading it.

Roberto Michel, French-Chilean, translator and in his spare time an amateur photographer, left number 11, rue Monsieur-le-Prince Sunday 7 November of the current year (now there're two small ones passing, with silver linings). He had spent three weeks working on the French version of a treatise on challenges and appeals by José Norberto Allende, professor at the University of Santiago. It's rare that there's wind in Paris, and even less seldom a wind like this that swirled around corners and rose up to whip at old wooden venetian blinds behind which astonished ladies commented variously on how unreliable the weather has been these last few years. But the sun was out also, riding the wind and friend of the cats, so there was nothing that would keep me from taking a walk along the docks of the Seine and taking photos of the Conservatoire and Sainte-Chapelle. It was hardly ten o'clock, and I figured that by eleven the light would be good, the best you can get in the fall; to kill some time I detoured around by the

Isle Saint-Louis and started to walk along the quai d'Anjou, I stared for a bit at the hôtel de Lauzun, I recited bits from Apollinaire which always get into my head whenever I pass in front of the hôtel de Lauzun (and at that I ought to be remembering the other poet, but Michel is an obstinate beggar), and when the wind stopped all at once and the sun came out at least twice as hard (I mean warmer, but really it's the same thing), I sat down on the parapet and felt terribly happy in the Sunday morning.

One of the many ways of contesting level-zero, and one of the best, is to take photographs, an activity in which one should start becoming an adept very early in life, teach it to children since it requires discipline, aesthetic education, a good eye and steady fingers. I'm not talking about waylaying the lie like any old reporter, snapping the stupid silhouette of the VIP leaving number 10 Downing Street, but in all ways when one is walking about with a camera, one has almost a duty to be attentive, to not lose that abrupt and happy rebound of sun's rays off an old stone, or the pigtails-flying run of a small girl going home with a loaf of bread or a bottle of milk. Michel knew that the photographer always worked as a permutation of his personal way of seeing the world as other than the camera insidiously imposed upon it (now a large cloud is going by, almost black), but he lacked no confidence in himself, knowing that he had only to go out without the Contax to recover the keynote of distraction, the sight without a frame around it, light without the diaphragm aperture or 1/250 sec. Right now (what a word, *now*, what a dumb lie) I was able to sit quietly on the railing overlooking the river watching the red and black motorboats passing below without it occurring to me to think photographically of the scenes, nothing more than letting myself go in the letting go of objects, running immobile in the stream of time. And then the wind was not blowing.

After, I wandered down the quai de Bourbon until getting to the end of the isle where the intimate square was (intimate because it was small, not that it was hidden, it offered its whole breast to the river and the sky), I enjoyed it, a lot. Nothing there but a couple and, of course, pigeons; maybe even some of those which are flying past now so that I'm seeing them. A leap up and I settled on the wall, and let myself turn about and be caught and fixed by the sun, giving it my face and ears and hands (I kept my gloves in my pocket). I had no desire to shoot pictures, and lit a cigarette to be doing something; I think it was that moment when the match was about to touch the tobacco that I saw the young boy for the first time.

What I'd thought was a couple seemed much more now a boy with his mother, although at the same time I realized that it was not a kid and his mother, and that it was a couple in the sense that we always allegate to couples when we see them leaning up against the parapets or embracing on the benches in the squares. As I had nothing else to do, I had more than enough time to wonder why the boy was so nervous, like a young colt or a hare, sticking his hands into his pockets, taking them out immediately, one after the other, running his fingers through his hair, changing his stance, and especially why was he afraid, well, you could guess that from every gesture, a fear suffocated by his shyness, an impulse to step backwards which he telegraphed, his body standing as if it were on the edge of flight, holding itself back in a final, pitiful decorum.

All this was so clear, ten feet away – and we were alone against the parapet at the tip of the island – that at the beginning the boy's fright didn't let me see the blonde very well. Now, thinking back on it, I see her much better at that first second when I read her face (she'd turned around suddenly, swinging like a metal weathercock, and the eyes, the eyes were there), when I vaguely understood what might have been occurring to the boy and figured it would be worth the trouble to stay and watch (the wind was blowing their words away and they were speaking in a low murmur). I think that I know how to look, if it's something I know, and also that every looking oozes with mendacity, because it's that which expels us furthest outside ourselves, without the least guarantee, whereas to smell, or (but Michel rambles on to himself easily enough, there's no need to let him harangue on this way). In any case, if the likely inaccuracy can be seen beforehand, it becomes possible again to look; perhaps it suffices to choose between looking and the reality looked at, to strip things of all their unnecessary clothing. And surely all that is difficult besides.

As for the boy I remember the image before his actual body (that will clear itself up later), while now I am sure that I remember the woman's body much better than the image. She was thin and willowy, two unfair words to describe what she was, and was wearing an almost-black fur coat, almost long, almost handsome. All the morning's wind (now it was hardly a breeze and it wasn't cold) had blown through her blonde hair which pared away her white, bleak face – two unfair words – and put the world at her feet and horribly alone in front of her dark eyes, her eyes fell on things like two eagles, two leaps into nothingness, two puffs of green slime. I'm not describing anything, it's more a matter of trying to understand it. And I said two puffs of green slime.

Let's be fair, the boy was well enough dressed and was sporting yellow gloves which I would have sworn belonged to his older brother, a student of law or sociology; it was pleasant to see the fingers of the gloves sticking out of his jacket pocket. For a long time I didn't see his face, barely a profile, not stupid – a terrified bird, a Fra Filippo angel, rice pudding with milk – and the back of an adolescent who wants to take up judo and has had a scuffle or two in defence of an idea or his sister. Turning fourteen, perhaps fifteen, one would guess that he was dressed and fed by his parents but without a nickel in his pocket, having to debate with his buddies before making up his mind to buy a coffee, a cognac, a pack of cigarettes. He'd walk through the streets thinking of the girls in his class, about how good it would be to go to the movies and see the latest film, or to buy novels or neckties or bottles of liquor with green and white labels on them. At home (it would be a respectable home, lunch at noon and romantic landscapes on the walls, with a dark entryway and a mahogany umbrella stand inside the door) there'd be the slow rain of time, for studying, for being mama's hope, for looking like dad, for writing to his aunt in Avignon. So that there was a lot of walking the streets, the whole of the river for him (but without a nickel) and the mysterious city of fifteen-year-olds with its signs in doorways, its terrifying cats, a paper of fried potatoes for thirty francs, the pornographic magazine folded four ways, a solitude like the emptiness of his pockets, the eagerness for so much that was incomprehensible but illumined by a total love, by the availability analogous to the wind and the streets.

This biography was of the boy and of any boy whatsoever, but this particular one now, you could see he was insular, surrounded solely by the blonde's presence as she continued talking with him. (I'm tired of insisting, but two long ragged ones just went by. That morning I don't think I looked at the sky once, because what was happening with the boy and the woman appeared so soon I could do nothing but look at them and wait, look at them and ...) To cut it short, the boy was agitated and one could guess without too much trouble what had just occurred a few minutes before, at most half an hour. The boy had come on to the tip of the island, seen the woman and thought her marvellous. The woman was waiting for that because she was there waiting for that, or maybe the boy arrived before her and she saw him from one of the balconies or from a car and got out to meet him, starting the conversation with whatever, from the beginning she was sure that he was going to be afraid and want to run off, and that, naturally, he'd stay, stiff and sullen, pretending experience and the pleasure of the adventure. The rest was easy because it was happening ten feet away from me, and anyone could have gauged the stages of the game, the derisive, competitive fencing; its major attraction was not that it was happening but in foreseeing its denouement. The boy would try to end it by pretending a date, an obligation, whatever, and would go stumbling off disconcerted, wishing he were walking with some assurance, but naked under the mocking glance which would follow him until he was out of sight. Or rather, he would stay there, fascinated or simply incapable of taking the initiative, and the woman would begin to touch his face gently, muss his hair, still talking to him voicelessly, and soon would take him by the arm to lead him off, unless he, with an uneasiness beginning to tinge the edge of desire, even his stake in the adventure, would rouse himself to put his arm around her waist and to kiss her. Any of this could have happened, though it did not, and perversely Michel waited, sitting on the railing, making the settings almost without looking at the camera, ready to take a picturesque shot of a corner of the island with an uncommon couple talking and looking at one another.

Strange how the scene (almost nothing: two figures there mismatched in their youth) was taking on a disquieting aura. I thought it was I imposing it, and that my photo, if I shot it, would reconstitute things in their true stupidity. I would have liked to know what he was thinking, a man in a grey hat sitting at the wheel of a car parked on the dock which led up to the footbridge, and whether he was reading the paper or asleep. I had just discovered him because people inside a parked car have a tendency to disappear, they get lost in that wretched, private cage stripped of the beauty that motion and danger give it. And nevertheless, the car had been there the whole time, forming part (or deforming that part) of the isle. A car: like saying a lighted streetlamp, a park bench. Never like saying wind, sunlight, those elements always new to the skin and the eyes, and also the boy and the woman, unique, put there to change the island, to show it to me in another way. Finally, it may have been that the man with the newspaper also became aware of what was happening and would, like me, feel that malicious sensation of waiting for everything to happen. Now the woman had swung around smoothly, putting the young boy between herself and the wall, I saw them almost in profile, and he was taller, though not much taller, and yet she dominated him, it seemed like she was hovering over him (her laugh, all at once, a whip of feathers), crushing him just by being there, smiling, one hand taking a stroll through the air. Why wait any longer? Aperture at sixteen, a sighting which would not include the horrible black car, but yes, that tree, necessary to break up too much grey space ...

I raised the camera, pretended to study a focus which did not include them, and waited and watched closely, sure that I would finally catch the revealing expression, one that would sum it all up, life that is rhythmed by movement but which a stiff image destroys, taking time in cross section, if we do not choose the essential imperceptible fraction of it. I did not have to wait long. The woman was getting on with the job of handcuffing the boy smoothly, stripping from him what was left of his freedom a hair at a time, in an incredibly slow and delicious torture. I imagined the possible endings (now a small fluffy cloud appears, almost alone in the sky), I saw their arrival at the house (a basement apartment probably, which she would have filled with large cushions and cats) and conjectured the boy's terror and his desperate decision to play it cool and to be led off pretending there was nothing new in it for him. Closing my eyes, if I did in fact close my eyes, I set the scene: the teasing kisses, the woman mildly repelling the hands which were trying to undress her, like in novels, on a bed that would have a lilac-coloured comforter, on the other hand she taking off his clothes, plainly mother and son under a milky yellow light, and everything would end up as usual, perhaps, but maybe everything would go otherwise, and the initiation of the adolescent would not happen, she would not let it happen, after a long prologue wherein the awkwardnesses, the exasperating caresses, the running of hands over bodies would be resolved in who knows what, in a separate and solitary pleasure, in a petulant denial mixed with the art of tiring and disconcerting so much poor innocence. It might go like that, it might very well go like that; that woman was not looking for the boy as a lover, and at the same time she was dominating him towards some end impossible to understand if you do not imagine it as a cruel game, the desire to desire without satisfaction, to excite herself for someone else, someone who in no way could be that kid.

Michel is guilty of making literature, of indulging in fabricated unrealities. Nothing pleases him more than to imagine exceptions to the rule, individuals outside the species, not-always-repugnant monsters. But that woman invited speculation, perhaps giving clues enough for the fantasy to hit the bullseye. Before she left, and now that she would fill my imaginings for several days, for I'm given to ruminating, I decided not to lose a moment more. I got it all into the viewfinder (with the tree, the railing, the eleven-o'clock sun) and took the shot. In time to realize that they both had noticed and stood there looking at me, the boy surprised and as though questioning, but she was irritated, her face and body flat-footedly hostile, feeling robbed, ignominiously recorded on a small chemical image.

I might be able to tell it in much greater detail but it's not worth the trouble. The woman said that no one had the right to take a picture without permission, and demanded that I hand her over the film. All this in a dry, clear voice with a good Parisian accent, which rose in colour and tone with every phrase. For my part, it hardly mattered whether she got the roll of film or not, but anyone who knows me will tell you, if you want anything from me, ask nicely. With the result that I restricted myself to formulating the opinion that not only was photography in public places not prohibited, but it was looked upon with decided favour, both private and official. And while that was getting said, I noticed on the sly how the boy was falling back, sort of actively backing up though without moving, and all at once (it seemed almost incredible) he turned and broke into a run, the poor kid, thinking that he was walking off and in fact in full flight, running past the side of the car, disappearing like a gossamer filament of angel-spit in the morning air.

But filaments of angel-spittle are also called devil-spit, and Michel had to endure rather particular curses, to hear himself called meddler and imbecile, taking great pains meanwhile to smile and to abate with simple movements of his head such a hard sell. As I was beginning to get tired, I heard the car door slam. The man in the grey hat was there, looking at us. It was only at that point that I realized he was playing a part in the comedy.

He began to walk towards us, carrying in his hand the paper he had been pretending to read. What I remember best is the grimace that twisted his mouth askew, it covered his face with wrinkles, changed somewhat both in location and shape because his lips trembled and the grimace went from one side of his mouth to the other as though it were on wheels, independent and involuntary. But the rest stayed fixed, a flour-powdered clown or bloodless man, dull dry skin, eyes deepset, the nostrils black and prominently visible, blacker than the eyebrows or hair or the black necktie. Walking cautiously as though the pavement hurt his feet; I saw patent-leather shoes with such thin soles that he must have felt every roughness in the pavement. I don't know why I got down off the railing, nor very well why I decided to not give them the photo, to refuse that demand in which I guessed at their fear and cowardice. The clown and the woman consulted one another in silence: we made a perfect and unbearable triangle, something I felt compelled to break with a crack of a whip. I laughed in their faces and began to walk off, a little more slowly, I imagine, than the boy. At the level of the first houses, beside the iron footbridge, I turned around to look at them. They were not moving, but the man had dropped his newspaper; it seemed to me that the woman, her back to the parapet, ran her hands over the stone with the classical and absurd gesture of someone pursued looking for a way out.

What happened after that happened here, almost just now, in a room on the fifth floor. Several days went by before Michel developed the photos he'd taken on Sunday; his shots of the Conservatoire and of Sainte-Chapelle were all they should be. Then he found two or three proof-shots he'd forgotten, a poor attempt to catch a cat perched astonishingly on the roof of a rambling public urinal, and also the shot of the blonde and the kid. The negative was so good that he made an enlargement; the enlargement was so good that he made one very much larger, almost the size of a poster. It did not occur to him (now one wonders and wonders) that only the shots of the Conservatoire were worth so much work. Of the whole series, the snapshot of the tip of the island was the only one which interested him; he tacked up the enlargement on one wall of the room, and the first day he spent some time looking at it and remembering, that gloomy operation of comparing the memory with the gone reality; a frozen memory, like any photo, where nothing is missing, not even, and especially, nothingness, the true solidifier of the scene. There was the woman, there was the boy, the tree rigid above their heads, the sky as sharp as the stone of the parapet, clouds and stones melded into a single substance and inseparable (now one with sharp edges is going by, like a thunderhead). The first two days I accepted what I had done, from the photo itself to the enlargement on the wall, and didn't even question that every once in a while I would interrupt my translation of José Norberto Allende's treatise to encounter once more the woman's face, the dark splotches on the railing. I'm such a jerk; it had never occurred to me that when we look at a photo from the front, the eyes reproduce exactly the position and the vision of the lens; it's these things that are taken for granted and it never occurs to anyone to think about them. From my chair, with the typewriter directly in front of me, I looked at the photo ten feet away, and then it occurred to me that I had hung it exactly at the point of view of the lens. It looked very good that way; no doubt, it was the best way to appreciate a photo, though the angle from the diagonal doubtless has its pleasures and might even divulge different aspects. Every few minutes, for example when I was unable to find the way to say in good French what José Norberto Allende was saying in very good Spanish, I raised my eyes and looked at the photo; sometimes the woman would catch my eye, sometimes the boy, sometimes the pavement where a dry leaf had fallen admirably situated to heighten a lateral section. Then I rested a bit from my labours, and I enclosed myself again happily in that morning in which the photo was drenched, I recalled ironically the angry picture of the woman demanding I give her the photograph, the boy's pathetic and ridiculous flight, the entrance on the scene of the man with the white face. Basically, I was satisfied with myself; my part had not been too brilliant, and since the French have been given the gift of the sharp response, I did not see very well why I'd chosen to leave without a complete demonstration of the rights, privileges and prerogatives of citizens. The important thing, the really important thing was having helped the kid to escape in time (this in case my theorizing was correct, which was not sufficiently proven, but the running away itself seemed to show it so). Out of plain meddling, I had given him the opportunity finally to take advantage of his fright to do something useful; now he would be regretting it, feeling his honour impaired, his manhood diminished. That was better than the attentions of a woman capable of looking as she had looked at him on that island. Michel is something of a puritan at times, he believes that one should not seduce someone from a position of strength. In the last analysis, taking that photo had been a good act.

Well, it wasn't because of the good act that I looked at it between paragraphs while I was working. At that moment I didn't know the reason, the reason I had tacked the enlargement on to the wall; maybe all fatal acts happen that way, that that is the condition of their fulfilment. I don't think the almost-furtive trembling of the leaves on the tree alarmed me, I was working on a sentence and rounded it out successfully. Habits are like immense herbariums, in the end an enlargement of 32×28 looks like a movie screen, where, on the tip of the island, a woman is speaking with a boy and a tree is shaking its dry leaves over their heads.

But her hands were just too much. I had just translated: 'In that case, the second key resides in the intrinsic nature of difficulties which societies ...' – when I saw the woman's hand beginning to stir slowly, finger by finger. There was nothing left of me, a phrase in French which I would never have to finish, a typewriter on the floor, a chair that squeaked and shook, fog. The kid had ducked his head like boxers do when they've done all they can and are waiting for the final blow to fall; he had turned up the collar of his overcoat and seemed more a prisoner than ever, the perfect victim helping promote the catastrophe. Now the woman was talking into his ear, and her hand opened again to lay itself against his cheekbone, to caress and caress it, burning it, taking her time. The kid was less startled then he was suspicious, once or twice he poked his head over the woman's shoulder and she continued talking, saying something that made him look back every few minutes towards that area where Michel knew the car was parked and the man in the grey hat, carefully eliminated from the photo but present in the boy's eyes (how I doubt that now), in the words of the woman, in the woman's hands, in the vicarious presence of the woman. When I saw the man come up, stop near them and look at them, his hands in his pockets and a stance somewhere between disgusted and demanding, the master who is about to whistle in his dog after a frolic in the square, I understood, if that was to understand, what had to happen now, what had to have happened then, what would have to happen at that moment, among these people, just where I had poked my nose in to upset an established order, interfering innocently in that which had not happened, but which was now going to happen, now was going to be fulfilled. And what I had imagined earlier was much less horrible than the reality, that woman, who was not there by herself, she was not caressing or propositioning or encouraging for her own pleasure, to lead the angel away with his tousled hair and play the tease with his terror and his eager grace. The real boss was waiting there, smiling petulantly, already certain of the business; he was not the first to send a woman in the vanguard, to bring him the prisoners manacled with flowers. The rest of it would be so simple, the car, some house or another, drinks, stimulating engravings, tardy tears, the awakening in hell. And there was nothing I could do, this time I could do absolutely nothing. My strength had been a photograph, that, there, where they were taking their revenge on me, demonstrating clearly what was going to happen. The photo had been taken, the time had run out, gone; we were so far from one another, the abusive act had certainly already taken place, the tears already shed, and the rest conjecture and sorrow. All at once the order was inverted, they were alive, moving, they were deciding and had decided, they were going to their future; and I on this side, prisoner of another time, in a room on the fifth floor, to not know who they were, that woman, that man, and that boy, to be only the lens of my camera, something fixed, rigid, incapable of intervention. It was horrible, their mocking me, deciding it before my impotent eye, mocking me, for the boy again was looking at the flour-faced clown and I had to accept the fact that he was going to say yes, that the proposition carried money with it or a gimmick, and I couldn't yell for him to run, or even open the road to him again with a new photo, a small and almost meek intervention which would ruin the framework of drool and perfume. Everything was going to resolve itself right there, at that moment; there was like an immense silence which had nothing to do with physical silence. It was stretching it out, setting itself up. I think I screamed, I screamed terribly, and that at that exact second I realized that I was beginning to move towards them, four inches, a step, another step, the tree swung its branches rhythmically in the foreground, a place where the railing was tarnished emerged from the frame, the woman's face turneds toward me as though surprised, was enlarging, and then I turned a bit, I mean that the camera turned a little, and without losing sight of the woman, I began to close in on the man who was looking at me with the black holes he had in place of eyes, surprised and angered both, he looked, wanting to nail me on to the air, and at that

instant I happened to see something like a large bird outside the focus that
was flying in a single swoop in front of the picture, and I leaned up against
the wall of my room and was happy because the boy had just managed to
escape, I saw him running off, in focus again, sprinting with his hair flying
in the wind, learning finally to fly across the island, to arrive at the
footbridge, return to the city. For the second time he'd escaped them, for
the second time I was helping him to escape, returning him to his precarious paradise. Out of breath, I stood in front of them; no need to step closer,
the game was played out. Of the woman you could see just maybe a
shoulder and a bit of the hair, brutally cut off by the frame of the picture;
but the man was directly centre, his mouth half open, you could see the
shaking black tongue, and he lifted his hands slowly, bringing them into
the foreground, an instant still in perfect focus, and then all of him a lump
that blotted out the island, the tree, and I shut my eyes, I didn't want to see
any more, and I covered my face and broke into tears like an idiot.

Now there's a big white cloud, as on all these days, all this untellable
time. What remains to be said is always a cloud, two clouds, or long hours
of a sky perfectly clear, a very clean, clear rectangle tacked up with pins on
the wall of my room. That was what I saw when I opened my eyes and
dried them with my fingers: the clear sky, and then a cloud that drifted in
from the left, passed gracefully and slowly across and disappeared on the
right. And then another, and for a change sometimes, everything gets grey,
all one enormous cloud, and suddenly the splotches of rain cracking down,
for a long spell you can see it raining over the picture, like a spell of
weeping reversed, and little by little, the frame becomes clear, perhaps the
sun comes out, and again the clouds begin to come, two at a time, three at
a time. And the pigeons once in a while, and a sparrow or two.

Translated by Paul Blackburn

Clarice Lispector

Love

Feeling a little tired, with her purchases bulging her new string bag, Anna boarded the tram. She placed the bag on her lap and the tram started off. Settling back in her seat she tried to find a comfortable position, with a sigh of mild satisfaction.

Anna had nice children, she reflected with certainty and pleasure. They were growing up, bathing themselves and misbehaving; they were demanding more and more of her time. The kitchen, after all, was spacious with its old stove that made explosive noises. The heat was oppressive in the apartment, which they were paying off in instalments, and the wind, playing against the curtains she had made herself, reminded her that if she wanted to she could pause to wipe her forehead, and contemplate the calm horizon. Like a farmer. She had planted the seeds she held in her hand, no others, but only those. And they were growing into trees. Her brisk conversations with the electricity man were growing, the water filling the tank was growing, her children were growing, the table was growing with food, her husband arriving with the newspapers and smiling with hunger, the irritating singing of the maids resounding through the block. Anna tranquilly put her small, strong hand, her life current to everything. Certain times of the afternoon struck her as being critical. At a certain hour of the afternoon the trees she had planted laughed at her. And when nothing more required her strength, she became anxious. Meanwhile she felt herself more solid than ever, her body become a little thicker, and it was worth seeing the manner in which she cut out blouses for the children, the large scissors snapping into the material. All her vaguely artistic aspirations had for some time been channelled into making her days fulfilled and beautiful; with time, her taste for the decorative had developed and supplanted intimate disorder. She seemed to have discovered that everything was capable of being perfected, that each thing could be given a harmonious appearance; life itself could be created by Man.

Deep down, Anna had always found it necessary to feel the firm roots of things. And this is what a home had surprisingly provided. Through tortuous paths, she had achieved a woman's destiny, with the surprise of conforming to it almost as if she had invented that destiny herself. The man whom she had married was a real man, the children she mothered were real children. Her previous youth now seemed alien to her, like one of life's illnesses. She had gradually emerged to discover that life could be lived without happiness: by abolishing it she had found a legion of persons, previously invisible, who lived as one works – with perseverance, persistence, and contentment. What had happened to Anna before possessing a home of her own stood forever beyond her reach: that disturbing exaltation she had often confused with unbearable happiness. In exchange she had created something ultimately comprehensible: the life of an adult. This was what she had wanted and chosen.

Her precautions were now reduced to alertness during the dangerous part of the afternoon, when the house was empty and she was no longer needed; when the sun reached its zenith, and each member of the family went about his separate duties. Looking at the polished furniture, she felt her heart contract a little with fear. But in her life there was no opportunity to cherish her fears – she suppressed them with that same ingenuity she had acquired from domestic struggles. Then she would go out shopping or take things to be mended, unobtrusively looking after her home and her family. When she returned it would already be late afternoon and the children back from school would absorb her attention. Until the evening descended with its quiet excitement. In the morning she would awaken surrounded by her calm domestic duties. She would find the furniture dusty and dirty once more, as if it had returned repentant. As for herself, she mysteriously formed part of the soft, dark roots of the earth. And anonymously she nourished life. It was pleasant like this. This was what she had wanted and chosen.

The tram swayed on its rails and turned into the main road. Suddenly the wind became more humid, announcing not only the passing of the afternoon but the end of that uncertain hour. Anna sighed with relief and a deep sense of acceptance gave her face an air of womanhood.

The tram would drag along and then suddenly jolt to a halt. As far as Humaitá she could relax. Suddenly she saw the man stationary at the tram stop. The difference between him and others was that he was really stationary. He stood with his hands held out in front of him – blind.

But what else was there about him that made Anna sit up in distrust? Something disquieting was happening. Then she discovered what it was: the blind man was chewing gum ... a blind man chewing gum. Anna still had time to reflect for a second that her brothers were coming to dinner – her heart pounding at regular intervals. Leaning forward, she studied the blind man intently, as one observes something incapable of returning our gaze. Relaxed, and with open eyes, he was chewing gum in the failing light. The facial movements of his chewing made him appear to smile then suddenly stop smiling, to smile and stop smiling. Anna stared at him as if he had insulted her. And anyone watching would have received the impression of a woman filled with hatred. She continued to stare at him, leaning more and more forward – until the tram gave a sudden jerk, throwing her unexpectedly backward. The heavy string bag toppled from her lap and landed on the floor. Anna cried out, the conductor gave the signal to stop before realizing what was happening, and the tram came to an abrupt halt. The other passengers looked on in amazement. Too paralysed to gather up her shopping, Anna sat upright, her face suddenly pale. An expression, long since forgotten, awkwardly reappeared, unexpected and inexplicable. The Negro newsboy smiled as he handed over her bundle. The eggs had broken in their newspaper wrapping. Yellow sticky yolks dripped between the strands of the bag. The blind man had interrupted his chewing and held out his unsteady hands, trying in vain to grasp what had happened. She removed the parcel of eggs from the string bag accompanied by the smiles of the passengers. A second signal from the conductor and the tram moved off with another jerk.

A few moments later people were no longer staring at her. The tram was rattling on the rails and the blind man chewing gum had remained behind forever. But the damage had been done.

The string bag felt rough between her fingers, not soft and familiar as when she had knitted it. The bag had lost its meaning; to find herself on that tram was a broken thread; she did not know what to do with the purchases on her lap. Like some strange music, the world started up again around her. The damage had been done. But why? Had she forgotten that there were blind people? Compassion choked her. Anna's breathing became heavy. Even those things that had existed before the episode were now on the alert, more hostile, and even perishable. The world had once more become a nightmare. Several years fell away, the yellow yolks trickled. Exiled from her own days, it seemed to her that the people in the streets were vulnerable, that they barely maintained their equilibrium on the surface of the darkness – and for a moment they appeared to lack any sense of direction. The perception of an absence of law came so unexpectedly that Anna clutched the seat in front of her, as if she might fall off the tram, as if things might be overturned with the same calm they had possessed when order reigned.

What she called a crisis had come at last. And its sign was the intense pleasure with which she now looked at things, suffering and alarmed. The heat had become more oppressive, everything had gained new power and a stronger voice. In the Rua Voluntários de Pátria, revolution seemed imminent, the grids of the gutters were dry, the air dusty. A blind man chewing gum had plunged the world into a mysterious excitement. In every strong person there was a lack of compassion for the blind man, and their strength terrified her. Beside her sat a woman in blue with an expression which made Anna avert her gaze rapidly. On the pavement a mother shook her little boy. Two lovers held hands smiling ... And the blind man? Anna had lapsed into a mood of compassion which greatly distressed her.

She had skilfully pacified life; she had taken so much care to avoid upheavals. She had cultivated an atmosphere of serene understanding, separating each person from the others. Her clothes were clearly designed to be practical, and she could choose the evening's film from the newspaper – and everything was done in such a manner that each day should smoothly succeed the previous one. And a blind man chewing gum was destroying all this. Through her compassion Anna felt that life was filled to the brim with a sickening nausea.

Only then did she realize that she had passed her stop ages ago. In her weak state everything touched her with alarm. She got off the tram, her legs shaking, and looked around her, clutching the string bag stained with the egg. For a moment she was unable to get her bearings. She seemed to have plunged into the middle of the night.

It was a long road, with high yellow walls. Her heart beat with fear as she tried in vain to recognize her surroundings; while the life she had discovered continued to pulsate, a gentler, more mysterious wind caressed her face. She stood quietly observing the wall. At last she recognized it. Advancing a little further alongside a hedge, she passed through the gates of the botanical garden.

She strolled wearily up the central avenue, between the palm trees. There was no one in the garden. She put her parcels down on the ground and sat down on the bench of a side path where she remained for some time.

The wilderness seemed to calm her, the silence regulating her breathing and soothing her senses.

From afar she saw the avenue where the evening was round and clear. But the shadows of the branches covered the side path.

Around her there were tranquil noises, the scent of trees, chance encounters among the creeping plants. The entire garden fragmented by the ever more fleeting moments of the evening. From whence came the drowsiness with which she was surrounded? As if induced by the drone of birds and bees. Everything seemed strange, much too gentle, much too great.

A gentle, familiar movement startled her and she turned round rapidly. Nothing appeared to have stirred. But in the central lane there stood, immobile, an enormous cat. Its fur was soft. With another silent movement, it disappeared.

Agitated, she looked about her. The branches swayed, their shadows wavering on the ground. A sparrow foraged in the soil. And suddenly, in terror, she imagined that she had fallen into an ambush. In the garden there was a secret activity in progress which she was beginning to penetrate.

On the trees, the fruits were black and sweet as honey. On the ground there lay dry fruit stones full of circumvolutions like small rotted cerebrums. The bench was stained with purple sap. With gentle persistence the waters murmured. On the tree trunk the luxurious feelers of parasites fastened themselves. The rawness of the world was peaceful. The murder was deep. And death was not what one had imagined.

As well as being imaginary, this was a world to be devoured with one's teeth, a world of voluminous dahlias and tulips. The trunks were pervaded by leafy parasites, their embrace soft and clinging. Like the resistance that precedes surrender, it was fascinating; the woman felt disgusted, and it was fascinating.

The trees were laden, and the world was so rich that it was rotting. When Anna reflected that there were children and grown men suffering hunger, the nausea reached her throat as if she were pregnant and abandoned. The moral of the garden was something different. Now that the blind man had guided her to it, she trembled on the threshold of a dark, fascinating world where monstrous water lilies floated. The small flowers scattered on the grass did not appear to be yellow or pink, but the colour of inferior gold and scarlet. Their decay was profound, perfumed. But all these oppressive things she watched, her head surrounded by a swarm of insects, sent by some more refined life in the world. The breeze penetrated between the flowers. Anna imagined rather than felt its sweetened scent. The garden was so beautiful that she feared hell.

It was almost night now and everything seemed replete and heavy; a squirrel leapt in the darkness. Under her feet the earth was soft. Anna inhaled its odour with delight. It was both fascinating and repulsive.

But when she remembered the children, before whom she now felt guilty, she straightened up with a cry of pain. She clutched the package, advanced through the dark side path, and reached the avenue. She was

almost running, and she saw the garden all around her aloof and impersonal. She shook the locked gates, and went on shaking them, gripping the
rough timber. The watchman appeared, alarmed at not having seen her.

Until she reached the entrance of the building, she seemed to be on the
brink of disaster. She ran with the string bag to the lift, her heart beating in
her breast – what was happening? Her compassion for the blind man was
as fierce as anguish but the world seemed hers, dirty, perishable, hers. She
opened the door of her flat. The room was large, square, the polished knobs
were shining, the window panes were shining, the lamp shone brightly –
what new land was this? And for a moment that wholesome life she had
led until today seemed morally crazy. The little boy who came running up
to embrace her was a creature with long legs and a face resembling her
own. She pressed him firmly to her in anxiety and fear. Trembling, she
protected herself. Life was vulnerable. She loved the world, she loved all
things created, she loved with loathing. In the same way as she had always
been fascinated by oysters, with that vague sentiment of revulsion which
the approach of truth provoked, admonishing her. She embraced her son,
almost hurting him. Almost as if she knew of some evil – the blind man or
the beautiful botanical garden – she was clinging to him, to him whom she
loved above all things. She had been touched by the demon of faith.

'Life is horrible,' she said to him in a low voice, as if famished. What
would she do if she answered the blind man's call? She would go alone ...
There were poor and rich places that needed her. She needed them. 'I am
afraid,' she said. She felt the delicate ribs of the child between her arms, she
heard his frightened weeping.

'Mummy,' the child called. She held him away from her, she studied his
face and her heart shrank.

'Don't let Mummy forget you,' she said. No sooner had the child felt her
embrace weaken than he escaped and ran to the door of the room, from
where he watched her more safely. It was the worst look that she had ever
received. The blood rose hot to her cheeks.

She sank into a chair, with her fingers still clasping the string bag. What
was she ashamed of? There was no way of escaping. The very crust of the
days she had forged had broken and the water was escaping. she stood
before the oysters. And there was no way of averting her gaze. What was
she ashamed of? Certainly it was no longer pity, it was more than pity: her
heart had filled with the worst will to live.

She no longer knew if she was on the side of the blind man or of the
thick plants. The man little by little had moved away, and in her torment
she appeared to have passed over to the side of those who had injured his

eyes. The botanical garden, tranquil and high, had been a revelation. With horror, she discovered that she belonged to the strong part of the world, and what name should she give to her fierce compassion? Would she be obliged to kiss the leper, since she would never be just a sister. 'A blind man has drawn me to the worst of myself,' she thought, amazed. She felt herself banished because no pauper would drink water from her burning hands. Ah! It was easier to be a saint than a person! Good heavens, then was it not real, that pity which had fathomed the deepest waters in her heart? But it was the compassion of a lion.

Humiliated, she knew that the blind man would prefer a poorer love. And, trembling, she also knew why. The life of the botanical garden summoned her as a werewolf is summoned by the moonlight. 'Oh! But she loved the blind man,' she thought with tears in her eyes. Meanwhile it was not with this sentiment that one would go to church. 'I am frightened,' she whispered alone in the room. She got up and went to the kitchen to help the maid prepare dinner.

But life made her shiver like the cold of winter. She heard the school bell pealing, distant and constant. The small horror of the dust gathering in threads around the bottom of the stove, where she had discovered a small spider. Lifting a vase to change the water – there was the horror of the flower submitting itself, languid and loathsome, to her hands. The same secret activity was going on here in the kitchen. Near the waste bin, she crushed an ant with her foot. The small murder of the ant. Its minute body trembled. Drops of water fell on the stagnant water in the pool.

The summer beetles. The horror of those expressionless beetles. All around there was a silent, slow, insistent life. Horror upon horror. She went from one side of the kitchen to the other, cutting the steaks, mixing the cream. Circling around her head, around the light, the flies of a warm summer's evening. A night in which compassion was as crude as false love. Sweat trickled between her breasts. Faith broke her; the heat of the oven burned in her eyes.

Then her husband arrived, followed by her brothers and their wives, and her brothers' children.

They dined with all the windows open, on the ninth floor. An airplane shuddered menacingly in the heat of the sky. Although she had used few eggs, the dinner was good. The children stayed up, playing on the carpet with their cousins. It was summer and it would be useless to force them to go to sleep. Anna was a little pale and laughed gently with the others.

After dinner, the first cool breeze finally entered the room. The family was seated round the table, tired after their day, happy in the absence of any discord, eager not to find fault. They laughed at everything, with warmth and humanity. The children grew up admirably around them. Anna took the moment like a butterfly, between her fingers before it might escape forever.

Later, when they had all left and the children were in bed, she was just a woman looking out of the window. The city was asleep and warm. Would the experience unleashed by the blind man fill her days? How many years would it take before she once more grew old? The slightest movement on her part and she would trample one of her children. But with the ill will of a lover, she seemed to accept that the fly would emerge from the flower, and the giant water lilies would float in the darkness of the lake. The blind man was hanging among the fruits of the botanical garden.

What if that were the stove exploding with the fire spreading through the house, she thought to herself as she ran to the kitchen where she found her husband in front of the spilt coffee.

'What happened?' she cried, shaking from head to foot. He was taken aback by his wife's alarm. And suddenly understanding, he laughed.

'It was nothing,' he said, 'I am just a clumsy fellow.' He looked tired, with dark circles under his eyes.

But, confronted by the strange expression on Anna's face, he studied her more closely. Then he drew her to him in a sudden caress.

'I don't want anything ever to happen to you!' she said.

'You can't prevent the stove from having its little explosions,' he replied, smiling. She remained limp in his arms. This afternoon, something tranquil had exploded, and in the house everything struck a tragicomic note.

'It's time to go to bed,' he said, 'it's late.' In a gesture which was not his, but which seemed natural, he held his wife's hand, taking her with him, without looking back, removing her from the danger of living.

The giddiness of compassion had spent itself. And if she had crossed love and its hell, she was now combing her hair before the mirror, without any world for the moment in her heart. Before getting into bed, as if she were snuffing a candle, she blew out that day's tiny flame.

Translated by Giovanni Pontiero

José Donoso

Ana María

1

'How odd for them to leave such a little girl all on her own in such a big garden!' thought the old man, mopping the sweat from his face with a handkerchief which he then proceeded to put back in the pocket of his tatty jacket.

The girl was, in fact, *very* little, she could hardly have been three years old. She was like a molecule which floated for an instant, vanishing afterwards amongst the trunks of the chestnut and walnut trees, way in the distance of the blue horizon that had been poured over the foliage. The old man's eyes looked again for the little girl: it seemed the chaos of vegetation had gobbled her up, that silence whose only inhabitants were the buzzing of the insects and the murmuring of an irrigation ditch lost amongst the undergrowth and brambles. He was worried for a moment when he couldn't spot her. Soon, however, his eyes found the little figure crouching in a pool of yellow flowers which, in the thickest part of the shade, seemed to imitate a spot of sunlight. The old man heaved a sigh of relief and muttered:

'Poor little thing . . . !'

He sat down under the willow tree which, hanging over from a corner of the property, shaded the pavement. With dry branches he set about making a tiny fire, where he brewed up his tea in a little pot. He took out a bit of bread, tomatoes, an onion, and ate, while thinking about how odd it was that he hadn't seen the little girl before. He'd always believed the piece of barbed-wire-enclosed land to be deserted, although at times he'd thought he could make out, amongst the trees at the far end, a kind of prefabricated house, small and not really suited to its location. He'd studied the garden intently on more than one occasion and had been surprised at never seeing anyone. Then after a while he stopped thinking about it.

Every day he would go along to eat his lunch under the willow tree and to have a nap beside this island of greenery, the only vegetation in that part of the city. And at two in the afternoon he would go back to the building site where he was working, two blocks away along the road in which almost all the plots were still undeveloped and dry.

The man lay face down next to the wire fence. Protected from the fierce midday heat, he would listen to the gurgling of the irrigation ditch, and, ears pricked for the slightest rustling of leaves, he would watch the garden. In the distance, perhaps springing up spontaneously as part of the vegetation, he saw the girl: diminutive and almost naked, she was standing near a broad tree-trunk which a tangle of red roses was climbing with animal-like urgency. He spent a little while studying her: how, as she played, she would disappear amongst the thickets, how she would suddenly drift away, how some especially dense shade would dilute the small white body. Later on, the man cleaned his little pot, and, after stamping out what was left of the fire, went back to work.

When he finished his day's labours, the old man did not leave with the group of workmen who walked home laughing and swinging their bags full of clothes. He lagged behind with the idea of stopping off by the garden on the off-chance of seeing the little girl. But he didn't see her.

At nightfall, he sat down to smoke in the doorway of the shack where he lived, right on the other side of the city. His wife, crouching at the entrance, was blowing on to a small brazier waiting for the coals to glow red hot before she placed a pan on top. The old man didn't know whether to tell her or not. Even after thirty-odd years of marriage he could never be sure what things it was possible to tell his wife without her flying off the handle, although for a long time he'd been indifferent to his wife's fits of anger. So he told her he'd seen a tiny little girl, all on her own in a very big garden.

'All on her own?' for a moment a few furrows softened his wife's face.

'And she had blonde hair . . .' added the man in a low voice.

When she heard her husband's tone, the hardness returned to the woman's face and she blew heavily over the brazier, causing a stream of sparks to spit out into the miserable night. Then she went inside to fetch the pan, certain, now more than ever, of the man's contempt. This was, doubtless, the appointed hour, when the man, weary of silently hating her failure as a wife, would call her a 'mule'. The women in the district all proudly called her this. Women who, overwhelmed by the need to feed scores of children, would always avoid any contact whatsoever with her, as she was so bitter and silent. Over the course of the years, she had hidden herself in a cloud of ill-humour and anguish waiting for the moment to retire and cede her place to another woman who would be more deserving of it. In the beginning, when they still retained a hint of their youth, the man had a certain amount of pity for her. But later it was simply too hard to reach her. And as they had grown old so much distance had come between the two of them, that the only tangible part of their relationship was one of silent bitterness.

That night the wife rudely served the plate of soup to her husband. He spooned it up, on this occasion not thinking it was the same old soup, the one which he had never in all the years of marriage actually managed to like. Then they went to bed. The woman would toss and turn and talk so much in her sleep that often the man would find it a real job to get any rest. But sometimes she would be all tense and stay awake for hours on end, and then she wouldn't toss and turn. The night the man told her he'd seen a tiny little girl, all on her own in a very big garden, the woman responded by being silent and calm, as if she were waiting.

Every day, at lunchtime, the man would lie down on the pavement in the shade of the willow tree, near the fence, gazing at the garden. Sometimes he would catch sight of the little girl, far away, almost naked, always on her own, floating in that island of plant light. But on other occasions he wouldn't get to see her because he would fall asleep, so frail was he in his old age in the face of the heat and the day's work. As there was no one else he could talk to about it, on several occasions he found himself saying something about the girl to his wife, whose spirits were getting lower and lower, until there was no longer even bitterness between them.

One day the man awoke with a start under the willow. He studied the undergrowth in the garden without seeing anyone. But suddenly, behind the fence, where the shade of a shrub weighed more heavily, he saw two huge, deep, blue eyes staring at him out of the darkness. Fear shook him.

They were the eyes of the little girl. Her body began to emerge from the green reflections of the leaves. The man, embarrassed, as if he were doing something wrong sleeping under the willow tree from somebody else's property, made to stand up to leave. But before he managed to, the little girl had approached the fence, crying:

'My lub' . . . !'

All the amazement that lay untapped in the old man smiled.

'Pwettie . . . !'

The little girl's eyes were so large and blue they seemed to glow in the little face framed by a blonde fringe. Both of them just stood looking at each other. Then the man asked:

'What's the little lady's name?'

She didn't understand straight away and the man had to repeat the question. This time the girl answered, smiling at him:

'Ana María . . .'

Unable to resist, the old fellow put a hand through the wires in the fence so as to stroke Ana María's hair. She came over all serious, as if she were meditating. Then, with a laugh, she looked straight into his eyes that were blurry with amazement, and she showed him a bag she was carrying over her shoulder. She cried:

'Angbag . . . angbag!'

'What a pretty handbag the young lady's got!'

'Pwettie! Pwettie you, my lub!' cried Ana María.

And, walking away from the wire, almost dissolved by the shade of the leaves, she waved goodbye to the old man. Then she disappeared amongst the thickets in the garden.

'Poor little thing!' said the man to himself.

That night he told his wife that the little girl's name was Ana María. He didn't tell her anything else. But the woman's body hunched in savage humiliation over the fire where the laundry was boiling. Later on, she told her husband there was nothing to eat that night. But this was a common thing for the old man, and he went early to bed, because when you're asleep you don't feel hungry. The woman went silently to bed, very quiet by his side.

2

In the house at the bottom of the garden Ana María's mother and father were lying next to each other in the narrow, unmade bed. The aqueous light traversed the closed green shutters and fell on the bodies glistening with perspiration, flooding the small bedroom. A persistent buzzing of flies and botflies kept the air throbbing, the air damp with the smell of exhausted bodies and cigarettes and used sheets.

The man hardly stirred. He moved a hand over his chest and stomach to dry the perspiration, and when he wiped his palm on the dirty pillow, he screwed up his face in disgust without opening his eyes. Then he half opened them slowly, as if the sweat were weighing too heavily on his eyelids, and he turned on to his side, studying his wife's body. It was beautiful, beautiful and white. Too big and too flabby, perhaps, but beautiful, and touching the sheet, the outline of the body was underlined by a fold of heavy, abundant flab. The man knew she was only dozing. On her lily skin, at the point where her neck met her chest, he saw one of his own discarded hairs, black, powerful, curly. He removed it slowly, leaving a slight reddish line on her skin, which gradually became paler. Then, with very delicate movements, he killed several tiny, green insects, which coming from the undergrowth in the garden, where everything grew and multiplied, had alighted on his wife's body. There was an almost invisible one under her arm, uncovered because she was sleeping with her arms crossed behind her head: he squashed it with premeditated pressure. The woman smiled. He stroked the hair under her arm, even whiter than the rest of her body. The woman turned towards him and they slipped into a long embrace.

Afterwards they dozed a little more. Until, opening his eyes wide, the man cried:

'It's two in the afternoon! I'm hungry!'

The woman stretched, muttering as she yawned:

'I don't think I've got anything to eat ...'

Both of them yawned together.

'I saw some eggs ...'

'Yes, but I actually gave the little'un eggs this morning.'

'Oh, never mind,' said the man, turning over in the bed and going off to sleep with one heavy leg on top of his wife's thigh.

She freed herself from that weight by sitting up a little. She left a stain of perspiration on the sheet. She leaned against the sturdy, broad shoulders of her husband and her fingers played with the man's muscles. Oh, no. On second thoughts, she decided she should make an effort. She took an ornamental comb which she found on the floor beside the bed, on the side with the shell full of half-smoked cigarettes, and with an expert twirl she gathered together her wet hair at the top of her neck. Then she put her feet into the dirty white high-heeled shoes, and, naked, headed for the kitchen.

There were indeed only eggs in the fridge. Seeing the dirty dishes from that morning's breakfast and the previous night's meal, she gave a nonchalant shrug of her shoulders and took out some clean plates so that she didn't have to wash the others. As she cooked, she put the radio on, a programme playing dance numbers. She tapped along to the rhythm of the music with her high heels and swayed her naked body as she beat the eggs.

'You've gone and woken me up with that music!' yelled the man from the bedroom.

'Oh! You've had enough sleep!'

The man got up. He started doing exercises in front of a full-length mirror. In between touching his toes he asked:

'Hey, where's the little'un got to?'

'She's around somewhere ...' replied the woman. 'It's Sunday, so she knows she mustn't bother us ...'

'She's too little to know it's Sunday.'

'But she knows she mustn't disturb us when you're here.'

The wife served up a dishful for her husband and one for her daughter. She poured her own into a cup because she couldn't find another clean plate and she couldn't bring herself to wash the others. She put a dressing gown on, her husband some underpants, and after shouting out to Ana María from the entrance to the house, all three sat down at the little table in the living room, where they generally ate.

When Ana María saw the eggs, she said:

'Don' want.'

But they didn't listen as they laughed together at the jokes in a magazine. Later, the woman saw that Ana María hadn't eaten and that she was staring at her with her huge blue and oh-so-transparent eyes. She felt uncomfortable and told her dryly:

'Eat it up . . . !'

Ana María looked at the eggs and said once more:

'Don' want . . .'

'Have some bread, then, and run along . . .'

Ana María went off.

'Did she eat this morning?' asked the man.

'Yes, I think so. I was in a bit of a daze, so I didn't really notice . . .'

'In a bit of a daze? How come?'

'You ask me why after a night like that! You beast!'

They laughed.

'Can't you wash the plates up . . .'

'I don't think so. Do you think I married you so I could be a servant to you and the little 'un?'

Leaving everything in the same mess as before, they went back to the bedroom. After a few moments of suggestive games and dozing, the man came out with an idea:

'Hey, shall we go to the pictures tonight?'

'Okay, but we'll have to make sure the little'un's asleep first, and locked in.'

'Well . . . just like normal then.'

'Yes. But she's acting very odd, I don't know what's up with her. Haven't you noticed? Sometimes I find her . . . I don't know . . . like she, well . . . sort of gives me a fright. I mean, the other day when we got back from the pictures she was awake, she was just pretending to be asleep, and that was, what, one in the morning . . .'

'And? So what?'

'I don't know, she's very young.'

'Don't be silly. What's the big deal? She's got all day to sleep if she wants to.'

'She's always been a bit odd. I'd even say I find her a bit backward. I mean, the only thing she like playing with is that bag which I keep my shoes in ... goodness knows what she sees in that ... Angbag, she calls it.'

'Mmm ... she's odd.'

'And even a bit of a pain sometimes when she stares at me with those sort of animal-like eyes of hers. I mean, just the other day I was sleeping in the canvas seat in the garden, you know the heat makes me so sleepy ...'

Laughing, the woman stroked the damp hair on her husband's chest.

'... so, I'd gone off to sleep. Suddenly I woke up. The first thing I saw, not very near by, in the shade of that lime tree there, was the little'un, or rather the little'un's eyes staring gormlessly at me from the shade. When she realized I'd woken up, she ran off.

'Oh! You're just crazy! What's wrong with that?'

'I don't know, but it's odd. And the other day. I mean, she'd been following me around all morning for me to pick her up or something, but without saying anything to me without coming up very close to me. But I didn't feel like doing anything, I was sort of tired, I don't know ...

'When aren't you, lazy bones!'

'... until I finally picked her up. Then she started to hug me and laugh and be all affectionate, but in a cloying sort of way, that it made me feel I don't know ... sort of scared or disgusted. But sometimes she's lovely too, ah. And she was saying "My lub" and "pwettie" to me, you know, the first things she learned to say, goodness knows where, because you never say that to me ...'

'Never? What do you mean?'

'No. Never ...'

'But I say better things to you.'

'Okay, but not those. So, she was being all lovely and affectionate and I was getting really very worried, when, do you know what she did?'

'No ...'

'She bit my ear.'

The man laughed.

'She bit your ear? And how did the little devil know you like that?'

'Don't be silly, not like that. Don't laugh, 'cos she didn't nibble it. She bit it really hard, as if she wanted to tear a slice off with those little sharp teeth of hers. It hurt so much I yelped and let go of her. And she raced off as if she knew she'd done something wrong. That was in the morning. She didn't come back at lunch time, or for the rest of the day. And as you know I can't stand going out into the garden, the other side of the trees, I didn't go looking for her. But when she came back at night, looking scared stiff, I punished her . . .'

'And what did you do to her?'

'How should I know? How do you expect me to remember?'

The man laughed again, this time at another joke in the magazine, which he'd been flicking through during the conversation. He felt, next to his own, the rather damp shape of his wife's body. They smoked, and one of them went to get the radio to listen to music. The green light of the shutters and of the garden began to pale.

3

The old man carried on going to eat his lunch every day under the willow tree. It was no longer a case of studying the garden intently because the little girl would always be waiting for him beside the wire. Somehow she seemed to guess the time, and if the man came along late, she would give him rather a harsh look. But soon she would smile muttering:

'My lub. Pwettie.'

The old man would strain to lift Ana María up over the fence so as to sit her down beside him. He would light the fire to brew the tea. Then he would eat bread, on rare occasions a bit of meat, onions, tomatoes, sharing his provisions with her, and she always seemed hungry.

A workman from the site happened to overhear the old man's conversation with Ana María. From then on, his workmates didn't give him a moment's peace.

'Hey, old lover! Come on! How's your love life getting on?'

He would hear out their laughter patiently. As he trundled the mortar barrow, his legs, quivering with age, would barely support him on his route down the plank. His eyes, blurry with dirt and sweat, could scarcely make out the young workers who gibed at him from the scaffolding:

'Hey, you little old devil! You'd better be careful, they'll lock you up!'

And thinking about what Ana María had said to him at lunchtime, he would blush under the grime on his face.

The girl had sat down next to him in the shade, suddenly opening her ever-present bag, to show him a pair of shoes.

'Soos! Pwettie littew tootsie?'

She also had, inside the bag, a crumpled but shiny ribbon. With clumsy hands the old man tied it round the girl's blonde hair, and she, thrilled, felt the sky-blue bow with her fingers. The girl showed him other things as well, some dice, a medicine box, a box of matches, a doll's head that had been smashed up. That was the last thing she took out of the bag, as if she didn't want her friend to see it, as if she herself didn't want to see it. It was a blonde, chubby-cheeked, head with a cheerful, flirtatious face.

'And this? What's this, young lady?'

Ana María's eyes suddenly filled with tears, which trembled inside but didn't fall, magnifying her eyes prodigiously.

'Bad girl . . .' muttered the girl.

'Why?'

Then she shook the broken toy vigorously, crying:

'Bad girl, bad girl, bad girl . . .'

And threw it into the undergrowth. At that moment her eyes overflowed and she remained still, looking at the old man, her cheeks streaming and eyelashes soaked.

The old man took Ana María in his arms, cradling her head on his shoulder, until the silent weeping abated. He wiped away her tears with his own handkerchief. Then the girl said to him, stroking his furrowed and unshaven face with her diminutive hand:

'Pwettie . . . pwettie, my lub . . .'

And afterwards the man went off contentedly.

In the evenings, smoking in the doorway of his shack, he would see the darkness fall on the makeshift roofs of the district. There, too, he would be thinking about the tiny little girl, all on her own in the very big garden. Without planning to do so, without recalling any incidents, he opened up his whole heart to allow Ana María's presence to flood into him. His wife loomed nearby yet barely glanced at him, convinced that she was going to leave and resign her place to another woman.

Some time passed and the building the old man was working on was completed. They laid off the men, who soon found other employment, but nobody wanted to give work to a creature as frail as the old man. He understood his situation and didn't really fret about it. Though it did concern him to think about Ana María, waiting for him by the fence over on the other side of the city just to have a little talk to him and for him to give her some bread and onion.

The woman did people's washing and that gave them something to live on. The old man was sure she wouldn't have a go at him for being idle, despite the fact that her silence had almost become tangibly solid. But the woman didn't say anything because she had no right to anything. She merely studied him as he sat in the doorway of the shack, in the morning, at midday, in the evening, meditating. With his haggard hands, one on either knee and with scarcely a hint of a smile, he seemed to be counting the seconds in each hour. The old man's lips would move almost imperceptibly. 'Poor little thing!' the woman could read in them, and in those words, uttered for another woman, she found her own condemnation.

Nevertheless, two or three times the man went to see the little girl. He would steal a piece of bread from his wife and, muttering under his breath about going to look for work, he would leave the house very early in the morning. The wife knew it wasn't true.

The old man would walk slowly, resting now and then beside some tree in a park, picking up a piece of newspaper from the ground to read as he rested. And when he felt refreshed, he would carry on walking, slowly, until he crossed the whole city and reached the garden where Ana María would be waiting for him, at the same time of day at which the old man used to lunch under the willow.

The first thing the old man would see were the deep, blue eyes shining furtively amongst the branches. When she saw him, the little girl would run out excitedly so that her friend could lift her over the fence. As they ate and talked under the willow, it seemed as if nothing in the world could disturb them.

The woman couldn't stand the situation any longer. The little that remained of her world that had never been abundant and which over the years had shrunk more and more, was collapsing. She spent the days working hard, ferociously, to kill within herself everything she dared to feel. But before totally submitting to the inevitable, some hidden embers of energy propelled her to make a stand.

One fine day she bought a packet of mixed sweets and, taking the bus, she headed for the garden adjacent to the building site, where the little girl lived. She settled down under the willow. Huge and green the garden certainly was, a luxury of trees and coolness and depth. Close to her, in the shade, remained the black marks of the fires where her husband had brewed the tea. She sat down to wait.

Suddenly she caught sight in the distance of the little girl splashing about in the irrigation ditch, her white body cut up by the reflections of the water. Upon this discovery, a tangled knot of amazement and hatred came together within the woman's heart. She got to her feet beside the barbed wire so that, seeing her in the distance, Ana María should run up.

But Ana María didn't look at her. She removed her feet from the water, and little by little, without the woman knowing quite how, circling round thickets and brambles, she seemed to be getting closer to the willow, still managing to conceal herself in some way.

Then the woman made out the deep, blue eyes gazing harshly at her from the shade, trapping her in their hostile blueness. With a final effort, the woman, from somewhere inside herself, unearthed a smile. But the little girl remained motionless, behind the thicket, gazing out at her.

The woman began to flag. It had all been in vain. All of it, for ever, in vain. In a last bid, she showed her the sweets, saying to her:

'Would the young lady like a sweet?'

The girl shook her head. The woman insisted:

'They're delicious . . .'

'Don't want . . .' replied Ana María.

Finally, the whole mask of anguish and failure collapsed upon the face of the woman. She got ready to leave. At that moment, the little girl took a few steps forward:

'Bad girl! Bad girl! Bad girl!' she cried, staring at her. And the woman slunk off in defeat.

When she got home she told the old man that a family who she worked for had asked her to go into service with them, so that she shouldn't be without food and somewhere to live. What's more, a neighbour wanted to rent the shack they were living in. She was leaving the next morning. There was silence. Then, the man thought that the woman was asking him from across the room:

'And you, what are you going to do?'

'I don't know,' he replied in a loud voice.

And the woman looked at him in surprise.

For a month the man had not seen the little girl. He was getting so old, getting wearier by the hour, that walking to the other side of the city was almost impossible for him.

But tomorrow, when his wife no longer existed, he would go and say goodbye to the little girl. After that, nothing else mattered. Perhaps the best thing would be to go off to some deserted place, to a hill, perhaps, and wait for night-time to lie down and die. He was sure that just by curling up on the ground and wishing for it, death would come.

The next morning he took the last piece of bread and walked more slowly than ever in the direction of Ana María's garden. It was a Sunday. The people who were sheltering in the shade of the trees in the parks did not look at him, just as if he no longer existed.

The little girl was waiting for him as usual beside the fence. And just like the first time, he was overwhelmed by amazement at seeing such a tiny little girl, all on her own in such a very big garden.

'Poor little thing!' he said to himself, walking over.

'My lub!' muttered the girl when she saw him.

He lifted her over the wire, and Ana María hugged him and kissed him, laughing as she did so.

'My pretty little lady,' cried the old man over and over again, stroking her dark hands. 'And her little handbag?' he muttered a few moments later.

Ana María's face clouded over suddenly. She shrugged her shoulders and said:

'No ... noth ...'

They remained together for a long time in the shade of the willow, until the old man thought it was time to leave. He placed her down on the other side of the fence. And, stroking her blonde head through the wire, he muttered:

'Goodbye, little lady ...'

She looked at him, startled, as if she understood everything.

'No, no, my lub, no ...' she said, her eyes widened with tears.

'Goodbye ...' he repeated.

Ana María held on to the old man's hand. But suddenly, as if she'd thought up a plan, she smiled. Her tears stopped and she said:

'Wite, wite ... angbag ...'

The man watched his friend vanish amongst the vegetation, as if it were the last time he would see the tiny little girl, all on her own, fleeing amongst the tree-trunks and the thickets in the very big garden.

Ana María opened the door to her house and entered the living room, muttering:

'Angbag ... angbag ...' searching in the kitchen, in the bedroom, in the larder.

But she couldn't find it.

Before going into her parents' room she hesitated a second. But she pushed open the door. In the green light populated by the sound of buzzing, the couple brutally undid their knot, and, when they saw the girl, they were embarrassed and furious and hastily threw a sheet over themselves. The woman's eyes fixed on to her daughter in the doorway.

'Stupid little girl!' she screamed, sitting up a bit higher.

Her hair was in a mess. She covered herself with a corner of the sheet.

'Don't you know you mustn't disturb us?' shouted the man.

'Angbag!' muttered Ana María, searching for it with her eyes all over the room, heavy with the intimate aroma of her parents.

'I've told you I don't want you to play with that bag. You'll end up losing it for me. Go on . . . clear off.'

'Give her the bag so she'll go away . . .' muttered the man, pulling the sheet over his body.

'Over there, on the chair . . . go on, clear off . . .'

The girl took hold of the bag and ran off without looking at her parents, who sank back into the bed, relieved, but uncomfortable.

Ana María ran across the garden, jumped, or rather flew, over the irrigation ditch, exposing herself to the medallions of floating light which were falling through the thicket, diluting everything. The old man was waiting for her beside the fence. The girl said to him:

'Upsadaisy, upsadaisy . . .'

The old man lifted her up, putting her down on his side. He was trembling a little because he was very old and he knew what was going to happen, and he didn't know that many things. Ana María sat down on the ground beside him and took the shoes out of the bag. She asked the man:

'Soos. Put tootsies . . .'

The old man knelt down so as to put her shoes on with his awkward hands. Then they got to their feet under the willow, the old man hunch-backed and dark next to the little girl with the bag over her shoulder. He looked at her as if he was hoping for something. Then Ana María smiled at him as she had done during the good times, from the bottom of her shining blue eyes:

'My lub,' she said to him.

And taking the old man by the hand she led him out from under the shade of the willow, into the fierce heat of the summer noon. She was guiding him, taking him with her, and saying to him:

'Le'ss go . . . le'ss go . . .'

The old man followed her.

Translated by Jeremy Munday

Gabriel García Márquez

The Handsomest Drowned Man in the World

The first children who saw the dark and slinky bulge approaching through the sea let themselves think it was an enemy ship. Then they saw it had no flags or masts and they thought it was a whale. But when it washed up on the beach, they removed the clumps of seaweed, the jellyfish tentacles, and the remains of fish and flotsam, and only then did they see that it was a drowned man.

They had been playing with him all afternoon, burying him in the sand and digging him up again, when someone chanced to see them and spread the alarm in the village. The men who carried him to the nearest house noticed that he weighed more than any dead man they had ever known, almost as much as a horse, and they said to each other that maybe he'd been floating too long and the water had got into his bones. When they laid him on the floor they said he'd been taller than all other men because there was barely enough room for him in the house, but they thought that maybe the ability to keep on growing after death was part of the nature of certain drowned men. He had the smell of the sea about him and only his shape gave one to suppose that it was the corpse of a human being, because the skin was covered with a crust of mud and scales.

They did not even have to clean off his face to know that the dead man was a stranger. The village was made up of only twenty-odd wooden houses that had stone courtyards with no flowers and which were spread about on the end of a desert-like cape. There was so little land that mothers always went about with the fear that the wind would carry off their children and the few dead that the years had caused among them had to be thrown off the cliffs. But the sea was calm and bountiful and all the men fitted into seven boats. So when they found the drowned man they simply had to look at one another to see that they were all there.

That night they did not go out to work at sea. While the men went to find out if anyone was missing in neighbouring villages, the women stayed behind to care for the drowned man. They took the mud off with grass swabs, they removed the underwater stones entangled in his hair, and they scraped the crust off with tools used for scaling fish. As they were doing that they noticed that the vegetation on him came from faraway oceans and deep water and that his clothes were in tatters, as if he had sailed through labyrinths of coral. They noticed too that he bore his death with pride, for he did not have the lonely look of other drowned men who came out of the sea or that haggard, needy look of men who drowned in rivers. But only when they finished cleaning him off did they become aware of the kind of man he was and it left them breathless. Not only was he the tallest, strongest, most virile, and best built man they had ever seen, but even though they were looking at him there was no room for him in their imagination.

They could not find a bed in the village large enough to lay him on nor was there a table solid enough to use for his wake. The tallest men's holiday pants would not fit him, nor the fattest ones' Sunday shirts, nor the shoes of the one with the biggest feet. Fascinated by his huge size and his beauty, the women then decided to make him some pants from a large piece of sail and a shirt from some bridal brabant linen so that he could continue through his death with dignity. As they sewed, sitting in a circle and gazing at the corpse between stitches, it seemed to them that the wind had never been so steady nor the sea so restless as on that night and they supposed that the change had something to do with the dead man. They thought that if that magnificent man had lived in the village, his house would have had the widest doors, the highest ceiling, and the strongest floor, his bedstead would have been made from a midship frame held together by iron bolts, and his wife would have been the happiest woman. They thought that he would have had so much authority that he could have drawn fish out of the sea simply by calling their names and that he would have put so much work into his land that springs would have burst forth from among the rocks so that he would have been able to plant flowers on the cliffs. They secretly compared him to their own men, thinking that for all their lives theirs were incapable of doing what he could do in one night, and they ended up dismissing them deep in their hearts as the weakest, meanest, and most useless creatures on earth. They were wandering through that maze of fantasy when the oldest woman, who as the oldest had looked upon the drowned man with more compassion than passion, sighed:

'He has the face of someone called Esteban.'

It was true. Most of them had only to take another look at him to see that he could not have any other name. The more stubborn among them, who were the youngest, still lived for a few hours with the illusion that when they put his clothes on and he lay among the flowers in patent leather shoes his name might be Lautaro. But it was a vain illusion. There had not been enough canvas, the poorly cut and worse sewn pants were too tight, and the hidden strength of his heart popped the buttons on his shirt. After midnight the whistling of the wind died down and the sea fell into its Wednesday drowsiness. The silence put an end to any last doubts: he was Esteban. The women who had dressed him, who had combed his hair, had cut his nails and shaved him were unable to hold back a shudder of pity when they had to resign themselves to his being dragged along the ground. It was then that they understood how unhappy he must have been with that huge body since it bothered him even after death. They could see him in life, condemned to going through doors sideways, cracking his head on crossbeams, remaining on his feet during visits, not knowing what to do with his soft, pink, sea lion hands while the lady of the house looked for her most resistant chair and begged him, frightened to death, sit here, Esteban, please, and he, leaning against the wall, smiling, don't bother, ma'am, I'm fine where I am, his heels raw and his back roasted from having done the same thing so many times whenever he paid a visit, don't bother, ma'am, I'm fine where I am, just to avoid the embarrassment of breaking up the chair, and never knowing perhaps that the ones who said don't go, Esteban, at least wait till the coffee's ready, were the ones who later on would whisper the big boob finally left, how nice, the handsome fool has gone. That was what the women were thinking beside the body a little before dawn. Later, when they covered his face with a handkerchief so that the light would not bother him, he looked so forever dead, so defenceless, so much like their men that the first furrows of tears opened in their hearts. It was one of the younger ones who began the weeping. The others, coming to, went from sighs to wails, and the more they sobbed the more they felt like weeping, because the drowned man was becoming all the more Esteban for them, and so they wept so much, for he was the most destitute, most peaceful, and most obliging man on earth, poor Esteban. So when the men returned with the news that the drowned man was not from the neighbouring villages either, the women felt an opening of jubilation in the midst of their tears.

'Praise the Lord,' they sighed, 'he's ours!'

The men thought the fuss was only womanish frivolity. Fatigued because of the difficult night-time enquiries, all they wanted was to get rid of the bother of the newcomer once and for all before the sun grew strong on that arid, windless day. They improvised a litter with the remains of foremasts and gaffs, tying it together with rigging so that it would bear the weight of the body until they reached the cliffs. They wanted to tie the anchor from a cargo ship to him so that he would sink easily into the deepest waves, where fish are blind and divers die of nostalgia, and bad currents would not bring him back to shore, as had happened with other bodies. But the more they hurried, the more the women thought of ways to waste time. They walked about like startled hens, pecking with the sea charms on their breasts, some interfering on one side to put a scapular of the good wind on the drowned man, some on the other side to put a wrist compass on him, and after a great deal of *get away from there, woman, stay out of the way, look, you almost made me fall on top of the dead man,* the men began to feel mistrust in their livers and started grumbling about why so many main-altar decorations for a stranger, because no matter how many nails and holy-water jars he had on him, the sharks would chew him all the same, but the women kept piling on their junk relics, running back and forth, stumbling, while they released in sighs what they did not in tears, so that the men finally exploded with *since when has there ever been such a fuss over a drifting corpse, a drowned nobody, a piece of cold Wednesday meat.* One of the women, mortified by so much lack of care, then removed the handkerchief from the dead man's face and the men were left breathless too.

He was Esteban. It was not necessary to repeat it for them to recognize him. If they had been told Sir Walter Raleigh, even they might have been impressed with his gringo accent, the macaw on his shoulder, his cannibal-killing blunderbuss, but there could be only one Esteban in the world and there he was, stretched out like a sperm whale, shoeless, wearing the pants of an undersized child, and with those stony nails that had to be cut with a knife. They only had to take the handkerchief off his face to see that he was ashamed, that it was not his fault that he was so big or so heavy or so handsome, and if he had known that this was going to happen, he would have looked for a more discreet place to drown in, seriously, I even would have tied the anchor off a galleon around my neck and staggered off a cliff like someone who doesn't like things in order not to be upsetting people now with this Wednesday dead body, as you people say, in order not to be bothering anyone with this filthy piece of cold meat that doesn't have anything to do with me. There was so much truth in his manner that even the most mistrustful men, the ones who felt the bitterness of endless nights at sea fearing that their women would tire of dreaming about them and begin to dream of drowned men, even they and others who were harder still shuddered in the marrow of their bones at Esteban's sincerity.

That was how they came to hold the most splendid funeral they could conceive of for an abandoned drowned man. Some women who had gone to get flowers in the neighbouring villages returned with other women who could not believe what they had been told, and those women went back for more flowers when they saw the dead man, and they brought more and more until there were so many flowers and so many people that it was hard to walk about. At the final moment it pained them to return him to the waters as an orphan and they chose a father and mother from among the best people, and aunts and uncles and cousins, so that through him all the inhabitants of the village became kinsmen. Some sailors who heard the weeping from a distance went off course and people heard of one who had himself tied to the mainmast, remembering ancient fables about sirens. While they fought for the privilege of carrying him on their shoulders along the steep escarpment of the cliffs, men and women became aware for the first time of the desolation of their streets, the dryness of their court-yards, the narrowness of their dreams as they faced the splendour and beauty of their drowned man. They let him go without an anchor so that he could come back if he wished and whenever he wished, and they all held their breath for the fraction of centuries the body took to fall into the abyss. They did not need to look at one another to realize that they were no longer all present, that they would never be. But they also knew that everything would be different from then on, that their houses would have wider doors, higher ceilings, and stronger floors so that Esteban's memory could go everywhere without bumping into beams and so that no one in the future would dare whisper the big boob finally died, too bad, the handsome fool has finally died, because they were going to paint their house fronts gay colours to make Esteban's memory eternal and they were going to break their backs digging for springs among the stones and planting flowers on the cliffs so that in future years at dawn the passengers on great liners would awaken, suffocated by the smell of gardens on the high seas, and the captain would have to come down from the bridge in his dress uniform, with his astrolabe, his pole star, and his row of war medals and, pointing to the promontory of roses on the horizon, he would say in fourteen languages, look there, where the wind is so peaceful now that it's gone to sleep beneath the beds, over there, where the sun's so bright that the sunflowers don't know which way to turn, yes, over there, that's Esteban's village.

Translated by Gregory Rabassa

Salvador Garmendia

The Melancholic Pedestrian

It's ten years ago today that I started to write my novel. In all this time, working day after day, I have managed to amass 970 pages of tiny handwriting, but I still have to admit that up till now I hadn't really begun.

The idea of writing the novel came to me some day or other, almost out of the blue. I'd just taken possession of my apartment and I still wasn't really accustomed to the furniture. It wasn't brand new, though it had been carefully looked after, so everything around me made me feel like I was wearing someone else's clothes and that everyone was staring at me. I really did feel scrutinized by those easy chairs with satin upholstery and smoothly sanded armrests, and by the hard old double bed with its headboard and posts carved with fillets of gold, and by the cute sideboard (a classic spinster's piece, more suited to a silly comedy set than to daily use) which still houses a set of china decorated with pastoral images, that I've never used. I thought from the outset that getting a place of my own would have to add some sense of permanent stability to my humdrum bachelor existence. It was there, amongst so many things of uncertain origin, that I should remain for ever and my days would be governed by those pale walls and the unmoving landscape of roofs and electric cables which the window framed with rigid monotony.

Well, one evening when I was coming home from the greengrocer on the corner cradling a bag of melons, the idea of the novel seeped into my head like warm steam. I would write a novel, no matter how long it took me. After all, I didn't have anything else to do all day, as the small income I receive covers all my needs as a single man.

Walking backwards and forwards through the hall, wringing my hands as I tend to do when something is turning over and over in my head, I began to think about the details. It would be, I was sure, a detective story. It was a logical, if sudden, choice as although I hadn't actually read many detective stories I didn't find any other genre particularly appealing; I also thought, and I really do believe this now, that only this kind of story would truly capture people's interest, if, that is, my novel were actually published and gained a few readers, something which really didn't worry me. From the outset, an image planted itself in my head and there it has remained fixed until this very day: I can see myself sitting at my table churning out pages, while a whole crowd of faces and indeterminate figures (so many over all these years I would not be able to properly describe any of them) sat and waited, completely motionless, for the final outcome of my work. In ten long years since, I haven't had to recount a single desertion, a single casualty: none of them has moved from their seat nor have I stopped writing page after page.

Right, so in all novels of this kind, good or bad, there must be a crime, the most perfect possible, as the main element in the plot and then straight away a whole chain of events which must lead, one after the other, to the identification of the culprit, always in the midst of a varied collection of suspects on whom the reader's innocent malice may be unloaded. So I needed a crime and, above all, a victim condemned to perish violently in the first few pages, together with the entrance of the investigative brain who would eventually have the final word but would still, before he completely disappeared, shoot a sly glance into the surprised face of the reader. I had no doubt at all about this: that man would be me; that's what I had decided and not out of any excessive vanity or because I harboured pretensions to heroism, but out of pure and simple convenience: in all likelihood it was going to be much easier for a completely inexperienced writer like myself to take note of my own habits, gestures and thoughts than to invent as I went along the peculiarities of a character created out of my imagination. So, if I needed to describe in detail any particular situation, I would play it out in front of the blank page, rushing over afterwards to note it all down, and always knowing in the back of my mind that I had the option of playing back any movements if memory failed me.

By the time I went out that first morning I had already changed into the character. From the outset, the new situation was clear as day and actually comforting. In some way the everyday street scene, which used to wash over me before, had taken on a new brightness and prominence both warm and stimulating. In myself I noticed an aura of unreality, the shiftiness of a conman, of a cold, deliberate dissembler, which allowed me to observe others with a touch of burlesque and good-natured humour at the same time.

As had become his daily habit in those days, the character took refuge on a bench in the jaded little park next to his block of flats. The spot was always pleasant and relaxing: the shade of a ceiba tree would bathe the bench, the concrete ground would be covered in dry leaves and opposite me rose, reminiscent of a postcard from some strange country, the marble bowl of a fountain and the two large, big-buttocked angels screwed into the base.

It was that very afternoon that I saw her for the first time. That's my victim! I could have sworn at that moment that there could be no other victim in the world. I sensed within her whole being, the very first time I clapped eyes on her, a feeling of innocent predestiny that was alive and touched by a certain tenderness. She tripped along with quick little steps, had a delicate figure of fine, nervous little bones, faded-mahogany hair with a lot of white, a fragile and lily-white neck. As for her age, she must have been in her sixties.

*

That day I began to write. I recounted in a simple and natural style that first meeting and on the following day the second, when, at the same time of day, making it seem a happy coincidence in habits, she passed by the same spot. I followed her for around three hundred metres along a street of dwarf trees which by now I must have walked a thousand-odd times; a rather drab street, excessively grey, awash with little hardware and iron-mongers' shops. I saw her go into an Adventists' chapel and a moment later I heard the sound of a harmonium and high-pitched voices giving a rendition of one of those soggy hymns that seem to be made of cold, whitish pasta.

She was the chapel organist, which, in my eyes, seemed the most appropriate occupation for her role as angelic victim.

That was enough for me for the time being. In the following chapter I didn't follow her all the way to the chapel: it would have been a tedious and unnecessary repetition. I remained on the bench, not thinking about anything, stroked by the cool breeze and at times I thought I could hear, very vaguely in the distance, the song and breathing of the harmonium; although that must have been a memory.

I followed her back. We went out of the park. It looked like we were going home. She stopped first in the pork butcher's next door (the building was a three-storey red-brick construction, more in the style of the less well-off areas) and she came out with a little packet and the vanished remains of a smile. A moment later as if in a dream, I saw her go into her building. It really became a scene out of a dream, that moment, for ever imprinted on my mind, when she disappeared defiantly through the doorway of the building. That image has repeated itself in my mind hundreds, thousands of times, always identically: a dog was passing her, panting; a huge woman,

heaving an equally misshapen knot of washing came directly towards me;
and as she went through the door, forced me up against the wall. But
everything that took place was very real as I found myself going up the
stairs after her and saw her stop on the first landing. That was where she
had her apartment, below mine.

Spying on my neighbour became my prime occupation for a long time,
together with the hours of writing. I understand your wish for details; but
putting down everything would be well nigh impossible. The truth is, her
regular movements were governed, with a certain timid strictness, by habit.
The same walks each day, identical movements. In this respect, I admit that
the only interest in my account lies in the stating of certain incidental
details, which, because they subtly affected the whole picture, caused
minor variations to the routine. Today I am able to state, and this is in full
possession of the facts, that the human eye is poisoned without us noticing,
a poison that manages to subtly penetrate what we look at. I cannot find
any other explanation for the fact that certain little things in the victim's
conduct should have seemed so suspicious, as if she, consciously playing a
part in the game, had been leaving little signs behind her (directed only at
her pursuer), uncertain clues which would lead me to the revelation of
some surprising form of depravity, of secret cruelty or deceit.

I do remember one particular time, in itself unique and extremely odd.
(It was one of the few occasions when I had the less than entirely pleasant
impression she wanted to give me the slip and act of her own accord.) It
happened one afternoon, around four o'clock. The sound of her door, to
which my ears were always alert in just the same way as a pet responds
to the slightest noise, forced me to stop my work. It was strange since she
never went out at that time. I only just managed to catch up with her as
she was about to board the bus, which, to my surprise was going to the
western part of the city. Neither she nor I used to go to that district, an
essential theatre of action for run-of-the-mill newspaper reporters in search
of a story. In an audacious move I sat down next to her. As I never stopped
looking at her out of the corner of my eye, I could see that she did not
glance at me once. As far as the rest of the world was concerned, we must
have seemed like two total strangers there, clinging to the precarious reality
of that vehicle, where so many different thoughts passed by without
bumping into each other.

Half facing the window, she devoted all her attention to the urban
landscape which was becoming progressively more chaotic, dirtier and
more confusing. Whole waves of human life took part in a long promenade
down Sucre Avenue: coming out of a modest chapel we saw a family group

at a baptism; further on, we stopped for a hearse and its miserable cortège of hire cars; and at Marshal of Ayacucho square we ran into an immigrants' wedding. In my district things were different. It seemed that people were happy they had fulfilled all the requirements of life and were getting on with prospering as much as they could without the slightest worry.

I noted, as well, that she was continuously crumpling up a lace handkerchief in her fingers. I could see her fingers were tiny and incredibly soft for her age, as her hands pressed between her knees.

I swear I shall never again go back to that street. I have never attempted to find it nor will I do so now. It will not be the way it was that day. Maybe it does not exist for anyone and will not appear the same to my eyes. A narrow sidestreet smelling of stale bread, hardly touched by the sun; the backs of warehouses, a few dark houses, not a single sound or human voice; at the end, a stretch of windowless wall and a narrow metal door which opened a fraction to let her through and remained shut for more than an hour. While I waited there I was overcome with the feeling that I was being besieged by a tedious dream, becoming more exasperating the longer I waited: it was terrifying it could carry on so long without vanishing or changing. Finally she walked past me, and although our faces met, I can swear she did not see me. Her eyes were red and, if I'm not mistaken, there were traces of tears on her cheeks.

Over recent months I visited her apartment once, using the master key. I made a detailed inventory of her belongings, making sure I erased any possible sign of my presence. However, I couldn't help committing one terrible indiscretion: I wound up a cuckoo clock which presided over the hall. I can't help thinking how surprised and confused she must have been when at nine o'clock that night, when she went to perform the unchanging rite of a person regulated by noise, she was only able to turn the key a couple of times. She could never have worked out what happened.

The next day there was a knock at my door, and instead of the red-faced Galician woman who did my cleaning, it was her on the landing. The clock! I screamed to myself and imagined the worst; however, she was only trying to get me to subscribe to *The Sentinel* and *Herald of Health*, a magazine which filled me with horror with its frightening coldness. I politely declined and even refused the free copy she offered me. (Her tiny, shrill voice, not at all unpleasant, took on, in the way she pronounced certain sounds, a colourless central European accent). 'That's okay, Sir,' were her final words and at that moment I realized I had to kill her. She seemed to understand and gave me authorization with a sweet, resigned smile of modest complicity.

Her expression, which at the time seemed totally normal, removed any possible lingering feeling of remorse I might have had.

Two weeks later, I found myself in her apartment again, under her bed. At the normal hour the latch creaked. Her child-like feet criss-crossed the carpet, accompanied by a clinking of crockery and metal and an inviting aroma: she was preparing her cup of tea. There was a moment I thought I could hear her humming, in the kitchen, something which resembled a Teutonic march. She would come out with a few syllables of the melody and, in the pauses, mimic the sound of the drum: ta-ra-ra, ta-ra-ra, ta-ra-ra ... shss bong! As soon as normal silence had resumed, I came out of my hiding-place. Through the half-open door I could see her with her back to me, sitting in her favourite armchair. Following the simple procedure of suffocation I used a cushion with a picture of a Bavarian village on it to take her life in a few seconds, and I dedicated a final look to her to record her image in my mind, which was scarcely deformed by a slight contraction of the jaw.

As I supposed, the person called to examine the body was an old doctor in the neighbourhood: cardiac arrest. Just a few of us from the building attended the burial. The old lady had a policy with an undertakers who held her lonely funeral according to the contract.

It's ten years ago today. A grey and peaceful afternoon. I've finished page 970, which tells of my last visit to the pork butcher's and the conversation with the owner, who (I discovered long after the event) was a fellow countryman of hers. They were born in the same village and they first met and played together as children.

Tomorrow I shall go down the street of the dwarf trees, the hardware and ironmongers' shops and I shall stand guard in front of the Adventist chapel, which now sports a new façade. Then I shall come home to pick up the thread of my story adding the new details.

Now I must squeeze into my dark suit and go and buy the bunch of carnations which, on each anniversary and in recognition of the many years of our life together, I religiously take to her grave.

Translated by Jeremy Munday

Julio Ramón Ribeyro

The Wardrobe, the Old Man and Death

The wardrobe in my father's room was not simply another piece of furniture, but was a house within a house. Inherited from his family, it followed us, huge and embarrassing, in move after move, until it came to its final resting place in his bedroom in Miraflores.

It took up almost half the room, and practically reached the ceiling. Whenever my father was away, my brothers and I ventured inside it. It was a real baroque palace, full of curlicues, mouldings, cornices, medallions and columns, carved down to the last detail by a demented nineteenth-century cabinetmaker. It was in three parts, each with its own characteristics. The left-hand side had a door as heavy as a house entrance. From its lock dangled an enormous key, which for us was in itself a protean toy, serving equally well as a gun, a sceptre or a blackjack. It was in this part that my father hung his suits and an English coat that he never wore. This was our obligatory point of entry to a universe smelling of cedar and mothballs. The central section was the one we liked most, because of all the different things it contained. At the bottom were four deep drawers. When my father died, each of us inherited one of them, and we established our authority over them just as jealously as our father had over the entire wardrobe. Above the drawers came a niche which held thirty or so favourite books. And the central part was topped off with a high, quadrangular door that was always kept locked. We never did find out what it contained: perhaps all those papers and photos one trails with one from childhood, taking care not to destroy them for fear of losing part of a life which in fact we have already lost. And finally, the right-hand side was another door, but this time faced with a bevelled mirror. It too had drawers at the bottom for shirts and underwear, and above it was an open space where a person could stand upright.

The left-hand side communicated with the right thanks to a passageway at the top, behind the book niche. This meant that one of our favourite games was to disappear inside the wardrobe through the heavy wooden door and pop out again a few seconds later from the door with the mirror. The top passage was also the perfect place to hide in hide-and-seek. Whenever we did, none of our friends could ever find us. Even though they knew we were in the wardrobe, they could never imagine we had clambered up it and were lying stretched out in the middle part, as if in a coffin.

My father's bed was placed exactly opposite the right-hand section of the wardrobe, so that when he propped himself up on his pillows to read the newspaper, he could see himself in the mirror. He would look at himself in it, but even more than that, he would look at all those who had seen themselves in it before him. He would say: 'That's where don Juan Antonio Ribeyro y Estada looked at himself as he tied his bow tie before leaving for a ministerial meeting,' or 'That's where don Ramon Ribeyro y Alvarez del Villar would look at himself, before he left to give his lectures at San Marcos University,' or 'How many times I saw my father, don Julio Ribeyro y Benites look at himself in it when he was getting ready to go to Congress to make a speech.' His ancestors were all caught in the depths of the mirror. He could see them, and see his own image superimposed on theirs, in the unreal space, as if for once, by some miracle, they could all inhabit the same time together. Thanks to the mirror, my father entered the world of the dead, but he also used it to bring his ancestors into the world of the living.

*

We marvelled at the subtle ways that summer had of expressing itself, its endless fine days offering themselves for our pleasure, games and happiness. It even mellowed my father, who since his marriage had stopped drinking, smoking and seeing his friends: when he realized that the fruit trees in the small orchard had produced in abundance and invited admiration, and that we had finally purchased a proper set of china, he decided to occasionally throw his house open to one or other of his former companions.

The first of these was Alberto Rikets. He was the exact likeness of my father, but in miniature. Nature had taken the trouble to edit the copy, just in case. The two were equally pale, equally scrawny, and not only had the same gestures but the same turns of phrase. All this was due to the fact that they had studied in the same school, read the same books, spent similar sleepless nights, and suffered the same lengthy, painful illness. In the ten or twelve years since they had last seen each other, Rikets had made a fortune working all hours in a pharmacy, which now belonged to him, unlike my father, who had barely managed to buy the house in Miraflores.

During those ten or twelve years, Rikets had achieved something else too: he had had a child, Alberto junior, whom he brought with him on the inaugural visit. Since the children of friends rarely get to be real friends themselves, we were suspicious of young Alberto at first. We thought he was skinny, clumsy and at times plain dumb. While my father was showing Alberto round his orchard, pointing out the orange tree, the fig, the apple tree and the vines, we took his son to play with us in our room. Alberto junior had no brothers or sisters, so he knew none of the games we invented and played together: he was no good as a Red Indian, and even worse at allowing himself to be plugged with bullets by the sheriff. None of us were convinced by the way he fell dead, and he could not understand that a tennis-racket could also be a machine-gun. We quickly decided it would be no good playing our favourite game in the wardrobe with him, so instead we concentrated on simple, repetitive pastimes, which left each of us to our own devices, like pushing toy cars across the floor, or building castles with wooden blocks.

While we were playing before lunch was called, we could see my father and his friend out of the window. By now, they were doing the rounds of the garden, because it was time to show off the magnolia, the geraniums, dahlias, carnations and wallflowers. My father had discovered the delights of gardening some years earlier, and the profound truth that was concealed in the shape of a sunflower or a rosebloom. That was why he spent his free days not as he had done previously, in wearisome readings that led him to reflect on the meaning of life, but in simple tasks such as watering, pruning, grafting or weeding, in all of which he invested a real intellectual passion. His love of books had been transferred wholesale on to his plants and flowers. He had created the entire garden, and like a character from Voltaire had concluded that his happiness came from tending it.

'One of these days I'm going to buy myself some land in Tarma, but not a tiny plot like this, no, a real farm: and *then* Alberto, you'll see what I'm truly capable of,' we heard our father say.

'My dear Perico, what about Chaclacayo instead of Tarma?' his friend said, referring to the luxury home he was having built there. 'The climate's almost as good, but it's only forty kilometres from Lima.'

'Yes, but my grandfather lived in Tarma, not in Chaclacayo.'

There he was with his ancestors again! And the friends from his younger days called him Perico!

*

Alberto junior sent his car underneath the bed, crawled in to fetch it back, and we heard his shout of triumph. He had discovered a football under there. We'd been having such a hard time trying to keep him amused, and it was only now we found out that if he had a secret passion, the vice of a squalid, lonely kid, it was to kick a leather football around.

He had already grabbed it by the laces and was about to kick it, but we stopped him. It was madness to play in our room; in the garden it was strictly forbidden; so there was nothing else for it but to head out into the street.

That street had been the scene of dramatic games we had played years earlier against the Gómez brothers, games that lasted four or five hours and didn't end until it was completely dark, by which time we could no longer see either the goals or our opponents, and the games became a spectral struggle, a fierce, blind battle in which all kinds of cheating, fouls and unfair play took place. No professional team ever put so much hatred, such passionate determination, or pride into their games as we did in those childish encounters. That was why after the Gómez family moved away, we gave up football for good: nothing could ever rival those epic battles, so we hid the ball under our bed. Until Alberto junior went and found it. If it was football he wanted, we'd give him a bellyful of it.

We made the goal against the wall of our house so that the ball would bounce back. We stuck Alberto junior in goal. He saved our first efforts bravely enough. But then we really started bombarding him with vicious shots just so we'd have the pleasure of seeing him sprawling on the ground, spreadeagled and beaten.

Then it was his turn to shoot and I was in goal. For a weakling, he had the kick of a mule, and though I stopped his first shot, the palms of my hands were stinging afterwards. His second shot was a perfect goal in the corner, but it was the third one that was the real beauty: the ball flashed through my hands, flew over the wall, sneaked through the branches of a climbing jasmine and over a cypress hedge, bounced on the trunk of the acacia tree and vanished into the depths of the house.

We sat on the pavement waiting for the maid to bring us back the ball, as usually happened. But nobody appeared. Just as we were getting up to go and look for it, the back door to the house opened, and my father came out, the ball under his arm. He was paler than ever. He didn't say a word to us, but strode over to the far side of the street and went up to a workman who was walking towards him whistling. When my father reached him, he put the ball in his hands and went back inside the house without even deigning to glance in our direction. It took the workman a moment to realize he had just been given a ball, but when he did so, he ran off so quickly we had no chance of catching him.

My mother was waiting at the door to call us to lunch. She looked so upset we realized something terrible must have happened. She waved us inside the house with a sharp gesture. 'How could you have done that!' was all she said as we filed past her.

It was when we saw that one of the windows in my father's room, the only one without bars on it, was half-open that we began to suspect what might have happened: Alberto junior, with a master stroke neither he nor anybody else could ever repeat even if they spent their whole lives trying, had managed to send the ball in an incredible arc that, in spite of walls, trees and bars, had hit the wardrobe mirror dead centre.

*

Lunch was a painful affair. Unable to scold us in front of his guest, my father choked on his anger in a silence no one dared to break. It was only at the dessert course that he softened a little, and told a few stories that delighted everyone. Alberto took his cue from him, and the meal ended in laughter. But that was too late to erase the impression that not only the lunch, but the invitation, my father's good intentions of trying to take up with his old friends again – something that was never repeated – had all been a complete fiasco.

To our horror, the Rikets left soon after; we were terrified our father would take the opportunity to punish us. But the visit had tired him out, and he went off to sleep his siesta without a word to us.

When he woke up, he gathered us in his room. He looked refreshed and calm, propped up on his pillows. He had had the windows opened wide so that the afternoon light could stream in.

'Look,' he said, pointing to the wardrobe.

It was indeed a sorry sight. In losing the mirror, the wardrobe had lost all its life. Where the glass had been, now there was only a rectangle of dark wood, a gloomy gap which reflected nothing and said nothing. It was like a shimmering lake whose waters had suddenly evaporated.

'The mirror my ancestors saw themselves in!' my father sighed, and dismissed us with a wave.

From that day on, we never again heard him mention his ancestors. In disappearing, the mirror had caused them to disappear too. My father was no longer tormented by his past; instead he peered with increasing curiosity into his future. Perhaps that was because he knew he hadn't long to live, and so no longer needed the mirror to get reunited with his forefathers – not in another life, he was not a believer – but in that world which captivated him just as books and flowers had before then: the world of nothingness.

Translated by Nick Caistor

Inés Arredondo

Subterranean River

For Huberto Batis

I've lived for many years on my own, as a solitary woman in this huge house, a cruel and exquisite life. That's what I want to recount: the cruelty and exquisiteness of life in the provinces. I'm going to speak about all those things that are normally hushed up, what you think about and what you feel when you don't think. I want to tell about all the things that have been building up in a provincial soul, things that have been polished, nurtured and practised without other people suspecting. You may think that I'm too stupid to try to relate this story which you already know but which, I'm sure, you don't know properly. You simply don't pay any heed to the river and its courses, the pealing of the bells, nor the yells. You haven't always tried to understand what they mean, all together in the world, these inexplicable things, terrible things, sweet things. You haven't had to give up what they call a normal life in order to follow the trail of something you don't understand, in order to be faithful to it. You didn't fight day and night to make sense of certain words: to have a destiny. I do have a destiny, but it isn't mine. I have to live life according to the destinies of others. I am the guardian of what is forbidden, of what cannot be explained, of what brings shame, and I have to stay here to guard it, so that it doesn't get out, but also so that it should exist. So that it should exist and a balance should be achieved. So that it shouldn't get out and harm others.

This is what Sofia taught me, she whom Sergio had taught, who in turn conceived of it when he saw the madness of his brother Pablo, your father.

I feel it was my lot to live beyond breaking point, the limit, on that side where everything I do seems, but isn't, against nature. If I stopped doing it, I would be committing a crime. I've always felt the temptation to run away. Not Sofia, Sofia even seemed proud, since she was able to build for madness. I merely manage to survive.

So that you don't have to come and see it, I'll try to explain what Sofia did with this house which used to be just like the others. It's easy to recognize because it's on its own, it's detached from the rest: on one side it's flanked by the big wasteland which Sergio didn't build on, and on the other by the ruins, the black ruins of your father's house. Apart from this, you can see a run-of-the-mill façade: a porch with three barred windows on the right and three on the left. But it's inside where the difference lies.

It's a very run-of-the-mill house, with three corridors in a U-shape, but in the centre, in place of the courtyard, there is a splendid staircase, with steps as long as the length of the central portico with its five semicircular arches. It drops slowly, step by step, opens out as a terrace, and then descends again to what in the past was the bank of the river when it was full of water. You can't begin to imagine how beautiful it is.

At the level of the terrace four rooms had been dug out: two on either side of the staircase, so they were actually underneath the side corridors and it appears they were always there, supporting the upper part of the house. Maybe that's so. These four rooms are richly panelled. Sofia thought that since your father couldn't have any comforts, not even furniture, he needed to have some extra special luxury. There are four rooms, but in fact only one has been used, the first on the left, as you go down towards the river. I've never stopped wondering why Sofia had to have four built, one for each of us, or was it simply the need for proportion with the location of the terrace and the staircase which required this number of rooms.

And your father had been in one of them when Sergio and Sofia hit upon the idea of building a place for him here, a place in the world that was his alone. They did not fetch him then, but afterwards they looked after him, sparing no pain. They listened to his inhuman cries, they focused on them.

That he should have escaped from the padded room was no one's fault in particular. Perhaps you think someone left the door open or the key within his reach, but if you'd ever seen the swollen river coming, heard its earth-shattering roar fill the air before you saw the first, terrible wave sweeping away houses, cattle, dead bodies, you would know that he had to leave that room like the river left its course, and destroy himself so that other life, other people's and his own, your life perhaps, might start afresh.

If you understood this you would know that the fact that he burned down a house, the one they'd all inherited from him, was not a coincidence, no more than is the fact that he died in the flames. You, for instance, can get someone to sell the wasteland, but the thought that there's a house here in your name, would make you come here. That's why the other one we're living in now won't be yours, I made sure of *that*. But Sergio's piece of land does belong to you even if you don't ever see it.

I don't want to tell you the story of your father's death, or Sergio's, I just suggest you learn to look at them differently, and that's why I'm telling you all this about the life we lived.

*

You could hear, in the light of the oil lamp, under the pale skin of moving lips, in the iron stillness of hands on laps, a thick, struggling whirring which filled the silence of the room, of the house, of the night. They were my brothers and sisters, but I still didn't understand. It was more that they were brothers and sisters, very brotherly and sisterly amongst themselves. They bore no physical resemblance at all, apart from their slim waists and the skin which seemed transparent on their eyelids. However, a harmony was preserved out of their difference: the way they moved; their hands; the deep eyes, ecstatic and watery, made them look very much alike, above and beyond their features and colouring. Their ages and education were also different, but no one would have thought so.

That voluntary resemblance was their defensive rampart. But I've already told you I won't speak about that struggle any more than is strictly necessary. In fact, it all started before I was able to understand it and I'll retell it for you just as it is imprinted in my memory, not filtered by the light of time or reflection.

*

The night the place was sacked turned out differently for us than for the others: we stood at the wide-open window, looking out, and our porch was the only one which nobody smashed up because Sergio, as soon as he heard the yelling coming from the road to Bebelama, walked slowly down and opened it, put the lights on all through the house, straightened his tie in front of the mirror in the corridor, took up position, his back negligently pressing against the window frame, and waited; Sofia went to sit on the window sill and they didn't exchange a word.

I saw them enter the square: on foot, on horseback, yelling and shooting, breaking down doors, laughing their heads off, for no reason, and I was scared; I went up to Sofia, took her hand and she smiled at me and sat me down next to her: then she turned round and carried on watching.

They shoved the priest out through the arches of the sacristy. It pained me to see his pale, shaken face move from light to shadow, from a guffaw to a rifle butt, to a swearword, stumbling over flowerpots, making the canaries screech. If you see it now, in the morning, that same sacristy with its arches, you won't be able to picture it. Only when flames are present can you see the huge space which the shadow of a man takes up.

'These guys only want the money. But he fancies the idea of becoming a martyr. I hate martyrs,' said Sergio. I felt his contempt for that pale face, that familiar face which we had seen every day since we were born and which was suffering. I shuddered violently, Sofia squeezed my fingers firmly and placed her other hand on my shoulder.

When they came into our house, I was frightened they would notice the almost ironic curiosity in Sergio's eyes, and there was one who went and stood right in front of him and was about to say something. If Sergio had smiled or moved, I don't know; but he didn't react at all, looking at the other man with his eyes which had a golden point in the centre, and the other man went off and slashed up a sofa. It's still here, faded and with its insides hanging out, and it's very soothing to look at it, I don't know why, maybe because it doesn't yell and it's remained the same for thirty years.

Looking back, I imagine we must have looked like a family portrait, the three of us in the window frame, but that moment was the first time I felt that we were, myself as well, detached, and that they couldn't touch us.

On the other side of the little square, Rosalía was screaming and a man was chasing her. Above the gunshots, you could hear the screams of the women, very high-pitched.

They left our house quickly, in truth, because nothing was locked up. That's something Sergio must have done days before and without us noticing, or perhaps while he was putting on all the lights, as if we were throwing a great big party. They left quickly, without speaking to us, and what they took with them they abandoned in a trail through the bars and streets, but we never made any attempt to recover it all, it was understood that it was no longer ours.

'I thought it'd be different,' said Sergio, when silence began to settle and a leaden light in the sky made me feel sick. As he passed by, he stroked the oil lamp. 'Great that no one saw how beautiful its pink light is,' he said.

He shut the door and we went off to bed.

The following nights, while the patrols went round and you could hear the 'who goes there's, a shot or two and the dogs, Sergio explained to Sofia the different festivals of the different gods. 'The sacred disorder,' I remember him saying, and such like. I could quote you other phrases, but phrases are not important. It's funny that what hurt him about that night was not what happened to the priest, or to Rosalía, or to those who were hanged, it was that the joy of those men was false, that they had got it wrong, that instead of those hollow guffaws they should have been shouting, yelling, and killing, and stealing, with conviction, with pain, 'because it was the closest thing to a party'. And it was true that he was sad because of those men.

We didn't learn about revolutions from that revolution, but about cults, and rites and ancient gods. That was how he taught us so many things: teaching us to understand not through examples that were similar but through the things that existed behind life.

He could tell you, for example, that your mother was your mother because she'd given birth to you, but that a real mother is the one who *chooses* you afterwards, not because you are a child, but because you are as you are; that's why he found it normal that a queen should hate or despise her son from when he was tiny. That was how we read the history of France, I remember it well.

In fact, Sofia and I would study what was on offer and he would speak to us about it at night, with no real rhyme or reason. He wasn't a teacher, nor did he like the sound of his own voice, he would stammer as he searched for words, he would rehash his arguments; I've already said: he would trawl through his mind, sometimes in front of us, out loud. But on the nights when he was quiet and gloomy, what was he searching for?

In the light of the oil lamp I heard about you, about Pablo, your father, who went away so young I can hardly remember him. You were a baby and your father was already in a sanatorium. He never saw you. Don't get close to him now. Remember, he's just a dead man.

I would also hear about the staircase. The flame didn't flicker, it would remain still, and its tenuous brightness would tinge with warm tones the pale skin of my brothers and sisters. Sofia would be sewing and embroidering, while Sergio held a book in his hands; sometimes he would read a bit. I heard them talking quietly about all of you, about madness, as if you were all memories. Sofia would get the letters in the morning, but would usually wait until night-time to tell us gently, as if it were an old story, that Pablo had a very strange disorder or that it had become necessary to put him away in a madhouse.

'Pablo was always happy and noisy, he liked singing and lifting our mother off the ground to spin her round and make her scream while he laughed. Happy and strong, very strong. Or maybe we saw him like that because he was much older. But now they say he has turned violent, that there are moments he destroys everything he finds, and that he wants to kill. Strength and happiness together, but exasperation which may corrupt and distort happiness, can turn into violence, or is it anger alone that takes possession of and blinds all the vitality of a man? Where does that anger come from and where does it filter through, in what place does it lurk? It falls upon him like a thunderbolt, it possesses him like a demon and he is just himself and he has to be locked up in a secure place, in a madhouse, where there are people who know about that desire for destruction and do not fear it.'

That's how she read the news. Sergio was quiet and she carried on talking, questioned him gently until he began to speak of madness, of the staircase, or things or people, always in a friendly tone and as if they were far away.

Later, when I was a bit bigger and Sofia tutored me, I found out that she would spend all day looking for the way, the words to tell us these things, always taking into account, first and foremost, Sergio's anguish.

'Self-control is important. To be aware, perfectly lucid, to give events, feelings and thoughts the appropriate form, not to let ourselves be dragged along by them, as is commonly the case. Sergio would let me know about that in his letters, from Europe, before coming home, and then there was the little necessity of fitting it all to human proportions, because exaggeration is always more powerful than man; it was self-discipline, almost a game, but when he spoke to me of his anguish, that it was forcing itself into his chest and wasn't allowing him to think, or breathe, because it was gradually invading him, possessing him from the very first wound which is just like a frozen knife in a rib of his chest, I understood that everything I had been taught about the importance of form had to be applied to that, and so between the two of us we searched for the lukewarm words to heal the wound, and we forbade ourselves any discordant expression, because the first cry would set the beast free.'

Although at that time I was still going to school and visiting my cousins, I realized from the outset that I shouldn't use the language of my brothers and sisters, nor ever allude to the conversation which took place at home. 'Why do they never go to parties?' my relatives would ask me. 'They shouldn't get themselves down about Pablo's misfortune,' they would add. I couldn't tell them they didn't get themselves down, quite the opposite, they were alert, and couldn't waste a second of their attention because they had to be on guard precisely against that misfortune.

*

'No! Why Sergio? The doctor can say what he wants, because he's a sad village doctor. He wants the simple answer to *everything*, he thinks what Sergio has is melancholia, he doesn't know what anguish is.

'Sergio would say: "I want to find something smooth, something harmonious, into which my soul can glide. Not these peaks, these useless wounds, this falling and getting up again; higher, lower, crooked, almost still, making you dizzy. You know what? I feel that I'm falling, that they're throwing me, inside, understand? They're throwing me out of myself and as I'm falling I can't breathe and I yell, and I don't know what's happening and I feel they're stabbing me, with a real knife, here. It's sticking into me, and I fall and I'm very still, I keep falling, very still, falling, to nowhere, to nothing. The worst of it is I don't know what I'm suffering for, who for, what I did to have this great remorse, it's not because of something I could have done, but because of something else, and at times it seems to me that I'm going to get it, going to know, to understand why I'm suffering in this horrific way, and when I get up on tiptoe and I'm just about to reach it, and my chest expands, there's another blow, the wound and I fall again, fall. That's called anguish, I'm sure."

'What's this got to do with melancholia. I can understand it, feel within me the anguish of my brother when he talks of falling, and his fingers suddenly go cold and they end up gripping mine with an agonizing sweat identical to mother's that afternoon when I wiped her brow and she no longer felt it. If anguish and gratuitous remorse are madness, everything is too easy and it is monstrously unjust that Sergio should suffer so much for nothing. Madness would then merely be an imbalance, a little thing, a small detour on the way, scarcely noticeable, because it doesn't lead anywhere; something like a quick sideways glance. It can't be. Why Sergio?

'He needs support. Something real, concrete, for him to grab hold of.'

*

So Sofia invented the staircase, or rather, she got Sergio to invent it. She made them picture it, and then calculate, measure step by step the proportions, the land, the slope, the weight of the house, which was to be on top of it, solid, as if the house and the staircase were one and the same and could live at one and the same time.

They achieved her plan in part. It's true that when you go into the house and cross the passageway and the porch for the first time, you stop at the edge of the stairway as if at the edge of an abyss, and your heart skips a beat because you could have taken one more step, your last. But by stifling that little cry which has never been heard and which only seems to be the noise of sudden loss of breath, all the visitors have tried to express amazement and not fear. Why fear? Being amazed, on the other hand, is natural, since they didn't expect to find *that* there, by which I mean the courtyard which has become a staircase without anyone knowing why and, mainly (everyone has said the same), because beauty and harmony are always a source of amazement, they take your breath away. Beauty and harmony is what Sofia took from Sergio's anguish, so that he should know that he had them, that they were in him despite the anguish, but maybe also to see them herself and give everyone tangible, concrete proof that her brother's brain was working better than the whole village's put together, since it's certain that even by joining forces they wouldn't have been able to create that very beautiful, gentle, white slope which descends to the old river bank more elegantly than the slope of a hill. No, Sofia wasn't thinking about the village, she didn't want to prove anything to the village, since, when they asked her about the staircase (what for?) she just shrugged her shoulders and ignored the question. However, she never missed the opportunity to get absolutely anyone to go and see the staircase, and she always watched with satisfaction for the moment when their breath was taken away.

*

'Without opening my eyes I can watch him, study his slim body silhouetted against the arches. Without stopping my embroidery I can watch him pretending to see the men working. He stands there staring and I know his hands are frozen. It's five in the afternoon, siesta time is over, but he hasn't slept, it's a long time since he knew what sleep was; he stretches out on the bed and looks at the ceiling with eyes that are wide open and empty. It's five in the afternoon and it's June, the sun is still high and it falls on him with its light which corrodes, with its heat which destroys, but Sergio doesn't realize, he's there, standing, pretending to watch the workmen, impeccably dressed in grey wool and a cravat. So much effort. Maybe that's what it all is: taking effort to an absurd limit, seeking out what is beyond the limit. He had to get up off the bed, go out of the room and inspect the work, he had to do it and he didn't forget it when he had his eyes staring at the ceiling. How could he have remembered it? How do you drag yourself away from that fixed point? Even I don't know how much that takes out of him each day, but he does it, and more, much more: he showers, gets dressed, combs his hair, puts on his aftershave as if the date with that little task were with duty personified. And now he's there, pummelled by the sun unknowingly, that is, all put together, watching without watching. But tonight, when I ask him to, when I beg him to, when I demand it, he will know how much progress has been made, and where, and if the work is going well. Tomorrow morning I'll make him go down to the river again so that he can again work out the problem of the sandy soil.

It's cruel, cruel for me to see him screw up his eyes as if I were digging a needle into him, see him bite his lips together, or keep his forehead unfrowned by force of willpower, so as to prove to me he isn't suffering. Yes, he keeps his forehead unfrowned so as to calm me down.

'Sergio, if you find it so easy to work out the problem, if by leaning over and touching the earth you can recognize it, if by looking at the river, you suddenly, albeit fleetingly, smile, why don't you always do that, every day?

'No, please understand, I don't want you to accept things as they are, because they are there, I want *you* to be part of them, to do that, to name them, to smile at them, Sergio. Look at me . . . ! Sorry, yes, I know you recognize me, but it makes me scared, scared to death to think that one day you won't pay any attention to me, like to the trees, to the building workers . . . and yet, at night-time, if I torment you, you know exactly what they did and if it was good or bad. It's another kind of attention, you told me. What are you looking at . . . ? Sergio, look at me!'

Sofia was right not to let Sergio be seen by the doctors. Your father, I know little about him, I didn't see him before, nor when it started. Maybe he really was a loony for the doctors, but they knew so little about his illness they let him come and pass it on to the brothers and sisters who weren't a bit like him, who were each other's brothers and sisters. Sergio did his mad act when he saw your father, when he tried to understand him. It's not that he felt pity, stupid sympathy, he simply wanted to understand. But that surely is the correct path which madness itself has traced for its true chosen ones. You have to hear the cries, the screams, without blinking, as did Sergio tirelessly day and night. It would have been better to have thought about something else. However, Sergio would remain fixed on the bestial scream which travelled through the silence, which spread over the surface of the night. Yes, that's something I do know: it did not penetrate it; your father's madness cried to itself, it didn't cry out to anything.

If they hadn't had him brought here . . . At least Sergio wouldn't have learnt that cry. The one which did for him. The cry, the howl, the scream which is concealed in everyone, in everything, without us knowing.

I water the plants in slow motion every evening so as not to stir it up, so that it should not awaken in Sofia, who now occupies the padded room which had been Pablo's and Sergio's. She screams it out and listens to it, I carry on watering my plants. I understand that she had to scream it, but I mustn't try to hear it. I mustn't because of you, so that you should never have to come, so that you shouldn't be tied to this watching which ends when there is no one to continue for. Don't ever come here.

Even when they tell you I have stopped keeping guard, stopped listening out, even then, don't come. Don't try to understand. To you alone I'll say that maybe I've stuck it out because I suspect, with trembling and fear, that what we are, within our world, can be explained, but what we have to go through is not just, is not human, and I don't want, as my brothers did, to understand what is outside our strange order of existence. I don't want to, but nature is stalking me.

Because in fact, to explain: what does a madman explain? What does he mean? He roars, sweeps everything away like the river, drowns things in his conscienceless waters, drags off bellowing beasts in an ancestral sacrifice, stunned, seeking, in its coursing, annihilation, repose in a calm sea which might be insensitive to his angry and destructive arrival. What sea?

It picks up its fury in the high mountains, fills with wrath in the storms, in the snows which it never sees, which are not part of it, it is engendered by wind and waters, it is born in gorges and has no recollection of its birth.

The peace of an estuary, of a majestic journey towards the ecstatic depths. No more babbling, no crying, singing for a moment before entering the immensity, the eternal chant, the regular and eternal rhythm. Gradually losing along the banks the anger of the origin, calming down next to the silent poplars, licking the dry land, and leaving it, hardly having touched it, in order to achieve the final chant, the imposing whisper of the final moment, when the sun will be an equal, the pacified enemy of the immense water, the water which governs itself.

Suspicious, frowning at itself, enemy of all, it gives itself up at last, peacefully, reduced to its own size, to death. Scarcely has it learnt to die as it kills, without reason, so as to achieve awareness of itself, at moments before its parting from its origin, from the history it does not remember, peacefully powerful before giving itself up, huge and quiet, swollen, imposing before the unsuspecting sea, which murmurs indifferently and gobbles it pitilessly.

Waters, simple waters, turgid and clear, vindictive vortices and translucent millponds, sun and wind, gentle stones on the bed, just like flocks of sheep, destruction, crimes, tranquil pools, fertile banks, flowers, birds and storms, force, fury and contemplation.

Don't leave your city. Don't come to the river country. Never turn your thoughts again to us, nor to madness. And never let it cross your mind to send us a little love.

Translated by Jeremy Munday

Antonio Benítez Rojo

The Scissors

Oh, that you would escape in the very instant in which you had
achieved your most perfect definition.

– José Lezama Lima

On the copy of his birth certificate – the first step in applying for a
passport – it was written very clearly: Jorge Emilio Lacoste. But in the
office they called him Yoyi, even though he was a grown man in his
forties. Of course, it would be different there in Washington, at the Library
of Congress; surely they would have a Latin American section, the books
all in order, neatly labelled on austere shelves, and he, *Mister* Lacoste,
expert in Cuban folklore, consulted by sociologists from Harvard, giving
lectures on native theatre, and of course the profitable contributions to
journals and art magazines. Maybe Romualdo would explain more in his
next letter, but everything seemed to be arranged: 'Now it's just a matter
of a few months, today I have sent you some money so you can buy the
ticket in dollars and so when you get to Madrid you'll have a little pocket
money until I greet you with a big hug in the USA.' Then he told about
the wonderful Washington spring, of course the cherry blossoms in bloom,
'but the other parks, too, squirrels snacking while sitting on people's laps
and flowers that look like tulips peeking out of the frost in the morning,'
and suddenly, almost at the end, before the affectionate suggestion to
practise speaking English and the signature in pink ink, there was something about a man named Fred who had very good connections, 'a really
incredible guy, and what friends ...' painters, critics, directors of libraries
and art galleries, and with a real dream of an apartment complete with
Persian rugs and concretist music, 'and located on none other than 16th
Street, the fabulous street where all the embassies are.' Well, there was no
doubt about it, Romualdo was mixing in and getting along just fine and
hadn't forgotten him in spite of the distance and now Legón, the imbecile,
was taking his lunchbag out of the drawer with that cowface of his always
surrounded by flies, probably because of the way he stinks, although it
hadn't done that other guy any good to wear a shirt and tie and perfumed

lapels, they sent him to a farm for giving his lover the receptionist's job and there *he* was, cutting out newspaper articles all day long, 'clipping' as it was called by the other guy, who gave a name to everything because it was ridiculous to think that this place was a documentation centre, and then those scissors, a piece of junk that ruined your fingers, and Legón dusting the table with his handkerchief full of snot, that's what you call a pig, imagine him having the nerve to say that the Revolution has freed *us* blacks, saying that to him, who had always passed for white and Romualdo used to take him to Tropicana and to play golf at the Country Club, that damned Legón who always fancied himself as a former slave, conceited ape, and all because he had taken a course on how to pretend to be a librarian, but in the end he didn't learn anything anyhow, only to do things backwards like putting Dominga in charge of filing – Dominga, of all people, almost an illiterate – while *he* was stuck with snipping little pieces of paper, he, the one who had a doctorate in Arts and Letters and had an essay published.

He looked up when the boy put the newspapers on the corner of the table and asked him for a cigarette. Then he distracted himself watching him deliver the mail around the whole office, stop next to the big window, and after Legón's gesture of consent, clap three times indicating that it was lunchtime.

The chicken was too spicy and on the way back he stopped by the first-aid cabinet for some bicarbonate. Back in his spot, he untied the cord that held the bundle of yellowed newspapers – in the afternoon he worked on information from six years ago – and started to cut theatre listings and articles on art. An issue that skipped a date and lacked the cultural page caught his attention, probably a filing mistake by someone although Legón didn't think it was important and told him to stick to his own job and not worry so much about what others did. The next one was a *Marina Daily News* from the year 1854, Dominga had gone crazy; of course, she wasn't prepared for the responsibilities and she would never be an executive but this was going too far, it was an error of a century, and how curious that pair of scissors lying in the fold of the sheet, probably belonging to some employee, very, very old scissors with an exotic filigree design. They cut well and he decided to use them a little.

The paper was pretty well preserved, but like other times – whenever he read old newspapers the same thing happened – his fingers trembled at first, just the amount of time needed to get used to the idea that those ads and news articles were about dead people, things that had disappeared, a world swallowed up little by little which suddenly surfaced in the name of an ocean, in the names of certain streets and cities, some now simplified by the omission of a letter.

That day the major news had been the events in the Russo-Turkish conflict; Omar Pasha was crossing the Danube with 50,000 men, two days' journey from Bucharest, and an Ottoman victory was clearly in sight; then the failure of Count Orloff in his compelling move: the Court of Vienna would not accept an alliance with Russia and declared its neutrality in favour of France and England. Next, a double column reported runaway slaves, listing indentifying traits and rewards, and immediately following that the local news: the amusing play 'Uncle Caniyitas,' Mardi Gras balls, and the première of *Don Pasquale*, at the Tacón Theatre. Since that night he was planning to go to the opera, coincidentally a revival of *Don Pasquale*, he read the article carefully in order to put on airs during the intermission conversations. After memorizing the Italian surnames and the details of the première, it occurred to him to tease Legón and prolong Dominga's stupidity by pasting the review in the folder of performances. He carefully cut out the article, but when he was matching up the edges, the scissors fell out of his hand, jabbed his thigh and suddenly were on the floor, under the table, broken. Unhinged. He looked around and picked up the separated blades and put them in his pocket. He'd find a way to put them together, a missing rivet, maybe the jeweller who worked upstairs in the building; he would return them tomorrow.

Out on the street he had felt cold and the tepid shower and the rocking of the chair made him slip into a sweet drowsiness. Almost without realizing it he went to his bed and fell asleep. He dreamt something that he couldn't remember exactly, maybe that he was brandishing the scissors at someone, in that case it would be Legón and strictly speaking you couldn't call it a nightmare, though when he opened his eyes he had noticed that sweat was running down his neck and he was breathing anxiously. The room was dark by then and he turned on the lamp at the head of the bed; it was a quarter to nine: if he didn't fly he would arrive late at the opera: the García Lorca Theatre was far from there, even without considering transportation difficulties.

'I repeat that it is full, there are no orchestra or balcony seats, only the gallery,' insisted the ticket clerk examining a seating plan marked with red x's. 'You should have come earlier.'

'But I'm a friend of the manager, he sent me an invitation. Check with him, I'm sure he can resolve the matter.'

'If you're referring to Del Monte, they got rid of him yesterday morning, and we still don't have a replacement,' the woman replied dryly.

Lacoste straightened his jacket with a tug to make it look as if he were going to leave in a huff, but he restrained himself and accepted a gallery ticket: after all, he was already here and besides it was free.

His seat was missing one of its arms and, as if that weren't enough, he could only see half of the front curtain. And that was in spite of the fact that they had just finished remodelling the building, a real disaster, bungling amateurs, they don't know how to do anything, you could tell from just looking at it, the theatre that Covarrubias opened, of course, things were different back then, the *belle époque cubaine*, and how he would have liked to live back then, the elegant balls, the gallantry, the colonial courtyards, the French fashions. He scanned the front seats: if only there were an empty one. But the orchestra, invisible to him, finished tuning, and above scattered coughing, launched into the Donizetti score.

Don Pasquale was a lively work, but the stage and the music seemed so far away from him that he left his seat before the end of the first act. The café was deserted and (on his way in) he ordered a soft drink and something to eat. When he was paying he felt the scissors in his pocket and thought that it was a shame he hadn't spoken to the jeweller; he would do it tomorrow for sure.

He spent the intermission nonchalantly leaning against the wall, explaining to a group of acquaintances about the hit performance of Steffenone and the bass Rovere in that very theatre back when it was called the Tacón, the raving final applause that extended the season – surely that's the way it had been – until the middle of March, an unforgettable show and more than a hundred years ago, and not to bore you but it's common knowledge that back then everybody knew all about opera. The bell signalling the end of intermission rang opportunely and Lacoste, deciding to really pay attention to the show – maybe he would get inspired to write a critical review – made one last comment and went back up the stairs. As he opened the door, a rush of hot air hit him in the face and suddenly something strange was happening to the lights. He sat down in a seat that could very well have belonged to the usher, the back harder, a wicker seat. Someone to his right brushed his elbow but then the curtain was opening and an inexplicable backdrop was hanging in place of the set of the first act; and of course it must have been an optical illusion but the stage seemed smaller, not as deep, I don't know, different, and suddenly that change in the cast, that new Norina fat as a barrel, and worst of all that gigantic Don Pasquale getting tangled up in the carpet, what a pair, where did they dig them up, and what a way to sing out of tune.

When he turned to ask his neighbour's opinion, he realized that it was all a dream, that at some point he had fallen asleep and now the man on his right was wearing an old-fashioned dresscoat the same style as his, though the shirt front was full of lacy ruffles and that dressed it up a lot.

Lacoste smiled thinking that he probably hadn't even gone to the theatre, that he could be in his bed after his tepid bath and the book in his rocking chair. Anyhow the air was too suffocating and down there Don Pasquale wasn't doing anything but bellowing. He would have preferred to dream about an English comedy, by Noel Coward, for example, or better yet something prohibited, a savage rite, an esoteric dance. And he was a little astonished at how easily he left his seat, put on his extremely tall hat and his gloves and descended the stairs.

In the lobby there were half a dozen mirrors. In one of them, which reached the floor, he contemplated his appearance, satisfied – he had always liked the kind of style that flattered the figure – and he tried out a few chivalric gestures without very good results: curiously his movements didn't turn out the way he imagined and ended up being crude poses. The stuff of dreams, he thought. Nearby, a petite odalisque on the arm of a pasha was attentively reading a playbill. Lacoste moved closer when he heard her mention Steffenone's name, but as hard as he tried he couldn't understand the meaning of the big red letters, although he thought he recognized some of them, the 'A' and the 'O'. He crossed the room looking for other surprises, and going down an outside staircase he entered a clear, cool night. Before him stretched, instead of the Prado, a beautiful colonial boulevard, very wide and busy. He leaned against a streetlamp that barely shone and, half-amused, half-annoyed, avoided the gaze of a man dressed up as Death who had stationed himself next to him. He headed towards another corner. It suddenly occurred to him that the dream made sense, that it wasn't so absurd: the Turks had been in the newspaper articles, the same as the opera performance, and, of course, that was the famous Isabel II Boulevard from the Miahle illustrations, and the tremendous shadows on the other side of the five lanes, the ancient city walls.

Since he wasn't waking up, he decided to go walking but not in any set direction, letting himself be carried by the dream and the night and thinking about Romualdo, about the trip to Spain. He reached a sort of circular plaza, and from a bench, next to a wide bed of pointed red stones, he entertained himself watching the carts and carriages, the extravagant groups of passers-by parading down the lanes. Two elegant mulatto women, with funny-nosed masks, slowed their pace in front of him laughing behind their fans. The younger of the two stopped, and after she let her purse fall, approached him asking if he was from the capital, because we've been following you from the theatre and you seemed sort of lost. Lacoste, without knowing why, answered that he was born in Puerto Príncipe, and had just recently arrived in Havana to sell a store. The mulatto woman said her name was Encarnación and she proposed flatteringly that he go with her to Lucindo Pérez's dance, there he would have a wonderful time and it cost so little, I think only eight *reales*, of course the main thing will be to introduce you to my girlfriends, a gentleman of such presence as you, sir, so sophisticated and so proper, you would see how well they would attend to you, like a king, besides, she would make sure he wouldn't get bored and guaranteed him dances and wine all night long.

Lacoste murmured that he would enjoy seeing a ritual dance, well, that kind of thing. But the women just shrugged their shoulders, took him by the hands and led him singing through the gates of Monserrate.

While Encarnación held his hand pleasingly tight, Lacoste congratulated himself for imagining such a good dream; shy since adolescence, he rarely approached women and suddenly that encounter, that coincidence of his mind with the articles in a forgotten newspaper.

Taking advantage of the darkness of an alley Lacoste put his arm around the waist of the other mulatto woman, Rosa, and from her learned that the dance at Lucindo's place was for Mardi Gras although neither Encarnación nor I like to wear costumes, but you look very nice the way you are, you make a lovely couple, flatterer you're saying that because of Rosa, look I saw how you let your hand slip down to her hip.

After walking within the city walls for a while, Encarnación and Rosa started to argue about the best way to get to Lucindo Pérez's house. Encarnación preferred to keep going along the wall and cut down Ricla, which was the most advisable thing to do considering the robberies there have been lately. Rosa, however, I won't take another step if you don't turn left and go down this street right here, and gathering her skirts she sat down on the kerb to cry. Recommending calm, Lacoste was about to offer a conciliatory plan to proceed in a diagonal, but someone hit him on the head from behind, knocking him to the cobblestones and now Rosa's hands were searching through his pockets and a gruff voice was complaining, between elaborate insults, that all he had was a broken pair of scissors, that he was the second broke client they had brought and if you don't do your job the way you're supposed to I'll thrash you.

Lacost managed to get to a doorway. For a moment the dream had turned into another where Fred and Romualdo, holding giant fans, were waiting for him in the underground airport of the Washington Monument. Though it was Fred and not Romualdo who, bowing politely, handed the

newspaper over to him in the yellow lift via Puerto Príncipe before the
trapdoor fell. Legón gave the clapping signal at once and Miss Rosa and
Miss Encarnación pulled the tulips and squirrel tails from their bosom and
ignoring the howling of Steffenone chained to the theatre seat, they
manhandled him viciously, leaving him defenceless and face down in the
dark doorway, the doorway of the first dream.

Still on the ground, while he tried to get the dirt off his face and clothes,
he thought that the best thing to do was to go back to the starting point,
retrace the spiral back to the front of the theatre. Then let go of the flying
trapeze and fall under the covers of his bed; then the sound of his Big Ben
alarm, cologne on his handkerchief, the easy familiarity of daily things.

Hanging on to a column, he stood up and went to the edge of the street:
among the stones of the gutter gleamed a blade of the scissors: he picked it
up automatically. But there was no sign of his spats, dresscoat, top hat, or
bow tie.

Luckily the way back wasn't difficult: all he had to do was find the wall
and follow it to one of the gates, greet the officer of the guard confidently
– or maybe explain to him that he had been robbed – and head for the
familiar territory of the boulevard.

He could also knock on a door and ask some old man with a candlestick
and nightcap how to get outside the city walls, yes, to ask someone was the
most sensible thing to do, *ask someone?* how foolish.

He walked with his shoulder to the walls: he was cold: probably the
window was open and a breeze blew across his hammock over in Puerto
Príncipe.

He stopped in front of the steps of a church. Since sometimes the cold
woke him up, he tried taking off his shirt. And on top of the shivering and
the headache he got the idea that after all he had never felt so much the
master of his existence; paradoxically that nightmare, while it thrust him
into another century, granted him little by little a vague and painful need
to choose a direction, a way to go on; and now realizing that he was
standing in the middle of the deserted street, at the foot of the black tower
of the church, with his shirt hanging from his hand, trembling in the icy
wind, wind thick with sea salt from the bay, it all seemed somewhat
ridiculous and improbable and at the same time frighteningly real; and he
couldn't keep thinking because the noise behind him turned out to be a
wagon led by four horses that was turning the corner, and he had to jump
up on to the steps and press himself against the studded door amid the
lightning crack of a whip, curses, and whinnies.

It was useless to put his shirt on: it was left torn and dirty on the other side of the street. Some voices that were getting nearer made him duck down next to the stairway banister. They were two men. Two white men dressed in frock coats who were laughing about somebody called Uncle Caniyitas. As they passed in front of him, a vague impulse prompted him to search in his pocket for the scissors blade. After a few moments it was quiet again.

Lacoste went back down the steps to the street clutching the blade and looked at his shirt again, and it must have been that strange fear, that velvety anguish swelling inside him, that must have been what was paralysing his memory, because he couldn't remember anymore the reason why he had taken it off.

Crouching next to the gutter, perplexed and numb from the cold, he realized his memories were fading away from him; a thick fog was isolating him from things felt and thought, dissolving them into darker and darker wisps, farther and farther away. Terrified, he struggled to make his way back, to reach at all costs a territory that would affirm him, a fortress to defend to the death his identity. He groped through the mist and recovered scarcely two notions: his name and a veiled feeling of guilt: Jorge Emilio Lacoste and something like original sin.

He opened his hand and somehow knew that in that piece of scissors gleamed remorse. Then, while he ran his finger along the filigree on the blade, he started to remember, little by little, trace by trace, point by point, as if a spider were weaving his memory. But in the centre, in the petrified hollow of the web, remained always the mystery of the great hall of mirrors and he couldn't remember how he had gotten to it, nor who had taken him up to that crazy perch near the ceiling where the din had awoken him, most likely the cries of those clowns on the platform, howling and running from one side to the other with paint smeared on their faces, which they weren't even ashamed of, they were so big and goofy, yes sir.

And now, from very far away, came a voice telling him to join together the blades of the scissors. But why put them together if he was the one who had broken them? He had dropped them on the floor four times in the store. He remembered that clearly. They had fallen flat until the ends broke apart and zap ... he had travelled through the air and landed with new clothes in the middle of the capital, so bewitched and bewildered that he didn't even know exactly who he was. Yes sir, that's what had happened. No more, no less, that's it. And how was he going to put them together if the other blade was lost, not even if he were a *babalawo*, a soothsayer, and knew everything. And if he wasn't under a spell then he must have been asleep and dreaming all that, of course, the great hall of mirrors and that screaming bunch of clowns and Death wanting to take him away, yes sir. And then those juicy mulatas, Rosa and Encarnación, and he had felt the ass of one of them. No more, no less, that's it. And then the rope on his hammock must have busted and crash, the party's over. That lousy rope, that dirty rotten low-down rope that wrecked the wine and roses at that guy Lucindo's dance and had given him that goose-egg on the head. And at least he was still in the capital. And who was going to tell him so and now it was high time to change. You always dream on and on about that getting rich jive. That's because of the money buried in the back of the store, yes sir. Under the old wall, of course. Nobody can tell me it's not true, I saw it being put there with my own two eyes, so many jugs smack full of *centén* coins and double doubloons, so much gold, yellow as a bunch of bananas, and Don Remigio saying you have to be prepared what with the war coming and the shootin' and the lootin' and this and that and the other thing. Yes sir. That's it. And you looking at those things. And the best thing to do is to go up this way and see if I find the mulatas or that party of Lucindo's.

He put on his torn shirt and turned the corner.

He thought that he had never had such a complicated dream. Nor one in which it had been so cold.

Some distant music made him switch to another street, quickening his pace: must be Lucindo's party.

And the dance must have been a really important one: near the house there was a line of carriages and quite a few people were gathered at the door and the window, both wide open.

He passed behind a group of carriage drivers; they were playing cards for the change in their tips, and they didn't even look at him.

Lacoste stood on tiptoe and managed to see over the top of the onlookers: there were a lot of people in the house, a lot of lights, a lot of flashy black men and a lot of mulatto women wearing big haircombs and marabou feathers. Only a few were wearing costumes. Others just used masks like the ones that Rosa and Encarnación wore.

There were also some white men, but they weren't dancing; leaning against the wall they drank all the time surrounded by women and trays of food and they looked very happy. Every once in a while an old, fat, smiling mulatto man went up to talk with them. Lacoste supposed that he was Lucindo Pérez, and he pushed his way through the doorway and entered the parlour.

At first no one noticed him. Almost everyone was dancing in front of the musicians or applauding the salty wit of a tall black woman, who wriggled under her skin like cigar fillers. The drummer, with a drumroll, ended the song and the black woman, perspiring and out of breath, left her partner and headed towards him, winking at him with her arms outstretched. Lacoste took a step forward, but suddenly the woman bent at the waist, clapped her hands in the air and, turning her back to him, went to a corner and almost died laughing, you should have seen it. Now everyone was laughing and they looked at him and laughed again and he knew that kind of dream already, yes sir, those dreams where you looked for a *centén* coin and what turned up in your hand was a cold toad that pissed on you, of course, seven years' bad luck and you were almost sure to die, and the store clerk hung up his suitcoat and quilted vest again and was making fun of him with an enormous laugh, of course, a laugh the size of his face and *he* was tossing and turning furiously in his hammock, yes sir, that's what was happening. But now it wasn't a toad in his hand but the scissors blade, and nobody was laughing at him anymore.

He knocked over a candlestick and ran out to the courtyard amidst the women's screaming. Out of the corner of his eye he saw Lucindo fling open a knife, but he was already scaling the backyard wall with the scissors in his teeth and before he knew it he was on the other side. He fled down a narrow cobbled street and then turned to the left.

He found Death, after a black cat, arching its back with its hair standing on end, had left him standing sort of dazed next to a pile of garbage. Without looking back, trying to get out of the dream, he bounded to the other corner and ran towards the glow of some streetlamps. There were the old city walls. And there, in front of him, was the gate he had gone through with the mulatto women. He passed by two soldiers who were asleep, and crossing the bridge over the trench, he reached the boulevard with the five lanes that he had so admired. In the doorway of the great hall of mirrors people were waiting for their carriages. He heard a gunshot and turned his head: Death and the soldiers were chasing after him, just leaving the city walls. As if that weren't enough, a carriage was coming down the lane next to him to block his way. He suddenly felt like breaking into hysterical laughter like the black woman at Lucindo's, clapping his hands and ending once and for all that stupid chase, getting out of his hammock and splashing his face with water from the pitcher to rinse off the sweat from that dream, that dream in which for no reason he was running away from a night of madness. But now it was too late, the carriage had already stopped and a purple hooded robe jumped down from the horse with its arms open ready for anything.

Still he tried to escape, and it was easy to elude the careless attack by swinging his body around, leaning his back against the hub of the wheel and desperately sinking the piece of scissors into the purple cloth.

After that he had time to jump on to the wooden wheel shaft and grab the reins in one swoop, line up the carriage on the street while the soldier with the grey moustache aimed a gun at him impassively. Then all that was left was to raise the whip above the gunshot, come crashing down painfully at the horse's feet and listen to Death, who, hood down, told the onlookers that he, Jorge Emilio Lacoste, was a runaway slave from a sugar mill in Puerto Príncipe, a mulatto thief and murderer whose identifying traits had been reported in the newspaper.

At that point he struggled again to wake up, to pretend that his shoulder barely hurt him, and when the soldiers violently dragged him to the edge of the circular plaza, before Death and the others gathered handfuls from the bed of stones, he thought that he would never escape from that dream, that returning was no longer possible and he would continue to dream it for the rest of his life.

Translated by Diane J. Forbes

Alejandro Rossi

Orion's Glow

'Yes, when she saw him full length without clothes, she realized he was black. She was terrified. She ran out through the passageways and left that huge, polite man, naked in the middle of the room. Yes, she fled like a frightened blast of wind and, according to her, never saw him again. Women, Lorenzo – to me they're much more decisive than we are.' 'Perhaps, Don Pío, they're less ashamed to admit they're afraid.' 'Could be, but, fear can be a strong force, you are right on that.' They heard the impatient clanging of the bell. 'That's the Chinks' boat. They'll be at Puerto Naranjo by daybreak. They're carrying vegetables, flowers, good fighting cocks if there are any. That's what they claim they're carrying. I bet there are a few scared girls in the old man's cabin, though; they cling together all night like young trees. The Chink gives them green tea and *casabe*.' 'But did she ever tell you she was terrified?' 'Yeah, but you should realize I met her a few years later and by then she'd turned the whole thing into a sort of silly joke. She thought it shocking things should come to such a pass, that they hadn't stopped before. She might have been sorry, felt foolish perhaps. There's something crude about putting on a good show, don't forget that.' You could hear the cries of the children calling goodbye to the boat now, mingling with the shrieks of birds coming home to roost. 'Those bloody kids'd say goodbye to the leaves the river carries along. Then they feel sad and angry and don't know why and fight together like starving dogs.'

'And the black guy, Don Pío?'

'The black guy? Big hulk, Washington Miranda, he was called – sounds like a declaration of independence, like a shield paraded in front of the enemy, or perhaps just to convince himself the future was bright, in spite of his kinky hair and smell. No doubt about it, he was an optimist, toe the line type, wanted to get on. He was a lawyer, he'd studied in Trinidad under the English, got his training in the Main Office, in the capital city, of course. Wearing a straw hat and a suit of matching colours. Later, he struck out for himself and handled things for some shipping company on the river; they did say he ran a couple of broken down whorehouses for Colonel Méndez, remember, him of the "Triumvirate of Traitors". For me, the big guy made several mistakes, but the main one wasn't his fault. I mean, that he looked like a mulatto. That was only one of those chance combinations of genes you find in this part of the country. You know, around here, and even more in river town, folks are made up in patches, a fine narrow nose like a young woman in a Florentine painting, and a blubber mouth from cane-cutter ancestors. White faces, yellow bellies; pale blondes with hair like bushes and tight asses that belong to lazy little black girls. Yes sir, Don Washington Miranda had skin like *café au lait* and hid it very well with his good suits – white man's suits – his expensive watch chain, and all sort of make-up tricks he'd learned from East Indian barbers and Chinese tradesmen – they're experts at disguising. But it was no good. Gracielita Valdemosa found him out at one point in time, he was only a refugee from the slums.' 'But Don Pío, didn't her mother suspect anything?' 'I don't know. I don't think she cared too much. Don't forget, Lorenzo, she was already a widow and worn out with life – her exhaustion was unbeatable. Her husband was well known, once, another of our mixed-up heroes; they shot him on the border in the Second Constitutional War, as they call it, a lot of talk, started as a slanging match between bad-tempered lawyers and ended up with guns and machetes in Santa Rosalia savannah, a sort of island with rivers all around. I never liked General Valdemosa, the one historians call the Orator General now. He looked more like a playwright with his beard, and he'd rather debate than fight. His aides were a pack of upstart lawyers in high boots, but his troops were a mangy lot shuffling about in rope soles. It was the way he died and his good frinds that made him a hero. In this area, though, he was bad news. He carried off workers, livestock, and for twenty years left us fighting those up north without knowing what for. His widow showed up at ceremonies in his honour and looked as though she was sleepwalking through the Grand March from Aida and those slap-bang speeches celebrating nobody knows what. Then she started going round and round those waiting rooms with toothless shoeshine guys and cuspidors in the corners, applying for a pension. Here we call them them 'pretty wars', when they're personal ones and participants cover the costs – our Orator General even had to hock his grand piano. His widow had a problem, given the circumstances; she was one of those dazzling beauties, I mean the sort that stun at first sight as opposed to those that melt hearts over time. She was the granddaughter of the wine importer, old Müller, but her blood was mixed with that of the Regueiros – slow, thoughtful blood, they had. You've got to admit, emigration's a laboratory, but it doesn't classify the women it's going to experiment with or we'd never get the results we do. There was good mettle in that family but no staying power. You find families like that, solid, but they don't take root. Towards the end, poor old Müller faced General Garmendia – the one who came up with the barbarity of us all drinking coconut milk. I think loyalty spurred her on at first. She went round the bosses' offices, in spite of the way they treated her, and recited her litany without adding anything, and left ten minutes later when she noticed how upset they'd all become. I don't know at what point she decided she was the important factor, not her husband's questionable glory. Perhaps she realized it was ridiculous to insist on a nickel and dime pension, or she might have started feeling her strength, surprised, since she was a beginner at the game. Anyway, she never made any major conquests, I can assure you; she was an innocent soul, really, in spite of having a body that swept all before it. Abascal was the one who lasted the longest, I think. He was an officer of the old school, very proud of his knowledge of classical events, a dandy, strictly Officers' Circle material, his uniform always well pressed and a gold ring on his little finger.' They heard the scuffle of Leoncia's slippers as she brought them two plates of fried bananas with rice. She put them down unceremoniously and added, in the indifferent tones one would expect of an ancient turtle, that she'd be back with their tamarind water in a bit. 'It's like jail diet, Lorenzo, but it's all my stomach can take. I don't think Leoncia can fix anything else now. If you like, she'll fix you a coffee later. And if you want to, I'll get the old telescope out and we'll go up on to the roof and look at the stars. They used to fascinate me, but I'm less interested in the heavens nowadays, not like when I was young and thought I could read my fate there. I'll settle for sitting in this armchair and hearing the *cocuyos* flap their wings and the river lapping. You know very well that in my profession it was a question of luck, though I practised it and earned my degree as one ought to. I was a mining engineer, looking for gold. It depended on some technical knowledge, some encouraging gossip, and what the heavens foretold. I found it in the rivers, and pot-bellied Indians brought it to me. I went up North once and claimed a mine that was a godsend. I buried myself in it for years and had the pleasure of following a vein that petered out to an imperceptible thread. I stripped that mine as if it had been a woman, but when all was said and done, it was a skinny bitch. She ruined my digestion and left me with a heart that feels fleeting passion and suffers from spasms. I'm not complaining though. Can you imagine how wonderful it was living from day to day on expectations and your heart galloping with excitement. I don't live on what I made; my aunt Angelina left me four sections of land and I live on that. Good Aunt Angelina, nobody could say the rosary as quickly as she could, sounded like a bee was trapped in the room. I'd tiptoe in and cover her eyes and shout 'Amen!' But that didn't stop the fastest Ave Marias in the county. You're looking at me, Lorenzo, as if you don't believe most of what I'm saying, you're not convinced that I'm all right. I am, though. Old age doesn't trouble me and I'm thankful not to have aches and pains. Pain cuts you off from everything, you concentrate on it, it's a bird of prey that never lets go. If you have a more or less peaceful old age, though, it gives you back that narrow space you had as a child. I find myself watching the ants march along, never tiring, or the birds wheeling. That minute tremor of life that surrounds you. A hummingbird's vibrant, hysterical; a lizard's electric, and those huge butterflies that we have here, they sway in the air, forgotten, innocent. You don't long for the same things, Lorenzo. Women become bodyguards who look after you from a distance. Women who stick around used to get on my nerves. I've got used to the girls around here, who flit around. They still haunt my fancy, and even though I've no weapons to fight with now, old Leoncia brings me little girls to bathe, slowly, carefully. I wash them with special soap I've still got left from the old days, big oval bath soap, not those fiendish little slivers you find in showers in the backyards around here. Then I dab them with eau-de-Cologne. They half smile and wriggle a bit when I tickle them unintentionally. Seems to me they go away happy enough, and it leaves me somewhat exhausted. Listen, if you're still hungry I'll tell them to bring you a cup of coffee, with milk. I was going to ask you, Lorenzo, if death frightens you, but I know at your age it's an abstract sort of challenge, a religious impertinence to keep you in line. I only worried about it when I was intensely happy. I'd see it like a thief coming to steal away those moments of grace. Now it's something else. What can it take away from me now? Fried bananas? My pewter plates? I'm seeing it as part of life for the first time. I see it in my repetitive days, my discouraged dreams, in a certain gratitude I feel for everything and for nothing. Look, look up, the sky in this region is overwhelming. It is more populated than this plain. Make me keep talking, Lorenzo, I like that.'

'I'm glad, Don Pío, since I have to admit they'd told me you were gloomy and silent.'

'So I am, especially when people treat me like some sort of relic, a piece of precious mineral, what's left of a past that can't be fathomed. They ask me things that leave me feeling very much alone. It's different with you, you're Francisco's grandson.'

'But it's only natural for them to look you up, Don Pío, you're even mentioned in one of the volumes of *Days of the Fatherland*, and unless I'm mistaken, it has you as a pioneer in the mining industry.' 'I thought it was a joke when I saw it – we're all pioneers in this area. Chink found a girl whose face was like an old woman's but her body was a young woman's, and Laureano, Laureano had a way with words, "just a cuckoo," he said, "in a cuckoo clock telling the time." But I told you, I was just in it for the gold, for what I could get out of it, of course, but there were hidden reasons, personal ones. I see myself sometimes as a nature warden alone, seeking the golden-haired beauty. Bear in mind, Lorenzo, that where I spent my youth illusion was stronger than reality. As if we all lived with the conviction that quiet rivers and the silence of the plains hid some mystery. I understand, though, to what purpose those hard-nosed scribes in port town fill out their red-backed ledgers. They mean to show the young folk that they had forebears, that there was a certain continuity, that all those disparate lights in that immense night add up to a Country. You don't hear me objecting; deep down I admire the hopeless measures they take.'

'I want to hear more about her, Don Pío. What happened then?'

'Abascal, a colonel, arrogant but respectable, he left her a little house near the cemetery. He pulled out step by step the way some folks get out of mass before it's over. Beauty, Lorenzo, isn't enough by itself; otherwise, we stop seeing it. It seems to me the widow didn't ask for much, didn't put up a fight. In cases like that, only a grand passion can save them. I don't know what she did next, though I can imagine. She was an excellent cook, famous for her *hayacas*, but you can't make a life from that. I know, I know the one you're interested in is the daughter, who was a skinny kid of seventeen at that time, with long hands and blue eyes like her asshole of a father. I can't tell you what I don't know, how she met Miranda, how he got into the game park. I imagine it must have happened very quickly; it wouldn't have done to give them time to think things over. I imagine his good manners, and let's be frank, his being such a big, kind man settled the matter in his favour. Good manners in a black, Lorenzo, can be most appealing. There's a gentleness in the way they look, they touch, that only they can manage. They got married, I imagine, in one of those churches near the water on the outskirts of the port itself, with a priest who dropped things, scared at performing a mixed marriage, and with Graciela's school friends around her, giggling and whispering. Afterwards, and this she did tell me, he took her to the Hotel Remanso, which is the only one with double beds, the only decent one in town; a wooden structure out over the sea, our noisy, rough sea that you almost have to shout to be heard over. The favourite spot of our many commanders, perfect for making plans, for undressing and singing boleros to young girls gone astray. That's where the scene took place, Lorenzo, that's where she'd run out on the black guy, left like a wounded animal lying on the ground. She went back by bus, stiff, not even leaning against the back of the seat. Don't you want to see the stars through the telescope? All right then, we'll let them be to blink on their own. People who've never lived here think of it as static, stunned by an irremovable sun. Another lie – it dates back to the famous Ocean Campaign, another of General Garmendia's idiotic schemes, the idea that our country's wealth is to be found in the riches of its coast. It was intended to stop people migrating inland. But static is what it isn't, just the opposite, rather. Here, Lorenzo, we live in a world that throbs, animals are short lived, flowers die in a day – it's biology in full flight, speeded up, as if we were in at the creation of the first species. All right, all right, I realize I haven't answered your question whether the widow knew if Washington Miranda was black passing for white. I'm certain when he showed up at the little house near the cemetery he hadn't a hope of marrying the daughter in the normal way her family would have gone about things. The port was a small town and the widow had too many rings on her fingers. Widowhood had worn her out. If we were philosophers, the ones in search of serenity, Lorenzo, we'd say that weakness, as well as strength, changes the course of destiny. Just listen to the wind. It's coming in from the mountains, from miles away, and after it's grazed thousands of trees, it's as though it came cold from inside the churches up north. I don't like it; it reminds me of crazy priests, fanatics, raping our peace and quiet here once again. She didn't tell it as it was; like I said, she preferred to turn it into a sick joke, though she spent months afterwards pale with shock, shamed into inertia. And that's how she was when your grandfather met her. When he said to me, "Nobody can survive so much bad luck," I knew he'd decided to take care of her forever. Francisco was one of those disconcerting men who stare life full in the face. He agreed to pay for one nephew to study because he was brilliant, keep a sister-in-law in New York because her marriage was on the rocks, send a brother who was depressive to Europe. He neither praised nor criticized, as if nothing weighed on him. I don't know if he felt pity for the unfortunates of this world, or some mysterious need to bring everything together. He dragged all along, never asking himself if things were out of the ordinary, whether good or bad. And don't forget, it was a time in the port town when asking about the whys and wherefores of anything could reduce you to total helplessness. Your grandfather would hear Professor Carrillo, our only pundit, shooting his mouth off about the rules and regulations of those goddamned little colonels, and agree, impatient, without enthusiasm, and the poor old beaver would rage on in one of his oratorial ecstasies about 'those besotted with evil'. Francisco, mind you, never said to me, "Pío, I've fallen in love with the fatherless girl who told

Miranda to go to hell." He bore it secretly, he visited her a couple of times a week and, I believe, he didn't touch her until much later. It was as if he allowed her to rest, as if he realized she needed undemanding normal conversation. That was the time Francisco was just starting out in the shabby Customs House in the port. They went to work as if they lived in a place with another climate, in worsted suits, sweating in gentlemanly dignity under ceiling fans. They'd mop their brows and wipe their hands on English tissues soaked in lavender-water. And you wonder what they used to talk about, don't you, Lorenzo? At first, good manners demanded he tell her about his trips to the United States, exaggerating how poor he'd been as a student, to make her laugh. Then he took her books, *Fortunata y Jacinta* perhaps, one of her favourites, and that would give them plenty to talk about. He might have shown her his Mark Twains, too; he was always talking about them. Or he'd translate for her – he was very fond of showing off his English – articles from American magazines he used to get. No demands; your grandfather was careful, intense. Very down to earth, too, he noticed the smallest details, how the armchairs were threadbare, the bottom was out of the rocking chair, the walls needed painting, the curtains were faded, the canaries' cages were old. At first, he'd look but he wouldn't see, out of respect for the young lady and the straitened circumstances she was living in. And as he grew closer to her, as he realized that his visits were magic, as he entered the enchanted zone of love in the universe of blinding light, he dared mention that he'd send a painter to touch up the drawing room, bring a new cage, and so take a house that was going downhill and put it on an even keel again. Of course, they knew your grandfather was married, married to a beauty from the port town, but I don't think that mattered; I mean, they had that sad decorousness that takes life as it comes. Who knows what he told her on the day he let her know he'd fixed up another house for her. We'll never know and I don't want to make things up. I'm sure, though, there wouldn't have been any arrangements or discussions of any sort. Gracielita slipped with no effort whatsoever to the other side of town, to Barrio Nuevo de la Costa. He wanted her alone, without the widow's eternal suffering. She said, right here, on one of those never-ending, quiet evenings we have here, that the day she moved was the first time he ever ordered her to do anything. "I advise you, Graciela," – he didn't like pet names – "to cut your nails and take up the guitar." Old men, Lorenzo, see love as a fantastic adventure. They dwell on, how can I put it? the surge of life, the pleasure, the longing to see how she turns suddenly when you call her, the delicate silence as she straightens her clothes, the way she touches you absent-mindedly as she passes, the way she folds the pillow, the gap in her teeth, the way she pays attention, but with a sideways glance to what you say, suddenly fastening a button on your shirt. Ah, son, you're in deep, in an uncharted world of minute obstacles. The mole beneath her arm, her dark, young nipples, her deep navel, and the light touch of her hand. It requires continuous attention, that I'll never achieve now. Perhaps that's why I'm not telling you about it the way I should; I can't imagine things clearly. Every reality needs an impulse, and mine's different now. From the depths of my soul I envy them this story, me, the man who only liked his women unattached, girls for the time being, adolescents, light sleepers. When I met her on one of my rare trips to the port town, she was definitely his woman. She lived like an Arab, appearing only at night. Your grandfather only visited her at night, worn out from his work, fighting against his weariness with increasing doses of whisky. I know that Francisco kept her against all odds, all the gossip and pleading. It's ridiculous to think that Gracielita felt hemmed in, drowned. Those are stupidities. Nobody wanted to go anywhere. That they lived through such difficulties only proved their love was divine. It wasn't a price they paid, large or small. That's how things were, and neither of them expected anything from the town. They'd walk in the patio, go into the overgrown garden at the far end and uncork bottles of champagne when the Dutch freighters went by, and make love, certain that their destiny was pure gold. What more do you want? What more could anyone want? Zanabria, the red-head soloist, still gave her guitar lessons, and she played like a feather. We'd drink slowly, not too slowly, though, talking, listening to her playing, and to the rockets the black kids on the wharf liked to send up. We were sure that life belonged to us. Sometimes they'd link hands and leave me talking to myself. Those were your grandfather's golden days, no doubt about that; he'd escaped from the sticky paper and red tape of the Customs House and left the smell of frying oil and the sound of raucous voices in the street. He was dealing with money in large sums now, his career as a banker and administrator had taken off. He'd begun associating with Genaro González, a name you'll be familiar with, you with your nose in history books about our country. Yes, the same one, Fatso González, the one they rebaptized "General Piety". His descendants must be happy, surprised, too. The official version, improved on as always, nevertheless a decent tale and one not to be ashamed of, is that he always had his pockets full of candy to give to the kids that surrounded him like hornets when he showed up in the plaza, and, of course, there was his famous generosity to those he defeated in battle. Remember the tale about the captains from the south, those rascals who came up with the

"Doctrine of Privilege"? They wanted to secede and came up with a really terrible national anthem. After defeating them, he should have shot them but instead he had them parade barefoot on the wharf and sent them off to some island out there, saying – what are those goddamned lines on his monument? "Our countrymen, though wrong-headed, still deserve to live." Those already killed in battle didn't count. The ones that remained were Carcía – what an idealogue, he talked on and on, shaking as if he had malaria, and López Miralt, the liberal priest, the one they called "the priest with a thousand girlfriends", and a few officers who didn't realize what was going on. Francisco helped finance the General, and perhaps he wasn't the worst we had; he took part in a few wars that were far enough away and seemed necessary – border disputes where nobody knows where the border is, and ridiculous ideas about secession that feed on men being alone and feeling hopeless. Our generals went into business and kept the country together. Your grandfather used to say to me, "Cut the crap, Pío, start a tobacco factory for the troops, I'll back you." I think he thought I was a bum; he called me his "errant friend". I did the impossible not to get mixed up with the military nor with gung ho politicians who produced a new reform every year. I can admire those pundits' intentions when they carry on about one Fatherland, but I could never accept those fanatics from the north as being on my side. I stayed in this region, where the rivers are smart and easy going, where slow living speeded up, among the thousands of birds and the plains shimmering like a mirror.'

'Was she beautiful, Don Pío?'

'Good question. No, she wasn't beautiful; you should never measure a man's love by his woman's beauty. We fall in love with a gesture, with a voice, with those things that tell us we've found a soul that runs parallel to our own. I used to wonder how she could be so attractive, since her nose was big. Now, I'd swear she was a woman without hidden doubts, one that would never ask you, if you follow, how to get a cork out of a bottle, but one who wouldn't worry either if your grandfather never said a word for three nights. A woman who never wonders if things might have been different. A woman for whom the greatest offence would have been for someone to put in doubt the happiness of her too brief nights with Francisco. She was neither a lapdog nor a pampered cat, Lorenzo, even if she had that age-old way of looking on men askance. Have I given you an idea of how extraordinarily intelligent she was? Photographs from those days are so conventional, they couldn't do her justice, they don't show her alertness, her tremendous capacity for enjoyment. You can scarcely see how noble her neck, how broad her high cheek bones, possibly Pomeranian inherited from old Müller. They only once came to this region, under the pretext of Francisco having to sort out a mixed-up mortgage for the nephews of Baldomero, no doubt resulting from General González's third campaign, the one they call "The War of the Flowers", a stupid bloody mess if ever there was one. I picked them up in Puerto Naranjo, they arrived in one of those phony luxury steamers, and looked very distinguished, but keeping their distance from each other, which I didn't understand at first. As if they were brother and sister, rather than living together in that little house on the coast. It was the first time they'd gone off together and they didn't know how to act as man and wife. After a few days, I remember her saying to me, "All that's missing here are giraffes." They were put off by all our disorder, our overabundance, like going into a huge vegetable market. They liked the bare rooms in our houses and the depth of our hammocks, a refuge, perhaps, when faced with overwhelming space. The variety of oddities astonished her, the quantity of unmatched volumes, works of Tacitus, Castiglione's *Courtier*, the poems of Villaespesa. She realized in a flash that what we have here isn't peace but only a truce. I recall her sitting in the rocking chair, waiting for Francisco, fanning herself, as if she wanted to change the air of the whole region all by herself. I get mixed up about dates, but I believe she was already pregnant. About the problems that followed, I'd better tell you straight, I know very little. To some extent the problem wasn't the child itself, but your grandfather's decision, one he wouldn't change, that her son should not be brought up by her, but grow up in the house downtown, legally protected, along with the others. It's very hard now to reconstruct the way Francisco had reasoned this out or what impelled him to act as he did, and anyway, I only learned half the story, and that after the fact. Perhaps he thought his son deserved something better in the port town, perhaps he wanted to save him from embarrassment, from growing up unsure of himself. It was a major operation and we can't reduce it to a matter of prejudice or fear of what society might do. It's very easy to make arrogant decisions about other people's lives, Lorenzo. The selfish hypothesis, but one that includes the idea of blind love, is that a child would take from his own freedom to enjoy her, would turn her into a woman like any other, and that clashed with his nights of champagne and a full moon in the squared-in patio. Seeing it that way is romanticizing, I realize that: he didn't want to break up the idea, his fancy, call it what you like, that he had a night-time princess. What I want is for us not to judge their lives but to dwell on them with the indulgence friendship gives us.' 'But what about her? What did she think, Don Pío?' 'Come now, how can you know? I can't imagine. She must have been dumbstruck when they told her, probably before having the baby, though the very idea of living out the life of the girl of his dreams that he was proposing, no matter how unfair, must have been flattering. Afterwards, a long time afterwards, she went to Rome and lived there for many years, very active, with her Spanish guitar. Francisco went to visit her regularly, the way the rich men of the port town would do. I don't know anything about those times. Could be it was the only way to make any sense of their lives, the illusions that romantic meetings bring. A way to hold off inevitable decay. And when she came back she survived your grandfather's accident in the most heart-wrenching loneliness. She wanted to come back to this part of the country, not to smell the innumerable flowers, not to face our astounding daybreaks, just to talk to me for a while. To talk about the wars and our phony peace, about rivers and how deep they are, but never about her life, though at times she mentioned Francisco, lightly, in passing, as if he were there at her side. I saw her here, in this ramshackle house, with my pewter plates and in the din the birds make. I can't tell you any more. I know it isn't much, but it's the best love story I know.'

'That's all right, Don Pío, thank you. It's helped me get a lot of things straight.'

'For me too. Heavens, Lorenzo, you're a born interviewer. You really took me in, with class. I assure you, I had no idea that you didn't know that Gracielita Valdermosa was your grandmother. Congratulations, you're the grandson of a great love, and that's worth a fortune. And what do you say if we look for the telescope now? Orion should be shining.'

Translated by Alita Kelley

Luis Loayza

A New Man

So they've separated. She's taken the children and gone back to the house in Miraflores that her mother kept all those years, despite it being far too big for a woman all on her own; he's rented an apartment in one of those new neighbourhoods I can never remember the name of, and is living with the girl. Who, I've been told, is very elegant, intelligent, very sensible: 'the cat's whiskers' as someone with a taste for old-fashioned expressions said. Were all this to have happened in my day – by which I mean before I first left Peru – it would have provided the perfect excuse to drag out morality, pity or talk of keeping up appearances as a way of doing them down. But it has to be said that in the years I've been out of the country – drawing up reports that nobody's ever bothered to read, chatting with a whole string of ambassadors – back in Peru people have been going to the movies a lot, and now they're very up-to-date. The talk over lunch at my cousin Maruja's the other day was all based on several unspoken assumptions: we're very modern, we respect other people's freedom, everybody has the right to do as they think best, nothing surprises us. And anyway, it seems there's been a lot of similar startling breakups in recent years, so they're hardly a novelty any more, though that doesn't make them any the less interesting. I had to listen to a lot of details and explanations, that I had admittedly mostly asked for, all of them recounted in a light-hearted manner steering clear of any condemnation. Above all, I mustn't forget that the young lady in question is a wonderful person; and all this praise almost had me convinced until I heard that she should have been with us at lunch: they were going to come – he would have accompanied her, of course – but had been obliged to leave town the night before on some urgent business that couldn't wait. Fine then, so they live together, they travel together, they're invited everywhere together; they're a universally accepted couple who only need to get married to really set the seal on things.

*

But to do that, he needs to get a divorce, and it's by no means certain Graciela will give him one. Alberto has offered to pay for their children's education and to give her a small allowance, but nothing more. There's the house in Orrantia, the apartment in Ancon, and above all, there are pots of money, but he's put all that into limited companies and suchlike, plus he's a lawyer so any lawsuit would be long drawn-out and complicated, and she'd most likely get nothing out of it in the end. I wonder how people manage to discover all these kinds of things: perhaps we're still rather provincial after all, at least as far as our interest in other people's lives is concerned. Be that as it may, the general impression was that so far, Graciela had refused a divorce, which wasn't very modern of her, but since we ourselves were, we could understand and excuse her for that.

*

The last time I saw them together was when I was in Lima two years ago. I was invited to dinner at someone's house, and from the hallway the first person I saw was Alberto, standing in a corner of the room, glass in hand. He didn't see me at first; I noticed something strange about him, but it took me a while to figure out what it was. The years had not touched him – that phrase, which we repeat so often out of politeness but which tends to be meaningless, or simply means that our friends haven't yet become complete ruins, was more than justified in this case. Alberto looked younger than ever before, slimmer, stronger, more relaxed. I was still in the doorway, greeting the host and taking my coat off, and I couldn't help catching a glimpse of myself in the mirror: a plump, grey-haired fellow in glasses. Alberto came over to say hello and to tell me they had come to town especially to see me, travelling from Chaclacayo, where they spent the winter. I felt obliged to tell him he looked younger than ever (and he's a year older than me, dammit!), so much so it was downright disgusting. He was suntanned, as if he had just got back from the beach, and when he laughed he revealed impeccable teeth. At that moment, Graciela appeared; I kissed her on both cheeks, and she scolded me for having completely forgotten her and her family, especially my godson, their second child, and it's true – true that he's my godson, and that I should remember him. I denied it, of course, thinking while I did it that on her, at least, the years had left their mark. She was still good-looking, certainly to my eyes; she had dyed her hair (what colour had it been before exactly?). I couldn't see a single wrinkle on her face, but her make-up was just too perfect, and in a woman of taste and means, age is sometimes simply a question of too much elegance, a certain jerkiness in the gestures, the lack of something, some natural quality she has no control over: the bloom of youth.

*

That evening I was sitting across the table from Graciela. Alberto was a little farther down, on my right. As usual, I had to put up with the jokes that diplomats everywhere face about the easy life they lead, and how interesting it must be to get to know other countries, even though all I could remember about my last posting was the unbearable heat and the mosquitoes. Graciela was complaining about having to live shut up in Lima where nothing ever happened. She had been to New York with Alberto a couple of times, but those were only brief business trips, and anyway Alberto preferred to go on his own. What she would really like was to make a long journey to Europe, where she had never been, but Alberto kept putting off the idea. Perhaps she would go and just take her eldest daughter, who had finished school. Perhaps they'd all go, the following year. Expecting some kind of witty response, I suggested she ran away with me, but instead she replied with a shrug I had never seen in her before that showed she was either sad, tired or was trying to tell me: 'I wasn't joking.' Disturbed, I looked away, only to catch Alberto's eye as he listened in to what we were saying. His look was alert but unconcerned. That was new too: the Alberto I had known had never been so sure of himself, or observed people so coolly from afar. Graciela's gesture had been a sad one, no doubt about it.

*

That night I spoke about them with the couple who were driving me home. 'Yes, Alberto's in fine form,' Paquita told me – Paquita, whom I remembered as a shy, religious girl but who now was a non-stop smoker and looked a lot like Bette Davis (in her later years). 'He's a new man.' I told her I'd like to be rejuvenated too, but that I just felt more and more weary. 'That's because you don't do any sport,' Paquita said. 'It's tennis that keeps Alberto in shape. He plays every morning before he goes to work.'

I wasn't entirely convinced. But, just in case, in my new posting I took to watching all the tennis tournaments (something was bound to rub off on me, if it was so effective) but nothing much came of it. Of course, whenever I sat down with my cigar and glass of cognac to watch the matches, waiting for my rejuvenation to begin, I thought about Graciela and Alberto, and I have to say that their separation came as no real surprise. It was as if I had begun to read one of those old-fashioned novels; and, after the opening, I had skipped a couple of hundred pages, but as I knew the characters, when I read the closing chapters I could imagine what had come before, and guess the ending.

*

The first chapters are Graciela in the house in Miraflores, the one she has gone back to now, and Alberto a student companion of mine at university. Graciela is some kind of cousin, so I have childhood memories of her, I can vaguely see her running around in a garden; then, small and fragile and with a shaven head as she recovers from a bout of typhoid fever in a room flooded with the intense light of December in Lima, surrounded by Christmas presents she's not the least bit interested in; or, later on, tall and proud in her blue Colegio Belén uniform. At that age, a few years' difference seems a lot, so we hardly talked to each other; years later, she told me she had always dreamt of being big like me, and always seen me as one of the adults. I used to go to her house not on her account but to see her father, Don Pablo, who treated me as a friend. I've said we were related in some way, but I was the poor relation. Don Pablo was extremely rich, or seemed so to me: he owned a country estate which sent him fruit and delicacies, and where I was always supposed to be going to spend my holidays so that I would grow strong and learn how to ride – a promise or a threat that was never carried out. He was also involved in business, which to this day is a word that remains a complete mystery to me; he had been a senator and was a friend of the President; above all, I was impressed by his two cars (we never even had one at home) which in the Lima of those days was an extraordinary luxury. I suppose to him I was, as they say, the son he had never had; at any rate as I was growing up I found it entirely natural for him to invite me and to hold long conversations with me, invariably listening to my childish stories with that exquisite old-school politeness of his. When I left he always gave me a book from his library (where the books were bound in Spanish cloth and gave off a pungent smell when you opened them), telling me he no longer had the time to read.

*

I met Alberto the year we both entered San Marcos University. He was a withdrawn young man, who seemed suspicious of everyone. We were both from families that had fallen on hard times, and this brought us together, as well as the books we had both read, and a spirit of revolt we found hard to conceal. He took this more seriously than me because once, speaking in confidence, he said he not only detested all that was detestable, but went much further and proclaimed himself a revolutionary – something which wasn't so common in those days – and used the word 'bourgeois' as if it were the worst insult imaginable. After we changed from literature to law I went into the foreign ministry, and Alberto started work in an important lawyer's practice. I saw him in lectures and when I left the Torre Tagle building, I would often call in at his office and we would go out to enjoy ourselves as far as our means would allow: nights out were a kind of initiation shrouded, as they were, in a sadness we could never admit to. One day when I met him at his office I was surprised at the friendly way the top lawyers were talking to him, as if he were already a colleague. A bit later in the street I said to him half-jokingly that they obviously thought highly of him, and that his future was assured. Alberto took it badly, as if I were being ironic. I remember we were under the arches of San Martín square, outside the French bookshop. He came to a halt and declared, in the tone of someone wanting to set the record straight once and for all, that he had nothing but contempt for the legal career and all it might have to offer him, but that the only way to fight the system (those weren't the exact words he used, but something to that effect) was to reach a position of power within it in order to destroy it. We never talked about the matter again, but for a long while I thought of him as a secret revolutionary, a leader of a plot of which he was the only member.

*

I had mentioned my uncle Pablo to Alberto soon after I met him, and he was immediately critical, saying that everyone knew of the shady deals he had got up to with the government. I'm afraid I didn't exactly leap to his defence, but changed the subject. Despite that, I introduced Alberto to Graciela when we met up on La Herradura beach one morning. In those days, girls were not allowed out much, but I saw a lot of Graciela as I had the run of her house, and soon Alberto began to come with me. He wasn't as shy as he had been, he was charming and witty, and Don Pablo got on well with him. Given that he married her, it might seem easy to imagine the rest of the story, but it wasn't that simple. The one who fell in love with Graciela was me, after all the years I had known her. One afternoon, while we were waiting for her father, I leant over her shoulder to read something or other, and almost without meaning to, almost as a joke, I kissed her on the neck. Mine was a Lima love, dull grey and desperate as the city drizzle, and I think she loved me back in the same feeble way. We had to keep everything a secret in her house, because I was sure (and I was right) that her parents wouldn't exactly be pleased that someone like me, who didn't have a cent and hadn't even finished his studies, was taking their daughter from them. They had a lot of affection for me, but Graciela could expect a much better catch. I realized that I agreed with them; and anyway, I wasn't sure there wasn't something dishonourable about marrying an heiress. The two of us counted the years it would take for me to get my first post, wondering whether the salary I would earn as third secretary was enough for us to get married, and made lists of all the cities we wanted to visit. We saw each other a lot, but only managed moments of stolen intimacy in parks or cinemas. We had frequent arguments; because in a fit of fake generosity I told her I didn't want her to waste her time (it may have been a cliché, but I really did feel it was an uncomfortable situation), because she got tired of all the anxiety, because her mother found out, because Don Pablo was forced to have it out with me – I've never forgotten his puzzled face or the lengthy pauses between his sentences – the upshot being I stopped going to their house for several months. We kept on with our chaste pretence however, probably more stimulated than dismayed by the obstacles, but we never took things any further, although we thought and talked about it rapturously – we had more prejudices or fears than exist in this enlightened age, and the truth is that it would have been difficult to organize anything – or so we thought. When I finally secured my first posting abroad, Graciela was all for getting married and coming with me, even if it meant breaking with her parents, but I convinced her it would be better to wait: either I didn't love her enough, or felt so secure about what we had that I didn't mind leaving her behind, or with the masochism of youth thought we ought to put our love to the test. The truth is, I can no longer remember quite why I did it. She was a beautiful girl; I remember how tanned her arms would get in the summer, the way she laughed, the tenderness that suddenly gripped my heart like a fist when she looked at me. For a few months we wrote to each other, then things gradually cooled off. I learned from some Peruvian tourist that she had got engaged to Alberto. It was Alberto himself who told me of their wedding in a very friendly letter; if I had been in Lima, he wrote, he would have asked me to be a witness.

*

I think it's understandable that from then on I never saw very much of them when I was back in Peru, although they always invited me to their house and even insisted I be the godfather of their second child. Don Pablo gradually lost his fortune, so that on his death he left his wife the house, and I suppose some kind of pension, but the estate, the businesses (and the cars) went to pay off debts. Alberto on the other hand became wealthy in the fifties thanks to some property speculation in the new suburbs. In those days he would tell me that what was needed in Peru was hard work to make the country rich; he still had his left-wing ideas, but it was reality that counted, not dreams. By then I wasn't particularly interested in his political views anyway, and I must admit that my meetings with Graciela, either at her house or at common friends', still left me so agitated that I consciously tried to avoid them. That was one of the reasons why, whenever I was supposed to have a period of home leave in Peru, I always left before I was supposed to, even if I had to take a posting no one else would accept, at the ends of the earth. Either because I was a coward or because I wanted an easy life, I didn't want anything to do with married women. The odd thing is, in spite of all my best intentions, I fell for one of them at the ends of the earth; and a few years later she left me, battle-weary and with an ulcer that almost finished me off. It was only then that in the midst of all these other problems, my feelings for Graciela changed and I could finally think of her calmly, as something from the past.

*

Then one fine day I realized that retirement wasn't far off, I could ask to be taken off the active list and come back to Lima. Perhaps Graciela, Alberto and myself could sit and talk about ourselves, all passion spent, just like a scene that's frequently in the final chapter of classic novels. But then again, if novels have changed, it's probably because they no longer reflected reality. Instead of being a disillusioned middle-aged gentleman, Alberto went around with a tennis racket under his arm, and a girl who could have been his daughter hanging from it. But I was more interested in Graciela, and as soon as I heard they had split up, I wondered how she was coping. It wouldn't be long before her children had grown up and gone their separate ways, and if the story about the divorce were true, she couldn't have much money – Don Pablo had left hardly anything – and it wouldn't be easy for her to find work. A couple of days ago, after leaving the lunch where I'd been told about everything that had happened, I called her from a public phone. As I dialled the number I began to worry I was making a mistake, that I should have phoned her as soon as I got to Lima. To tell the truth, I was worried how she might react – I detest scenes on the telephone. My worries proved unfounded, because she replied as she had always done, with pleasure in her voice (the kind of pleasure that it's good manners to display to a friend one hasn't seen for a long time) and asked me to come to her house the next day, around four in the afternoon because the children would be out and we could talk undisturbed.

*

I would have liked to have been busy yesterday until it was time to see her, but by two o'clock I had nothing to do, so I went for a long walk round

Miraflores. I could scarcely recognize it: for every tree they've chopped down (and there are lots of them, all the avenues have disappeared) it seems hundreds of cars have sprung up; there are apartment blocks everywhere, all more or less the same, taking the place of those old, dark houses and gardens I used to like so much. None of this was to my liking, which just goes to prove what a reactionary I've become, as a nephew of mine was telling me the other day. so by the time I arrived at Graciela's house I was feeling slightly down; in the back of my mind I confused her image with that of her mother the last time I had seen her, at Don Pablo's funeral: tearful, dressed in black, looking exhausted. But I was wrong again, because Graciela was wearing a bright-coloured dress and seemed pleased to see me. She was waiting for me in the garden; I kissed her on both cheeks; she was wearing the same perfume she always wore.

*

When we went into the house I crossed the living room to Don Pablo's library, where nothing had changed. I sat in the leather armchair, with Graciela opposite me. 'You're looking very well,' I told her, and she said I was too, but at that moment I took off my glasses and rubbed my brow with a tired gesture, so she added: 'as well as can be expected, that is.' I pretended to be outraged at her cheekiness: my advanced years have always been a joke between us.

*

She started out by asking about me, the places I'd been to, the changes I noticed in Lima each time I returned. Then she talked about friends we had in common, their marriages, divorces, misfortunes, successes, their settled lives and premature deaths. But although I was interested in all she had to say – Graciela has always had her own view of things, and can uncover the lie beneath apparent honesty, or the hidden virtue that redeems an unlikely character – I felt we ought to be talking about something else. I asked her how the children had taken it. She replied that they had taken it quite calmly. The two elder ones were at university: her daughter was thinking of marrying her boyfriend, and my godson was trying to get a grant to go and study in the United States. It was only the youngest boy who seemed to have been affected by it; he didn't say much, he was very quiet anyway, he'd always been very close to her, her favourite, and had never got on with Alberto, though that was nobody's fault.

'Especially lately, now he's been swept away by passion.'

'No need to exaggerate,' said Graciela. 'This isn't the first time he's been swept away, far from it. But I prefer not to talk about that. Things are better like this, that's for sure.'

There was no bitterness in the way she said it; she was simply stating a fact.

'I've heard Alberto's become rejuvenated, a new man.'

'It's true. I'm sure he's looking fine, I haven't seen him in a long while.'

'They say it's because of the sport. Tennis.'

'Tennis?'

She was about to add something more, but stopped. I looked at her eyes, which began to sparkle with laughter, and we laughed together again.

'It's all part of a plan,' she said.

We've always understood each other, and this time too I knew exactly what she meant. There would be no rejuvenation for either of us.

*

It wasn't true, as I'd been told, that Graciela was refusing a divorce. Alberto was negotiating it with the lawyer, and they had almost reached an agreement. She didn't know what she was going to do; for the time being she intended to stay in her mother's house with the children, they had all they needed there. She'd like to work if she came across something. She still had a good many friends, and saw them a lot. She felt better than she had done for a long while; she preferred not to dwell on the last years with Alberto.

*

That's how far we'd got when her mother appeared. She had been snoozing the whole afternoon but wanted to have tea with me. In the dining room they still had the tea set with blue figures where even after all these years a little Chinaman had still not crossed the bridge. Graciela's mother has always been slightly suspicious of me, especially since she learnt that her daughter was in love with me, and she seemed determined to settle old scores.

'What d'you make of the divorce then?' she asked me. 'We never used to hear of such things.'

I was in the middle of a piece of toast, and Graciela looked at me with amusement.

'You're partly to blame, you know: you were the one who brought your friend Alberto home.'

'That's life,' I said.

At that, Graciela had a coughing fit, because in the good old days we had had our own secret language and 'that's life' was the stupidest phrase we could possibly imagine, one that could be used on any occasion. Her mother glanced at her in alarm, and said this girl will never grow up; she wanted me to agree, but I was on Graciela's side.

*

Before I left, I announced I was going to take a book from the library, in honour of Don Pablo. I picked one at random, and Graciela accompanied me to the door. We came to a halt in the front garden; she asked me how long I would be in Lima, and I replied only a few more days, my ambassador can't do a thing without me. We stood there silently for a moment, looking at each other. Graciela is still very beautiful. I was about to say something but then thought better of it; I've always mistrusted my first impulse, and it's too late to change now. She didn't ask me to call again, and I don't think I'll go and see her before I leave. I have started to read the book I brought from their library. It's by a Frenchman who travelled in Peru in the middle of the last century: he thinks the inhabitants of Lima are very unpleasant people, and blames the weather.

Translated by Nick Caistor

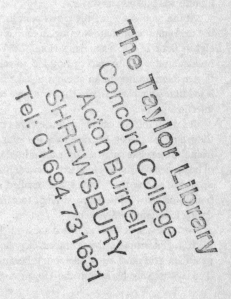

Sergio Pitol

Bukhara Nocturne

I

For instance, we would tell her that at nightfall the cawing of the crows and the flapping of their wings made travellers go insane. But just to say that the birds came to the city by the thousands was meaningless. You had to see how that sinister clot of feathers, beaks, and scaly feet coagulated on the tall eucalyptus trees and the leafy chestnut trees, whose branches were all on the point of splintering. Seeing it made you realize the absurdity of trying to reduce certain phenomena to numbers.

Does it really mean anything to say that a flock of thousands of crows or, if you prefer, hundreds of thousands of crows noisily fluttered around in the skies of Samarkand before landing on its tree-lined parks and avenues? It doesn't! You had to see that pitch-black mob to realize that numbers ceased to matter, that an unformed but perceptible notion of the infinite was pushing its way in.

'At the moment when the crows pour in,' Juan Manuel pointed out, 'it's not uncommon for some Norwegian tourist to jump off the balcony on the eighth floor of the Tamerlane Hotel, or for some Bolivian diplomat on holiday in the city to start cawing too, to wave his arms up and down and flutter them, to hop in an attempt to take flight. Until a nurse comes and leads him someplace where they can give him the indispensable sedative injection.'

'It's the ferocious cawing that the crows make,' I went on, 'at the instant they're cut to pieces. Because over there, at nightfall, what you see falling from the trees like smashed fruit, are gutted birds with broken wings, pieces of heads, feet, a cloud of feathers – I swear it's a damn spectacle! Meanwhile, up above in the thick leaves, the terrified survivors hop from branch to branch or just huddle in an attempt to camouflage themselves, not even daring to attempt to fly away.'

'Because a species of desert crane with long, thin beaks and powerful teeth,' he interrupted, 'the dentiform ciconiida, swoops down and cuts them to shreds. You must know all about it because, according to what I've read, it makes its way here from the Libyan coasts and takes control of large sections of Calabria. The terror makes the birds emit their most deplorable caw. Have you ever seen them attack? During his convalescence, the Hungarian Feri almost went insane because of the din during those melodious massacres.'

She looked at us with a certain annoyance and then, having decided to participate in our dialogue, nonchalantly declared: 'I think it's actually Lapland sea gulls that live on the flesh of other birds.'

'Lapland sea gulls? The larus argentatus laponensis,' asked Juan Manuel with absolute seriousness. 'Truth be told, I've never heard anything about that species. But of course you know that in ornithological matters, I'm a complete novice ... Are you sure it's called the Lapland sea gull? My reference books are very rudimentary and make no reference to it. I'll have to consult some more technical source.'

'The screech of the crows sometimes sounds like the cry of a child. At other times, most times, it sounds like the scream of someone being hung.'

We forgot about birds, and without the slightest transition began to ramble on about the holy, mysterious and opulent city of Samarkand. About its history, its architecture, its culture. The only thing that really mattered was that she not speak, that she be kept quiet the longest time possible.

'It has neither the charm nor the cultural prestige of Bukhara,' we admitted a few days before she set out on her journey. 'Bukhara is the city of Avicenna. Samarkand the city of Tamerlane and Genghis Khan. That's the difference, and it's enormous. Do you realize that?'

II

I'm sure that the first time I was in Warsaw my ignorance about Bukhara was absolute. Perhaps I'd seen the name in some novel. Is there a 'Wizard of Bukhara' in the *Thousand and One Nights*? It's possible I'd accidentally seen the name on the window of some rug shop. But ever since the day when Issa turned up with her travel pamphlets, Juan Manuel and I set about, each on his own, tracking down all the facts we had at hand on the Uzbek cities of Central Asia so we could infuse the stories with greater verisimilitude.

Barely a few weeks ago, just before starting out on that trip, I heard a Mexican theosophist who was passing through Moscow say that Bukhara was one of the navels of the Universe, one of the points (I think he said there were seven) where the earth makes contact with heaven. I don't know if there's anything to all that, but when I reached the city at sunset and made out the concave configuration of the sky-blue dome, I did feel I was at the very centre of the planet. It's possible that when I passed through the walls that surround the ancient city all those things worked to make the sensation of magnetism and magic the city emanated more powerful: I approached the marketplace, the casbah, the inextricable streets of the Jewish ghetto with the same astonishment that certain books and movies produced in me during childhood.

The heart of Bukhara seems not to have known any change during the past eight centuries. I walked with Dolores and Kyrim through that labyrinth of alleys along which two can only walk abreast with difficulty. Extremely narrow paths that surprisingly open on to wide plazas where stand the mesquites of Poi-Kalyan, Bala-i Jaúz, the Mausoleums of the Samanides and Chashma-Ayb, the thin and herculean minaret of Kalyan, and the remains of the ancient bazaar. At certain times, late at night, the traveller strolls through deserted side streets flanked by one-storey – on rare occasions, two-storey – houses, devoid of windows, with wooden doors covered (every centimetre) by carving, all different because each one in its way tells the history and recites the genealogy of the family living there, reworked every 150 or 200 years with the same designs, legends, and signs they bore in the eighteenth, the fifteenth, or in the twelfth century. On those streets, the strolling traveller hears the echo of his own footsteps as if they were coming from other eras.

I study the postcards I bought in Bukhara. The truth is I don't fully recognize those places. I could or could not have been there. I'm dazzled, nevertheless, by knowing I experienced the marvels I shuffle before my own eyes like a skilful cardsharp. I barely manage to reproduce the city. Above all, I remember the noise of my own footsteps, conversations with Dolores and Kyrim, the air of intoxication, of delight that invaded me each time one of those narrow streets opened up to make room for the soft forms of a mausoleum. I remember the music of Islam that filtered through some windows, it too, possibly, very little transformed from the days when the ancestors of the current inhabitants erected a religious centre that soon became a commercial emporium where caravans converged from the different corners of Turkestan and from even farther away: China, Byzantium, the incipient Russia. They communicated by signs, they uttered words that only a few understood; under the arcades of the bazaar and in the adjacent areas, they laid out their wares and showed money, knotted cords; they exchanged, in a series of extremely hectic market days, reeds filled with gold dust and pieces of silver, coins from Toledo mixed with those minted in Crete, in Constantinople, coins from the entire Orient.

After a night's walk through Bukhara, the grandeur of Samarkand, experienced the next day – so much gold, so much splendour, how long its walls were, how high its domes! – seemed in comparison something made by *nouveaux riches*, a rare delusion of grandeur, a prelude to the Hollywood of a certain era. As if Tamerlane had intuited the subsequent existence of D. W. Griffith or Cecil B. De Mille and had amused himself by showing them the way!

But not everything was silence and quiet in the Bukhara night!

The month of November was beginning. The cotton harvest was coming to an end in Uzbekistan, and weddings were being celebrated in its rich cities. There was a moment when Bukhara sank in the din and in madness. And it was then, contemplating the marriage processions, when I must have felt the rustle, the first slight touch, not being able even to identify it, of a story that took place twenty years earlier, when Juan Manuel and I were talking in Warsaw with an Italian woman, a rather detestable painter, and we suggested she travel to Samarkand. Now it occurs to me that Bukhara had to be the city we should have recommended to her. Everything we invented to arouse her spirits seems possible to me in Bukhara. When we spoke to her about Samarkand, what outlined itself in our imagination was the other city.

As we walked up alleys in our attempt to reach the centre of the city, the true navel of the universe to which the theosophist had to be referring, Kyrim told to great effect horrible stories he'd heard in the house of some of his parents' friends. In all likelihood, those stories are transmitted from generation to generation and will pass on to the centuries to come. They describe hair-raising crimes, bodies carved up in the most complicated fashion, and the narrator is quite successful at revealing the cruelty that takes possession of the desert tribes in the most unusual moments. But, as in the *Thousand and One Nights*, such tales lack real blood. They're a kind of metaphor of inevitability, the fortunes and misfortunes that make up human fate (because Allah will always be the wisest!). Instead of horrifying us, they produce a kind of looseness and repose.

It isn't difficult to imagine that when Issa, the Italian painter, made the journey to Central Asia, she saw Bukhara and Samarkand. It's possible it was there she contracted the illness that deprived her of sanity and whose details we never managed to find out about completely.

III

We told her stories whose extravagance exasperated her more often than not, although sometimes they did amuse her. We made her forget her stupid sentimental conflicts with Roberto, the Venezuelan student whose lover she had quite inexplicably become. It was one thing to go to bed with him and quite another that she bring him everywhere, have him speak his nonsense, and even celebrate it. But if that was absurd, even more so was the fact that Roberto should respond to such a passion. That neurotic woman, bitter and rapacious, bore not the slightest resemblance to the young blondes with round little faces with whom he was always seen: the jolly waitresses from a beer garden located not far from the Plac Konstitucij.

When Juan Manuel went to Warsaw, we would meet to talk in the small indoor café at the Bristol Hotel. After we met the painter, there came a moment when we almost stopped seeing her. Issa drank too much, talked too much, and the only thing she liked to talk about was her own life, to rehearse her past glories (which we supposed were false!), and, at a certain point, to make us hear the long list of grudges she held against her lover, who promised to pick her up and almost always stood her up.

Before getting to know her, I'd seen her a few evenings dining in the restaurant of the Bristol Hotel. Always alone. With a desolate air, but one charged with disdain towards the world around her. She was a very rich woman, related to powerful industrialists from the north of Italy. She painted. Rather, she once painted in former times. She'd shown her work in several important European galleries (which must have cost her a fortune). No one knew exactly what she was doing in Warsaw. Apparently she'd come chasing after a Polish lover and stayed on out of inertia. Perhaps she was afraid to return to the bosom of her family and her city burdened with failure and hoping that through some miracle her work would be recognized.

One night, I had to have dinner with her. She told me her 'friend' would be by to pick her up, but we waited there until the restaurant closed, and he never came. From that moment on, I couldn't get rid of her. Against my will, she turned me into her confidant, her audience. The fatigue she caused me was overwhelming.

Jealousy began to disturb her in an alarming way. She wept in public, made scenes. One day she turned up with a less gloomy air than usual and announced she had decided to cure herself of this love that gave her so little satisfaction. The best method, she thought, was to distance herself.

No, she did not think it was time yet to return to Italy. What she needed was to travel, to see new places, and that day, when she went down to the Wagon Lit office, she found no satisfaction. She'd bought a ticket to join a tour group going to Moscow, Kiev, and Leningrad. She walked in carrying a few tourist pamphlets. She would fly to Moscow in three weeks or so. She explained that she wasn't working well, that she'd started a large oil painting that could be her masterpiece, but that she'd suddenly been overcome with diffidence; the cramped space in her studio was drowning her. The trip was going to help her recover the energy she would need to break with that boor she loved. Then she could go back to work with what she said was her accustomed rigour.

Juan Manuel, who was spending a few days in Warsaw, began to leaf through one of the tourist prospectuses: It announced the itinerary Issa had chosen and another that included several more cities, among them Samarkand. A full-page colour photo showed the whole of Registan.

'How could you not choose this route?' he exclaimed after reading a few paragraphs in the brochure. 'Lack of money or lack of curiosity? Do you know if you'll ever have another chance to visit those places? Just think! Did you know that Samarkand is contemporary with Babylon? The only city of its time still inhabited today! Samarkand is a place where the strangest things happen. Remember Feri, the Hungarian pianist who lived last year in the Dzienkanka student residence in Warsaw? He spent his summer vacation with some of his friends who came from those regions. When he came back, he told hallucinatory stories.'

We began to use every trick in the book, what we usually do when we talk about places like that, mixing together commonplaces, easy visions, imprecisions that confuse the Caucasus with Byzantium, Baghdad with Damascus, the Near East with the Far East, speaking about Yakut and Samoyed princes, barbarian rites and atrocious refinements that took place in Samarkand, all the time using young Feri as informant and protagonist. He did have extraordinary experiences from the moment he stepped off the train and discovered that the friends who were supposed to meet him, his old friends from the Budapest conservatory, were not on the platform. Instead, he found one old man and one young man, both with thick beards, wearing capes with astrakhan collars, caps of the same skin, and black, knee-length boots. They seemed to be studying him carefully, as if trying to recognize him, identify him. Feri thought they might be members of his friends' family who for some unforeseen circumstance were substituting for them now. He approached them and asked, in rather crude Russian, if they'd come to meet him. He clarified the matter by saying he was Feri

Nagy and gave the name of the young men who'd studied with him in Budapest. They answered affirmatively in Russian. Then they entered into a solemn dialogue between themselves in their own language, a dialogue Feri thought excessively formal. The younger man picked up Feri's suitcase and with a ceremonious gesture invited him to follow them.

Feri said they plunged into the Asiatic city, a real marketplace of narrow alleys, low walls, regally carved doors that allowed a glimpse of interior patios dotted with pomegranate trees, rose bushes, and infantile hordes capable of producing a din almost as deafening as the crows he later saw every dusk in the gardens of the city. The fat, big-headed children peered out at the doors, emitting strange sounds in their language, as if to warn him he should go back, that there was still time to return to the station and take the first train out of Samarkand. According to what he said, the sound resembled a sentence that in Hungarian means 'Go back to your house, Satan!'

One of us discovered the house they reached, in no way different from the others. On one corner, a blank wall and a door; on a second floor, a minimal window protected by iron bars. They entered, crossed the patio, which was also planted with rose bushes and pomegranate trees and only different from the others by the absence of children. The old man and the young man with the coats with astrakhan collars walked in very upright posture, and, with an identically military air and movement, they climbed a narrow staircase that led to a terrace. They crossed that terrace and reached a very simple, almost monastic, room whose furnishings consisted only of a narrow bed and a small table with a washbasin on it.

The old man clapped his hands once or twice and launched into a harsh tirade that clashed with the severity of his manners. A young woman appeared with a pitcher of water and filled the basin. Feri never liked washing up in the presence of others, but there was nothing else he could do but take off his shirt and wash his face, neck, and arms in front of the two men. They stood at the door of the room, having taken on an air more like guards than hosts. He took a shirt out of his suitcase and was just about to get dressed when the young woman came in again with an Arab djellaba. Following the signs, almost orders, the old man made, he had no choice but to put it on.

'He felt completely ridiculous. You met Feri, didn't you?' Juan Manuel asked again. 'No? He was just a boy, very timid, incapable of putting up any resistance whatsoever. I can easily imagine him in that situation, obeying every order they gave him without even arguing. Besides, in what language could he speak? Every time he tried to say something in Russian, they said yes to him, of course, naturally, but still went on talking to each other in that language of which he didn't understand a single word.'

Then they went into the main room. A young man Feri's age, dressed in European fashion – to the extent that anyone would have taken him for a boy from southern Europe, Palermo or Athens for instance – greeted him and sat him down next to the princess.

'What princess?' Issa finally asked with just a trace of interest.

They had to explain that Feri had ended up in a house belonging to a family of Circassian nobles.

'In Samarkand there are still to be found the descendants of some of the most ancient families in the world.'

They were seated on carpets amid mountains of pillows and cushions. Everything in the salon was elegant and at the same time very dirty. This was not an obvious elegance, and it took work to detect it, to know in what and where it resided. Only someone who had put things behind him could notice it. An ordinary mortal would only have found confusion, filth, and chaos. The old princess wore rich brocades, but she was barefoot, and the stench her body gave off was unmistakable: a mixture of sweat, dirty feet, never-washed clothing, rancid oils, and vulgar perfumes.

On the other hand, the men looked very clean. Only the grandson was dressed in European style. The others, women and men, were costumed in the most outlandish fashion imaginable. Almost all wore knee-length black boots, some had golden tunics, others jackets and trousers made of leather and suede with caps and collars of astrakhan. The women wore baggy trousers barely hidden by tunics of very bright colours. The overall effect, according to Feri, who as an observer was terrible, looked like a magnification of a Persian miniature.

'Does that say anything to you?' I interrupted, speaking to Issa. 'To me, it actually says nothing. A Persian miniature? What could that mean? Persian miniatures can illustrate all kinds of situations, from the harem to hunting. Hungarians, you know, are Asiatic, which is why our dear Feri Nagy had begun to feel right at home. He didn't need words to communicate with them. He never managed to describe the gathering very well because for him there was nothing strange about it. It was all as natural to him as attending a birthday dinner at the Gellert in Budapest, except that he did not like the princes, or the old lady, at all.'

'But where was he? In the bazaar?'

'You haven't understood a thing, because in your heart you are just like Feri. It's all the same to you to be one place or another. You find everything natural. How could they be in the bazaar? For hours now, we've been trying to explain to you that a meeting was being held in the house of some Circassian princes.'

'For openers, I'm sure private homes don't exist there, any more than princes of any kind. What I think is that the only thing this Feri has done is tell you a ton of lies which you two have believed.'

'It's possible. But I assure you he did not invent the scars. We saw them.'

'Yes, we did see them. And we can add that they weren't kids' stuff. All right, let's proceed in an orderly fashion.' They began to pass around platters – lamb stews, aromatic herbs, and, at the same time, without any order at all, candies made of honey, pine nuts, pistachios, hot seeds, bowls of soup, and the food was accompanied by a peach brandy, exquisite according to Feri.

Up until a certain moment, the old lady, despite the fact that she was right next to him, kept herself distant from him, acting arrogantly towards him, disdainfully, as if he were an upstart introduced in her salon thanks to who knew what ploys. But after the second or third drink, she began to smile at him, to say incomprehensible things to him, to pass him sweets with her pudgy fingers whose nails were of an evidently perpetual blackness. The young man dressed in European clothes did not eat: in a corner, he beat out a monotonous rhythm on a little drum and intoned a very languid, very soft oriental song. At times, his face acquired an almost feminine expression.

The food, that combination of fatty meat with honey would only have made me nauseous, but Feri was delighted. Everyone came over to him, surrounding him, smiling, pouring him glass after glass of brandy, passing him lambchops or sweets with their hands, sticking dates in his mouth. Feri is one for the books! By now, he was completely used to the stench that at first had disgusted him so much. Not only that, be breathed it in with delight, as if it were a complement to the honey in the candy and the aroma of the brandy. Yes, at a certain moment he felt he'd reached the promised land. He tried to stand up and make a toast, but he discovered his legs would hardly obey him. Feri's clumsiness is proverbial, and as a drinker, forget it, he's terrible.

He sat down again, to conceal his deficiencies. The others by then were piled up around him, smiling, eager, in expectation of his words, his gestures. Down every face, down every open collar flowed an abundance of sweat. Only one girl, the same one who had brought him the water and the djellaba in the small bedroom, withdrew just then to a far corner of the salon and began to whisper between her teeth a melody that was in counterpoint to that of her companion, the boy dressed in European clothes. The expression on the faces of this pair of musicians was severe, absent, as if both were in a trance. How different they were from the family members, who would break out in noisy laughter and then just as suddenly fall silent. There is no doubt they were waiting for something to happen. Their eyes were shining, their teeth were shining. Feri had never seen teeth that white and gleaming in his life.

Incapable of standing up, he pushed his chest out, extended an arm, raised his glass, and toasted love, the nightingale's song, friendship, the colour of the pomegranate, and this afternoon's gathering. His voice – have you ever heard it? What a shame! It seems impossible you never met him! Feri was the king of the Dzienkanka residence, a boy with a really melodic voice, a deep baritone that was well cultivated. When he spoke Hungarian, it was as if he were singing.

Those, it seems, were the words the princes were waiting for. No sooner had he stopped talking than the drums resounded with frenzy and the rest of the company gave a savage cry, although the proper adjective probably isn't savage but ancient; it was an archaic howl. A hand passed him another glass, without any doubt the old lady, who took advantage of the moment to emit a lewd laugh and caress his cheek with her calloused, dirty hands. That was the last thing he remembered about that night.

When he woke up, he was naked in the narrow cot in the room he'd first entered on arriving. He thought he was going to die. His body ached in a terrible way. Not all of it, because there were parts, his legs for instance, that had no feeling whatsoever. For an instant, he had the horrifying thought they'd been amputated. Overcoming tremendous difficulties, he moved an arm and felt his thighs: they were in their proper place. He raised his head a bit and could see his entire body, stained as if a bucket of pomegranate-coloured paint had been poured over it. It didn't take much effort to figure out that the stains were dried, blackened blood, that his body had been horribly hurt, that some of the wounds, several days old by the look of them, were of a terrifying aspect, that most certainly several days had passed since they'd been inflicted, and they were on the point of becoming infected.

He stood up as best he could. He covered his body with a sheet. He didn't have the strength to get dressed. He walked down the stairs, crossed the patio, deserted at that hour, and reached the street. It was dawn. He walked a few blocks. There was already light in some windows. He heard steps near him. He made one final effort and shouted with all his might. Then he collapsed in a faint. He woke up in the hospital. He couldn't tell if hours or days had passed since he lost consciousness. His only amusement (if you can call that amusement!) while he waited for his wounds to heal – they weren't so serious despite their appearance, although the ones in his groin were very painful indeed – consisted of going out on the balcony during the afternoon to watch the sun set and to observe the surprising arrival of the desert cranes to make their harvest of crows.

When he was released, he desperately searched for the house where the banquet had taken place, but was unable to locate it. Several times he went to the station when trains were arriving in the hope that chance would again put him face to face with his hosts, but they never appeared. Feri is like that, completely oriental: he'd found his small heaven and didn't want to lose it. Finally he was forced to leave the city and return to Warsaw. By then he was living in another world. He didn't want to continue his studies. He talked about elixirs, about pleasures we would never understand, and since no one paid him any attention, he went home. He lost interest in the piano, we were told, and it's a shame because he was really a talented boy.

'I don't have the slightest doubt,' said Issa, 'that this Feri has done nothing more than amuse himself at your expense. He wouldn't have dared to tell me such a lot of nonsense.'

'Perhaps. You Europeans know how to get around better in these affairs. In any case, whatever the people may be like, the mere act of seeing the monuments makes the trip worthwhile. Think about the bazaars, the fabrics! After all, it's a matter of perceiving another continent!'

'Perhaps it is worthwhile.'

And one day she announced that she'd changed her ticket, that she'd be leaving within three or four days, and that when she returned, she'd tell us about her experiences in Samarkand. We never got to hear them.

IV

Some time or other, Juan Manuel made me read a text by Jan Kott that he'd just translated: *A Brief Treatise on Eroticism*. I track it down on my shelf of Polish literature and, in the English edition, find the quotation I was thinking about the day after our nocturnal tour through Bukhara, when we were getting ready to fly to Samarkand. Together with Kyrim and Dolores, I recalled the marriage ceremonies. I'll try to translate: 'In the darkness, the body explodes into fragments that become separate objects. They exist *for their own sake*. Only my sense of touch succeeds in making them exist for me. Touch is limited. Unlike sight, it does not involve the whole person.

Touch is invariably fragmentary: it divides things. A body experienced through touch is never an entity; if anything, it's a sum of fragments.'

I'd tried to remember that quotation when we left Bukhara, and as I read it, it pleased me to confirm that I hadn't been mistaken about the sense. We were at the airport in an outdoor waiting area. Under the grape arbour, there was a series of small wooden tables and benches, scattered throughout a large garden. A group of German tourists filled the place. All of them were old. The baby pink of the masculine faces spread a network of tiny veins and other blood vessels over their noses and towards their temples; the stout legs of the women who resembled the jacks in a deck of Spanish cards repeated that same network, but the violet-coloured knots they formed had a much less innocent air to them. Some stretched out on the benches that early-November morning to catch the last rays of that year's sun. That setting made up of grape arbours, rose bushes, and tourists splayed out in the sun created the most distant atmosphere conceivable from that of an airport. Everything there negated the idea that within thirty minutes, Dolores, Kyrim, and I would be aboard a device that in less than one hour would deposit us, along with the blond horde, in Samarkand.

Suddenly, the intrusion of those men and women, possibly from the Bundes Republik, annoyed me. Everything about them – their noisy guffaws, their explosive voices, the awkwardness of their movements – seemed to me vulgar and, for that very reason, repugnant. Fifteen hundred years ago, when Bukhara already existed as a city, the ancestors of those intruders were using their teeth to tear apart the deer their forests sheltered. In spite of the quality of their clothes, their costly cameras, their obvious desire to constitute a superiority, their gestures and manners, compared to those of the locals, implied newness in history, something bizarre and profoundly garish.

I was possessed by a blind wave of ill-humour. It was not only that the presence of these outsiders sullied the city; after all, I too was an outsider, no matter how hard I tried to affirm the idea that deep down we Mexicans were also Asiatics. What irritated me most when I summarized the memorable events of the previous evening with my two travelling companions Kyrim and Dolores – the nuptial ceremonies we'd witnessed – was that I'd forgotten essential details I could only reconstruct, and only imprecisely at that, from the account the two of them gave. I tried to hear again the screams, the drums, I tried to visualize the leaps and capers of the young people, the harsh redness of a jacket, the mad, almost parodic, steps of a dance, eyes that shone because of a drunkenness produced not only by alcohol but by a multitudinous, shared excitement. I saw a tunic made of golden brocade that contrasted with the jeans and modern jackets worn by the majority of the celebrants. But the fire eluded me, the great bonfire that most certainly signified, I thought as I heard my friends' account of events, a proof of purification, of vigour. Kyrim, who'd spent a good part of his life in Tashkent and, of the three of us, the only one familiar with the region, explained to us that those ceremonies have nothing to do with Islam but instead go back to earlier historical periods. They were reminiscent of the period in which the region saw the high point of the cult of Zoroaster.

We'd left the old city behind. We were walking back to the hotel along a wide boulevard and decided to sit down on a bench to rest. I mentioned that nothing would give me more pleasure than to go to the theatre that night. By contemplating the spectators and observing their reactions to the show it would be possible to get an idea of Bukhara's social fabric. To see how the audience entered, where people sat, how they dressed, in which section there were mostly adults, in which mostly young people, why and how they laughed, what was the intensity of their applause. I'd done the same thing elsewhere: I'd seen a Turkman opera in Ashkhabad, a puerile and moving piece called *Aína* and, in a theatre in Irkutsk, a drama very like Faulkner's *As I Lay Dying*, written by a contemporary Siberian author. I had no desire to see Uzbek or Tadzhik, or Russian theatre in Bukhara. But how I wished I could see the reactions of the audience to something most distant, most alien, *The Merry Widow* for example, the degraded foam of rites rendered marvellously banal! To be there at the same time as a touring operetta from Tashkent, Dushanbe, or Moscow would have been a heavenly experience!

All of a sudden, we heard an uproar in the distance, an abrupt howl and a beating of drums followed by an awe-inspiring silence. We stopped talking. In the distance, coming from one of the fortified entryways into the walled city, there appeared a group of people illuminated by torches. Suddenly the crowd was right before us. Two boys and an old man preceded the procession; behind them, a group of drums and two or three trumpets of huge size. Even farther behind, a motley crowd of some two hundred or two hundred and fifty people who hopped in place as if they were bouncing on the pavement.

The faces and expressions of the dancers were very sober, almost inexpressive. Then they began to run for a good distance. We stood up and followed the procession. The three dancers (always one old man and two young ones) who led the march were replaced by others. They danced frenetically, swaying in the air, twisting their bodies as if they were on the verge of falling down, only to straighten up again and reestablish perfect balance before touching the ground. After some hundred metres, the three would rejoin the crowd and another trio would emerge to take the part of soloists.

Sometimes, the procession marched extremely quickly, while at others it would drag along at a slow pace, according to the rhythm set by the trumpets. Then the drums would resound, and the human mass would seem to stop for a moment, hopping in place, not saying anything, their faces transfigured by ecstasy. When the immense trumpet began to play again, the mob made a strange kind of roar, something bestial, primitive, an echo of the earliest stages of mankind. And then they all would rush forward, but without ever losing the rhythm of the dance, until they again stopped, listened to the drums and, once more, repeated the entire ritual. Only the soloists, dancers and acrobats, who led the parade performed without stopping, both in the moments of rest and in those when they all moved forward.

We followed them a short way, walking alongside them on the sidewalk, astonished, surprised, as if in a dream.

Kyrim suggested that for our last walk of the evening we visit a park where the ancient tombs of the Samanites were located. We walked through a small birch grove. In the distance we could hear the din from the procession mixed with Uzbek or Turkman music playing on some radios. There was no one around us. We were the only people walking through that wood. The darkness made the tombs invisible. The stories Kyrim had just told us about murders and mutilations in the back alleys of the old city began to weigh on us ominously. When we left the park, we again heard the din and saw the mob in the distance. Apparently it was no longer moving forward. A glow illuminated a low building, wider than the others, just as sealed off to the outside, opposite whose door a much larger group than we'd seen marching was now milling around.

We walked towards them. The group really had stopped moving forward. They were jumping up and down and shouting in an amazing frenzy around what the next day, as Dolores and Kyrim made me remember, was a bonfire. For the life of me, I cannot explain how in just a few hours I could forget everything related to that pyre, which was the central element in the scene. By the same token, I could remember, as if they were still before my eyes, the intensity of some of those drunken faces, the hopping and leaping, a fragment of a gold brocade tunic, a scarlet jacket, the monotonous beat of the drum, the shouts, the expression of the young groom, whom they held by the arms and shook to the rhythm of the dance, the placid faces of some women who peered out from the patio where they were in all likelihood standing guard over the bride's purity. We had returned to the beginning of time. An unknown intensity returned me to the earth. I wished I could jump up and down with the natives and shout along with them. When Dolores and Kyrim spoke to me about the great bonfire where the howling mob made the bridegroom jump up and down a few times, I was taken aback by how partial my vision was. How could I have forgotten the fire, not notice it when it was the central element in the party?

As in Jan Kott's treatise on eroticism, fragmentation of vision was something that could apply to all kinds of intense sensorial experience. Just as the world, if it were apprehended only through touch, would come apart, its elements would separate, disconnect from one another. Only one or two details, because of their strength, would nullify the others. For example, why a piece of red brocade under a monstrous face? Or a certain turban, greasy with filth and not the bonfire, which even now I cannot reconstruct exactly? Then, this I do remember very well, the groom entered the building through the door, walking between two rows of burning torches that formed the roof of the universe. He was turned over to the women, who must have led him to the bride. As soon as the procession entered the house, the shouts and the noise from the drums and trumpets ceased, and we could hear a languid, undulating music – the leap from the man of the forests to the refinements of Islam. For reasons irrelevant to the story, we did not accept the invitation of some young men to participate in the festivities. As far as I was concerned, the important thing had already taken place.

And it was in the Bukhara airport (as we waited for the plane that was to take us to Samarkand and talked about the fire and I was in agony over forgetting about it) when the old memories that had been trying to make themselves felt since the previous night began to arise: the student years in Warsaw, the unforgettable conversations with Juan Manuel in the Bristol café, the way we'd aroused the interest of that annoying, overweening, and ridiculous painter whom everyone else fled like the plague to extend her trip farther into the Soviet Union to Central Asia, the nonexistent adventure of Feri and, above all, an immense nostalgia for lost youth. My hatred for that flock of tourists absorbing the sun intensified, and for an instant I felt a tiny flash of disquiet about the possible participation in this story of the trip made by the Italian woman to that same region some twenty years before.

'It was certainly not our fault. Nothing can make me feel responsible,' I

said. I saw that my friends were staring at me, not knowing what I was
talking about.

V

What could we feel we were guilty of? Of the fact that little by little Issa got
more and more excited over what we were telling her about the exoticism
of the places she would later visit, about the artistic remains of the past
that she would soon see, about the picturesque customs and the strange
landscape she would be given the opportunity to experience? Because it
was impossible she would really believe the story about Feri, the young
Hungarian pianist we'd invented to amuse her, to dazzle her, to liberate
ourselves at least for a short while from her complaints, from the list of
wrongs done her, in the absence of Roberto, by her unfaithful lover, who at
that moment, when we were chatting in the café, was probably dancing
with one of the waitresses, whose aura of sweat and beer seemed to attract
him so much. Was that our fault? It would be absurd even to think it. Not
even at that moment did such an idea pass through my head.

The painter's trip would take three weeks. It was restful just knowing
we'd be free of her. When the holidays were over, Juan Manuel went back
to Lodz to continue his studies, and I accepted an invitation to spend some
time in Drohicin, a small ecclesiastical city in southeastern Poland, where
the solitude allowed me to write and rewrite a collection of stories I was
thinking of publishing when I returned to Mexico. I'd suddenly begun to
take literature seriously. I naïvely thought that from then on I would be
able to devote myself almost exclusively to writing.

One of the stories, of a vaguely gothic cast, was slightly inspired by the
Italian painter. I began to imagine her locked up in a house in that
mysterious city. The theme was very simple, and as I elaborated it I tried to
explain something to myself that usually leaves me dumbfounded when I
meet it in reality; the passion certain women have for repugnant men. The
protagonist of this tale, an Italian artist who spends some time in Warsaw,
meets a man of Polish extraction (he could be an Australian or an American), morally and intellectually a very primitive person with absolutely no
sensibility, with no family in Poland but with a firm desire to live in
Drohicin, the city of his ancestors.

The narrator, who'd met the protagonist in an earlier phase, runs into
her in a restaurant in the plaza of the old marketplace, in the company of a
man who's already older, whose enormous bald head is disproportionate to

his insignificant body. He sits down at their table. The boor doesn't allow anyone else to speak. He tells anecdotes of a hair-raising vulgarity, reels off a list of stupid remarks about every possible theme, and constantly mocks what he considers his girlfriend's intellectual pretensions. The fool, whose huge bald head reddens in those moments as it drips thick sweat, greets the few words she does manage to interject in the conversation with crude comments and guffaws.

A few moments later, the narrator gets up, disgusted with the couple. Even more repugnant than the man's manners is the woman's submissiveness, the devout expression on her face as she listens to his banalities. The moral and mental imbalance in the couple astonishes him as much as the perfect balance they seem to have established.

Years later, visiting Drohycin, he remembers it's the city the painter had mentioned as her future home. He begins casually, first with reluctance and then with unrestrained curiosity, to make enquiries about the couple. A crime has taken place. He would never discover the motives. The conclusion, rather macabre and inexplicable, remained in a mere play of conjectures.

Back in Drohycin, I telephoned Juan Manuel, and we agreed to meet in Warsaw. He arrived depressed and ill-humoured. Over the past weeks, he lived through a love affair with a film student who had just been given an important part in a famous director's new film. Overnight, she'd been transformed into a star. Juan Manuel was spending his time in cafés and restaurants engaged in very literary disquisitions on the difference between physical and mental reactions in the moments when love ends. Everything we accept rationally, she said, aware she was not rediscovering the Mediterranean but with absolute conviction, is refuted by the senses. Sometimes we wondered why Issa never looked us up to annoy us with her impressions of the trip. It never occurred to us to find her.

It wasn't until one of Juan Manuel's later trips that we ran into Roberto in one of his jolly taverns. He was slightly drunk. At first, we didn't understand much of what he was saying. Only after making him repeat the story several times were we able to tie up the loose ends. Issa had returned. She was in the hospital. The doctors had told Roberto a very strange story. It seemed that one day at dawn she'd been found in one of those Asiatic cities she'd visited, wrapped in a sheet and with her body completely mauled, as if a pack of animals had attacked and bitten her. The truth was that she was cut to pieces.

They had to hospitalize her to cure her contusions and wounds. Then they put her on a plane, but when she was back in Warsaw she had to be hospitalized again. No one understood what she was talking about. She would introduce strange phrases into the conversation in God-knew-what language. Roberto went to see her twice, but Issa would not allow him or anyone else to approach her bed. The doctors kept her asleep most of the time on sedatives. Her mother and nephew had come from Italy to take care of her and bring her home as soon as she'd recovered a bit. What bothered Roberto most was that the painter owed him almost four hundred dollars because of a leather coat he'd bought her in Bulgaria. The family would not even allow him to mention the subject to her. That was a lesson to him, he repeated, that he wouldn't be such a jerk the next time. He'd only fool around with the local cattle.

That was all. We were a bit apprehensive about finding her. What sense did it make visiting her when she couldn't and wouldn't see anyone. We never found out what happened to her or where she'd been. I wonder if she actually visited Bukhara. If the mishap that had affected her so strongly had taken place there. They brought her back to Italy some time after that, and we never heard any more about her.

A loudspeaker began to announce the next flight. The Aryan beasts and we along with them began to shake off our lethargy, to check flight numbers, to walk reluctantly towards the fence that separated the garden from the landing field.

Translated by Alfred Mac Adam

Luis Rafael Sánchez

Getting Even

For Clem and Greg Rabassa

I'm saying what's that black man doing with those two blue eyes and they're laughing till they just about pee in their pants my daughter Puchuchú and the black man that's with her. She says he bought them and she's making like she's trying to get them away from him and she uses the playing to screw her bellybutton into the black man's bellybutton and he grabs my daughter Puchuchú by the ass. Laughing gets to them and drives them wild. I say black folks don't wear blue eyes and my daughter Puchuchú says they wear them if they got them and they got them if they can buy them and they buy them if a real snazzy white man needing a fix sells them and a fix costs plenty and a fix costs fifty bucks an ounce and 'cause Fortuna had fifty dollars he bought himself a white man's blue eyes 'cause Fortuna my he's a real special black man. Laughing gets way down deep inside them right to their bones. I'm saying white folks hang on to their goods and if they was to sell their blue eyes they'd sell them to some other white folks. Laughing does them in and makes them fold up just like accordions do when they're playing those outlandish *plenas* from Santurce or *plenas* by poor ole dead Cortijo. I'm saying if it was a white man that sold him the blue eyes he must have smelled just the way only white folks do. Laughing's now got them stomping all over the linoleum, and there goes a great big juicy kiss. My daughter Puchuchú is fixing to ask me I don't know what but the punishment she's taking for laughing so hard won't let her. Laughing that pours out loud rushing like water makes my daughter Puchuchú let loose a little fart that knocks her down and this guy Fortuna falls over trying to pick her up and now that he's got her facing him anyway no matter she's a sopping mess he reminds her Puchuchú Pretty Baby let's get with it 'cause since last night I can't take it no more. The blast from laughing knocks them down again and 'cause they're dying from laughing I tell them mind you don't die from laughing and I grab on to the railing so's a sudden burst of laughing don't drag me off like a whirlwind to where they're at. My daughter Puchuchú and this guy Fortuna that's with her laugh so hard seems like the laughing's going to knock the shack down and still Puchuchú gets the strength she don't even have and asks what do white folks smell like Mama. Laughing turns their bellies inside out 'cause my daughter Puchuchú always laughs with her belly and it looks like this guy Fortuna does too else he just caught it from my daughter Puchuchú 'cause he's unbuttoning his *guayabera* shirt and he's rubbing his kinky-haired skin like his belly was aching. I'm saying I don't know about white folks and I don't go around with white men and when it was time for me to get together with somebody I got together with your Papa who was a real good-looking black man and solid like a brick house and he was a black man my real special and always ready for action with a hard on. This guy Fortuna lets out a howl that knocks him over on to my daughter Puchuchú and my daughter Puchuchú strokes his deal real sweet like. From under this guy Fortuna and shouting I peed from laughing my daughter Puchuchú again asks me what do whites smell like. I'm saying Puchuchú don't bug me 'cause you know better than anybody about how white folks smell 'cause in the morning on Saturdays you bring more than one white man up to the shack and every Saturday afternoon the same Saturday-afternoon white man comes and I tell this guy Fortuna it was a stinking white man that got her into trouble and I'm telling this guy Fortuna it's 'cause she became a whore that does business only with white men that's why her Papa took off on me and left home. This guy Fortuna just like that stops laughing and just like that he takes her off from on top of him Puchuchú that's less drastic or is trying to act less drastic and she tries to force a laugh and she's still acting like she's laughing but the laugh don't come out not even a sound. This guy Fortuna real cool like buttons up his shirt and just as cool he smooths down his deal and deep inside this guy Fortuna you can see something's over or is about to end 'cause he's looking like a man beaten or done in. My daughter Puchuchú that's less drastic or is trying to act less drastic springs from a laugh to a smile and from a smile she springs to begging him with her hand and when this guy Fortuna pushes her away she springs like a cat into a fight hollering like mad now see here you jealous Nigger why you ain't my ole man or nothing like that now see here you jealous Nigger why I told you that with those doings on Saturdays I was looking to make some dough turning a trick now see here you jealous Nigger why I told you Mama's been crazier than a fuckin' loon since Papa left her for a white woman. My daughter Puchuchú can't hide her desperation that's blossoming like a drooling banana tree and she can't leave off dirty words neither coming on gushing and loud. I say Puchuchú child we black gals that was born in Black Assville don't talk

dirty and I'm telling this guy Fortuna you can screw around with black
men but you fall in love with white men and it's on account of white men
that she's paining like she was white and I go on stringing more phoney
tales alongside these phoney tales that I make up about dudes coming and
going and I don't stop listing them till my daughter Puchuchú stops me
with a hard shot that knocks me over. This guy Fortuna shakes his head
and says you're crazier than your crazy Mama and he slinks towards the
door. My daughter Puchuchú springs like a cat springing and she hangs on
to this guy Fortuna's powerful shoulders and she's whimpering soulsick
when she pleads with him Fortuna don't run off on me and she's paining
done in when she begs him Fortuna give me just one little chance and
she's dragging herself all broken up when she whispers Fortuna why you
know my style's just fine for you we're good together and I'm gonna quit
whoring. I'm saying from the floor I'll tell you again Puchuchú child we
gals born in Black Assville don't dirty our mouths with all those ugly words
and soon as I say that my daughter Puchuchú's kick smashes my face in
'cause now she can't do nothing else but screech at me and spit on me and
kick me and threaten me with first I'm gonna do you in before you do me
in and threaten me with I'm gonna set you right again with one clean shot.
This guy Fortuna must be leaving 'cause of the quick footsteps going down
from the shack. I'm not saying no more Puchuchú child we gals born in
Black Assville and I'm not saying no more what's that black man doing
with those two blue eyes and I'm not setting no more not even one syllable
on my big fat lips 'cause my big fat lips been split by a rap in the mouth
and from my big fat lips a thick gush of blood comes pouring out. My
daughter Puchuchú sees the gush of blood and just like that she slinks
back and it seems she's leaving 'cause I can make out footsteps soft and
slow going down from the shack. When the footsteps are gone I can't hide
my joy that's blossoming into a drooling smile and I decide bit by bit to
get up and bit by bit get the swelling down with some ice and bit by
bit get back my health and get me in good shape again for the next time
and right on up to the very end keep on acting like a fuckin' crazy bitch
so's I don't go crazy for sure.

Translated by Clementine Rabassa

Nélida Piñón

House of Passion

She had followed her since she was small. Antônia had witnessed her birth, accused her father with a look, cleaned up Marta, lost in the placenta. She smelled sour, then Marta learned to hide her face in the useless breasts, catching the breathing. Later on, she suffered with the decomposition of that body – martyrized skin, as she defined it with surprise – feeling the sex through the dress.

She trailed after Antônia to discover her secret, her lack of submission to any virtue. Her face closed, barely showing her teeth, her words had to be listened to carefully or they would become lost and no one would hear them. Marta would call, 'Antônia, food, water, and be quick.'

Just to see her run, so that no one would think that she was dead, forgotten among creatures. Antônia seemed to imitate animals in her way of walking, her scarred face, pity all over her, the way she kept her hair created the image. She stinks – Marta said those words and took pity on the animal that served in the house. She couldn't imagine that sex wide open, some man sinking in there like a snake. She feared an Antônia free for such things. A bad-smelling woman could give pleasure the same as a rare species, those skinny, nervous women who can climb walls because they're so agile, truncated lizards. She felt that Antônia's sex was suppurating, she kept repeating it, but not from the illnesses of men, because nature would respond mysteriously and darkly to such evil things.

In the morning Antônia did the milking. She touched the udder of the cow as if she were loving it, making some kind of love on that fallen flesh that recalled a man's machine. Marta blushed at the comparison. Antônia's way of drawing out the milk was more like a beautiful ejaculation.

Then Antônia would lose herself. She liked ant trails, avoiding Marta. And even when they were close to a tree, in the kitchen, because one demanded of the other the displeasing smell of their respective excited skins, they scarcely spoke.

Marta knew that Antônia probably loved her as one loves a table, a chair, small objects, an extravagance that could divide the earth. But Antônia did everything to make Marta forget her. She wouldn't allow herself to be loved even for brief moments. Marta bringing her a flower, she delicately refusing, placing the flower on Marta's own breast. She was not to be rendered homage, she had told her sternly before. Antônia might well confess: my smell doesn't reconcile itself with yours, because she had told her once that to stink was also to survive. From condor to man, from mountains to dust. She'd been born dirty and she was used to it. Greater cleanliness would have transformed her beauty.

The father watched the closeness of the two women, one almost animal excrement, the other the child of his perdition. Understanding that the union of strange beings was a natural end, he too followed his daughter, faithful and dishonoured, bearing in his heart the grief that successive discoveries brought out in him. Marta was lost in Antônia – in whom was he also lost?

The father took care that Antônia should not be offended. When he spoke to her he never looked right at her, and he only noticed her when, looking for Marta, he saw Antônia close by. But Marta recognized Antônia as one of the strongest resources in the home. It would be good if she lived longer than her own mother, whose death she had seen close up. Antônia told her that the woman had trembled as she expired, just like a chicken. She made it clear so that Marta would make the vision grow in her breast.

Antônia slept in the barn, in the straw. Marta brought her coffee just one time. And it's not love, she murmured, so that even she wouldn't get her feelings all mixed up. She wanted to surprise the woman, ugly and dirty, in her beast's lair. For a long time she had wanted to plumb the most secret undergrowth of that body, get into its veins like some tiny thing, smell her nauseating stench, the aged flesh, search out her thoughts perhaps.

The woman didn't sense her arrival, not for a moment did her savage routine warn her of the danger. She slept with her clothes on, saving the trouble of any changing. With her legs open, it was possible to put a branch or a rake in through her gates, not to poke or to dig, but to return to hell the production of ardent animals. A free head, Marta felt. A desire to tread on the woman, not to touch her body, her audacity drew back envisioning other deeper contacts, but to dominate her condition and step on her the way one crushes a fallen leaf, rubbish. She could not resist the fruit power, the star power that that singular woman conferred on her. So much so that she was driven by the pretext of bringing her coffee to warm up her perhaps sclerotic veins.

Antônia opened her eyes. She spied Marta, accepting her presence. That creature who surprised her by mistrusting her existence. 'Come here, you bitch.'

Marta went closer, she too seemed to expose her body to the thorns, the pains, suffering in general. She had invaded Antônia's realm, it seemed proper to her to accept the insult. It was difficult to conquer a peopled territory through the shadows, everything so hostile. She was guided by the woman's smell, fetid, unpleasant, so many substances had decided to concentrate there so that Marta would not be lost. She imagined the woman swallowed up by the depths of the earth, the naked earth in all its splendour. A weighty breathing asking forgiveness because Marta had finally commanded her to exist.

Antônia didn't get up. She enjoyed that freedom for the first time. Marta was so close, almost in the other's hole, that she could barely stand the adventure of that woman. Passing to hatred or killing was not difficult for her. Like squashing a bug, climbing a tree, picking a piece of fruit and flinging it far off. Never forgetting to return the pit to the ground, what a strange thing it produced, because everyone was androgyne, volatile, and concrete, and she inadvertently sucked.

Antônia had to die, she thought one last time. And she went away because of the malignant love, the kind they offered her. She knew she was destined to love unpleasant, forbidden things, the sun then, until she opened her convalescent eyes and chose the more rooted heat of the earth, which was really rooted in the soil of the intestines, so much so that in the midst of pain and wounds Marta had gone off to hunt it, for she never doubted its trail. Heat was man's crystalline destiny. And she lay down beside the woman as if she could make love to a repulsive creature, then to save her own soul.

They were still for a long time. Antônia, with accelerated breathing, an insect speedily registering the quality of the flight, murmured that only Marta understood, saying no, I rescued you from out of the placenta, the red product of marketplace and woods, I extracted you from the vagina of the woman and it would be easy to sink you back where you'd be forgotten, burying your head in the water, or back to the darkness you came out of, but I saved you the way one saves a nervous fish, the scales slide like a razor, the way one chooses what still hasn't been proven, and Antônia murmured those things as if they'd been lying broken among her teeth for many long days, a meal preserved in alcohol, not pieces of a snake kept in liquor, and she shook her head harshly in a way Marta had never seen her act before, Marta, who had learned how to surprise Antônia a long time ago, when, actually, the secret archives of the two had been started, the years then passed, it was on a cold morning, Marta decided to follow her: Antônia went into the henhouse to collect the daily eggs: she and no one else performed that chore: she would fight with anyone who tried to emulate her, even Marta was expelled when she tried to take her place, not caring in her brief fury that Marta, judging herself wronged, would complain to her father: perhaps through her father to understand a sacred wisdom, and because of which he didn't answer, that only Antônia should gather the warm eggs, pushed out of the fragile and hesitant bodies of the hens: and she followed her in the same way that she had followed her into the barn in order to see that woman conciliating sleep, although Antônia had seemed hesitant of late, would have lost the virility that Marta appreciated, without knowing why, Antônia was an androgyne, she wagered in her sex, and she glowed with the invention of what any concept would deny, her origin had doubtless abandoned some island, a native of doubtful sex, tall in stature, long hair, man and woman as it mattered, to adopt the sinuosity of a river, lost on so many frontiers, and Marta was careful so that Antônia in those moments would not produce in her body another birth, as if creating other weapons, suffering the apathy of a new world: she sought secrecy for the intense observation, perhaps Antônia would suddenly raise up a round belly, almost a pregnant creature: she went into the henhouse closing the door, Antônia revealed a certain beauty that Marta never cared to admit, the beauty of the wild boar for those who understand that perfection, and Marta assessed the open face of the woman with a sudden joy, as if she saw not the customarily repugnant old woman before whom she had let herself be burned by the sun that she loved and for whom she always opened her legs in search of greater torment: Antônia calmly gathered the eggs in a basket, acting without any worry of hurting or damaging them, but she looked at the creatures as if they were Marta, to whom she helped give birth, even though the look she cast at Marta was always furtive, one would not imagine that it was close to love and represented it: perhaps Marta condemned Antônia's lust in gathering the eggs, until Antônia, unable any more to bear an affliction that Marta suddenly understood and had accompanied from the beginning, to which a vehement metamorphosis was owed, at the point of suddenly being changed into a fat woman, close to the tearing of her pelvis, scattering fruits into the world in the midst of the pain – she went to where the hen had left among red feathers and delicate blood a newly constructed egg: she contemplated the warm hay, precisely where the creature had put down the basest part of her body, for Marta the most pleasing and burning, to the point of wanting to insert her finger along the same trail that the egg had known, not to feel the warmth that the closed and silent thing preserved, but to reconstruct in some way the apprenticeship of a hen, which Antônia could clarify perhaps under the power of love, she would say, you can be sure, Marta, her giving birth is different, she doesn't do her best the way a woman does, her pains run in opposite directions and there's no indication of the most honourable among them: she pitied the hen, Antônia lost in contemplation of the nest in which the creature had settled her extremities, had only been there long enough for the time of her pain, her placenta was timid, it had excrement, feathers, and a modest line of blood: Antônia picked up the egg, raising it to the level of her face, smelled the swollen thing, newly abandoned in the world, and, after smelling it, she kissed the egg as in a sacrifice, or in full flight, an object almost converted into a winged piece by her own exhalation: unable to bear, however, the love that broke away from that hot, humid thing that one hen among so many others had manufactured there, to the extreme of the old woman's feeling the product of the hen projecting itself in her face, in Antônia's face there was probably excrement, viscera, everything the hen, intimidated by duty, was to place in its making – Antônia was gliding towards the centre of the earth where the hen had also been born, all of her species conceived in that way, in a nest covered with hay, feathers, a smell which Antônia absorbed in the end and which now lived in her skin: she stayed there for a long time, stern, until her legs opened wide over the hay and imitated a hen in laying position, Marta had a precise look at everything Antônia was practising to assimilate the bird, anyone who saw her would not doubt her transcendence as much as the fact that the old woman was abdicating her human form on the pretext of being the hen who gave up the struggle after an enormous effort, her face showed the rigours of procreation, her cheeks trembled, her teeth, she was so dilated by the effort that Marta murmured: let the creature open her womb for the ground: she wanted to go get her, pull Antônia out of her supreme pretension, explain her minor performance, but the old woman was flapping her arms like wings, her mouth was a beak, her crest was fallen, lost among false clouds: even though Marta had not been negligent in the perfection of those instants, Antônia was delirious – and that was always her excuse – no longer bearing the pain she was acting as if successive eggs were coming out of her shaken vagina, children, chayotes, green, half thorny, she shouted, however, cries just like a hen's, she cackled, a rooster spreading light, telling of dawn, a hen, no doubt, going to fetch with her hands, in that hidden region, the egg fruit of her passion: she stood up quickly, first withdrawing from her buttocks and adopting as her own the same egg that had been there: later on, in the kitchen, Marta pointed to the egg that the old woman held like a child and said, 'The prettiest one of the lot, Antônia.'

Antônia looked at her as if sliding down a mountain, fainting and tumbling. She asked Marta to stay, just a few minutes. And seeming to be offering her a bird, a habit never cultivated by them, she fried the egg and made her eat it: in the same way as she had demanded her body beside hers in the barn and they stayed that way, quiet and in surrender, so that the woman's respiration would become stronger than Marta's, when the most profane secrets would be transmitted: Marta dragged her fingers in order to know some god who existed by himself, her only responsibility to be proud of the earth, she touched Antônia's hand and thought that that instrument at least once had been introduced into the womb of her mother, had not hesitated to draw her from there with life to give her afterwards to the world, or perhaps to return her to the vegetable world, with which she would be more closely associated, something discreet, but which came to constitute her own shape: she thought that other responsibilities should be credited to that hand, a reason to bring it to her body so that it would rest calmly on her breasts, grown now, rigid when caressed, a natural modesty that moved her: Antônia rested on Marta's breasts, the earth breathing outside, they knew, especially Marta, that her thin skin would explode when the milk flooded it, it would be necessary to want offspring, any kind of offspring, and she a fertilization of gods: Antônia slipped her hand down and touched her sex and said with a barbed-wire voice, I'm old, ugly, but your joy will come out of here: Marta arose, anointed by Antônia's conse-cration, she still feared that the miracle would never take place in the end if Antônia weren't capable of foreseeing: they both tried to transmit the most vehement truths to the innocence of the atmosphere, for Marta wanted Antônia to take part in her burning: they were enemies and they loved each other, the egg that fed her that morning would join her flesh with fury as if she had had it in her tissues until then, that nourishment that Antônia had abdicated in her favour.

'So, Antônia, is that the joy you promise?'

Antônia sneezed, just like an animal, hairy, ugly, she pretended to sleep now, obliging Marta to desist in the spectacle that her always smelly body represented: but when Marta, with some gesture, looked for a kind of untranslated light, which had finally arisen, perhaps conquering the end of the night, giving relief to the house, to the trees, to what was made dark and later lighted, Antônia still told her, and it was like a threat, 'We know about the egg. What about your sun sex?'

Translated by Gregory Rabassa

Luisa Valenzuela

Panther Eyes

Part I

They're moving along the corridor in the dark. Suddenly, she turns round and he screams. What's up? she asks. And he answers: Your eyes, your eyes are phosphorescent like the eyes of wild animals.

Come off it, she says, look properly. And there was nothing there, of course. She, facing him, and complete, soothing darkness. Then he stretches out his hand to find the switch and puts on the light. Her eyes are closed. She closed them when she was hit by the initial flashlight, so he thinks, but he can't calm down.

So, the conversation between the two alters from the moment of that vision of her phosphorescent eyes. Green eyes with their own light and now so brown, hazel as it says on identity cards; hazel, that's to say normal there in the everyday light of the office. He would like to offer her a job, a green phosphorescence intervenes between them (a will-o'-the-wisp). Outside something as unconstructive and constructed as Corrientes street. Inside in the office, sounds of the jungle made by a pair of shining eyes. Okay, okay, if we begin like this we'll never find out where our objective account of the chain of events is going. The window is open. We want to point out the fact of the open window to give some kind of explanation for the sounds of the jungle, although, while noise can be explained by noise, the light of the eyes in the corridor can't be rationally explained because there is a closed door between the light of the open window and the prevailing darkness.

She turned round to face him in the corridor, that's beyond question. And then, those eyes of light; what was their aim in looking at him? What were they seeking in him or what were they demanding? If he hadn't screamed ... On floor 14, in the office, he asks himself questions while he speaks to her – he speaks to a pair of eyes – and he doesn't really know what he may be saying right then, what is expected of him and where is – was – the trap through which he has slowly slid. Eyes of a wild animal. He wonders while he speaks to her with the window open behind him. If he could have suppressed the scream or investigated a bit more ...

Part II

At three in the morning you, lady, are woken by a suspicious noise and you stay very still in bed and hear – feel – someone moving around in your bedroom. A man. The man, who violated the door, no doubt will now want to violate you. You hear his velvety steps on the carpet and feel a slight quiver of air. The man is coming nearer. You don't dare move. Suddenly something inside you becomes stronger than terror (or is it terror itself?) and you turn round in the darkness to face the man. Seeing what presumably is the glow of your eyes, the man shrieks and leaps out of the window, which, since tonight is muggy, is wide open.

*

Of many questions, there are two that are pertinent at this point:

a) Are you the same woman as in the previous story?
b) How will you explain to the police the presence of the man in your house when the inquiry begins?

Answer to a)

Yes, you are the same woman as in the previous story. For that reason, and bearing in mind previous events, you wait until 9 a.m. to dash off to see the optician. The optician, who is a consummate professional, does a whole series of tests on you and finds nothing untoward with your eyesight. It's not my eyesight, you dare to tell him without offering any further explanation. The optician then examines inside your eyes and comes across a black panther there. He can't explain this phenomenon to you, he just records the fact and leaves the analysis to his more imaginative and learned colleagues. You return home speechless and, to calm yourself down, you start pulling out facial hair with a pair of tweezers. Inside you, the panther roars but you don't hear it.

The answer to b) is unknown.

*

Green eyes of black panther, phosphorescent in the darkness, are not reflected in mirrors as might have been imagined in the beginning, if there ever had been a beginning. The man of the first part of this story is now her boss and of course he can't even pluck up the courage to tell her what to do for fear she will suddenly turn off the light and leave him once again to face those eyes. Luckily for him the panther does not appear out of any other of her bodily channels and the days pass by in that certain peaceful-ness which makes a habit out of fear. The man takes his precautions: each morning when leaving the office he makes sure Segba Electricity has not planned any power cut in the area, he has a powerful torch within arm's reach in the top drawer of the desk, he leaves the window open at all times so that the very last ray of daylight can enter and doesn't allow himself the slightest dark thought with her as he did with his previous secretaries. And he'd like to. He'd like to take her out dancing one night and afterwards to bed. The terror of once more facing those eyes prevents him even enjoying this kind of activity. The only thing he does allow himself is to wonder if he really did see them or if they may have been the figments of his imagination (an optical illusion of the optical other). He goes for the first option because he doesn't believe his imagination is so great. He uses music to appease her, she doesn't seem to be ready to spring upon him as she takes down his letters.

Buenos Aires can't allow itself (allow him) the luxury of conscious hallucination. We who have been treating him for a while can confirm that his fear has nothing illusory about it. We don't much like him but let's see if with time we can give him the opportunity to redeem himself. She isn't great shakes herself, to tell you the truth, the black panther saves her, but this sort of panther *que non parla ma se fica*, that doesn't speak but watches, can have little chance in a person so consumed by apathy. She begins to develop oscurophobia or whatever it's called and only goes to very brightly lit places so that no one should find out about her useless secret. The panther sleeps with its eyes open while she is awake, perhaps it wakes up during her sleep but that's something that it hasn't been possible to confirm. The panther doesn't require any food at all, no display of affection. The panther is now called Pepita but that's all. The boss is starting to look at her with a kind eye, but mark you, never into her eyes. She and the boss end up having it off in broad daylight on the office carpet. The relationship lasts a good while.

*

There is a choice of endings:

– Once a year Pepita is stirred by jealousy. The boss does what he can but she ends up with only one eye.

– She ends up pushing the boss out of the window because of that saying about the eyes being the windows of the soul and vice versa.

– Pepita moves from eyes to liver and she dies of cirrhosis.

– She and the boss decide to get married and the electricity bills they receive are incredible because they never dare to be in the dark.

– Pepita begins to mess him around and she has to leave her beloved to go off with a wild animal tamer who abuses her.

– Ditto but with an ophthalmologist who promises to operate on her.

– Ditto but with a vet because Pepita is ill and she's frightened she'll lose her sight if the panther dies.

– Every day she washes her eyes in a Flor de Loto eyebath and is happy because Pepita has converted to Buddhism and practises non-violence.

– She reads that in the US they've discovered a new system for combating black panthers and travels full of enthusiasm to find, once she gets there, that it's something completely different.

Translated by Jeremy Munday

José Emilio Pacheco

The Queen

Oh queen, resentful and in mourning ...
   – Porfirio Barba Jacob

Adelina put down her eyelash curler and started applying her mascara. A streak of perspiration stained her brow. She mopped it up with a Kleenex and went back to putting her make-up on.

It was ten in the morning. Everything was soaked in the heat. The porfirian waltz played by an organist gave way to the racket of a car with a loudspeaker with incomprehensible voices blaring out.

She got up from the dressing table, opened the wardrobe and selected a floral dress. Crinoline was not in fashion any more but, according to its designer, there was no better material to conceal a body like hers.

Indulgently, she looked at herself in the mirror. She crossed the interior patio, stepping over the baseball bats, gloves and caps which Oscar had scattered around the flower pots, and got on the bathroom scales. She took her shoes off, got on them again: she weighed seventy-eight point four nine now. The scales must be broken: it was the same weight recorded a week before when she began the diet.

Again she walked across the patio, a pool of light. One day, as Oscar predicted, the ground would collapse if she didn't lose weight. She imagined herself falling into the clothes shop. The Turks, her father's tenants, hated her. How Aziyade and Nadir would laugh when they saw her buried in yards and yards of poplin.

She went into the dining room and saw, as if for the first time, the drowsy family portraits: herself at six months, winner of the 'Strongest baby in Veracruz' competition. At the age of nine, in the Carrillo Puerto theatre, reciting Juan de Dios Peza's *Mother or Mummy*. Oscar, a little baby, floating in an enormous cot, handed down by his sister. Oscar the previous year, the pitcher in the Gulf Junior League. Their parents on their wedding day, he still wearing his cadet's uniform. Guillermo in the bow of the *Durango*, now with his captain's insignia. Guillermo shaking the president's hand on manoeuvres. Hortensia in the background with a parasol, so proud of her husband and so uncomfortable between the governor's wife and the MP Goicochea. Adelina, at fifteen, dancing with her father to 'Over the Waves' or 'Green Club' or 'Fascination'. What a day. Better not to remember. Who told her to invite the Osorio girls. And the chamberlain who didn't get to the Casino: he preferred to expose himself to the hostility of Guillermo (his implacable and martially sadistic teacher at the Naval College) than showing himself up waltzing with Adelina.

'This is so sad,' she heard herself say. 'I'm even talking to myself. It must be because I haven't had any breakfast.' She went to the kitchen. In the blender she made herself a banana and condensed-milk shake. As she savoured it she flicked through *Hurricane of Love*. She hadn't seen that number of 'The Weekly Novel' left by her mother next to the fire – Hortensia is so selfish. Why does she keep hiding the picture stories from me as if I were a little girl?

'There is no law other than our desire,' declared a character in *Hurricane of Love*. Adelina felt a slight disquiet about the naked torso of the man who appeared in the picture. But nothing comparable to when she found, in her father's briefcase, *Corruption in a Boarding School for Girls or the Seduction of Lisette*. If Hortensia (or, worse, Guillermo) had caught her …

She went back to the bathroom. Instead of brushing her teeth she rinsed her mouth with Listerine and rubbed her front teeth with the towel. She was walking towards her room when the telephone rang.

'Fatty …'

'What do you want you lousy little dwarf.'

'Calm down, it's a message from *notre papa*. Why are you all so het up this morning, Adelina? You must have put on another hundred kilos.'

'What's it to you, you stupid idiot. Just tell me what you've got to tell me, I'm in a hurry.'

'Hurry? Oh, yeah, no doubt you're going to be the carnival queen in place of Leticia, aren't you?'

'Look, that mentally retarded *black woman* is not a queen, is not anything. It's just that her family fixed all the votes and she slept with everyone down to the roadsweeper on the organizing committee.'

'The truth is you're dying of envy, fatty. What wouldn't you give right now to be in Leticia's place getting yourself ready for the procession.'

'The procession? Ha, ha! I'm not bothered about the procession. I couldn't give a damn about you, Leticia and the stupid carnival, screw the lot of you.'

'Very nice words. Tell me where you learnt them, I haven't heard them. I hope my Mum and Dad hear you.'

'Piss off.'

'Come on, calm down, fatty, what's up with you, what have you been on, you haven't let me get a word in ... Look, my Dad says we're going to stay and eat here in Boca del Río with the vice-admiral; that the station wagon's coming to pick you up straight away because later there'll be no way through.'

'No, thanks. Tell him I've got a lot of studying to do. Anyway, that silly old vice-admiral really annoys me. Always with his little practical jokes and stupid funny stories and Dad having to tell him how good they are.'

'Do as you please but don't stuff yourself too much while no one's watching you.'

'Fuck off and stop being such a pain in the arse.'

'Bet you don't speak to my Mum like that, bet you don't, eh? You'll pay for this, I'll make you ...'

Adelina hung up. She felt like crying. The heat was all around her. She opened the child's wardrobe decorated with Walt Disney transfers. She took out a lined notebook and a green biro. She went over to the dining room table and wrote,

Dearest Alberto,

for the thousandth time I'm writing a letter in this book which I'm never going to send you and which will always tell you the same things. My brother has just gone and insulted me on the phone and my Mum and Dad didn't want to take me to Boca del Río. Well, Guillermo no doubt did, but Hortensia has him under her thumb. She hates me, out of jealousy, because she can see how much my Dad adores me and how worried he gets about me.

Although if he loved me as much as I believe, don't you think? he would've already sent me a long way away, to Spain, Canada, England, I don't know where, a long way away from all this hell which my soul can no longer bear without you.

She stopped; crossed out 'this hell which my soul can no longer bear without you'.

Albert, dear, in a little while I'll be going out and will see you again, even if you don't look at me, when you pass by on Leticia's theme float. She doesn't deserve you, I really mean that. You look so ... so I don't know what with your cadet's uniform. There's never been, in all of history, a cadet like you. And she isn't as beautiful as you suppose. Yes, all right, maybe she's attractive, I don't deny that: she must have had something to get to be the carnival queen. But her type are, how can I put it?, very vulgar, very common, don't you think?

And she's so flirtatious. She's full of herself. I've known her since we were in nursery school. Now she's good friends with the Osario girls and beforehand she used to speak very nastily of them. They band together to make fun of me only because I get better marks. Of course, that's normal: I don't go to parties or things like that, I'm not one for parading round the Zócalo square or going out all day with lads. I just think about you, my love, at the moment when your eyes will at last turn to look at me.

But you, Alberto, do you remember me? No doubt you've already forgotten we met two years ago (you'd just started at the Naval College) once when I went with my Dad to Antón Lizardo. I waited for him in the station wagon and you were there sorting out a jeep and you came over. I don't remember any other day as beautiful as that one when our lives met never to separate.

She crossed out 'never to separate'.

We had a nice long chat and I wanted to give you my transistor radio to remember me by. You didn't accept. We arranged to meet on the Sunday to go walking round the Zócalo.

I waited for you all day long, anxiously. I cried so much that night ... but then I realized you didn't come so that no one could say you were courting me out of self-interest because I'm the daughter of such an important person in the Navy.

On the other hand, I shall never be able to understand, I'm being honest here, why on New Year's Eve in the Spanish Casino you danced all night with Leticia and when I went over and she introduced us you said 'pleased to meet you'.

Alberto, it's getting late. I'm going out to meet you. Just a few words before I say goodbye. I promise you this time I will lose weight and next carnival, hear it now, I'm going to be THE QUEEN! (My face isn't ugly, everyone says that.) Will you take me swimming to Macombo, where I saw you once with Leticia? (You two didn't see me, fortunately. I was in my bathing costume and ran to hide amongst the pines.)

Ah, but next year, I swear, I'll have a prettier and slimmer body than hers. Everyone who looks at us will envy you because you'll have me on your arm, isn't that right, Alberto?

Bye, my love, till very soon. I'll be seeing you in a little while. All yours,
    Adelina

She went back to her room. When she saw the time on the Bugs Bunny alarm clock she left the notebook on the bed, touched up her make-up in front of the mirror, crossed herself and raced down the mosaic stairs. Before opening the door of the porch she breathed in the damp, rusty smell. She passed by the Turks' silk shop: Aziyade and Nadir weren't there; their parents were getting ready to lock up.

Rounding the corner she bumped into two of her brother's team-mates (hadn't they gone with him to Boca del Río?). They saw her all made up and asked if she was going to take part in the carnival costume competition or if she had launched her bid to be The Ugly Duckling.

Adelina didn't answer and walked off, her heels clicking as she went, in the smell of the smoke from rockets, jumping jacks and firecrackers. There was no traffic, the people were walking down the middle of the street carpeted with confetti, streamers, and beer cans and bottles.

Hooded figures, musketeers, clowns, Roman legionaries, ballerinas, circus artistes, Amazons, court ladies, pirates, Napoleons, Aztec warriors, and groups and families in masks, little cardboard hats, Zapatista sombreros or not dressed up at all were making their way towards the main street.

Adelina speeded up. Four girls turned to look at her and she left them behind. She heard them all laugh and thought they must be making fun of her like Oscar's friends.

Then she walked between the tables and stalls in the arcade, packed with *marimbas*, groups from Veracruz; people selling crabs, lottery tickets. She didn't discover anyone she knew (decent people don't mix with those from out of town, especially at carnival time) although several women turned their noses up at her. She wanted to take her compact mirror out of her handbag to see if she'd overdone the make-up (this was the first time she'd used her mother's stuff) but where would she hide to have a look at herself?

With great difficulty she managed to reach the corner she'd been heading towards. The heat and the formless noise, the promiscuous closeness of so many strangers filled her with confused uneasiness. There was applause at the appearance of the traditional *charro* horsemen and their Pueblan women, and amidst the ear-splitting shouting and music the first float came past: gay men dressed as peacocks. Then came mulattos dressed as Vikings, eagle-horsemen covered in streamers, stevedores in bikinis and mamba dancers' plumes. And there followed: members of the Ku Klux Klan, cavemen, the court of Louis XV (they were shoved and manhandled), Snow White and the Seven Dwarfs, Blue Beard and his wives, Maximilian and Carlota followed by their pages; cannibals, redskins (perspiration drenched their backs), giants and figures with huge heads, Romeo and Juliet, Pierrot, Harlequin and Columbine (she closed her eyes).

Then the procession of theme floats, some pulled by tractors, others put together on the backs of lorries: the Brewery float, Miss Mexico, Miss California, the National Film Awards, the Gypsy Camp (little girls who were whimpering because of the heat, the fear of falling off, and having to stand still), the Romance of the Volcanoes, the Conquest of Mexico, the Thousand and One Nights (a nightmare of cardboard, sequins and rags. Immediately afterwards there was a damp breath of tequila: 'Come on, big girl, here's the king' and an enveloping embrace. Adelina turned round furiously but in whose direction? how was she to discover the guilty one amongst the raucous, enthusiastic crowd?), the Pirates of the Gulf on Treasure Island, The Fiery People of Vera Cruz, Guadalupe of Chinaca, the Warrior Race, My Sweet Darling, Valentina with Pancho Villa, the Divers in the Land of the Mermaids, the Astronauts and the Little Green Men.

From an unexpected balcony, the Osorio girls falling about laughing, making themselves heard amidst the paraphernalia of the carnival: 'Fatty, fatty, come on up. What are you doing down there, rubbing armpits with the plebs and the commoners down from the capital?'

Everyone seemed to spy her, to look at her. Adelina swallowed hard, grimaced. At last, the float with the queen and her princesses. Leticia the First on her throne under the crossed swords of the cadets. Alberto next to her, very close. Leticia all aflush, all giggly, peering out from under the artificial curls supporting her crown, waving, blowing kisses.

'People are so different when they're properly made up,' Adelina said to herself. The sun made the stones glint on the sceptre, crown and dress. Applause was ringing out. Leticia the First acknowledged them happily five metres above her on a cardboard throne which was destined for a rubbish dump the following morning.

'You'll see, you'll see next year; we'll be swapping places,' muttered Adelina. But a paper bag thrown from who knows where burst on her head and bathed her in red aniline at the very moment that the queen passed. There was a collective roar of laughter. Leticia herself could not help noticing her amongst the crowd and laughing. Alberto relinquished his statuesque pose and sniggered.

It was a split second. The float moved away. Adelina cleaned her face with her sleeves. She gazed up towards the balcony where the Osorio girls were signalling how sorry they were about what had happened and were inviting her up.

Then she was bathed by a cloud of confetti which stuck to the wet skin. She pushed her way through, tried to run. But the procession had ended, the streets were overflowing with commoners from the capital, with camp men, with druggies, with aggressive, hooded strangers who continued throwing confetti into Adelina's mouth, half-open as she panted, who were dancing in front of her to block her way, who were squashing their hands on to her breasts, who were blowing party-blowers into her face, who were goading her with carved sticks from Apizaco.

And Alberto was moving farther and farther away and didn't get off the float to defend her, to avenge her, to open up a way for her with his sword. And Guillermo in Boca del Río, his head by now spinning after his eighth beer, was giving advance applause to the vice-admiral's lewd old jokes. And out from under some Frankenstein and Dracula masks sprung Aziyade and Nadir to have a bop with her, to chase her and hassle her as she fled, singing, humiliatingly and distressingly singing at her an improvised and never-ending little ditty: 'Over Adelina / they threw aniline-a / coz she didn't take her Dietina / coz she didn't take her Diiiiii-eeeee-tiiiiiiiiii-na.'

And she slapped them and kicked at them and the boys tried to hit her and a devil and a court-lady separated them. Aziyade and Nadir went off softly singing the verse. Adelina managed to continue her flight until at last she got up the stairs and found her room in a mess:

Oscar had been there with his friends from the baseball team, Oscar had been there with his group of mates, Oscar hadn't stopped in Boca del Río, Oscar had gone to see the procession ...

She saw the exercise book on the floor, opened and sullied by the fingers of Oscar, by the hands of the others. On the pages of her last letter were fingerprints, the ink was blotched, the paper torn, there were large stains of red aniline.

How they must have laughed, how they must be laughing right now, throwing bags of aniline in people's faces, handfuls of confetti in people's mouths, breaking eggs on the heads of passers-by, of people who had dressed up, of spectators.

'Damned, poofy, shitty dwarf, fucking bastard. I hope they beat you up, I hope they give you a real going-over and you come home screaming like a poof, I hope you die, I hope you die and that bitch Leticia and those nerdy Osorios and the cretinous little shitty cadet and the stupid carnival and everyone.'

And as she spoke, she shouted, gesticulated with bereaved rage, she began tearing up her notebook of letters; then she began stamping on the bits, hurling against the wall the jar of make-up, the bottle of mascara, the Sanborns fragrance.

She stopped and in the mirror framed by the Walt Disney figures she saw her blonde hair, her green eyes, her pale face covered in aniline, grease, confetti, mascara, sweat, make-up, tears. And she threw herself on to the bed weeping, destroying herself, telling herself, 'You'll see, you'll see next year.'

Translated by Jeremy Munday

Alfredo Bryce Echenique

A Brief Reappearance by Florence, this Autumn

To Lizbeth Shaudin and Herman Braun

I couldn't believe it. I couldn't believe it, yet I wondered if deep down I hadn't always expected something like this to happen to me with Florence. The memory I had of her was from happy times, but happy in my own way, the way I chose. And perhaps the remains of the dreamer that still is in me had firmly if intermittently believed – it's possible, who knows – that I would meet her again some day. I admit there were long periods when I didn't actually remember her, didn't think of it as something absolutely essential, but I also recall dozens of times when I walked along that street and stopped for ages in front of her house, the palace which had once been the residence of Madame de Sévigné, and which at the time I was teaching at, that decrepit school when I first met Florence was already the Carnavalet museum, but also, in one wing, Florence and her family's residence. In 1967, when my mother came to visit me in Paris, I took her to the museum, and we stopped at the foot of a staircase that led up to the part they lived in. I told her a bit about Florence and the years I was her teacher, about how we used to play in the snow, and as my mother began to take it all in, I also told her about the things that deep down were part of me.

But that was as far as it went, mostly because I was hardly of an age to go knocking on the door of someone who had stayed as almost a girl in my adult memory. And yet . . . and yet I don't know, but I went on believing for many years in another meeting with Florence. And now I come to think of it, perhaps that's why I wrote so many of the real details about her: the place, my nationality, the games we played, and even the names of people she could easily identify. Yes, perhaps I wrote that story out of the vague hope that some day she might read it and seek me out because of all the things I said about her in it, perhaps I really did write it as a vague, improbable, but subtle way of calling out to her, of seeking her out, just in case she was still the same Florence of old, the joker, full of life, the pianist, hypersensitive. I can't state it categorically, but the idea fascinates me: A man does not dare search for a person he remembers with passion. Too many years have gone by since they last met, and he is afraid she has changed. In fact, he is more afraid of that than the difference in their ages, or their social status, etc. He writes a story, publishes it in a book, throws it into the sea in a bottle that contains another bottle that contains another bottle that ... If Florence sees the book and stops, it's because she recognizes the author's name. If Florence buys the book, it's because she remembers the author and is curious about him. if Florence reads the story and calls me, it's because she's taken the trouble to find my name and address, because she remembers me, and because the story can continue, but this time here in my own house. It's a fantastic idea, and there's just a hint of Machiavelli about it, *ma contenutissimo, pas d'offense*, Florence, as well as having its *andante ma non troppo* side, no offence, Hortense. Whatever, above all it's a literary idea, and is deeply in tune with the remains of the dreamer in me, it's wonderful. Cheers, James Bond. But James Bond wouldn't have been moved by it, all bulletproof vests and technology. I change my mind, and drink to Inspector Philip Marlowe. And like him, sit on the shabby chesterfield in my office, thinking of all the years I haven't seen Florence, because that helps me think of all the years I've spent without so much happiness knocking on my door. It's not James Bond or Philip Marlowe: *The Old Man and the Sea* is the one for me.

*

Then one day it all happened. All and everything. Who knows. I couldn't believe it, and it took me a moment to understand, to realize, to recognize the falsely husky voice she was putting on to scold me for being so stupid, for not having recognized her at once. At last, Florence shouting at me that her house was full of bottles. I shouted at her: Writer! Nobel Prizewinner! and we ended up converted, by telephone, into the characters of this story.

Then of course life had to mess it all up, even though I fought tooth and nail. She too, I must admit. That's why she'll always be Florence W. and Florence. In a whisper, and with disillusion in my voice, I have to say that Florence had married. And I have to add, though I'm not sure in quite what tone of voice, that the wedding took place a month ago, after what seems at first sight like a whirlwind romance, so that only three months ago should we say ... no, much better to say nothing. The wedding was a month ago, period. The fortunate spouse (I could simply call him 'the lucky guy', but that snobbish 'fortunate spouse' is better suited to the class of busybodies whose only merit is to know how to appear at the right moment) is much younger than me, a doctor, sportsman, and highly intelligent. The truth is, I felt both affection and respect for him, and if there'd been more time we might have become friends, but there wasn't much more time because I left before the story began to lose its charm or magic, or whatever it is you call the thing that takes away a story's enchantment. In love as in war ... well anyway, I left trailing my blood in the sand. It had never been my intention to feel the way I did for Florence that night in her house; not even when she called me on the phone, I swear. If I had wanted to see her again for so many years, it was because I like to wager that there are people who never change. I won my bet, of course, but I ended up leaving, as the gaucho said.

Okay, but let's go back a bit, which is something one can do in stories. Here I am, jumping for joy in my flat, not caring a bit that Florence has got married a month earlier. Her husky voice made me laugh out loud. No, Florence could never change! It was because Florence did not understand what she was part of that she put on that husky voice, and shouted at me on the phone, accusing me of everything, of having no hope, no sense of fantasy, nothing. Florence had not changed! She was expecting me the next day, no, I want to see you tonight, I'm trembling with the urge to see you! I can't wait till tomorrow! It can't be true! But it is, and I've dreamt of seeing you again too! D'you remember the school? D'you remember when my sister committed suicide? I think it was thanks to you we got over it at home! Every day I'd get back and begin telling them all you had said! They started to laugh again ...! Another day ... yes, tomorrow, why not, we'll meet tonight so tomorrow I can take you to see my father and mother! They always wanted to meet you! They're going to be so happy to know you're still here! You'll see! They'll invite you thousands of times! But Pierre and I are going to invite you even more often! I've tried to translate the story for him. It annoys him, he can't get it, he'll never get it! It's as if it were just between you and me! You've brought those years back to me, and made me so happy! It's easy to see why Pierre doesn't get it! Those years were *cosa nostra*! But don't worry about Pierre! I adore him, and you will too! I'm going to tell him you didn't recognize me on the phone! Yes, but it took you a while! The next time, I'll kill you! Well, I'm still a weakling, but Pierre will kill you next time!

Hours later, I was still jumping up and down. Okay, the news about Pierre wasn't much to make a song and dance about, but on the other hand, not jumping up and down wasn't going to make him go away. And anyway, Florence was the same, only she could have thought of putting on that husky voice just so she could shout at me for not recognizing her straight away. Now that I think about it, that was why I stopped jumping up and down like an idiot. What about me? Was I still the same? I hadn't seen her for ten years. Ten years since she had seen me as well. And in the story I had described myself as she saw me, how she saw me in those days. A shabby guy, with a shabby coat, who lived in a shabby world. And how had I seen her? In spite of our points of contact, as few as they were tender, Florence was an inaccessible adolescent, still almost a girl, an inaccessible being who returned each day to Madame de Sévigné's palace. The moment had arrived for a great flight of fancy. I wanted to be happy, and by now I'd learnt to accept the fact that these things are pretty short-lived. I dressed as if I were going to a palace.

So the person who landed that night outside Florence's flat was some kind of mixture of all that, necktied to the nines, face hidden behind a surprising bunch of flowers, what would happen when they opened the door and his mug appeared from behind all that lot? It was a bit over-exaggerated, but I know that's what'll be the death of me in the end. I'll be perfectly lucid though, just as I was that night outside Florence's flat, noticing a few things that were wrong. The neighbourhood was very different from the one she used to live in. So was the street, the building, and the less said about the staircase the better ... no one as elegant as myself had ever climbed that staircase, and I was nothing more than an edited version – heavily edited, it's true, but still basically the same – of the character in my previous story. What on earth was happening? What had gone wrong? I would never know if I didn't ring the bell. In any case, I stood trembling behind the flowers as if nothing was going on. That's what I call keeping faith.

And keeping it until it was all too late. Whether or not the flowers I had brought were precisely the sort Florence hated, they were already in one hand and the other was poised on the bell. Whether or not the knot of my tie had slipped to the ground, one hand was busy with the flowers, and the other was on the bell. Whether or not Florence was going to think me completely ridiculous, I had the flowers in my right hand, and my left was on the bell. Whether or not Florence had married Pierre: the right on the flowers, the left on the bell. She opened the door. For a long time, nothing happened after she did so. I peered round the bunch of flowers so she could see me once and for all, and when I saw her I wondered what on earth had become of the elegant Arab butler of my earlier story. It was incredible: I kept noticing things that were wrong, but I still kept the faith, even though Florence did not bother to remove the cheap cigarette she was smoking from the corner of her mouth, nothing on earth would make me believe this was Florence, not for anything. But I was wrong. Everything, yes everything, started up when she smiled and asked me if I'd made a pact with the devil, or what? We burst out laughing when we both realized that she was no longer a fifteen-year-old girl but a grown woman of twenty-five, and I was no longer the ancient, twenty-five-year-old teacher, but a man over his head in an exaggerated situation. Then, in the background, just where he should have been, Pierre came on the scene. I don't know if Florence did, but I realized we only had a few seconds left.

'Take this, it's heavy,' I said to her, handing over the bouquet.

Now it was Florence's turn to be hidden by the flowers.

'Come on in,' she said, 'don't stand out there all your life.'

I wanted to embrace Pierre, but of course I didn't know him yet, and the French are rather reserved on these occasions. I didn't want to seem over-sentimental, so I merely shook his hand, but I did show a great interest in all the branches of medicine he practised. It turned out he didn't practise any, he had just graduated and didn't even have a consulting-room yet. But you will practise, I told him, you will, and you'll see how everything from now on ... everything from now on ... I changed the subject to sport. Florence had told me Pierre was a keen sportsman, so I changed to sport and showed a great interest in all the branches of sport he practised. He told me he only played tennis, and that only occasionally nowadays, it was very difficult in Paris, there was no time for anything, and he had his medical thesis to complete as well. But you will practise, I said, you will, and you'll see how everything from now on, everything from now on ...

'He has a tennis racket and a medical thesis!' shouted Florence, in a desperate effort to alleviate my suffering.

The effort exhausted her, and the cheap cigarette was increasingly evident in the corner of her mouth. The husky voice she had put on for the phone turned out to be her real voice at twenty-five. Her desperate shout convinced me, even though I hadn't wanted to accept it until then. And yet, now ... oh! if I had to go on writing about Florence all my life ... it would have to be with that voice that showed you were exhausted after your despairing shout, Florence. Okay, now it was Pierre's turn.

'Why don't you sit down?' he said, 'take it easy while I bring you something to drink.'

I almost embraced him, but decided instead to obey him as one does a doctor, and to sit down as one does in a consulting-room. Florence fell on to the same sofa, smoking like crazy. Pierre went to fetch glasses, ice and a pitcher of sangria in the kitchen, because all this was far from being

Madame de Sévigné's palace. I don't know about Florence, but I realized we only had a few seconds left.

'Shout at me again,' I shouted at her.

'Shut up,' she shouted.

'Calm down, children,' Pierre called from the kitchen.

'Shut up,' Florence shouted at him.

'Can't you stay calm for a minute in there?'

That was the son of a bitch Pierre again. Florence pulled all her long, curly, blonde hair in front of her face so she could hide behind it. I was worried to think that the cigarette was still lit in there, and began to take precautions, going firefighterly to her rescue, until I realized it was Florence I was getting close to, and pulled away again. I chose to speak instead.

'Come back,' I said, in a voice I hoped wouldn't carry to the kitchen.

'Upset, Florence, are you upset?' I asked, since I had chosen to speak.

I must confess that was the stupidest phrase I have ever uttered in my entire life. I didn't know what I said it for, I still have no idea, but I include it here because I deserve it. You choose to speak. Look where it gets you. Upset? Are you upset, Florence? I deserve it. What a booby! Upset, Florence, are you upset? To think that with just five words, and one of those Florence, you can say such nonsense. That's what I did, and just when we had only a few moments left.

What follows I leave for psychoanalysis. Where on earth did I get such an idea? Who on earth could think such a thing? I'd completely forgotten about it until Pierre told us to sit down while he fixed us all a drink, but as soon as I felt something cold on my left buttock, I remembered horrified that I had brought my hipflask – my elegant little Gucci hipflask, part of a matching set with my briefcase and my wallet, the leather-covered bottle that holds just enough for two. Straight out of the interpretation of dreams. Only I could think of such a thing. And only I could discover that it was leaking out in my back pocket. I didn't shut it properly I said to myself, and wiggled my bottom a bit, but that only made the leak worse. With the result that by the time Pierre reappeared from the kitchen, there can't have been more than one drink left in it.

'Look, Pierre,' I said: 'I had some fantastic whisky at home. The kind you can only get in Scotland.' And I struggled to remove the leaking hipflask from my pocket.

'Let's drink it!' Florence shouted.

'There was only enough left for one,' I said. 'And I brought it for Pierre to try.'

'And it didn't occur to you I might be interested as well?' Florence complained, seriously put out.

I would have liked there to have been only seconds left between us, so I could explain all the unexplainable to her, but there was Pierre, and he had the hipflask in his hand. Like an idiot, he thanked me for it, and began to help himself.

'There's more than one shot here. There's at least one and a half.'

'Drink the lot,' said Florence. 'We'll have the sangria. We've got enough to get drunk on while Pierre hogs all your whisky.'

She stared straight at me while she said those last words, and pulled her already dishevelled hair down across her face again. But this time she only did it half-way, to disappear only partly. Pierre gave her a kiss as best he could, Florence gave him a kiss as best she could, because Pierre was busy sitting down in the armchair opposite, and I lifted my glass and said 'Cheers!' thinking: little doves, stinking little turtle doves.

'Cheers!' Florence replied, lifting her glass a little too high.

'Cheers!' I said again, lifting my glass a little too high.

'Cheers!' said Pierre, lifting my whisky and adding: 'But can't you two stop trembling and relax before you spill everything?'

'In my case,' I said, to set things straight, 'it's Parkinson's disease. I was born with Parkinson's disease.'

Florence groaned and ran out to the kitchen. I said something must be burning, Pierre smiled brightly in agreement, so I said again that something of Florence's must be burning, to see if he would flash me his bright smile once more. He told me my whisky was first rate.

Pierre was at least ten years younger than me. I realized this all of a sudden, and just as suddenly felt the need to confess something to him, to tell him there had been whisky for two in my hipflask, and you weren't one of them, Pierre. I felt defenceless, I had no sense of hatred to cling on to, and worst of all, Florence was calling me from the kitchen. I chose not to hear her, I tried to look as if I could not hear a thing, I started to drink more and more sangria, I served Pierre some sangria for when his whisky ran out, I kept trying to look as if I couldn't hear a thing, I almost said that if she was calling me it must be because something was burning, to see if Pierre smiled in agreement once more. Because by now Florence was really shouting at me from the kitchen.

'Why don't you take her glass out with you?' Pierre said, with a bright smile.

I was about to say: but what'll become of you if I go? but the risk-taker in me chose instead not to say a word. Defenceless, with the empty hipflask back in my soaking pocket, I went out to the kitchen with two full glasses of sangria. I entered the kitchen just as I am, and so will never know how I looked when I went into the kitchen with two shaking drinks in my hand. I only know that together with me went the dreamer and the observer that are also part of me, and I'll always remember that the latter completely gave way to the former when from the door I caught sight of Florence, ladle in hand. She had been waiting for me for centuries, and this time it's true, there were tears in her eyes.

'So what's burnt?' I asked, loud enough for Pierre to hear.

'Nothing; nothing's burnt, it's all ready to serve.'

'We should tell Pierre nothing has burnt.'

Florence asked me to give her the two glasses, put them on the table, and came to embrace me. No, there were no kisses or anything like that. The only thing I could feel were her arms hugging me tight, and her wet cheeks, and I suppose that was all she could feel as well. I don't know how long it lasted either, but we almost fell over several times, and we only once managed to say something when we tried to say something.

'Look,' she told me, 'I want you to know that whatever happens, whatever nonsense I say, however much I put my foot in it, however much it seems that tonight it's all coming crashing down . . .'

I hugged her tighter.

'The only thing crashing down round here is me, Florence. Pierre is a saint.'

When she heard me praising Pierre, Florence hugged me as tight as she could.

And now of course it was Pierre's turn. We heard his voice from the other side.

'How about eating, Florence? I'm starving.'

'Florence, why don't you tell the pope to stop blessing us? He spends his whole goddam life blessing us.'

We let go of each other.

During the meal I learnt that Florence had prepared her favourite dishes for me, and that Pierre liked wine as much as I did. No other way of explaining how we ate and drank so much that night. I also learnt that Florence's husky voice was the product of years of smoking two packs a day of cheap black non-filter cigarettes, and that she only occasionally played the piano these days. Florence was no longer the pianist I had written about in my story. In fact, I don't know what was left of Florence, not even she herself could have told me what was left of Florence. And yet

I went on eating and drinking like a pig in the absolute certainty that I had won my bet with reality. That was because there was not a single moment in which Florence had changed, not even sitting at that table in this rather shabby flat.

But what on earth had happened to the palace, and what was she doing living with Pierre in a flat like this? I don't know at what point I managed to ask Florence these questions, causing her to burst out laughing, but the fact is that Pierre, who was in charge of logic that night, and even allowed Florence and me to fight a battle with our napkins in imitation of the wars we used to fight in the school of my story, Pierre who also allowed Florence to play me music by Eric Satie and Fafa Lemos on the tablecloth, while I corrected the position of her hands, because that was no way for a good pianist to hold them, and then she deliberately plonked them down again, so I could correct her again, Pierre, Pierre, there's nothing more to say about Pierre, Pierre was the one who took it on himself to explain everything.

'We can't go on living at her parents' expense, can we? I've only just graduated and earn next to nothing at the moment. We've rented the flat until I can find a proper job. Eventually I'd like to find a much bigger place, where I can have my consulting-room too.'

'As you can see, he doesn't want to let me out of his sight for a moment.'

'He's quite right, Florence.'

Pierre gave his blessing to this exchange, but Florence and I already knew that there was no way the night could come crashing down now. We had even commented on my immortal phrase: 'Upset? Florence, are you upset?' Florence told me yes she had nearly died of shame on my behalf when she heard me say it, and took the opportunity to cackle with the laughter she had suppressed the first time around. We became mortal enemies, but Pierre patched up our friendship. We were forcing poor Pierre head first into my earlier story, getting him mixed up in things that had nothing whatsoever to do with him. I even went so far as to confess what had happened with my hipflask, although I did try to point out it was done without any ulterior motive, not one outside psychoanalysis at any rate, and describing in great detail how uncomfortable I had felt when it started leaking out in my back pocket. Thank heavens! shouted Florence, looking at me and bursting out laughing again, confessing in turn that she had also felt extremely uncomfortable when she saw the stain spreading on the sofa, and thought it was something else entirely. Thank heavens! she shouted again, unable to stop laughing. And finally, over dessert, I confessed I had dressed up for dinner with Madame de Sévigné, and Pierre in his turn confessed they had dressed to have dinner with the teacher from my story, who was bound to be even shabbier after ten years' hardship in Paris.

'It was Florence's idea,' Pierre went on. 'She told me to put on the clothes I wear to mend my motorbike in.'

That earned him a slap from Florence. Whereas I was rewarded with both her hands squeezing the forearm of my black velvet jacket, while she stared hard at me with the same look as when there were only seconds left for us.

When we had finished eating, Florence decided the time had come for the story, she wanted to hear me read the story. She went to get it, I sat down again on my stain on the sofa, and Pierre in the armchair opposite me, both of us with our glass of wine. By the time Florence returned, clutching the book in both hands against her chest, there was a rather strained atmosphere. I at least had begun to feel uncomfortable and I got the impression that Pierre's fixed smile was not enough by now to make everything seem normal. Florence was trembling, but all of a sudden seemed to decide there was no use worrying, and handed me the story. Start reading she said, throwing herself down on the carpet in such a way that her head and arms were touching my knees, while her feet reached Pierre so that she could tap him with them now and then to keep him calm. But none of us was calm.

Reading made me feel there were only seconds left again. But this time for the last time. Yes, this really was it, and both of us were well aware of that. Reading was to listen to Florence and to laugh and play just like in that story, and in this one I am writing now. It meant listening to her clap and stroke my knees whenever in my reading I referred to her as an unforgettable person. It meant receiving her slaps and punishments whenever I referred to her as an unbearable person. She kept giving Pierre taps with her feet as well, which helped calm me down, but as I was reaching the climax of the story, she lay listening to me without moving at all. She leant her head back on my knees, took my right hand in between hers, and did not move until I had reached the end.

'Now inscribe it to me,' she said. She still had not moved. 'Dedicate it to me, please.'

'Fine, but you'll have to let go of his hand for that, because I don't reckon he's left-handed,' said Pierre.

So she let go of my hand, with a strange, sad, weary look that made it seem she were returning from far away, as if she found it hard to come back from some distant, pleasant land. So I took hold of both her hands, then let them go, and she took hold of mine again for a second, then let go again. All done in the worst possible taste, with the room spinning all round me, and all of a sudden Pierre more than ever in the armchair opposite me. Florence shook her head with all her heart and crawled over to him. It was Pierre's turn, and of course he already had the pen ready for me to do Florence's dedication with. The son of a bitch had succeeded in getting me drunk with his sang-froid. And when he gently tossed the pen to me from the armchair opposite, where Florence was hugging his legs, the pen arrived from an armchair to my right, an armchair to my left, and a million other armchairs, in all of which Florence was hugging his legs. I caught it perfectly, and my honour was saved.

I was still dedicating the book to Florence when I woke up dreadfully late the next day, remembering I had spent hours dedicating and dedicating every blank space in the book, I even wrote something on the cover. I think, no, I don't think, I'm sure, that every one of the thousand phrases I wrote was on the same level as my immortal phrase: Upset? Florence, are you upset? And I had a hangover that was exaggerated even for someone who has been through such an exaggerated situation, even though that didn't stop me beating my head desperately against my pillow. Upset, Florence are you upset? I'd become history, I felt I'd become past history, I was feeling I had become a thing of the past when the phone rang. It was Florence of course, to tell me nothing had happened, and then fall silent for a long while. I almost told her I couldn't remember a thing anyway, but that she hadn't changed at all, only now she was a woman and an enchanting one at that.

'Do you want me to hang up first?' I said, and hung up.

Translated by Nick Caistor

José Balza

The Stroke of Midnight

In the rearview mirror he thought he glimpsed a luminous fragment, receding in the distance: smooth vertical surfaces, aluminium-hued façades: the towers of the city. He had a sense of innumerable windows and even a section of motorway: an imposing metallic vision. But he knew it was an illusion of the little mirror (or of his mind); the urban landscape was five hours behind them, and only the open road lay ahead. They passed through a brief downpour, heavy enough to make it hard to see the road (even with the wipers on high speed), but so violent that they sensed how, in a few kilometres, the forest would open radiant on both sides, and the road markers would gleam, their white paint incandescent.

And that's what happened: as suddenly as it had started, the rain stopped. Moments before, a truck's headlights – burning through the iridescent mist that rose from the concrete – had made him wince, disorientated. Now all that was gone: just pure sun, limbs arched over the road, shadows, and bright green grass, alternating against the horizon. In front of him, the undulating road – its black ink outlined precisely against bone-white margins of gravel – showed the way.

He was feeling a little tired, but also already relaxed. In less than five minutes they would branch off to the right from the main road, then take the provincial route. In one quick look he took in the approaching exit, the mirror (which showed a distant truck), the dashboard clock (three p.m.), and the beautiful face, tilted slightly forward and away towards the vent window. The dark glasses kept him from recognizing Clara's exact expression, but he reached out for her hand, and – attentive as ever these last three months – she responded instinctively, without meeting his eyes.

What to think of this girl, with skin so fresh it seemed laminated with mother-of-pearl? How to repay the minutes and months of togetherness, of generosity? He was no longer young, and yet he had won her love. They had met coming out of a conference room with two mutual friends. Discussion of the meeting ensued, as they made for the nearest café; and there, seated between their friends, they had spoken for the first time. Was it six months already? He'd noticed her grace, her easy movement; her speech was spontaneous and confident; he'd admired her dark eyes and her pleasant mouth, bright with lipstick. When the other couple left, he'd risked immediate rejection – but it was his only chance – and asked her to dinner and a movie the very next night.

He'd been sure she wouldn't accept. So young, so independent. She seemed to consider a few moments, then agreed. From then on they would meet occasionally, attend concerts together; gradually he entered her circle of friends. Her vibrant sensuality, her improvisations seduced him. It's true she became a little more serious around him, but his age didn't bother her. Once she had whispered to him, teasing, 'Don't worry, I like a little paunch on a man.'

He hadn't really noticed it himself, but instinctively he sucked in his stomach. She laughed, and for the first time she kissed him. Later she'd agreed to come home with him.

Then everything happened with speed and ardour. She was having her period, so there was no need to take precautions. Afterwards they went out to eat with some of his friends. But during those first months he was very careful. He couldn't stand the thought of being burdened with a pregnancy. Neither could she, apparently.

'Here's where we get off, Clara.'

The sign indicated various towns and distances. The traffic light changed, and so did the scenery. Off to his left were the distant cities and the sea; he bore to the right, where the earth bunched up into mounds and sank into gullies: a swampy expanse of fascinating greens: August plums, amid a few wind-tossed leaves. The road cutting through the landscape like a squiggly line.

The car, in low gear, stirred up insects that were sleeping in the sun. In front of them rose huge butterflies, flashes of shimmering colour. A cloud of dragonflies or flying beetles or wasps enveloped them briefly. He gave a mock shout of alarm and Clara gestured as if at a movie. Then the afternoon sun swallowed the insects and the translucent green accompanied them right up to the cabin door.

Actually, they'd had to detour one more time. The local road continued, searching out small towns. To the right, the red clay gave way to a narrow path towards the mountains. The mud and jutting rocks made the car's passage seem almost miraculous. A little curve, then another. Cujie trees, two or three wild palms, and the foliage of the plum trees. Finally, the white façade.

Beside him Clara expressed shock at the crudeness of the landscape and at their sudden isolation. In a few seconds they felt they had lost all contact with the known world. He himself had never really understood why he bought this house. Three years before, he'd been travelling with some friends, one of whom had wanted to visit some campesinos in the area and had directed them off the main road. They were received warmly and with a great deal of liquor, but at times he detected beneath the hospitality of the natives a certain grimness, a superstitious reserve. That unexpected visit to the countryside had coincided with an interest he'd developed in acquiring property away from the city, as well as with some available cash. But he never really knew just how he'd ended up buying this house. Through carelessness, through manipulation by the campesino who'd offered it to him, as submission to a claim made by what remained of his youthful self? For the same price he could have bought something much closer to the beach, but his friends who knew this little settlement urged him on, and – a little drunk – he had decided. Eventually, there would be public services out here. In the meantime, only vegetation, drought in the summertime, and interminable rain in the heat of the monsoon. He'd only been here – alone, or with friends – in the gentle, clear light of January or December. He was unprepared for the harshness of August. A week earlier, when he'd proposed this trip, Clara had been so enthusiastic (her vacation was just starting) that he'd begun to believe he'd really enjoy spending a few days here.

The car rocks to a halt, skidding and swaying a little (would they be able to get back out with it, without getting help from a tow truck or one of the neighbours?), and they sit for a moment contemplating the simple façade: two windows, the porch, metal columns, the zinc roof. The habitable portion is small, but it's surrounded by a nice little orchard of wild plums, which gives way to the towering forest.

A year ago, in the summer, he came here with his brother, who roundly criticized his judgement in making this purchase. He found the lack of utilities and the isolation too inconvenient (and, according to him, no real chance of things improving in the future). But they stayed there two days, talking all the time and going out only to eat in a restaurant along the main road. During their second evening there – a magnificent damp tapestry of stars, pure phosphorescence glowing among the white trunks of the plum trees – he now recalls two things his brother said.

'It's amazing how the landscape itself seems to affect our choices. You picked out this spot almost haphazardly, and yet there, out front, we can see Polaris – just like at our parents' house and just like from your apartment in the city. You seem to instinctively orientate yourself towards the north.'

His brother's observation delighted him: in the immensity of the planet, something permanent, always facing the same direction, even in different houses. A coherent stellar axis, there beneath those almost dripping stars.

The other thing he remembers of his brother that night was an odd personal comment: 'You know what always happens to me? All the women I go to bed with get their period at the same time of the month.'

They had both laughed, but he didn't reciprocate: the same thing had happened to him.

Clara and he opened up the house, unpacking and arranging things so they could move about comfortably. The cooler, with ice and drinks; whisky on the sideboard, fruit and other snacks on the table. An elegant hammock on the porch, another inside. Sleeping pads on the floor, with sheets. The campesino hired to look after the place appeared, subservient and discreet. They toasted together the last evening light. He told them that the little water tank was full and that the electric lights worked. Even so, they got out an oil lamp, with matches. And for when they were alone, candles in homemade candlesticks, a tablecloth, and a little cassette player.

The sky was doubly darkening, with dusk and with the approach of menacing clouds: it all merged into a thick blanket of liquid cotton.

Distant thunder. The campesino left as abruptly as he'd come, bidding them good evening. They both felt alone and complete: alone together in the immense wilderness. They didn't need music; he took his drink over to the hammock. He peeled off his shorts and waited for her. Clara wasn't wearing lipstick for the first time since he'd known her; her silky lips came to him and, among the brusque movements of their suspended bed, she kissed him everywhere. Her skin was still moist from the shower. He didn't think of himself as an older man. She loved him as he was, regardless of the difference in age. At each pass of her mouth, his muscles tensed in response. They descended from the hammock to the sleeping pads. Their bodies joined in a rhythm at first synchronous, then frenzied. Remembering her cycles, at the last minute he jumped up and found a condom.

Perhaps they slept, whispering, laughing. When they got up to get a drink, to fix supper, it was quite late. The storm, surrounded by the powers of night, had never arrived. There was almost no breeze. They turned on the light bulb outside the door and lit the candles. Hordes of insects began to enter from the mountains: buzzing, flying, between the darkness and the light. Tiny, some crawling, some winged. A dark moth, lightning bugs, crickets. At first they were amused, but soon it started to bother them. They lit a repellant coil, but to no effect. The avalanche was extraordinary; they were buried beneath it. There were few mosquitoes, but after a while they discovered a scorpion, some winged ants; they identified the sound of a snake amidst the frogs. In the distance, a night bird sang. And, high overhead, the surprising passage of an aircraft. Was it a shiver of fear he felt just then, a sudden thought of escape?

They went back inside for protection. They had enough tapes to last for days. Should they combine the wine with that adagio from Schumann's *Second*? Or slip into the melancholy of Billie Holiday? They did both, then went on to a bolero by Benny More, then to faster rhythms, dancing like fools. Clara loved traditional Caribbean music.

Around midnight they were laughing at something, hopping around, chasing each other. Clara did impressions and told funny stories from her office. They weren't exactly drunk – rather in an exalted state of intimacy. Eventually it began to rain, a torrential downpour. Thunder sounding as if from caverns; lightning bursting above them. The music stopped. Naked, damp with sweat, they lay upon the smooth sheets. It was still a little before midnight. Clara held back, awaiting his advances. His pulse slowed, his whole body ached for pleasure, his muscles relaxed. This time he kissed her, interminably, listening for her to sound the notes of surrender.

When he returned his mouth to Clara's, when he began to push, her warm friction drove him wild. It almost felt like she had never before made love: he penetrated a tightly stretched web, it almost hurt to go in. And it was wonderful. Clara opened herself completely, even though it seemed to hurt. Each millimetre, a glory. His heart vibrated with passion, as did his brain and his penis. He felt her breathe deeply, and he went in all the way. The torrent beat on the roof, an obscure drone.

Both inflamed, they were just one step away from another climax. For a moment he recalled the fact that he'd always vowed not to father a child. To stay with Clara now or to withdraw (with both of them right on the edge): this was a test of his freedom. He had never attempted a long-term relationship. He could tell that neither of them would be able to hold back orgasm, that most complex of physical fulfilments. Her undulations and her moaning quickened; there was no way he'd be able to wait for her, then come outside of her, later.

The viscous thunder excited even more. They were lost in a place only real in the present. Their pleasure was mounting, peaking. And then he said to himself: both of us know what's happening now, for once I'm just going to have to accept it. It doesn't matter that at this moment a child is being formed. It's the first midnight of August, it's raining like crazy, and we're facing Polaris. But, no, actually he couldn't tell himself any of this, because his body thought nothing. Clara was his, and he could ask for nothing more. From his heart he let go the last lightning bolt of pleasure, he lowered his belly, he would flood her. He thrust with insatiable ardour: everything; now. She laughed or cried; they came together as if in a knot.

And just in this final moment, some tiny little insect, which had managed to get inside, flew through the dark like an arrow. He barely felt – caught up in his orgasm – something land on his ear, then the creature's violent invasion. A sting, a bite? A mild pricking sensation inside his ear. Then everything converged.

Translated by Bruce Morgan

Moacyr Scliar

Van Gogh's Ear

We were, as usual, on the brink of ruin. My father, the owner of a small grocery store, owed a substantial amount of money to one of his suppliers. And there was no way he could pay off the debt.

But if Father was short of money, he certainly wasn't lacking in imagination ... He was an intelligent, cultured man with a cheerful disposition. He hadn't finished school; fate had confined him to a modest grocery store where, amid bratwursts and other sausages, he bravely repulsed the attacks of existence. His customers liked him because, amongst other things, he granted them credit and never exacted payment. With his suppliers, however, it was a different story. Those strong-willed gentlemen wanted their money. The man whom Father owed money at that point was known as being a particularly ruthless creditor.

Any other person would have been driven to despair. Any other person would have considered running away, or even committing suicide. Not Father, though. Ever the optimist, he was convinced that he would find a way out. This man must have a weakness, he would say, and that's how we're going to get him. By making enquiries here and there, Father dug up something promising. This creditor, who to all appearances was a boorish and insensitive man, had a secret passion for Van Gogh. His house was full of reproductions of works by the great painter. And he had seen the movie about the tragic life of the artist, with Kirk Douglas in the star role, at least half a dozen times.

Father borrowed a biography of Van Gogh from the library and spent the weekend immersed in the book. Then, late on Sunday afternoon, the door of his bedroom opened and he emerged, triumphant:

'I've found it!'

Taking me aside – at the age of twelve I was his confidant and accomplice – he then whispered, his eyes glittering:

'Van Gogh's ear. The ear will save us.'

'What are the two of you whispering about?' asked Mother, who didn't have much tolerance for what she called the shenanigans of her husband.

'Nothing, nothing,' replied Father, and then to me, lowering his voice, 'I'll explain later.'

Which he did. As the story went, Van Gogh had cut his ear off in a fit of madness and sent it to his beloved. This fact led Father to devise a scheme: He would go to his creditor and tell him that his great-grandfather, the lover of the woman Van Gogh had fallen in love with, had bequeathed him the mummified ear of the painter. Father would let his creditor have this relic in exchange for the cancellation of his debt and for additional credit.

'What do you think?'

Mother was right: he lived in another world, in a fantasy world. However, the main problem wasn't the absurdity of his idea; after all, we were in such dire straits that anything was worth a try. It was something else.

'But what about the ear?'

'The ear?' He looked at me astounded, as if the matter had never crossed his mind. 'Yes,' I said, 'Van Gogh's ear, where in the world are you going to get it?'

'Ah,' he said, 'no problem, we can get one from the morgue. A friend of mine is a janitor there, he'll do anything for me.'

On the following day he left early in the morning. He came home at noon, radiant, carrying a parcel, which he then proceeded to unwrap carefully. It was a flask of formaldehyde with something dark, of an indefinite shape in it. Van Gogh's ear, he announced, triumphant.

And who would say that it wasn't? Anyhow, just in case, he stuck a label on the flask: *Van Gogh – ear.*

In the afternoon the two of us headed for the creditor's house. Father went in, and I waited outside. Five minutes later he came out, disconcerted, and really furious. The man had not only rejected the proposal but he had also snatched the flask from Father and thrown it out of the window.

'Disrespectful!'

I had to agree with him, although I thought that such an outcome was to a certain extent inevitable. We started to walk along the tranquil street, with Father muttering all the time: disrespectful, disrespectful. Suddenly he stopped dead in his tracks, and stared fixedly at me:

'Was it the right one, or the left one?'

'What?' I said, without getting it.

'The ear that Van Gogh cut off. Was it the right one or the left one?'

'How should I know?' I said, already irritated by the whole thing. 'You're the one who read the book. You're the one who should know.'

'But I don't,' he said, disconsolate. 'I admit I don't know.'

We stood in silence for a while. I was then assailed by a nagging doubt, a doubt I didn't dare to articulate because I knew that the answer could be the end of my childhood. However:

'And the one in the flask?' I asked. 'Was it the right one or the left one?'

He stared at me, dumbfounded.

'You know what? I haven't the faintest,' he murmured in a weak, hoarse voice.

We then continued to walk, heading for home. If you examine an ear carefully – any ear, whether Van Gogh's or not – you'll see that it is designed much like a labyrinth. In this labyrinth I got lost. And I would never find my way out again.

Translated by Eloah F. Giacomelli

Antonio Skármeta

The Cyclist of San Cristóbal Hill

> ... and I did plunge so very far,
> that I soared so very high,
> that I did seize the prey ...
> – St John of the Cross

And on top of that, it was my birthday. From the balcony of the Alameda I saw, unhurriedly crossing the sky, the Russian Sputnik the newspapers had been talking so much about and I didn't take the slightest bit of notice because the following day was the first climb of the season and my mother was ill in a room that was no bigger than a wardrobe. I just had to keep on pedalling away in the air with the back of my neck against the floor so as to tone up my muscles and so that I could kick into the pedals tomorrow with that special style of mine they'd devoted an article to in *Stadium*. While Mum was delirious with fever, I started walking up and down the hall eating up every single crumb of the cakes aunt Margarita had given me, desperately separating out the bits of candied fruit with the tip of my tongue as they were disgusting and spitting them to one side. My old man came out every now and then to try the punch, but he would stay there five minutes each time giving it a stir, and sighing, and then he'd squeeze the pieces of peach floating shipwrecked in the mixture of cheap white wine, and brandy, and orange, and Panimávida mineral water.

Both of us needed something to speed the night along and bring the morning in with a rush. I decided to stop exercising and to polish my shoes; the old boy was pacing up and down probably with the idea of calling an ambulance, and the sky was clear, and the night very warm, and Mum was saying, half asleep, 'I'm burning up', not so weakly that we couldn't hear her through the open door.

But that was a night brimming with stars. The vivid crest did not seem to be getting dimmer. Passing your eyes over each star was like counting cacti in a desert, like biting the skin round your nails until they bleed, like reading a Dostoevsky novel. Then Dad would go into the room and repeat the same implausible arguments in my mother's ear, that the injection would reduce the fever, that it was getting light now, that the doctor would be coming very early in the morning before going fishing in Cartagena.

In the end, we set about cheating the darkness. We'd latch on to the milky effect the sky has in the middle of the night and we'd try to pretend it was the early morning (if I'd been pressed a little I could have made out some cockerel or something else crowing right there in the night).

It could have been any time between three and four when I went into the kitchen to get the breakfast. As if in unison, the whistle of the kettle and the screams of my mother began to get louder. Dad appeared in the doorway.

'I can't bring myself to go in,' he said.

He was fat and pale and his shirt was soaked through. We could make out Mum saying: get the doctor.

'He said he'd be round first thing in the morning,' replied my old man for the fifth time.

I was transfixed by the way the lid was jumping up and down with bursts of steam.

'She's dying,' I said.

Dad started feeling all his pockets. A sign he wanted to smoke. Now he'd have a hell of a job finding the cigarettes and then the same thing would happen with the matches and then I'd have to light it from the gas.

'You really think so?'

I raised my eyebrows as far as they would go, and sighed.

'Give it here, I'll light it for you.'

*

As it got closer to the flame, I noticed, perplexed, that my nose wasn't singed by the heat as had happened on every other occasion. I handed the cigarette to my father, without turning my head, and deliberately placed my little finger on the small ring of fire. It was as if there was nothing there. I thought: my finger's died or something, but you couldn't think of the death of a finger without laughing a little, so I opened my whole palm and this time touched the gas rings, every one of the little holes, with my finger tips, rummaging in the very roots of the flames. Dad was walking up and down the far end of the hall making sure he knocked all the ash on to his lapel and filled his moustache up with flecks of tobacco. I used the moment to take things a little further, and I started to toast my wrists, and then my elbows, and then my fingers again. I turned off the gas, spat into my hands, as I could feel they were dry, and took the basket with yesterday's bread, the jar of marmalade and a new pack of butter into the dining room.

When Dad sat down at the table, I must have started crying. With his neck bent over he sank his gaze down towards the bitter coffee as if all the resignation on the planet were focused there, and then he said something. I didn't manage to catch it, because actually he seemed to be having a strange conversation with a part of himself, a kidney maybe, or a thighbone. Then he put his hand through the gap in his open shirt and tugged at the tangle of hairs on his chest. On the table there was a basket of slightly bruised cherries, apricots and peaches. For a moment the fruit became virgin and pristine, and I started to gaze at the wall as if I was being shown a film or something. Finally, I grabbed a peach and rubbed it on my lapel until it shone very acceptably. My old man, prompted to follow suit, picked up a cherry.

'The old girl's dying,' he said.

I fingered my throat. Now I was turning over and over in my mind the fact that I hadn't burnt myself. I licked the few remaining bits of flesh off the stone with my tongue and with my hands I began to squeeze the crumbs on the table. I began to pile them up in little mounds, and then I'd flick them between the cup and the bread basket with my index finger. At the precise moment that I was pushing the stone against the inside of my cheek, and was imagining I had a big bit of peach on my tooth and was trying to look serious, at that moment I believed I'd discovered why I'd become unburnable, if you can use that word. It wasn't that clear, but it was the same sort of evidence which makes people forecast rain when the teru-teru wind starts to blow: if Mum was dying, I would have to leave the planet as well. That moment with the flame had seemed like a trailer for a horror film, or maybe I was just thinking a load of rubbish, and that really the only thing that had happened was that my cinema trips had addled my brain.

I looked at Dad, and when I was just about to tell him about it, he pressed his chubby palms in front of his eyes until there wasn't a gap to see through.

'She'll live,' I said. 'People get all het up when they have fever.'

'It's like the body's defence mechanism.'

I cleared my throat.

'If I win the race we'll have some money. We could send her to a decent hospital.'

'That's if by any chance she doesn't die.'

I spat the stone out over my shoulder; it was ever so smooth after all that polishing. The old boy seemed to perk up enough to take a big bite out of an extremely juicy-looking peach. We heard Mum moaning in the room, but this time there were no words. I gulped the coffee down, almost comforted that it hurt the top of my mouth. I stuffed a roll into my pocket, and when I stood up, the ball of crumbs rolled off to have a drink in what seemed to be a pool of wine that looked fresh but wasn't. Since Mum had become bedridden any stains on the little table cloth had remained, abandoned there for a month, at the very least.

I tried to sound matter-of-fact as I said goodbye, sort of American-like I thought.

'I'm off.'

In reply Dad simply turned his head and assessed the night.

'What time's the race?' he asked, taking a sip of coffee.

I felt a real bastard, not just one of those harmless baddies you get in comic strips.

'Nine o'clock. I'm going to do a bit of a warm-up.'

I took the clips out of my pocket to tie round my trouser bottoms, and grabbed the bag with my kit in, all the time humming a Beatles song, one of the psychedelic ones.

'Maybe you'd be better off getting some sleep,' suggested Dad. 'That's two nights in a row...'

'I feel okay,' I said, walking towards the door.

'Okay, then.'

'Don't let your coffee get cold.'

I shut the door as gently as if I was off to smooch with a girl, and then I undid the padlock on the bicycle, taking the bike down from the bars of the banister. I put it under my arm, and without waiting for the lift I ran down the four flights to the street. There I stopped for a minute stroking the tyres not knowing where to start. By now an early morning breeze had got up, a little cold, and halting.

I got on, and with a single kick of the pedals I slid over the kerb and went off along the Alameda till I got to Plaza Bulnes. I circled the fountain in the square, took an immediate left as far as the *Negro Tobar* nightclub and got under the awning to listen to the music coming out of the basement. It really annoyed me that I couldn't smoke; I was not allowed to spoil the image of the perfect athlete our trainer had hammered into our heads. Whenever I turned up smelling of fags, he'd smell my tongue and say you're out. But above all this, I felt like a foreigner in that Santiago morning. Maybe I was the only boy in Santiago who had his mother dying, the one and only sod in the galaxy who hadn't been able to wangle himself a girl to liven up Saturday nights when there wasn't a party, the one and only creature who cried when he was told a sad story. And suddenly I worked out what number the quartet were playing, and it was Lucho Aránguiz's trumpet that sang the 'I can only give you love, babe, that's all I can give'. One, and then two silent couples walked past the awning, moving like the ash that a mischievous schoolboy had tipped on to the pavement, and there was something gloomily unforgettable about the whispering of the fire hydrant on the corner, and there appeared to rise, out of the silvery sea on the stand, the milkman's cart, slow despite the urgency of his horses, and the wind was carrying off cigarette wrappers, ice-lolly papers, and the drummer was dragging out the number like a long rope with nothing attached to the end – sha-sha-da-da – and out of the basement came a young drunk to wipe his runny nose, his eyes rolling, red with smoke, the knot of his tie askew, his hair tumbling over his temples, and the orchestra started up a tango, *sophistiqué*, the same old story, the same searching, full of hope, and the buildings of Avenida Bulnes might at any moment collapse, and then the wind would blow even more wildly, it would make weathervanes out of ships, lighters and masts out of scaffolding, it would make barrels of alcohol out of modern heaters, it would turn doors into seagulls, wooden floors into foam, radios and irons into fish, the beds of lovers would burn, evening dresses, underwear, bracelets would be crabs, and would be molluscs, and would be fine sand, and to each face the hurricane would add its own, the mask to the old man, the broken laugh to the schoolboy, to the young virgin the sweetest pollen, all driven down by the clouds, all smashed against the planets, plunging into death, and myself in their midst pedalling the hurricane with my bicycle saying don't die Mum, me singing 'Lucy In The Sky With Diamonds', and the useless police with their whips lashing imaginary stallions, sitting astride the wind, lashed by parks as high as kites, by statues, and me reciting the last verses I had learnt, rather reluctantly, in the Spanish class, doing a pornographic doodle on Aguilera's exercise book, hiding Kojman's provisions from him, sticking a pencil in Skinny Leiva's backside, me reciting, and the young guy tightened his belt with the same lack of haste as a man thirsting for tenderness leaves a lover's bed, and suddenly I was singing frivolously, getting away from the words, as if each song were merely a storm before the quiet, and then I staggered down the steps, and Luchito Aránguiz went into a solo and a half on the trumpet and he started racing along, and it all turned to jazz, and when I tried to look for a bit of early morning air to cool down my mouth, my throat, the fever which was tearing me apart between my stomach and my liver, my head just hit against the wall, violently, noisily, and I got flustered and scratched around in my trousers and I took out the packet and I smoked happily, greedily, as I slid down the wall until

I lay my body on the flagstones, and then I crossed my arms and gently went off to sleep.

I was woken by the side-drums, bass-drums and bugles of some crusader who was going round and round the Santiago well, off to no war, though everything seemed decked out for a festival. I only needed to get on the bike and speed off a few blocks to witness the resurrection of the ice-cream sellers, the devout old ladies, the peanut sellers, the smooth-skinned adolescents with their fashionable shirts and boots. If the San Francisco clock was not lying on this occasion, I had exactly seven minutes to get to the starting line at the foot of San Cristóbal hill. Although my body was wracked with cramp, I hadn't lost the precision of the rhythm on the rubber of the pedals. What's more, there was a keen sun in the east and the pavements were almost deserted.

When I crossed the Pio IX, things began to hot up. I noticed that the riders who were lining the hill warming up were shooting admiring glances at me from the corner of their eyes. I caught sight of López of the Audax team blowing his nose, Ferruto of the Greens pumping up his tyre, and the boys in my team listening to the instructions from our trainer.

When I joined the group, they gave me a disapproving look but they didn't have a go at me. I took advantage of the situation to play the prima donna.

'Have I got time to make a phone call?' I asked.

The trainer pointed to the changing tent.

'Go and get changed.'

I handed the bike to the kit manager.

'It's urgent,' I explained. 'I've got to phone home.'

'What for?'

But before I could explain why, I pictured myself at the drinking fountain opposite amongst children going to the zoo and white-faced drunks dialling home to ask my Dad ... what? Has the old girl died? Has the doctor been? How's Mum?

'It's not important,' I replied. 'I'll get changed.'

I dived into the tent, and took my clothes off with an air of determination. Once I was naked I started to scratch my thighs and then calves and heels until I could feel my body responding. I meticulously squeezed my stomach in with the elasticated belt, and then I covered with the flannel socks all the bright-red marks from my nails. As I was adjusting my shorts and tightening the elastic on the shirt, I realized I was going to win the race. Having been up all night, with my throat parched and tongue bitter, with my legs as stiff as a mule's *I was going to win the race*. I was going to win it against my trainer, against López, against Ferruto, against my own team-mates, against my father, against my schoolmates and teachers, against my own bones, my head, my stomach, my wild living, against my death and my mother's, against the president of the republic, against Russia and the United States, against the bees, the fish, the birds, the pollen of the flowers, I was going to win it against the galaxy.

I grabbed an elasticated bandage and bound it twice round the instep, sole and ankle of either foot. When I'd wrapped them up like a single fist, only the ten toes protruded fleshy, aggressive, flexible.

I went out of the tent. 'I'm an animal', I thought when the starter raised the pistol, 'I'm going to win this race because I've got claws and hooves on both legs'. I heard the crack of the pistol and with two sharp, attacking thrusts on the pedals I took the first slope in the lead. As soon as the incline reduced, I actually had the sun dribbling slowly down the back of my neck. I didn't need to look very far behind to discover Pizarnick of the Railway team, sticking to my backside. I felt sorry for the lad, for his team, for his trainer who must have told him 'if he takes the lead, stick with him as long as you can, nice and easy, use your brain, okay?' because if I'd wanted to I could have set a pace there and then that would have had the lad spewing up within five minutes, his lungs churned up, he would have 'hit the wall', shocked and stunned. At the first bend the sun disappeared, and I looked right up at the virgin on the mount, and you could see her gently distant, incorruptible. I decided to be smart, and, suddenly reducing pedal speed, I let Pizarnick take the lead. But the boy had his racing bible on his saddle: he slowed until we were level, and then a blond-haired Stade Français lad zoomed past. I tilted my neck over to the left and smiled at Pizarnick. 'Who's he?' I said. The lad didn't return my look. 'What?' he gasped. 'Who's he?' I repeated. 'The guy who went through.' He seemed not to have noticed that we were a few metres behind. 'I don't know him,' he said. 'Did you see what bike it was?' 'A Legnano,' I came back. 'What are you thinking about?' But this time I didn't get a reply. I realized he'd been thinking all the time whether, now that I'd lost the lead, he should go with the new leader. If he'd asked me, I could have warned him; pity his bible was broadcasting through only one antenna. One steeper slope, and it would be goodnight compadres. He kicked and kicked until he closed on the blond guy, and almost in desperation he looked behind to gauge the distance. I looked either side for another rider to have a chat with, but I was only about twenty metres behind the leaders, and the rest of the riders were only just poking their noses round the bend. I placed my fingers over my pounding heart, and, with just one hand in the middle, I guided the handlebars. How could I be so alone, so suddenly! Where were the blond guy and Pizarnick? And González, and the boys from the club, and the Audax Italiano crew? Why was I getting short of breath now, why was the space closing in over the roofs of Santiago, so devastatingly? Why was sweat searing my eyelashes and forcing itself into my eyes and blurring everything? That heart of mine was not beating strongly enough to get blood to my feet, or to make my ears burn, or to firm up my bum on the saddle, and strengthen my kicks. That heart of mine was betraying me, it was turning its nose up at the steep climb, blood was spurting out of my nostrils, injecting dizziness into my eyes, it was coursing through my arteries, it was spinning in my diaphragm. It was weighing me down to an anchor, to my body limp like a rope, to my lack of grace, to my abandonment.

'Pizarnick!' I shouted. 'Stop, man, I'm dying!'

But my words hurtled back and forth between my temples, between my upper and lower teeth, between my saliva and carotid arteries. My words were a perfect circle of flesh: I had never said anything. I had never spoken to anyone on the earth. I had been constantly seeing the same image in shop windows, in mirrors, in winter puddles, in girls' eyes thick with mascara. And maybe now (pedal by pedal, push and push, bursting, bursting a gut) the same silence would be entering into Mum (and I was going up and up and down and down), the same blue death from suffocation (on and on, turn and turn), death by blocked nostrils and gurgling sounds in your throat (and me a whirlwind weaving motoring gears head down), terminal white death (no one could beat *me*, Mum!) and the gasping of some three, four, five, ten cyclists who seemed to be passing me, or it was me catching up with the leaders, and for an instant I had my eyes half-open over the abyss and I must have squeezed my eyelashes together tightly harshly like this so that the whole of Santiago shouldn't cast itself adrift and drown me as it carried me high and then threw me, dashing my head against a cobbled street, on to rubbish tips full of cats, on scummy street corners. Poisoned, with my free hand thrust down my throat, then biting my wrists, I had the last moment of lucidity: a certainty that was senseless, untranslatable, captivating, slowly blessed, saying yes, fine, I'm great, pal, this end was mine, this annihilation was mine, all I needed was to pedal faster and win the race in order to cheat my death, I was still in a position to control the little which remained of my body, those wiggly, fevered toes on the end of my feet, toes angels hoofs tentacles, toes claws scalpels, apocalyptic toes, terminal toes, shitty little toes, and to throw the handlebars to either side, east or west, north or south, heads or tails, or nothing, or perhaps to always remain northsoutheastwestheadstails, moving in immobility, resounding. So I covered my whole face with this hand and I slapped off the sweat and I shook off my cowardice; laugh you fool I said to myself, laugh you're not a man, roar your head off because you're out in front on your own, because no one uses their feet like you do on descents.

And with one last surge which swept upwards from the soles of my feet, filling, with beautiful, boiling, hot blood, my thighs and hips and chest and neck and brow, with a crowning glory, with an attack of my body on God, with an irresistible course, I felt the gradient level off for a split-second and I opened my eyes and I kept them open in the sunlight, and then the tyres really did speed off smoking and screeching, the chains sang, the handle-bars flew like a bird's head, sharp against the sky, and the spokes of the wheel were splitting the sun into a thousand pieces, scattering them everywhere, and then I heard, I heard – my goodness I did! – the people cheering me on from estate cars, children screaming on the side of the bend in the descent, the loudspeaker giving the positions of the first five places; and as the freewheeling started, amazingly quick on the new road surface, one of the organizers drenched me from top to toe laughing as he did, and twenty metres further on, dripping wet, laughing, easy, someone looked at me, a red-haired girl, and said 'little duck, soaked to the skin,' and that was the moment to stop messing about, the road was slippery, it was a case again of being smart, of slamming on the brakes, of dancing round the bends like a tango or a full-orchestra waltz.

Now the breeze that I was creating (the sky was calm and transparent) was clearing the dust out of my eyes, and I almost broke my neck when I twisted round to see who was second. The Blond Guy, of course. Only if he had had a pact with the devil would he have been able to beat me in the descent, and that is for a very simple reason which is explained technically in the sports magazines and which can be summarized like this: I never used to use the brakes, I would merely place my shoe on the tyres when they were going round corners. Bend after bend, I was the only tightly knit creature in the city on my bike. Frame, metal, leather, saddle, eyes, lamp, handlebars, were at one with my back, my stomach, my rigid clump of bones.

I passed the finishing line and dismounted while the bike was still moving. I accepted the backslapping, the hugs from the trainer, the photos the *Stadio* boys took and I knocked back the Coca-Cola. Then I took the machine and rode back along the side of the road in the direction of the apartment.

Hesitation in front of the door, one last moment of wariness, perhaps the shadow of a doubt, the thought that it might all have been a trap, a trick, as if the twinkling of the Milky Way, the sun in the streets, the silence, had been the trailer for a film that would never be shown, either in the centre or in the local cinemas, or in any man's imagination.

*

I pressed the buzzer, two , three times, short and urgent. Dad opened the door, a fraction, as if he'd forgotten that he lived in a city where people go from house to house knocking on doors, pressing buzzers, visiting each other.

*

'Mum?' I asked.

The old boy opened wider, smiling.

'She's fine,' he put his arm round my back and pointed to the bedroom. 'Go in and see her.'

I made a heck of a racket clearing my throat and turned round in the middle of the hall.

'What's she doing?'

'She's having lunch,' replied Dad.

*

I walked towards the bed, quietly, fascinated by the elegant way she was bringing the spoonfuls of soup up to her lips. Her skin was very white and the lines on her forehead had turned to deep furrows, but she was moving the spoon gracefully, rhythmically ... hungrily.

I sat on the end of the bed, engrossed.

'How did you get on?' she asked, nibbling a soda biscuit.

I smiled broadly.

'Okay, Mum. Okay.'

*

The pink shawl had got a piece of noodle on the end. I bent forward to remove it. Mum stopped my hand as I did so and gently kissed me on the wrist.

'How do you feel, old girl?'

She now put her hand round the back of my neck, and then tidied the fringe on my forehead.

'Fine, my boy. Do your mother a favour, will you?'

I frowned, questioningly, at her.

'Go and get some salt. The soup's a bit bland.'

I got up, and before going into the dining room, I went into the kitchen to see my father.

'Did you speak to her? She's in good spirits, isn't she?'

I stood and looked at him, gleefully scratching my cheek.

'Do you know what she wants, Dad? Do you know what she asked me to get?'

My old man blew a puff of smoke.

'She wants some salt, old boy. She wants some salt. She says the soup's a bit bland and she wants some salt.'

I spun on my heels and went over to the sideboard in search of the salt cellar. When I was about to take it out, I saw the uncovered punchbowl in the centre of the table. Without bothering with the ladle, I thrust a glass in right down to the bottom and, happily throwing it all over myself, I gulped the liquid down into my stomach. Only when the kick came did I notice it was rather strong. The bloody old man's fault, he never remembers to cover the punch pan. I took another glass, what the heck.

Translated by Jeremy Munday

Mario Levrero

Notes from Buenos Aires

31.1.86 I opened the door. No, not exactly. I mean, the door was there, I was in front of the door. I was on this side, the door was there; it was shut, and so I opened the door. But I don't mean it was locked; I didn't have the key. Nor did I have to use the handle, because in fact it wasn't shut, it wasn't shut at all. I didn't actually open the door, but the door was there; I pushed it, and it swung on its hinges. Not enough, first go; to squeeze through I would have had to push it again, a bit harder. But I didn't; nor did I squeeze through. I opened the door, and I stood there, waiting.

7.10.86 Sitting on a bench in the square I watched the pigeons; that's not at all original, since you can hardly see anything else; but I mean that I managed to fill out my opinion about pigeons, something which up till now had simply been a vague feeling of unease. Just as rats have a bad press, I concluded, pigeons have a good press, both cases being arbitrary and incomprehensible. I had been able to closely observe a rat that was trapped a while ago in the little rear courtyard of my house, and I found it to be an intelligent, witty, gentle and friendly creature. Pigeons, on the other hand, are ridiculous, gluttonous and extremely promiscuous, as well as lacking any trace of intelligence and sensitivity. It amazes me that people feed them. A whole industry has even grown up around it; here in the square there are several people selling a mystery 'pigeon food' (which in fact looks very much like corn). They sell it in little rectangular packets, and it really does seem to sell because I've seen them here every day for a long time and they haven't shown any sign of wanting a career change.

There's a kid of thirteen or fourteen who comes over as a really shrewd and successful operator; he sets up his trestle with a piece of wood on top, and then gets down to making little towers with the rectangular bags; he starts off with two, side by side, a few centimetres apart, and then he bridges them with another two, at right angles to the previous ones, and another on top in the same position as the first two, and so on; he does it quickly and skilfully and with an air of concentration that doesn't take anything away from his dynamic impression. I think he'll go far.

Anyway, I hate the pigeons' little stumbling way of walking, similar to hens and to some obese and obtuse women; and my final conclusion was that, probably, what I find so loathsome about pigeons and hens is that sort of extreme female caricature. But deep down in my soul, something whispers to me that most probably it isn't a caricature but is the expression of the female essence (something which, out of respect for my illusions, I can't accept). That's the way things are with me.

1.3.87 What's happened to me this summer is that I've lost track of time. I've ended up feeling that I've lived forever in this humid summer, this too hot and too humid summer, and I've felt I might have to live in it forever. At times, for me, it's seemed like an unwanted eternity.

More than ever before, during this time of helpless waiting, I invented illusions to ward off anxiety; I've even got to the point of hallucinating. And I've fallen in love, in an insistent, obsessive, adolescent way; this obsession has filled countless sleepless nights. In a way it cheers me that I've rescued the possibility of loving, which I'd believed to be lost amidst age and the cynicism of age. Although I've felt my chest seething with that anguish of love, pained, ill-treated, a sort of punch-bag. I've also noticed sweetness. hidden in certain mysterious twists of that pain, which more than once led me in a blind search for pain so as to get some of that sweetness I've lived, then, as if I were drunk, amidst the effects of heat, humidity, love, daydreams, pain and sweetness, staggering through the streets, or glued to the security of the walls, or with my eyes fixed on a point just in front of the tip of my shoes, fearful of the deceptive nature of my senses and of the precariousness of my balance. I've seen the city as if through a misted-up window or two-dimensional as in a film or with the blurred distance of a memory. Time is a warm mass revolving on its own axis, holding everything in, letting nothing out; a time that scatters but also retains the dispersed threads. Nothing devolves, but nothing evolves; nothing can be born, what appears to be born, has already been, over and over again, each act, each gesture, each thing all has the taste of having already lived many times over.

I never thought I'd get her; I didn't try to bring her into any pleasantly complicated story; I didn't try to rescue her from her own daydream. It was enough for me, when I verbally abused her, to see her blush slightly. I know there's something terribly perverse in this satisfaction but, after all, it's useless to talk about perversion and morals in the summer we're having right now, when the weather itself is an obscenity with a capital 'O'; what I have is a poor imitation, a vague reflection of the perversion of the earth.

3.1.88 I'm winning her bit by bit. One Saturday she gets off the plane, takes a taxi to the house, we make love, eat, argue a little or simply chat, and she leaves. When she comes back, two or three weeks later, it all happens again but never identically, because we are never identical to ourselves.

Between one visit and the next I think about her, I try to construct her, but each visit adds new bits that destroy what I've made. There are contradictory images, like two identically shaped pieces of a jigsaw but with a different picture on them. I don't know which one to choose for my model. Then, on another visit, you see that the jigsaw was much bigger and that one of the two pieces goes somewhere else, in another part of the picture. But I don't know which picture is the one I have to do. There's no guide.

My time ends up more and more becoming time for constructing her. It's useless. She comes back again, and again destroys what I make. I'm getting worn out; my work seems useless to me, I think I'm wasting my time, and yet I can't do anything else. There's an upside: as I no longer think about myself, I've become a little braver, less apprehensive. There's also an upside for her: she knows that, were I to finish putting together the picture, finish constructing her in her image, I'd get bored with her, I'd stop loving her. That's maybe why she takes on so many commitments and complicated family matters that prevent her coming more often, or stopping longer when she does come.

*

During her absences (which is the majority of the time) we speak a lot on the phone, though I'm not entirely sure that it's a real help. More like a resource for my illusions, but anyway it's the only thing I have.

Firstly, there are problems in getting through. Often they're down to my own phone, a fickle device if ever there was one. You can get the engaged tone at any stage, even when you pick up the receiver. Sometimes it takes me more than half an hour just to get through. On other occasions, I don't manage to.

Then there's the sound of the direct-dialling pulses, a kind of taximeter which conveys a sense of urgency, which is a second-by-second reminder of the money I'm spending, the fleetingness of the current moment, the vanity of terrestrial things. I get nervous and I don't say exactly what I was intending to say, I speak about the time, I speak about the very problems of getting through, I ask her how she is. Sometimes I forget to tell her that I love her, that I miss her very much.

She makes a splendid contribution to complicating the situation. In spite of the fact that I know full well she can't speek freely on most occasions, because our relationship is secret and because there's almost always someone near her; in spite of knowing that, I get all confused. When I get round to telling her that I love her or that I miss her, her reply might be, for example, '*and how are things with yourself, Miss Catalina?*' said in a cold voice or at least not in the voice she usually reserves for talking to me in. I get embarrassed and hesitate a few moments, wondering perhaps about my true identity, or if she's really recognized me, if she's understood what I said, if my voice could have altered so much. On the few occasions when I'm totally lucid and alert, I use a bit of humour '*fine, Roberto*' and I get back to what I was talking about but, of course, she can't have a normal conversation and in response to my passionate outbursts she replies mechanically with small talk or with extremely professional arguments which, I must say, are usually very sharp and can be really interesting and can get me off my subject. And then I waste a few more minutes of my dialling time, minutes like rivers of shining coins which I'm pouring into the street and then, of course, I can't pick up the threads of my subject which, in the meantime, has gradually lost its momentum; my passion has gradually ebbed away or diverted me down a cul-de-sac to questions about my identity and other commonplaces, and at last, I say goodbye with a melancholy '*bye, Roberto,*' and hang up.

18.1.88 Here, in the square, there's a man, I could say an old man, who is defying the sun. He's well built and although he's poorly dressed he has a noble presence, that rare spiritual aristocracy that I have only detected in certain humble people (and which makes me feel comtemptible). (Once, this man asked me for a cigarette; the city had clad me with a sort of selective indifference, shut off to everything that didn't interest me; so I wouldn't pay any attention to these requests; but this man got to me with his attitude and presence; giving him the cigarette I felt I was the one who was receiving something. I offered him another, and he turned it down.

Now I see him in the square, every day, at noon when the sun beats down. The square is deserted, and, whenever I'm forced to cross it at that time of day, I frequently get a bit of a nose bleed at night; every step under that blistering sun feels like a hammer-blow on your skull. But he sits there, in the middle of the square, far from the shade of the trees and from any shelter at all, in the glare of the sun, with his shirt open and his body streaming sweat. I was about to go up, once, to tell him not to be mad, that he was committing suicide. But I saw an expression, on his face and in his whole body, which made me stop: stubbornness, defiance, hatred, pleasure, conscience, rage.

Each day he gets darker. The skin on his face and on his whole head is like a piece of coarse, tanned leather. It may be suicide, but it is, above all, a struggle, something very private between him and the sun, goodness knows what secret story it is that I am unable to comprehend.

*

Jars of ketchup come with a special top; after screwing it on like any other normal top, you have to put a bit more effort in to manage a tighter turn to secure it. This is important, because the jar needs to be shaken vigorously before use, otherwise a thin liquid would come out instead of thick sauce.

So, after using the ketchup, okay, she merely places the top on the jar, without even giving it the first normal turn as you would any screw-top. I wonder if it would be possible for us to live together.

*

Today I had to cross, simply had to cross, the square again, and I saw the Man who Defies the Sun again, sweating and getting darker, sitting it out. I know for a fact it wouldn't be of any interest to him to learn that I'm on his side even though I might not be able to guess at the meaning of his struggle.

And a few blocks beyond the square, I bumped into a woman whom I associated, for the purposes of contrast, with this man. I'd first seen her before I moved, in a pork butcher's in what was my local area. She was in front of me and was exhausting my patience: for a start, the back of her neck irritated me. She had ridiculous hair, very short, very high up her neck, straight, as if drawn by a ruler. There must be good reasons why, in general, people don't go around with their necks uncovered; the impression I got was of an obscene, perceptive mollusc that was studying me. The woman had thick glasses, an unfathomable age and apparently was deaf and had trouble speaking. She ought to have aroused feelings of pity and the sort of underground and not-always-expressed solidarity one feels with the handicapped; but it didn't happen. She irritated me. I perceived her as an evil presence, something which, in the atmosphere that was already fairly charged with the impatience of those who had come into the shop, I vaguely associated with perverse rituals, twisted eroticism, criminal groups. She spent a long time very closely examining the things she wanted to buy, haggling over the price of each and every one, asking questions, touching, sniffing, picking out crumpled notes extremely slowly from a stingy little purse. She had an umbrella over her arm. And before letting go of each note, she would touch whatever it was she was buying once more and would ask the price again.

Some time later I saw her in the street, she was walking along as if her mind were elsewhere, she would stop every few steps, as if confused, open her handbag and check her purse, she would move the umbrella from one arm over to the other. I felt like following her.

Today she was standing on the corner of a street, with an attitude I could only class as shifty. Despite the sun that was splitting the paving stones, she was carrying the inseparable umbrella over her arm, and was standing there, with an absent-minded and confused look, doing nothing in particular but not giving the impression of resting or waiting for anything. I made a detour to walk behind her and look at the back of her neck. Her hair was exactly the same as two years ago in the butcher's, straight and defiant.

On my way home I saw the man was still there, rock solid, defying the sun.

5.2.88 On holiday, at the seaside. Last night I dreamt I was with her on the beach, near some concrete steps that went up to the promenade. On the right you could see the sea, where there were a few big ships, which stood out very sharply. Much farther away, on the horizon, there was another ship; it was also big, but you couldn't make it out clearly. It was sort of enveloped in fog or, rather, sort of made of fog. I could see it, as if it were in a blurry coarse-grained photo. Along with the images there was reasoning: the ships were close, they'd soon be arriving; I was, in a sense, looking into the future, because the ships had still not arrived. But how was it possible to see that other ship, on the horizon, if it would take almost a year to get here? I woke up in a sort of panic, asking myself about the relationship between perception, space and time, and, with the anguish that came from feeling, comprehension eluding me.

7.2.88 Last night I found out there's a spider in the bathroom of the apartment I've rented. The spider is one of those with a large body and long legs which taper towards the ends. It had spun a web from a small ceiling rose with two little lights in it over to the medicine cabinet and mirror which is above the washbasin. It isn't a sophisticated, classical web, but a series of fine threads, more or less parallel to each other although with unexpected cross-overs and joints. I saw it last night because I had to get up to go to the toilet, in the middle of the night; during the day I'd never seen it. Since the web did have a somewhat worrying look about it, I went to get the aerosol fly-killer, I shook the container as per the instructions and took the top off; that was when the spider performed the trick which saved its life: it scuttled along the web towards the light, and I saw it disappear, little by little, before my eyes, as if it were slowly erasing itself from the outer edge; its legs got shorter, its body seemed to squash up, and then it disappeared altogether with a funny somersault. I was left standing for quite a while with the fly-killer in my hand and mouth wide open.

Then I discovered it had passed through a little hole that's in the metal of the rose, next to the wall, a thin piece of steel that runs behind the lights; the hole is only a few millimetres in diameter, just about enough to hold a screw to fix the device to the wall, and which hadn't been used by the installer. When its legs had gone through first, the position of its body had meant that I couldn't see the hole, and hence the impression that it was erasing itself. It was both the conjuror's trick and the realization of how tiny it actually was, that stopped me from using the fly-killer; but above all I think it was the trick.

*

Tonight I didn't find it. I threw little bits of toothpick into the web to make it think some kind of insect had fallen in, but it didn't come to investigate. I fear it may have moved, and that it may turn up in some less convenient place – like, for example, my bed.

*

In sacred and philosophical books of various places and times, it is usual to attempt to teach good behaviour by means of examples: and in these examples it is common to come across two people who always seem to be the same: the Wise man and the Foolish (or Stupid) man. The wise man is careful, prudent and modest; the foolish man is careless, imprudent and boastful. After a good deal of this type of reading, I have gradually assimilated these people like old acquaintances, and I have almost managed to visualize them: the wise man is calm, clear-headed, with a profound and good-natured look in his eyes and with the beginning of a smile on his lips; the foolish man has coarse features, shifty and slightly bulging eyes, and an ironic and big-headed smile. They are always together, and one without the other can almost be said to be impossible; they are like Pinky and Perky. Of course, I have always identified with the wise man, just as I usually identify with the good guys in the movies; I read, nodding with approval, about what the wise man does, whereas I look forward with anticipatory relish to the reappearance of the foolish man. Everything goes wrong for the foolish man, he's the one who waits for it to begin raining to mend the roof, he never learns his lesson.

However, some time ago I began to awaken to stark reality and in recent days I have come to a clear and rather unpleasant conclusion: when books of wisdom speak about the foolish man, they are speaking, without a doubt, about me. I'm not prudent or modest, nor do I think things out in advance. I buy shorts in summer and pullovers in winter. When I open my mouth it is to say something out of place and to make people uncomfortable. And I identify with the wise man, a clear case of lack of humility. It was tough admitting it, but that's the way it is. Now, when I read these texts, when the foolish man appears he has more normal features and his attitude is not ironic, but disconcerted. '*Poor bloke,*' I think.

2.3.88. My idol has fallen. The Man who Defied the Sun in the square is still in the square and in the sun but today he's got a ridiculous hat on, made of plaited straw or plastic imitation-straw, light, soft, feminine, with a flower design on the weave of the plait. True, he hasn't lost his dignity and the way he wears the hat is very natural and shows no sign of embarrassment; but it's clear that tragedy has become comedy.

Translated by Jeremy Munday

Policarpo Varón

The Feast

What I really wanted to do was to watch the pool game. But things don't just happen on their own. It was too hot, so I ordered a cold lemonade and sat down in a corner. At times, of course, I had to stand up because the people watching would climb almost on top of the table, for the tricky shots, and would get in the way. I'd crane my head over the top and almost finish up with my head stuck up the bum of the little fella who was almost always cueing at the table, a crafty little fella, I can't remember his name now. Then the spectators would go back to their places. That was the scene when the man walked in. Can't say I knew him. The rough brandy must have gone to his head, because he caused one hell of a row when he came in. So I said, 'It's time to go.' But the man was making a beeline for me. 'He's gonna give me one,' I thought. Then the man began, 'Have one with me, Abelardo,' and he got hold of my arm and pushed me over to a table and said to me, 'Come over here, it's on me, I'll get you one, don't you go turning me down, mate.' I humoured him as he kept on at me: 'Come on.' 'I don't drink,' I told him, but the man wouldn't ease off. It was no from me and yes from him. I decided to wriggle free and leave but he kept a tight hold on me. I had to really struggle because he was very well built. The beers were on the table by now. The man picked one up and threw it in my face. I said, 'I'm certainly not taking *that* lying down' and I gave him a fistful right in the face. The man goes off to a corner and I tell myself, 'Now you'd better get out of here.'

I looked for the door but the police were already coming up the street. They were a sight: short-cropped hair, shirts open, hardly with their caps on their heads, slinging their rifles over their shoulders and the corporal giving them orders, hurrying them up, but these policemen seemed very sleepy. Who wouldn't have been, when it was mid-afternoon with the heat at its fiercest, when you just can't get comfortable. The corporal was turning round and was no doubt telling them, 'Get your bloody arses in gear, can't you see there's a fight going on?' and the men made out they were hurrying. When they arrived, they almost couldn't get in because half of humanity was already there. The police had to push people out of the way with their rifle barrels. I was right next to the door. The man had just got to his feet in the corner and was rubbing his backside and nose and it was there that the corporal went up to him (I'd swear the corporal was smiling) and said looking away, 'What's going on here' ... Then the man spoke. He told him I'd hit him. The corporal, unmoved, told me, 'You come with us,' and he pushed me out into the square. The policemen followed me up to the barracks. Everyone was in their doorways whispering, no doubt saying, 'They've taken Abelardo.' One of the policemen removed the old door, the large, lead-green, corroding door, without any hinges. He didn't open it. He took it off its frame and said to me, 'Get in there,' and he showed me a room that smelt of the devil full of stones, cockroaches, leaves, shit and urine. I went in because otherwise they were going to shove me in on the end of a rifle-butt. The same policeman put the door back on its frame and said, 'And don't try and get out, mate, because we'll blow your legs off if we don't lay you out in a coffin first...'

I had a bit of a clean-up near the door, piling the mess on one side with my shoes, and I sat down next to the little holes the children had made when there were no policemen in San Bernardo of the Winds, and in that room, which is now a prison, slept cows, dogs, pigs and the men who were going away, and it was there the youngsters would have a crap at night when they were playing in the square because there weren't no policemen then, what I mean is, there weren't no one what would make their life hell.

*

Last night I finally twigged. The first lights had come on at the street corners. I'd kept myself amused for quite a while killing mosquitoes and that's why I didn't twig that the people had gathered by the barracks and the police were standing in the corridor and had the safety-catches off their rifles. It was already food time and I thought no one was going to remember poor Abelardo. But when the first shouts came, when I heard some familiar voices chanting insults at the policemen (the policemen were saying 'disperse', but the people just stayed there right up at the front, and the policemen were scared stiff to shoot because there were a lot of them, around a hundred at least, or more, and just eight of them and each one had only six bullets to hand), when I began to hear all this, I mean, when I realized the people were in the square shouting, I got right up close to the holes in the door again and it didn't bother me that the mosquitoes might suck my blood. Course I wasn't going to be swatting them if I was watching what was going on in the square. The people stopped shouting when they heard the noise of an engine coming up from the river: two beams of light lit up the group for a moment and then went out. Then the engine stopped

droning and several doors clunked and everyone turned around for a
moment to see a tall shape, in glasses, pot-bellied and hairy, approaching.
'It's the lawyer,' I heard. A lawyer, who had come in the morning from San
Bonifacio to spend his Sunday by the river, by merely opening his mouth
was going to get me out of this hole. The lawyer walked up to where the
policemen were and they pointed their guns at him. He spoke for a few
minutes with the corporal and the corporal said that I would not be moved
from that spot by any god or person. So the lawyer had no other option but
to turn on his heels and drive off with his wife and children for the capital
... After a while the noise of the engine faded away beyond the fields and I
knew I was going to have to spend the night there in jail without eating,
putting up with the smell of shit and the mosquitoes and I wasn't very sure
of still being alive in the morning.

It was the following day that the police reinforcements arrived. They
arrived in a grey truck, kicking up the dust in the square. Those new
policemen proved to be more alive. With bayonets drawn they forced a way
through and positioned themselves between the people and the barracks.
Then the lieutenant or whatever he was, who was in charge of them,
stepped a few yards forward and shouted to the people that they had ten
minutes to disperse. But the people turned a deaf ear, started to mutter and
in no time at all you could hear them having a real go at the police,
jumping up and down with their arms in the air and fists clenched; faces
becoming redder. It made you laugh (although we weren't in a mood for
jokes at that moment) because the insults really were very funny. It was
those shouts which got under the skin of the lieutenant or captain,
whatever he was, and especially as the people were having a go at him in
particular. I could see that the lieutenant wasn't as brave as he had made
out at the beginning. He shouted to the people that the ten minutes were
almost up, that if they didn't leave he was going to fill them full of lead,
and the people instead of withdrawing moved forward almost on top of
him. So the lieutenant had no alternative but to shout, 'Fire,' and the
policemen, at first as if they didn't want to, squeezed the triggers.

I saw them fall. The women ran as fast as they were able and the
children too and the policemen moved forward in a crouching position
shooting all the time and the square began to fill up with bodies. Some
over the square and others stretched out in the dust and on the leaves of
the tamarind, ceiba and cashew trees. All night long I heard the screams of
the dying. My heart bled for all the people who were strewn over the
square: men, women and youngsters just beginning life. But I didn't have
the strength to move, my knees couldn't support me, I was getting stiff and

numb from crouching on my haunches ... the policemen finished off the wounded and went after those who had run, breaking down doors and firing on animals, poor things who had nothing to do with it. This is what the policemen were doing when the priest appeared, redder than normal, administering blessings to the fallen, sweaty, moving amongst the dead, touching them with something and praying quietly and then I saw him stand up and say something to the policemen and to the lieutenant but the lieutenant said to him, I could hear the conversation that's why I can tell you the gist, more or less, 'Shut your mouth, father, and clear off to the church,' and the priest hoisted up his robes so as not to get them dirty in the blood and the dust and, with long steps, he went back to where the lieutenant had sent him.

The bodies had been lying for several days out in the square in the dust and the leaves. The colour of the bloodstains had changed in the sun, the bodies had become bloated, had turned pale and were beginning to smell. It was then, with the stench, that the first buzzards arrived. There were just a few circling high above the village. But within a short time more began to gather. They came from all over: from San Juan de Picalá, from San Sebastián of the River of the Stones, from Ambalema and, little by little, they created a black cloud which circled quite low, almost sitting on the rooftops. As evening drew in (when you can't tell if it's day or night; the witching hour, as they say), they began coming down slow, opening their wings, making a spitting kind of noise with their beaks and letting their feet run over the roofs. Then the smell began, the fearful smell of buzzards. I said, 'Now you're really up shit creek.' And all night long there was that flying, that swooping of buzzards. 'All the buzzards in the world have come here,' I thought. As they didn't have enough room in the trees or on the rooftops, they too were making life difficult for themselves.

And in the morning, a large old buzzard, going grey with age, not totally black, with his long red neck, came down and walked amongst the bodies and stood on top of the bloated stomachs and scrubbed his beak in the hair and faces and several times crapped his white muck. Finally coming to rest on top of a body in the centre of the square he sunk his beak in with all his force, steadying himself with his legs, pulling his body backwards and tearing out the flesh.

When that first buzzard had eaten, he craned his neck and looked at the others. And then yes, as if responding to a sign, the others flew on to the bodies, the black cloud swooped and the village was all a flap of wings, a tugging and a hammering of beaks ... I was gripped by panic (and you all know that Abelardo Cruz's knees don't give out on him for no reason whatsoever), and with my heart in my mouth I pushed open the door of the jail. The buzzards, startled, flew off and they watched me from the trees and the rooftops stumbling across the square and taking the path down to the river ... Then they fell again upon the corpses. Nobody was going to disturb them now, because there was nobody left alive in San Bernardo of the Winds and the policemen had abandoned the place some time before ...

Translated by Jeremy Munday

Rodolfo Hinostroza

The Benefactor

My name is Francisco Orihuela. Usually that is enough for people to know who I am and what I do. My novels have been translated into nineteen languages, I have won several literary prizes, some quite important, such as the one Planeta Publications gives out, the Romulo Gallegos, and the Medici – I was even being considered quite seriously for the Nobel a few years ago. Sales of my work run to the millions. I have been president of the Pen Club, my face appears in newspapers and magazines all over the world, either in photos or cartoons.

Now that you have my credentials, let me tell you that Francisco Orihuela is nothing more than a façade, a hoax. The name is real, but not all it stands for on the top rung of the literary ladder where some would put me. There is only one person in the world who knows my story – knew, that is, since I am afraid he died some ten or twelve years ago, in Europe, perhaps in Italy, perhaps a poor man – and it is to this person I owe what I am and all that I have – money, fame, and the despair that has been with me since he vanished. I have never seen his face, never heard his voice, do not know his name or his nationality, and have only a few definite proofs that he existed, passed fleetingly through the world and for some years through my life. For the want of a better name, I began referring to him as The Benefactor, or simply 'B', and now that I have almost lost all hope of ever meeting him I feel I should use the meagre literary talents I possess to try to explain methodically – probably quite tediously – my relationship with him and the cataclysm that shook my life when he first came into it one autumn afternoon twenty years ago.

I remember how I received a Western Union cable one afternoon after five. It announced laconically, but sure of its facts, that I had just won first prize for the novel, as judged by the Spanish publishing house Planeta, for my book *Saint Appolonia's Back Teeth*. I will never forget how I sat nailed to the chair by surprise, since I had never written any such book, my only contributions to literature being three or four articles on Indians in the review published by the University of Trujillo, where I was then Professor of Peruvian literature. I had never written a work of fiction in my life and was quite satisfied with my teaching and research, in spite of the scanty financial remuneration that goes with being a professor at a provincial university.

There had to have been some mistake. Still, it seemed strange that my name and address, which I was certain nobody in Spain knew, should have become mixed up with those of the true prize winner, for whom I felt a lightning flash of envy, which disappeared as fast as it came. I thought the matter over, shelved it as unsolvable, and told myself that another cable would be on the way to straighten things out and clear up the ridiculous situation. My wife and daughter were on vacation in Lima at the time, and I had arranged to go on a hunting trip with a few friends to the hills of Otusco, since there was a long weekend coming up. I went to bed early, they collected me in a landrover next morning, and we headed up the steep mountainsides where deer graze and quail have their nests.

Five days later we returned to Trujillo. I had shot a deer, which was beginning to stink, and I intended adding it to my trophies. My share of the game birds came to a dozen quail and a couple of wild ducks. At the door of my house I found a strange pile of newspapers, telegrams, and hurriedly scribbled letters and cards, all confirming that I was indeed that year's winner of the Planeta Prize. Everybody was looking for me to offer congratulations.

After speaking on the phone with the public relations manager in Barcelona I was even more at a loss. He told me there was no possible mistake, congratulated me ceremoniously, and read out the results of the voting, with the final ballot in my favour. He listed the other works that had reached the finals and read the jury's decision in all its flowing rhetoric, leaving no doubt that Francisco Orihuela had won the famous prize with his novel *Saint Appolonia's Back Teeth*. All I could do was thank him; it would be useless to insist that I was not the winner. I did have the presence of mind, however, to ask him for a copy of the manuscript, explaining that a few urgent corrections needed to be made; he refused, politely but firmly, and offered rather to send a copy of the galley proofs in about six weeks time so I could make the corrections then and still meet the publication deadline. Ideally, the book should come out as soon as possible – and he invited me to Barcelona for the celebration.

The newspapers that I leafed through all carried the same old photo of me – some on the front page. If they were to be believed, I was little short of a National Treasure, one more illustration of the top rank Latin America has come to hold in world literature.

While absentmindedly going through the cards from friends and relatives I found a letter from the Banco Exterior de España which was short and to the point. In the envelope was a cheque for ten thousand dollars – the concrete part of the prize. I am under no obligation to explain my behaviour, but I will say that was five years' salary for a professor of my standing and a small fortune for me. All I had to do was play it as it lay and it would be mine. If something had gone wrong, it was in my favour; if the mistake still had not been caught after all the publicity about the prize, perhaps that meant the true author, for secret reasons I could not imagine, must be in a position that made him unable to accept it. I wondered if he couldn't show his face in public for political or family reasons and so had chosen me, an unknown provincial university professor, to stand in for him.

There would be a price to pay, of course, and if I lent my name and claimed the money I would have to assume responsibility for setting things straight once he got in touch with me. Something was not quite right about the whole affair, but the phone soon began brr-ing non-stop, and I realized that if I was going to accept the prize I would need to take care of a number of details; otherwise, the whole world was going to learn about the mystery.

In the first place there was the plot of 'my' novel, which I knew nothing about. Its title – half-comic, half-Catholic – rang a bell; if I could remember the meaning I might be able to form an idea of the subject matter and invent plausible replies to questions the press and people at the university would be sure to start asking. An hour in my study thinking about it and I had it! Saint Apollonia's teeth was the irreverent name Spanish soldiers used to give to dice – so, unless I was very much mistaken, the novel must have something to do with gambling. It took me quite a while to come up with a vague plot involving gambling which sounded convincing – one that was blunt and straightforward yet basically allegorical; up-to-date, but traditional at the same time. Until I had a chance to read the galley proofs it was going to be mostly a matter of parrying the first thrusts by my friends and the press without contradicting too blatantly what would later show up in the novel. It was a risk but one worth taking. At last I started answering the phone.

For a couple of weeks I suffered a continuous siege from the press, friends, workmates, relatives, cultural associations, and book salesmen. Prudence dictated that I not go down to Lima until I had read 'my' novel. Everyone swallowed the barely coherent explanations I gave, except, of course, my wife, who returned to Trujillo to submit me to a domestic third degree which put me on the defensive. She knew I was incapable of writing any kind of novel, and I knew her strait-laced leftist attitudes too well to trust her – money didn't interest her, but she was a stickler for the truth. I was acting in a way radically opposed to her standards, and it was not long before this drove us apart.

The proofs came at last in a huge manila envelope. My hands trembled as I ripped it open and pulled out pages smelling of printer's ink. My one and only satisfaction came from not having been wrong as regards subject matter. The novel was, indeed, about gambling, exactly as I had guessed, but it was not long before I began to have second thoughts about claiming to be the author of what turned out to be three hundred and fifty wildly chaotic folkloric pages of a notebook set during the Spanish conquest of Peru. The novel begins with the famous tale of the sharing of the booty, the treasure from the Temple of the Sun in Cuzco, capital of the Incas, and the madness which possessed the soldiers at that time. Mancio Sierra de Leguísamo, the main character, a man devoured by a passion for gambling which never leaves him throughout the whole novel, loses at dice (the teeth of the title) his share of the booty – the enormous solid gold disc representing the sun god, El Inti. The disc was divided into quadrants and thirty-second parts by black lines drawn in a crayon-like grease, and Mancio lost it, piece by piece, as the night went on, in his madness doubling the stakes after each loss. By dawn he had lost everything.

It was not exactly a historical novel since it lacked documentary rigour (among other things), and used anachronisms quite systematically. To give it its due, it could be called 'historical fiction', but it was something of a shocker, with a clear eye on sales. Mancio Sierra was drawn sketchily, and the gambling was only an excuse to have him travel to Potosí, with all its opulence, and to experience the sinful life of Zaña and the hidden Andean valleys infested by bands of Indians turned fanatic through some gnostic rites and where Conquistador generals behaved like highway robbers. Our gambler wended his way through these tortuous paths with only one aim in life – to win back the lost sun, or enjoy a similar stroke of luck.

At times the novel reaches peaks of brilliance, I admit, but not often enough to redeem its many defects. The end lacks all verisimilitude. Mancio, thanks to the intercession of his Inca princess wife, arranges to play *huara*, a native game of chance with magical implications. His opponent is none other than the Inca Sayri Tupac, who is hiding out at the time in the secret city of Vilcabamba, where no Spaniard has yet set foot. Mancio bets military secrets and perhaps his life in yet another night similar to that in which he lost the golden sun. This time he takes part in a ritual game of chance pregnant with symbolic meaning, interrupted by women possessed, foretelling the final fate of their people (who at the time had still not been conquered). Mancio knows this game belongs to him, that he will win a fortune; he plays in a frenzy, and by dawn has won the Inca's gold and emerald breastplate, which he subsequently loses on the road to Lima in a den of cut-throats and whores.

The text is a piece of grand guignol, exaggerated, phoney, unauthentic, cynical in tone, but with all the earmarks of a bestseller. My feelings were contradictory; on the one hand it didn't seem right that so uneven a piece of work should win such an important prize, on the other, any success it had would be to my good, since officially I was the author.

There was another problem too. It is true that a literary text has no reason to reflect the author's life, but the distance between this flying serpent of a novel and my controlled, orderly existence was so great that it could not be long before the people who knew me – fellow professors at the university and especially my wife – would start to wonder. Perhaps my wife would feel, like me, that the author couldn't possibly be Peruvian; linguistic quirks pointed to this, as well as ignorance of Peruvian geography. I would have to leave Trujillo before the novel came out; subjected to all eyes, the target of never-ending speculation, the pressure would have made me confess my guilt for sure.

I had to reach a decision, not an easy one but it took me only a day. My ambition had been growing like some late-blooming, all-consuming plant during these past few weeks. It dictated its own terms and demanded I eliminate by any means at my disposal anything constituting a threat to my new situation. The root of the matter, the ten thousand dollar prize money, had impressed me enormously, and I knew it was nothing compared to the sum that the author's rights and translations into seven languages could bring in. The invitation to Barcelona to launch the book would provide the solution, and that is why I have not stopped travelling since the damned book came out. It was a great success, very impressive, first in Barcelona then at book fairs in Madrid, Frankfurt, Bologna. I was carried to and fro by editors, press attachés, agents, though once all that was over (and the routine never varied) I had plenty of free time and quite enough money. I enjoyed feeling anonymous in foreign countries where old streets teem with young people. One morning I woke up on a canal in a crate filled with straw, embracing a pretty half-dressed blonde in the middle of Copenhagen. One autumn I spent an afternoon which I can never forget playing chess with someone I didn't know on a quay behind Notre Dame. At dawn in Barcelona, next to a drunk who was singing, I witnessed a flight of swifts crossing the towers of Gaudí's Sagrada Familia. I basked in my glowing celebrity; it was a thing I had neither worked nor struggled for, and this gave me a curiously detached air which people found agreeable.

My training as a literary critic made me able to comment on the novel with an objectivity usually denied those who create; I liked to exaggerate its defects with a forthrightness rare among writers – this won me a reputation for being hard-nosed and realistic. Soon the publishing house asked me to edit a collection of Hispano-American writing and I quickly accepted the offer. I put an ocean between my present and past lives and tried to exploit to the full everything I was being offered; it was a miracle that was not going to be repeated.

Once the novel's impact was over I would need to find something else to live on, since the time would come when I would be forgotten as a writer. The history of literature abounds with authors who have written one or two brilliant books then disappeared overnight, to reappear perfectly respectably a few years later as university professors, businessmen, diplomats. I prepared to follow their eminent example and during the first year edited five first-rate texts on Native American subjects, little known but with high prestige value.

I was living in a bachelor apartment on the Via Augusta and getting a divorce when my agent Jordi called me early one morning to congratulate me on my second novel. He hadn't been able to put the manuscript down all night and couldn't wait to tell me that for this beauty we'd easily get a twenty-five thousand dollar advance from one of the publishing houses.

I was still trying to make up my mind again regarding my benefactor and his secret intentions when a messenger from Jordi came round with a photocopy of the manuscript for me to make some corrections. It was in an ordinary blue-file cover, with three hundred and nine typewritten pages and my name on the first one, well centred, with the title underneath – *Montezuma's Peacock* – and the date – the current month.

The beginning was as lively as that of its predecessor. Pascual Reyes, a Mexican cook, is on the way to Santiago de Compostela via Paris in the middle of the French Revolution, when his master, a nabob, falls dead of apoplexy on reading *The Declaration of the Rights of Man*. Citizen Pascual, alone and free, is possessed by the spirit of the social and culinary revolution at that historic moment when bourgeois interests were equally divided between gastronomy and the guillotine.

B latches on to the theme from the very start, always playing up the cruel side of events in the way I was coming to expect of him; the Mexican takes the first twist in his professional helical ascent during the September massacres of 1792. Théroigne de Maricourt, a woman famed for the strength of her hysterical passion, pulls out the throbbing liver of the Marquis de Foix, one of her ex-lovers, and asks Pascual to turn it into a sublime dish. In a fit of Republican inspiration, he prepares a pâté from the noble liver, and uses it to stuff song birds served flambéd in armagnac, with steamed salsify and chervil. From this we more or less get the tone of the whole novel; as it and the revolution advance, more impressive dishes make their appearance, either cooked or written up by Pascual. There is Robespierre duck, guillotined and roasted, basted in its own blood; lobster thermidor; *vol-au-vent directoire*; imperial boar macerated with gunpowder, pepper-corns, and cayenne pepper. The text consists increasingly of recipes given in loving detail, with every ingredient and specific quantities and painstaking instructions for the preparation, which were quite inexplicable to me. Why does one have to freeze the cream, for example, before using it to stuff fish, and why must one always prepare onion soup with pre-heated water, never cold? Why do you cut parsley with scissors, never with a knife? It is difficult to consider the work as a historical novel in spite of the fact that throughout its pages of side dishes and main courses, splashed with soup, smeared with sauce, crabs bursting, pheasants belching, we see the bulging shirt fronts of the great characters of the French Revolution and those who took part in the most famous Napoleonic battles. Every event invariably ends in an immense allegorical eating party.

At the end of two hundred unbridled pages, and a hundred and fifty recipes, we reach the denouement. This fittingly takes place at the Congress of Vienna, the party that went on for several months in celebration of Napoleon's defeat by the forces of reaction. One evening Carême, Talley-rand's brilliant cook, serves *Faisan truffé à la Saint Alliance* at a banquet to commemorate the alliance between Metternich and the Tsar. It is a tremendous success, which infuriates the bonapartiste Pascual, who begs Metter-nich to give him a chance to beat Carême at his own game by serving a dish such as the human palate has never known. The banquet takes place at the P– Palace and the cream of European aristocracy is there. After the appetizers, soup, and main dishes, the *pièce de résistance* is brought in: peacock – that is to say, turkey à la Montezuma – adorned with the feathers that had graced the crown of the unfortunate Aztec ruler, bathed in a thick brown sauce with reddish highlights, the colour of fighting cocks' feathers, and giving off a thousand exotic scents. '*C'est l'Amérique*' cries Talleyrand, who has just sold Louisiana to the United States, raising his glass. The eaters, overcome with emotion, finally lift their forks to their mouths; the outcome is not a reverent silence but a unanimous roar as princes, counts, barons, duchesses, spit fire from their inflamed gullets, their nails digging into the table cloth, their eyes popping, and their wigs suspended in air, like so many cartoon characters. A fiery torrent had flooded the palates, tongues, livers, brains, veins, blood vessels of Europe in the form of the fragrant and avenging *mole poblano*, with its seven different types of hot chilli pepper, each damnably hotter than the last, in its chocolate sauce sprinkled with sesame seeds. The cursed intriguer Metternich rises from hell, recovers his speech, and splutters 'Bring me that cook.' The martyr, however, has foreseen his intent; Pascual has hanged himself from a beam, *à la Vatel*, with full samurai honour intact.

So ends a long-winded recipe book interspersed with utterly outrageous acts defying all credibility. I cannot deny that the book possesses a certain charm, perhaps as a secondary effect of all the exaggeration, but why would B choose to write about France if he was from Latin America? Why hadn't he drawn on our land for inspiration, since it has so much to offer? Here we obviously have another 'victim of cosmopolitanism' and other literary sins which the French critics would no doubt soon pick up on. Even though I sensed that this novel would be a bestseller too, and in several languages, it went against my very grain, not to mention putting me in a very tight spot once again, this time because I did not know one damned thing about cooking.

A week later saw me installed in a nice little hotel on the Rue des Saints-Pères, catching up on culinary matters before the novel came out. If B had decided to go on with the game, I had no option but to swim with the tide, always provided, and I took this for granted, that the conditions of our unspoken agreement had not changed. I have never felt more alone in my life than I did during the four miserable months spent eating in the world's best restaurants with nobody to share dishes which took my breath away. I hadn't a friend to guide me through the thick forest of flavours where day by day I risked losing my way, trusting only to my hunter's instinct to bring me through unscathed. I was coming to realize, though, that Paris had many other things going for it. It was cosmopolitan and offered anonymity and respect for privacy, though this might be considered heartless indifference. It could be the ideal place to live for someone forced to take part in constant play-acting, as I was.

It was in one of the restaurants, La Closerie de Lilas, that I met Diana, a beautiful Jewish girl who was studying painting and had little or no interest in literature. She couldn't tell a sonnet from a sausage, but, to put it bluntly, she was wonderful in bed, and that was enough to make me fall in love and promise her in my bad French that as soon as I returned from Spain we'd live together.

In Madrid the novel was a success from the minute it came out. Once again I was involved in the marathon of interviews, round tables, panels, and book signing sessions, but by now I'd had experience and could carry it off with a panache which won me a number of admirers. This, I suppose, I alone can take credit for. Even if I wasn't the author, I certainly knew how to wear my fame with dignity, not to mention irony.

It took some nerve to overcome a paranoid feeling that someone was going to yell 'Phoney' in the middle of the whole show and knock down the house of cards. The second novel had obliged me to put on an even better performance on the tightrope over a cesspool, and I couldn't wait for the circus to be over so I could return to anonymity and the feeling of protection Paris and Diana offered.

The next two years were, if not happy, at least peaceful. We installed ourselves in Sceaux in the fashionable suburbs, and went into Paris from time to time to shop, see new shows, visit the few friends we had. Diana had her first show of watercolours in a gallery on the Left Bank and I, missing university life, was considering trying for a doctorate on the work of José María Arguedas, whose recent suicide had deeply affected me.

I was not happy constantly being compelled to play the role of the famous author who had taken me over. It forced on me a second nature, whereas before I had been of a piece; it caused me anxiety as to my own identity. I found myself growing mean with money, since in spite of all my earnings through author's rights, translations, etc., I feared expenses would be very high at the time of the hypothetical reckoning I was going to have to make with B some day. I hadn't progressed very far in what I knew of B's identity nor his motives for remaining hidden and using me as a straw man, and there was no way to make enquiries without incurring dangerous risks.

The third novel arrived at my agent's office from Italy. I flew to Barcelona by the first plane and literally grabbed the manuscript from Jordi, claiming I'd sent him my only working copy by mistake. The postmark indicated it had been mailed in Sperlonga ten days before I held it in my hands. The text which I read in the train on my return to Paris was called *Ancestors of Eniac*, a strange title which was explained only much later when I was forced to bone up on computers. If I understand the book correctly, there are two parallel story lines connected by the structural nexus that opens and closes the novel, enclosing a multitude of subplots loosely tied to the

central theme. It was based on actual historic events and dealt with them
as before with little regard for chronological order and with the same
exaggeration and shock value which spoiled the best scenes.

The book begins with a long, purring interior monologue as Mary
Shelley ruminates on her recollections of Lord Byron's challenge to Shelley
that they 'each write a ghost story' during stormy days in the summer of
1816 in the Villa Diodati overlooking Lake Geneva when the fury of the
elements made outings impossible. The poets soon grew tired of the project,
and it was the sweet, long-suffering Mary who created the Frankenstein
monster on some feverish nights when her miscarried children, the obsessive beauty of Lord Byron, the utopian preaching of her father William
Godwin and the wild whiplash of lightning intermingled.

The novel starts as a praiseworthy attempt to understand the genesis of
Frankenstein, with recourse to Freudian theory, and is most convincing,
but soon it takes off in other directions. Byron's mistresses begin to parade
through, striking obscene poses, and B settles for describing, in minute
detail, a carnival orgy in the poet's house in Venice where he and the other
men present put on a poor show when faced with the sexual appetites of
the beautiful Italians.

Little by little the story line is taken over by women relating their
adventures and misadventures to other women, melodramatic enough to
bring tears to the eyes. There are no fathers not abusive; no husband not
impotent or cuckolded; children are carried away by sickness or neglect;
paranoic priests and magistrates, raping venal soldiers, fatuous penny-
pinching poets; not one ridiculous little male is left intact by these caustic
women of the last century, though one must admit they suffer like brute
beasts and go to extraordinary lengths in their attempts to escape their sad
condition. I was suddenly overcome with a horrible doubt. What if B turned
out to be a woman? The two previous novels seemed to go against this
idea, but this had such a fervent tone of militant feminism that I began to
wonder, recalling the recent events of May '68 and wondering if B had
perhaps shared some of the ups and downs of the women in the novel. I
cast aside this idea quite soon but could never free myself of it entirely,
which caused me further discomfort as regards my strange relationship
with B.

As always, the novel ends on a grotesque note. Lord Byron's daughter,
the mathematician Ada Lovelace, who has worked side by side with her
lover Charles Babbage to construct the world's first steam-run computer, is
amazed to see her beautiful machine turn into a monster before her very
eyes. More than a computer, it sounds like an enormous textile factory

running on gears, axles, pulleys, stick shifts, pistons, and steam whistles from which a yellow vapour escapes. For an hour it runs perfectly, then a mistake, originally confined to the final digit after the decimal point, gradually works its way up with each turn of the main axle, first to units, then, implacable as a salmon swimming upstream, to the hundreds, the thousands, the millions. The gigantic machine would calculate nothing but mistakes, even in the smallest, most humble operation. The defect lay in the way the pieces had been milled, and, as the machine ground away, each thousandth of a millimetre mistake was transferred to a higher gear and yet a higher, until all the gears of the machine were misaligned, turning it into the work of a madman and totally useless.

This was the most difficult of B's works to understand – nothing was clear. Are we, the men, or are women responsible for creating monsters? Or is it simply about the war between the sexes? It is as baroque as the previous books, though somewhat more cruel and less humorous. I didn't like it at all, and even less did I like what was going to happen when it was published. I wanted nothing to do with feminism or computers or the English, and I wasn't going to change in that respect to please B or anyone else. What was going on in B's stubborn mind didn't matter a damn to me; I decided then and there not to take part in the launching of the new novel and to leave it up to my agent and the editors alone. Since I'd been invited to give a talk on Arguedas at the university in Phoenix, Arizona, I took advantage of that to check out the possibilities of worming my way into the academic world of US Spanish departments. Paris wasn't going to be a healthy place for me when this novel came out.

We settled in Albuquerque, where I found a position, which lasted for a year, as writer in residence at the university. I spent my time doing research on the Quechua sources of Arguedas's poetry and systematically avoided any discussion of my novelistic work past, present, or future, limiting conversation to my academic field – the Indians of Peru. Diana adored the immense red desert scenery and pure blue sky like the one over Trujillo, and the four-lane highways. She spent the whole of this first period painting excellent watercolours – her other talent. She had met a group of painters boasting Indian blood, and one day we were taken to see a spectacle organized by a sculptor from the region. In the deserted countryside hundreds of lightning conductors had been placed in the ground to form an immense square. Our luck held, and that afternoon a storm came up; the lightning created extraordinary forms, branching out, like a Gothic cathedral in raw savage electricity as it fell on the conductors while we viewed the spectacle from the watchman's shack.

Montezuma's Peacock won the Medici Prize for the best foreign novel that year, and the following year it won the Romulo Gallegos, but I managed to get out of going to either ceremony by pretending to be ill. Black Sparrow Press published in translation a collection of my essays on Indians with the title *Identity Path*, and it was very well received in academic circles. I was almost happy. Three years had gone by since the last manuscript had appeared, and I nursed a hope that B had forgotten me once his whim was spent. Then the envelope arrived. As when a spy's shoulder is tapped he is reminded that he can never escape his calling and lead a normal life, so it was with me. Jordi enclosed a copy of the manuscript with his letter, 'just in case you want to make any changes', and congratulated me, 'not without fear, now that you've set out to write the great trilogy which will doubtless figure as your life's work'. He enclosed Volume 1, entitled *The Long Journey*.

A trilogy! Shit! B was coming on strong. He gave the names of the forthcoming volumes, *Men of the Borderlands* and *The Return*, and the name of the whole work, *Gamov's Law*. I began reading the first volume and was surprised to find no historical references whatever. The novel – we have to call it something – takes place entirely in our own times. It is no less baroque than its predecessors, only stranger, and narrates hundreds of different life stories, all most unusual, taking place over the entire planet. The protagonists move from the slums of Mexico City to the snowcapped peaks of Nepal, from the sands of Goa to the skyscrapers of Stockholm, from Telegraph Avenue to Rue St. Jacques, drawn by insatiable whims, loves (unrequited or badly requited), humorous moments, and the unforeseen disasters of life. It is an ever moving fresco in which the stories are acted out, some in relief against others, until they either become entwined or piled up haphazardly; tales might wander on alone like a *novela ejemplar* for various pages, then meet up with a new landfall of sentiment or a treasure chest full of surprises worthy of the *Thousand and One Nights*. The four hundred and fifty pages of manuscript had neither head nor tail. To put it another way, the text lacked any visible story line or character who could give it a token of unity, or at least a uniform style. Nevertheless, for once I was totally fascinated. The book, which I believe I understood, was telling of the ups and downs of human existence with all that it had of the tragic and comic. As I read the text, for B both these extremes, in the measure in which they repeat themselves infinitely, will meet at a grey centre point by virtue of statistical laws. I don't know how to describe my reactions, but after reading it my attitude to B changed radically and my lack of curiosity about him gave way to a warm desire to meet him and to be more than his unconfessed accomplice; I wanted rather to be his friend.

For the first time we bombed. *The Long Journey*, launched with a big splash in Barcelona, fell to earth with a phhht and sank amid general indifference helped, it's true, by the ill will of some of the critics who declared the novel was impossible to follow. Only then did I really appreciate the abyss which lay between 'them' and 'us'. At a round table on Spanish TV I was particularly aggressive when discussing the work with a couple of carping critics who talked nothing but imbecilities. My master argument stressed that this was only Volume 1 of a trilogy, and that the following volumes would clarify everything (or almost everything). It was my only public appearance. From then on I spent my time in the barn we had rented on the outskirts of Albuquerque waiting for Volume II. I discovered places where wild rabbits and a sort of pheasant made their homes and organized hunting parties with students from the university. At night I reread and tabulated the novels with a view to forming an overall reconsideration of B's work from my present perspective. I prepared for a long wait, which I assumed would be a couple of years, but one year and two months later the second volume arrived from the hands of my agent. It was called, as we'd been told, *Men of the Borderlands*.

Here everything started to clear up and shed new light on previous events. It followed, generally speaking, the themes developed in the first volume, but a good number of the unfinished stories came to an end and new ones began; above all the structure of the novel began to stand out. It had something of the soaring grandeur of a Gothic cathedral but with its carved figures shaken by violent passions in the pure transparent air. I began to feel, to my total astonishment, that B was telling my own story from the moment I received the prize that afternoon in Trujillo, long ago now, up to my present seclusion in the US southwest. There are many discrepancies, perhaps deliberate to protect my identity, or because B simply didn't know much about my life. In one passage however he speaks of a 'reconciliation' as in the Elizabethan drama, and generous unforgettable phrases are voiced by the character who stands for me. Nothing is said about the end of the tale, but I was left assuming everything would be explained in the third and last volume and that everything would come out all right.

Those few pages eased my torments. The feeling of bastardy which had been with me since the beginning of the affair was now removed, and I remember weeping at length on Diana's bare shoulder; Diana, who understood nothing. I wept too because I no longer needed her. I was no longer afraid. I was free.

The critics praised the book to the skies this time, and so saved the first volume from oblivion. The general consensus was that a masterpiece was being launched with sails unfurled to a place in the sea of world literature, and according to Jordi the Nobel Prize before long.

As everyone knows the last volume never appeared. It never reached my hands nor those of my agent. B disappeared from my life forever, and the twelve years I have waited for him have been long enough for all my dreams to fade. I had been at the peak of our career; my feelings of guilt, of being a double, of usurping another's place, had left me and I was enjoying the pleasure of our tacit reconciliation. I was sharing the pleasure of celebrity with B and spent our money freely. The closest I've ever come to knowing happiness was during the first two years following the publication of *Men of the Borderlands*. I travelled back and forth between New York, Paris, and Rio with no fixed abode enjoying my wanderer's life. Yes, I was very near to being happy.

B must have died. Nobody leaves a masterpiece unfinished unless the wings of death have wafted over him. With no hope of ever meeting him or knowing him if I did I visited all the places the books had been mailed from: Speriongha, Athens, Puerto Pollensa, Poros. I breathed the air he breathed, looked on scenes and people he might have seen, and experienced a depth of feeling I could scarcely have imagined.

Some years ago in my despair I tried to write the third volume myself. Everyone had tired of waiting, I was no longer a Nobel candidate, I was washed up. I'd my fame and money but was otherwise an empty shell, absent from myself, robbed of all vitality and nerve. I'd had time to form an idea of what the third volume might be. *The Return*. It would be as mystic and outrageous as B would have liked, and lead towards a place where all the signs in the earlier novels, especially the inexplicable feminist one, converged. It would reveal B's spiritual development and the touchstone of his thought.

The title of the trilogy, *Gamov's Law* refers to the physical law which says that the universe, on having reached its maximum point of expansion from the time of the big bang, will begin to contract until it forms the Cosmic Egg, the beginning and end of all things. Certain anomalies appear at the end of the second volume – the mother comes back to life, faults show up in Time, incest becomes general. I thought I could imagine what the third volume, the one B had given the title *The Return*, might be like. It would deal with the universe in a state of total contradiction, established laws and the direction of our lives would be modified, time would run backwards so chance would be abolished, the dead would rise from their graves and all humanity from the beginning of time would gather on our planet and head towards the centre point of the universe. The whole Cosmos would acquire meaning and spiritual significance.

That was one possible version. Perhaps there would be another ending. Whatever the answer, I could never write the novel; many years have gone by and I haven't managed to. I'm only a critic. B was a creator.

It's been more than a year now since I had this new house built, the modern one on the beach at Huanchaco a few kilometres from Trujillo, where I'm writing these lines. I've come back. B took me away, a great almighty hand, and his silence brought me back; I've never discovered why he chose and then abandoned me; I think it will always be a mystery. I've found my daughter Judith married to a doctor; they've made my return bearable. I've two little grandchildren and I've written some nursery rhymes for them, little punning songs. That's all I've kept of B – a love of words. That, and a feeling of anxiety in the afternoon around the time the mailman comes.

Translated by Alita Kelley

Sergio Ramírez

The Centerfielder

The flashlight passed back and forth over the prisoners' faces and stopped on a man, stripped to the waist and glistening with sweat, sleeping face up on a cot.

'That's him. Open up,' said the guard through the bars.

The rusty lock made a noise as it resisted the key, which was tied to the end of an electrical cable the jailer wore around his waist to hold up his pants. Inside, the guard slapped the rifle butt against the wooden cot; the man sat up, using a hand to shield his eyes from the light.

'Get up, they're waiting for you.'

The man groped for his shirt; he shivered, though it had been unbearably hot that night and the other prisoners were either sleeping naked or in their underwear. The one hole in the room was high up so that air circulated only near the ceiling. He found his shirt, and slipped his bare feet into his laceless shoes.

'Speed it up,' the guard ordered.

'I'm coming, can't you see?'

'No lip, huh, or you'll get it.'

'Yes, I know.'

'You sure do.' The guard let him go first. 'Get going,' he said, jabbing the rifle into the prisoner's back. The cold steel made him shrink back.

They entered the courtyard; in back, near the wall, the leaves of the almond trees shone in the moonlight. The meat market beyond the wall began killing steers around midnight and the breeze carried back the odour of blood and manure.

What a great yard to play ball in. The prisoners must choose sides among themselves or challenge the guards to a game. The centerfield fence will be the wall, some three hundred and fifty feet from home base. If the ball was hit that deep, I'd have to make a running catch by the almond trees and, after snagging the ball by the wall, the infield would seem far off and I'd barely be able to hear the yells for the relay and I'd see the runner rounding second while I'd jump up for a branch, straddle it in one motion, and I'd reach the branch level with the wall bristling with pieces of broken bottles and I'd bring my body across carefully, first my hands, then my feet, and jump down on the other side even if I cut myself as I dropped and I'd land on the pile where they dump garbage, bones and horns, tin cans, broken chairs, rags, newspapers, dead animals, and as I ran along, I'd be caught by thistles, fall into a rushing creek, but I'd get up, with the barrage of rifle fire sounding hard and dry, but kind of dull behind me.

'Stand still. Where you think you're going?'

'To piss.'

'You're so scared you're pissing in your pants, shithead.'

The town square resembled it, with the guarumo trees by the church atrium, and me patrolling centerfield with my glove. I was the only fielder with a cloth glove – the others fielded barehand – and at six p.m. I'd still be out there and though I could barely see, no hit would get by me; I knew the ball was coming by its hum and it would drop in my hands like a dove.

'Here he is, Captain,' the guard said sticking his head through the half-opened door. The air-conditioner hummed inside.

'Let him in and get out.'

He heard the door lock behind him and he felt caged in the bare room with a gold-framed picture and a calendar with huge red and blue numbers hung on a whitewashed wall, a chair in the centre of the room, and the captain's desk in back. The air-conditioner had recently been set in the wall because the plaster was still wet.

'What time did they pick you up?' asked the captain without raising his head.

He remained silent, confused, hoping with all his might that the question was for someone else, perhaps someone hiding under the table.

'Are you deaf? I'm talking to you. When did they catch you?'

'A little after six, I think,' he said so softly that he wondered if the man had heard him.

'Why do you say a little after six? Can't you remember the right time?'

'I don't have a watch, sir, but I had eaten dinner, and I eat at six.'

Dinner's ready, my mother shouted from the sidewalk. One more inning, mum, I'd answer, I'm coming. But son, can't you see? It's dark already, how can you go on playing? Yes, I'm coming, one more inning, and the organs and violins started playing for the church rosary just when the last out reached my hands and we'd won the game again.

'What work do you do?'

'I'm a shoemaker.'

'In a shop?'

'No, I fix them at home.'

'You were a ball player?'

'Yes, I was.'

'They called you "Flash" Parrales, right?'

'That's because I had a quick snap when I threw home.'

'You were on the team that played in Cuba?'

'Yes. Twenty years ago. I played centerfield.'

'But they dropped you.'

'When we got back.'

'Your throw home made you quite a star.'

He was about to smile, but the man eyed him angrily.

The best play I ever made was when I caught a fly by the church, glove stretched, my back to the infield, and fell flat on my face on the steps with the ball. My tongue bled, but we had won the game and they carried me home on their shoulders and my mother, who was making tortillas, left the corn meal to cure me, feeling sorry and proud of me just the same, you'll always be dumb as a mule, son, but an athlete.

'Why did they drop you from the team?'

'I fumbled a fly and we lost.'

'In Cuba?'

'Yes, against the team from Aruba. It was a little dove that slipped through my hands and two runs scored. We lost.'

'Several players were dropped.'

'Well, we drank too much. You can't drink and play at the same time.'

'Hmm.'

'Can I sit?' he wanted to ask, for his legs were wobbly, but he stood pat as if they had glued down the soles of his shoes.

The captain wrote for what seemed ages. Then he lifted his head; a red insignia glowed on his army cap.

'Why did they bring you in?'

He shrugged, looking helpless.

'Aha. Why?'

'I don't—'

'Don't what?'

'Don't know.'

'So you don't know why?'

'No.'

'I've got your record right here.' He showed him a folder. 'I'll read you a few lines so you'll know all about your life,' he said standing up.

'In the outfield, I can hardly, if ever, hear the ball hitting the catcher's mitt.

But if the batter connects, a dry whack explodes in my ears and all my senses perk up. And if it's a fly heading towards me, I wait for it with love, patience, spinning under it till it reaches me and I catch it at chest level as if my hands had made a nest for it.

'Friday, 28 July, at 5 p.m., a green Willys jeep with a canvas top stopped in front of your house and two men got out; the dark-skinned man wore khaki pants and sunglasses and the blond wore blue jeans and a straw hat. The one with glasses carried a Pan Am bag, the other a guard's duffel. They stepped into your house and didn't leave till ten, without either bag.'

'The one with glasses,' he began, then stopped to swallow a huge wad of saliva, 'happened to be my son.'

'I know that.'

There was silence again, and he felt his feet growing wet in his shoes, as if he had just crossed a stream.

'The bag they left had machine-gun ammunition and the duffel was full of explosives. How long had it been since you had seen your son?'

'Months,' he whispered.

'Speak louder. I can't hear you.'

'Months. I don't know how many. He left the rope factory after work one day and we didn't see him again.'

'You weren't worried?'

'Sure, a son's a son. We asked about, we searched, but got nowhere.' He pressed his false teeth together; they seemed to be slipping.

'But you knew he was holed up in the mountains?'

'We heard rumours about it.'

'What did you think when he showed up in a jeep?'

'That he was coming back. He greeted us, but left after a few hours.'

'And he asked you to keep an eye on his things?'

'Yes, he'd send for them.'

'Ah.'

He took out more papers, typed on a purple ribbon, from the folder. He shuffled through them and put a sheet on the table.

'It says here that for three months you dealt ammunition, small arms, explosives, propaganda, and that enemies of the state slept in your house.'

He said nothing. He only pulled a handkerchief and blew his nose. He looked thin and worn out under the lamp, as if he had turned into a skeleton.

'And nothing smelled fishy, huh?'

'You know how it is, sons—'

'Sons of bitches, like you.'

He lowered his head and glanced at his shoes, tongue out and soles caked with mud.

'How long?'

'What?'

'Since you've seen your son?'

He looked him in the face and took his handkerchief out again.

'You know that they killed him. Why ask me?'

Last inning against Aruba, 0 to 0, two outs, and the white ball floated towards my hands. I went to meet it, I waited, I stretched my arms and we were about to be joined forever when it struck the back of my hand, I tried trapping it as it fell, but it bounced off and I saw a man, far away, dusting himself off at home plate, and all was lost, I had to soak my injuries in warm water, mum, because you always knew that I could field even if I'd die doing it.

'Sometimes you want to be good, but can't,' the captain said walking around the table. He slid the folder in a drawer and turned around to shut off the air conditioner. Unexpected silence flooded the room. He unhooked a towel from a nail and wrapped it around his neck.

'Sergeant—' he called.

The sergeant snapped to attention at the door and once the prisoner had been removed, he turned to the captain.

'What should I put in the report?' he asked.

'He was a ballplayer, so invent any crap you want: say he was playing ball with some prisoners, in centerfield, when the ball hit the wall and he climbed up an almond tree, jumped the wall, and we shot him as he ran across the meat-market yard.'

Translated by David Unger

María Luisa Puga

Naturally

Woody Allen has done so much harm to society. So many people have identified with him. Men and women. And they're running around loose all over the place. They're terrible, and so hard to detect. At least in the beginning. It's nearly impossible then.

It's my fault, I know; who asked me to stick my nose in where it wasn't called for? Though he was the one that got me into it, that's for sure. He got me right into the middle of things and then, so naturally that it was bewildering, he began to use the plural.

That's how all at once I inherited a whole family in which the only one who had no role to play was me.

There was himself and his mother, who had come from another country to spend her vacation with her son and meet her grandson. They hadn't seen each other for five years. Her grandson was two. And the boy had a mother, of course. But the mother and father had separated a year ago. The boy's mother had a new boyfriend, who had a son of his own and was also separated. And so on. How obnoxious, that couple.

Is it necessary to mention that I'm divorced, too?

Well, one day I met the little boy. I put it that way because the boy was the one I noticed first: so tiny and quick, with smiling eyes and a constant babbling that was unintelligible but very expressive.

I had just learned to drive, although I didn't have the car that day because I was downtown when it happened and I didn't even know how to get out of Coyoacán yet.

I really hadn't paid much attention to him, and that's the truth. I have to confess, it was because he was much shorter than I am. Just a prejudice, I know. And when I did see him I imagined him married to a feminist who was in therapy or something every Saturday. With rimless glasses. A sociologist. And that he had to take the child to his office at the publishers on a Saturday morning ... and so jubilant – a very modern father and all that. It seemed logical to me.

We were going to have a meeting about starting a literary series. Suddenly he said something about a book and dashed up to the floor above, returning in a few moments with the book in his hand. Hair all mussed, eyes shining. Rather short and stocky. And the little kid running back and forth in his diminutive way. They were so alike. Made me feel good.

Later we both hitched a ride together to Coyoacán.

In the back seat the child slept on his father's legs. He was talking, hugging the boy, caressing his ear. His hand. The boy's face against his breast. Something liquid ran through my body. I like that, I thought. He had already told me that he was separated and that the boy was with him on weekends. He was taking him to Parnassus, in Coyoacán, his favourite spot. During the week the child was with his mother.

When we got to Coyoacán the boy woke up in the midst of an awful stench.

'Do you have any diapers?'

I should have realized then: the gestures, the shoulder bag with such a clutter of things inside it, the monologue out loud, stammering and anxious to be daring

But I didn't realize.

His pants needed washing, and while he was ironing them in my bedroom I was playing with the child in the living room. The boy drew, we chatted: 'Boo ri lao! Now ift ee lao!' And while ironing he was giving my books, my things, my apartment the once-over. He would appear in the living room and ask about things, everything. He kept ironing.

Afterwards: Where are you going to eat?

I really should have realized.

My clumsy handling produced some tugging and jerking that filled the child with glee, and me with laughter, and I assume all this appealed to him, too. That we ought to go to the movies some day. Okay some day.

He called a week later. Oh, I'm so sorry, but I can't, not today. But let's get together at Parnassus Saturday morning for coffee.

How marvellous the world suddenly becomes when you're with a child! It turns interesting. It's closer to you, and it gleams. It loses its utilitarian air. I had forgotten, and suddenly I remembered. He ... does he like *me*? I didn't really know. Once he put his hand on my shoulder. Yes. Later on he talked for a long time staring right into my eyes. No. And the boy in the middle, so little, so steady in his wee size. Mischievous, talkative.

But in the afternoon: Let's go now. I have to ... And I left.

Weeks like this until one day I invited him to a party.

A look on his face that I didn't like: a smile that was deliberately sweet, deliberately tender. Probably nervous. Uptight, for sure. But why smile, I wonder?

He would arrange for someone to stay with the boy. He was sharing an apartment with a friend who wasn't in town at the moment.

I didn't have anything in mind. I didn't want to. We agreed that I would go to his place by taxi around nine; I didn't dare drive at night yet.

Alone at my place, I began to have my doubts and dozed off. At ten the phone rang. I'd fallen asleep, I told him. A quick little laugh from him, very psychoanalytical. Will you invite me for breakfast tomorrow, I asked. I don't know, I'll have to see. He was planning to meet with some friends. He would have to talk with them on the phone ... Okay, I'll come by early in any case.

I dreamed about him all night long. He approached, got lost, I lost him, he went right past me. I was really torn up. I saw an immense house covered just with blue carpet, walls, beds, tables, little platforms, stairs, everything. And the whole thing was crowded with people who were arguing vigorously, vehemently, waving their arms. Did I mention yet that he was Argentinian?

I got up very early, and even though I'd never gotten out of Coyoacán in the car before, I drove down Avenida Gabriel Mancera, pretty nervous.

I got lost, naturally, and my anxiety increased. And he didn't have a telephone. The address, the number of the building and of his apartment had been buzzing around in my dreams all night long.

When he opened the door, the sun entered my whole body. In a room that was practically bare he and the little boy were wandering around with such a lost and vulnerable air that I hugged him as if a war had been keeping us apart for years.

And I spent the day there, getting acquainted with them. Learning to love them, slowly. Feeling very surprised.

I was beginning to drive better and at any hour of the day. It was quite natural for him to ask me to take him here or there. To pick up the child, to drop him off for the night. He never succeeded in understanding how scared I felt. Sitting beside me, he would just chat about anything at all, with that tone of nostalgia, of disinterestedness in the present that one uses to recall one's childhood. Naturally he was always telling me how to get there. We would spend the whole time with my hands damp with sweat. I used to feel that the city was lying in wait, waiting for an opportunity to come down on me.

During the week we stayed at my house. My apartment is very small, and the presence of the two of us filled it up wholly. We were always going around in bewilderment. We didn't know where to put ourselves. I would try to cook and he was kissing me on the back of the neck. He was giving me a hug while I would be trying to set the table. Until we went to bed, and then the time became softer, turned into one single, smooth element through which our calm voices slipped easily.

And it was inevitable that our respective lives should surge up in their reality. The time that I spend writing. That he devotes to earning enough money to support the child. To live. The confusion then because of the differences in our rhythms. The disagreements. The first arguments. Because right off there was the uncertainty, the fear of getting hurt. The fact is that one is quite ready to be loved, but for loving, I mean in order to love, you have to have certain guarantees.

I'm speaking of those moments when, in an incipient relationship, the other party turns out to be so deeply Other. Completely unknown. One almost feels a sense of relief: that has nothing to do with me.

The little boy was the one who was coupling us together. That tiny child, along with the car, I believe. All that driving around, crammed inside a Volkswagen that I was just learning to manipulate, and with him the guide, since the truth is that I suffer from topographical idiocy.

But the history of couples is so tedious, so repetitive. One always has the impression that circumstances are about to throw a revealing and definitive light over the whole thing. That's where the urge comes from to say, Look, the fact is, I . . .

However, to reach that point, that was where his mother came in. A tiny woman with an enormous load of distress on her back. A furtive, penetrating blue gaze, for she was able to personify worry, but also, suddenly, an unaccustomed joyfulness. Openly very childish.

She would stay with the boy's mother, since after all, that was the reason she had come: to get acquainted with her grandson.

Well, I thought, so now here we go. And, truth to tell, it wasn't even that I had time to actually think this. I became aware of it only in passing because there was so little time. The situation was so new and had advanced so rapidly in such sideways directions: before his own mother arrived, he asked me one Saturday morning to meet the mother of his child. Why? And he said something that afterwards he would say quite often, always leaving me without an argument: they are a reality, an actuality. They exist, the boy and his mother. But that day her boyfriend was there too.

The child smiled in an elusive way. He didn't try to get close to anyone. He seemed content. His mother was getting his bag ready with the diapers, and it seemed like we were all going around in circles without knowing what to say. Very cordial. Meticulous in our respective descriptions of the weather.

I became attentive again by the time we had tucked ourselves into the car Where to? Me the driver. And the brand new mother, the *compañera*: where to? Wherever he would like, for the boy.

Therefore, when his mother arrived, and not the evening after, since he, in a very natural way, had already arranged that we would all go – in my car – to meet her (I was the first one to want to back out, but afterwards the others did too), then it was necessary to get acquainted with her, and again there we were, not knowing what to say, and especially his mother, who was staring at us eagerly.

But what with one thing and another he did just as he wanted with us. Just a sip. No one wanted a sip. We would have preferred a deep swallow. But no, just a sip. But leave, anyone? Not on your life. A sip, then.

That night I decided I didn't like the situation. I discovered myself feeling very much alone in this relationship. I don't know why I stuck with it. Just morbid, I think.

And he?

He had so many things to think about: his mother, and whether she was getting along or not with the boy's mother. The boyfriend had the good sense to go away on a trip. Not me. I allowed myself to be convinced that it was fundamental to be there for his birthday. His mother would prepare a special dinner.

I don't have a mother. I mean that literally, though it's probably true in the other sense of the word, too. I don't have a mother and I don't know what one does with them. What one says to them. Besides, I had thought that the really important relationship must be the one with the boy's mother. That's why I was there, but not so much. Not at all. And he was coming and going from one house to the other, from one situation to the other, hair constantly mussed, full of comments and complaints. Of necessities, all of them absolute, for the situation. 'Joint situation,' he called it.

What a hassle, right?

One day he told me he felt very insecure. Besides, everything was coming apart in his hands, and he was stumbling over everything. Just like Woody Allen, he said.

It all came to a head one day when we were to meet at a restaurant. I arrive, and the whole family is there. The only one missing is the boyfriend of the boy's mother, the one who had gone on a trip, I already mentioned that. The whole family. Just a little outing. And there he was, all mussed up and looking out for everything. The centre. The little boy bouncing around from one set of knees to the other.

At that moment I now felt myself completely out of place. But intrigued, oh yes, even though I was uncomfortable because I obviously had nothing to do there (there, where all the roles were being played to perfection) but still I seemed almost fettered by a curiosity that I insist was simply morbid.

The conversation, of course, flowed affably, extraordinarily so. The attention we all gave to everyone – oh, how fabulous. Except for him, naturally, for he was doing his utmost on all fronts without remaining quiet for a moment. Prowling around us all, stretching the net in which he had us trapped. Could it all have been on purpose? Frankly, I don't know. It didn't seem so. But his poor mother was suffering. At times she would look at him as if imploring assistance, a clarification, anything. Not finding it, she devoted herself to the child, and she did so brusquely, with a grandmotherly asperity that got us all to quiet down in confusion, because the boy wasn't doing anything wrong. He was the best one there. Why didn't she leave him alone?

The truth is, she was a mother par excellence. A MOTHER. The kind there is only one of, and her son had placed her in a situation that was none too clear.

That was why our affable, social, distant conversation was the only recourse, and oh how bored we were with each other.

That day ended quite badly, though as least cordially, and after our courteous goodbye kisses we all went off to our own homes. It was then I saw him leaving in a very subdued mood while his mother helped his son's mother, and he couldn't find anyone to go to. To complain to.

I had to know by this time, didn't I? that this relationship wasn't going anywhere. Or rather, that it was: it was going to consolidate the great lack of organization under which he lived. I had nothing more to do than to be steady. Steady and serious, for when he would have to hand the boy over to me because he needed his arms free.

The boy and I amused each other. We just switched off the others. Those big adults who were wearing themselves out so, trying to exist in harmony, naturally. With his tongue fully loosened and his slight size, he climbed up into my lap and we pretended to talk about a circus we had seen a few days before.

Yes, it's true, we were always bumping into each other during the week, and we didn't stop to linger over the fact – it was gradually becoming more frequent – that there wasn't that much to say. Especially me, since he always had some plans for taking the boy here or there, or taking his own mother shopping, or else – why not let's all go to the movies?

And at night, making love – this love that would have to nourish so much, that would need to have surged up out of something more than this (joint) situation, although his mother had gone back home now, after instructing me to take care of her son, and the boy's mother to take care of the boy.

I made clear my doubts about how things weren't going along well, and he was shocked. At the beginning he had told me: I propose to take as much care with this relationship as a master craftsman does with his work.

The truth is we had tried to be on clear and even terms with one another. A relationship among equals. That would be ideal, wouldn't it? The boy's mother with her boyfriend, and we two. Why not? The most natural thing in the world. The boy had learned to call both of us 'mother'.

He was surprised when I told him I didn't feel I was getting to know him. I knew the father of the boy, and also the ex-boyfriend of the boy's mother. And a little bit about the son of the small woman with the blue eyes. I had learned to drive, that was true, but I didn't feel as though we were going anywhere.

And when I called him a few days later and told him I was getting out, he replied, You're cruel, that's not the way to say things.

Translated by Leland H. Chambers

Hernán Lara Zavala

Mirror Images

Thin, very dark-skinned, with Zapata's moustache and Einstein's hair, Manuel Mateos entered Mikado's with Jorge, his only friend amongst the group of forty-something Mexicans, all older than them, with whom he had travelled to Japan. Forty-somethings in search of a second chance, of a second youth, men who left their wives at home because travelling with the wife was, as they said, like taking sarnies to a banquet. Mateos and Jorge were in Akasaka, the geisha district, near Ginza street. They had split from the rest of the group in order to see Tokyo without the Mexican displays of excitability, without the 'hi, gorgeous's, or, 'skinny but good', without the inevitable hot chile at meal times. They were under no illusions, with no greater expectations than having a pleasant night out. Mikado's was huge and heaving. The tables, located on different levels, faced a stage where a magician was doing tricks. The youthfulness of the hostesses, some dressed in kimonos, others in Western clothes, contrasted with the senile faces of the majority of the parishioners: politicians out on the town and executives claiming to have a business appointment.

The girls, showing no interest, passed back and forth in front of the two young men who, obediently, were waiting for a table. In the end they sat them down. They ordered two beers and when the waiter asked in English if they would like anything else Jorge had the idea of asking for a couple of hostesses.

The magician finished his number. A Japanese singer was giving a perfect rendering of 'Eleanor Rigby' when up to the table came a woman dressed in a kimono with a face as round as a full moon, with simian features and a ghostly white complexion. She sat down next to Jorge who, when he saw what she looked like, couldn't help revealing his disappointment. The girl noticed, was taken aback for a second but recovered her composure. Timid and friendly, she forced a smile: my name's Kazu she said.

The waiter brought the beers. Kazu ordered rum and coke. We're a woman short, Jorge pointed out. I don't want my friend to be on his own, he said, poking fun at himself. The waiter nodded reverently and dutifully. Where are you from, asked Kazu. Mexico. Ah, Mekishco, the Olympics!

How do you feel being so far away? Are you happy in Japan? What would you be doing in your country at the moment? Probably the same as here, commented Jorge sarcastically: drinking beer and listening to Beatles songs.

The other hostess wasn't beautiful either though considerably more attractive than Kazu: small, slim, with a fringe covering her forehead that almost touched her almond eyes and a broad and pleasant smile. Her name was Noriko and she too ordered a rum and coke. That was what they were told to do: order the most expensive thing. They exchanged questions. When she found out they were Mexicans she confessed she was a fan of Los Panchos. No, she didn't speak Spanish but she loved Mexican music. She studied English at Tokyo University in the mornings and at night she practised what she learnt, she joked. They chatted for a while until, out of the blue, she got up from the table and excused herself. Mateos watched her go and noted that Noriko sat down at another table, with another man. They were looking straight at him. He called the waiter and getting increasingly indignant, complained that his hostess had walked off and asked either that she return immediately or that they exclude her from the bill. Shortly afterwards Noriko returned. Mateos demanded she stay with him. She gazed uninterestedly into his moustache for a long moment and smiled. Kampai, she said clinking her glass against Mateos's. At that moment you began to like her.

As soon as the show finished some couples got up to dance. Mateos asked Noriko. One moment, please, she requested and Mateos's dark eyes focused on the gap between the little Japanese girl's index finger and thumb. Noriko got to her feet and went away once more showing her long, straight hair which hung down her back. Now she was making her way towards a large and busy table. There she sat down next to an elderly man who, without looking at her, nodded agreement to her explanations. They've gone and dumped you, said Jorge laughing at him in an attempt to relieve his own boredom. Ten to fifteen minutes went by. Mateos saw Noriko resignedly coming towards his table giving a wave to people here and there. She was wearing a short gold dress and matching shoes. Okay, she said, and they walked towards the dance floor. They were absorbed in their dancing when a couple came up to them and the man, who seemed to know her, addressed Noriko in Japanese while scrutinizing Mateos defiantly. Somewhere Mateos had read the Japanese don't take kindly to seeing their women with Westerners and although he, with his obvious Mexican appearance, didn't know whether or not he should include himself amongst that group, he concluded, from the look the guy was giving him, that he didn't find it at all funny seeing them together. What did he say to you? Mateos asked when the other couple moved away. A load of rubbish, replied Noriko without attaching any importance to the matter. Who is he? Dance, she replied. Is he your friend? He is my 'friend', she replied and left it at that.

When they got back to the table Jorge had had an argument with Kazu. She was grumbling that if they wanted they should get another woman over in place of her. Jorge yawned, his mouth was wide open; two tears appeared in the corner of his eyes. The waiter came over with the bill. It was closing time. At eleven? I'm sorry, government rules. Good, said Jorge. I'm pretty tired. They paid and while they were getting their change Mateos asked Noriko if they could see each other again, somewhere else. She looked at him in amusement and, well, why not, gave him a card with her phone number: call me, she said.

*

Mateos waited for her one September Sunday at half past eleven at night, at the stage door to Mikado's. Alongside him other men, all Japanese, waited patiently while Mateos smoked one cigarette after the other and didn't take his eyes off his watch. The women came out periodically in groups through a small exit into a passageway leading out to the street and they disappeared off into the night, a night which heralded dark clouds and storms. Noriko was taking her time. Or had she already come out and he hadn't recognized her? Japanese girls: all look alike. Or maybe she hadn't really taken him seriously and had avoided him. He decided to hang on as the girls continued coming out. Gradually the group thinned out and he was left on his own. At nearly midnight he recognized her: dressed in trousers and flat shoes. And she looked very young. Even younger than you, who at that time were in your early twenties. She walked past him without stopping. She made a sign to him: follow me and don't speak to me. Without knowing why Mateos remembered the man who had approached them on the dance floor. However, he walked behind her. When they reached the corner they turned right; they walked without speaking, like two strangers amongst the crowd in the street and the heavy traffic that had converged on the different night spots. When Noriko finally turned round to face him she explained that her employers didn't like people waiting for them at the exit as it was forbidden to meet up with the customers right outside Mikado's, an argument which seemed doubtful to Mateos after having seen all those who had been waiting next to him. Had she been trying to give someone the slip? The guy who had come up to them when they were dancing?

Mateos suggested they go over to a taxi to take them somewhere they could have a quiet drink. A long line of hire cars was waiting. But Noriko didn't want to take a taxi and led Mateos on foot through the dark, deserted streets on the outskirts of Akasaka. The couple left behind the neon lights, the city landmarks and the bustle of the streets. They walked for over half an hour, seemingly going nowhere in particular. Mateos went on the defensive: so many stories seen, read and heard about scams and cons perpetrated on naïve tourists surprised in the darkness of the many skies of this small but complex world. A sudden feeling of insecurity took hold of him. You looked behind you. Some way off a man seemed to be following them. Careful!: we are not all brothers. The tourist is the international nerd. They reached a strange building. Noriko tapped on the little window. Two guys looked out. She identified herself and they let them in. They went down to a dark basement packed with young people who kept staring at them: hostile or merely curious? They sat down. The looks, the secrecy of the place, the smell of marijuana and not knowing his partner, the language and the city made Mateos feel lost. Noriko ordered noodles which she devoured skilfully with chopsticks. Mateos thought he could see in the bar the guy who had been following them. Seeing his little-boy-lost expression, Noriko laughed in amusement. Mateos finished the whisky he had ordered and then another and another. It was nearly three in the morning when they left. Once in the street Noriko asked him what he wanted to do. Sleep with you, replied Mateos. Where? In my hotel, he suggested. Impossible: the security's very tight and they don't let in any non-residents. At yours? I live with my aunt. A taxi passed by, Noriko stopped it and spoke in Japanese. You were completely at her mercy.

They arrived at a small ryokan built of wood and with a tiled roof. The woman in charge, a friendly faced old lady dressed in a kimono, spoke directly to Noriko and led them through the sliding doors and between the thin walls to a room. They took their shoes off before going in; the floor was tatami; they passed into a room with a table in the centre and a dressing table in a corner. On the table there were two large bottles of beer and some biscuits; on either side, two cushions served as seats. The woman slid one of the doors across and showed them the bedroom where the only furniture was a meticulously prepared futon and a bedside radio. A passageway led to the bathroom. The old woman turned on the tap to fill the bath. She took two blue-and-white striped kimonos and a pair of towels out of a drawer. Mateos paid, the woman said thank you and took her leave with a smile and a bow. They sat down in the living room. Mateo poured the beers. Noriko took a biscuit and explained, her eyes gazing into his: their name is Nori, like me. They're coated in a seaweed which is supposed to have aphrodisiac properties. Mateos examined the biscuit, smelt it. Try it, Noriko pressed. Mateos drank a swig of beer: he sunk his teeth into the biscuit, you sank your teeth into the bait.

*

Strange voices woke him. Startled, Mateos looked around. Nobody, save Noriko who was fast asleep. He could hear however, the quiet, though insistent, voice of a man. He concentrated: he was speaking in Japanese. Was there one person or several? The whispering was coming from the adjoining room. They must be the guys who had been following him and who perhaps had just been waiting for him to fall asleep. What for, to rob him? To beat him? Pretty certainly Noriko herself was an accomplice, otherwise, why all the mystery? He noticed some sliding doors at floor level, near the futon. He woke Noriko: Who's over there? he asked in a low but firm voice. I don't know, she replied drowsily and shut her eyes again. Without moving from his side, Mateos stretched his arm out over Noriko's body and, very carefully, slid back the doors: in the half-light he could make out two bodies. He shut the doors at once. You remained at the ready.

*

He woke very early in the morning. A calm silence dominated the room. The sunlight was filtering tenuously through the windows. He looked at Noriko: she was sleeping peacefully. Mateos remembered exactly what her body had been like when he touched it during the night: fragile, slight, malleable: her skin was smooth and silky and around her private parts there was plenty of straight, black pubic hair. Her breasts were small and her nipples large and dark. After drinking the beer and eating up the noris they had gone to have a bath. Mateos had tried to take her to bed first but she told him they would make love the oriental way, having a bath first. Noriko, sitting on a stool, sang in Spanish 'Quizás, quizás, quizás' without the slightest inkling of the meaning of the words that she was pronouncing clearly and correctly while they bathed. When they finished they put on the striped kimonos and got into bed. They made love and Mateos hadn't been aware at what moment he fell asleep. Mateos's gaze woke her up: Noriko blinked two, three times. Shadows and premonitions were vanishing. Who was following us. Who spent the night behind those doors, enquired Mateos. Noriko sat down on the futon and started laughing putting her hand over her mouth. Open them, she challenged. Armed with courage Mateos slid the doors back: behind them was, indeed, a couple: both wearing striped kimonos; she was Japanese, he foreign. You focused on the man: he was the image of fear. But fear of what? Of silly little things: of the food he was eating, the air he was breathing, the ground he was standing on, the people who surrounded him. He could see that the woman was taking off her kimono and then, very delicately, she removed his. Their naked bodies embraced. She, smiling, commented: in Japan we are sensual, aren't we? Yes, agreed the man, while you were confirming that he was thin, dark-skinned, with Zapata's moustache and Einstein's hair.

Translated by Jeremy Munday

Angeles Mastretta

from *Big-Eyed Women*

Aunt Natalia Esparza

One day Natalia Esparza, she of the short legs and round tits, fell in love with the sea. She didn't know for sure at what moment that pressing wish to know the remote and legendary ocean came to her, but it came with such force that she had to abandon her piano school and take up the search for the Caribbean, because it was to the Caribbean that her ancestors had come a century before, and it was from there that what she'd named the missing piece of her conscience was calling to her without respite.

The call of the sea gave her such strength that her own mother could not convince her to wait even half an hour. It didn't matter how much her mother begged her to calm her craziness until the almonds were ripe for making nougat, until the table cloth that they were embroidering with cherries for her sister's wedding was finished, until her father understood that it wasn't prostitution, or idleness, or an incurable mental illness that had suddenly made her so determined to leave.

Aunt Natalia grew up in the shadow of the volcanoes, scrutinizing them day and night. She knew by heart the creases in the breast of the Sleeping Woman and the daring slope that capped Popocatépetl.* She had always lived in a land of darkness and cold skies, baking candies over a slow fire and cooking meats hidden beneath the colours of overly elaborated sauces. She ate off of decorated plates, drank from crystal goblets, and spent hours seated before the rain, listening to her mother's prayers and her grandfather's tales of dragons and winged horses. But she learned of the sea on the afternoon when some uncles from Campeche passed through during her snack of bread and chocolate, before resuming their journey to the walled city surrounded by an implacable ocean of colours.

Seven kinds of blue, three greens, one gold, everything fit in the sea. The silver that no one could take out of the country: whole under a cloudy sky. Night challenging the courage of the ships, the tranquil consciences of those who governed. The morning like a crystal dream, midday brilliant as desire.

* Popocatépetl: volcanic peak near Mexico City

There, she thought, even the men must be different. Those who lived near the sea which she'd been imagining without respite since Thursday snack time would not be factory owners or rice salesmen or millers or plantation owners or anyone who could keep still under the same light his whole life long. Her uncle and father had spoken so much of the pirates of yesteryear and those of today, of Don Lorenzo Patiño, her mother's grandfather, whom they nicknamed Lorencillo between gibes when she told them that he had arrived at Campeche in his own brig. So much had been said of the calloused hands and prodigal bodies that required that sun and that breeze, so fed up was she with the table cloth and the piano, that she took off after the uncles without a single regret. She would live with her uncles, her mother hoped. Alone, like a crazed she-goat, guessed her father.

She didn't even know the way, only that she wanted to go to the sea. And at the sea she arrived, after a long journey to Mérida and a terrible long trek behind the fishermen she met in the market of that famous white city.

They were an old man and a young one. The old man, a talkative pot smoker; the youth, who considered all of this madness. How would they return to Holbox with this nosy, well-built woman? How could they leave her?

'You like her, too,' the old man had told him, 'and she wants to come. Don't you see how she wants to come?'

Aunt Natalia had spent the entire morning seated in the fish stalls of the market, watching the arrival of one man after another who'd accept anything in exchange for their smooth creatures of white flesh and bone, their strange creatures, as smelly and beautiful as the sea itself must be. She lingered upon the shoulders and gait, the insulted voice of one who didn't want to 'just give away' his conch

'It's this much or I'll take it back,' he had said.

'This much or I'll take it back,' and Natalia's eyes followed him.

The first day they walked without stopping, Natalia asking and asking if the sand of the seashore was really white as sugar, and the nights as hot as alcohol. Sometimes she paused to rub her feet and they took advantage of the chance to leave her behind. Then she put on her shoes and set off running, repeating the curses of the old man.

They arrived on the following afternoon. Aunt Natalia couldn't believe it. She ran to the water, propelled forward by her last remaining strength, and she began to add her tears to the salty water. Her feet, her knees, her muscles were aching. Her face and shoulders stung from sunburn. Her wishes, heart and hair were aching. Why was she crying? Wasn't sinking down here the only thing she wanted?

Slowly, it grew dark. Alone on the endless beach, she touched her legs and found that they had not yet become a mermaid's tail. A brisk wind was blowing, pushing the waves to the shore. She walked the beach, startling some tiny mosquitoes that feasted on her arms. Close by was the old man, his eyes lost on her.

She threw herself down in her wet clothes on the white bed of sand and felt the old man come nearer, put his fingers in her matted hair and explain to her that if she wanted to stay, it had to be with him because all the others already had women.

'I'll stay with you,' she said, and she fell asleep.

No one knew how Aunt Natalia's life was in Holbox. She returned to Puebla six months later and ten years older, calling herself the widow of Uc Yam.

Her skin was brown and wrinkled, her hands calloused, and she exuded a strange air of self-confidence. She never married yet never wanted for a man; she learned to paint and the blue of her paintings made her famous in Paris and New York.

Nevertheless, her home remained in Puebla, however much, some afternoons, while watching the volcanoes, her dreams would wander out to sea.

'One belongs where one is from,' she would say, painting with her old-lady hands and child's eyes. 'Because like it or not, wherever you go, they send you back home.'

Aunt Leonor

Aunt Leonor had the world's most perfect belly button: a small dot hidden exactly in the middle of her flat, flat belly. She had a freckled back and round, firm hips, like the pitchers of water she drank from as a child. Her shoulders were raised slightly; she walked slowly, as if on a high wire. Those who saw them tell that her legs were long and golden, that her pubes were a tuft of arrogant, reddish down, that it was impossible to look upon her waist without desiring all of her.

At age seventeen she followed her head and married a man who was exactly the kind one would choose, with the head, to accompany one through life. Alberto Palacios, a wealthy, stringent notary public, had fifteen years, thirty centimetres of height, and a proportionate amount of experience on her. He had been the longtime boyfriend of various boring women who became even more tiresome when they discovered that the good notary had only a long-term plan for considering marriage.

Destiny would have it that Aunt Leonor entered the notary office one afternoon accompanied by her mother to process a supposedly easy inheritance which, for them, turned out to be extremely complicated, owing to the fact that Aunt Leonor's recently deceased father had never permitted his wife to think for even half an hour in her lifetime. He did everything for her except go grocery shopping and cook. He summarized the news in the newspaper for her and told her how she should think about it; he gave her an always sufficient allowance which he never asked to see how she spent; he even told her what was happening in the movies they went to see together: 'See, Luisita, this boy fell in love with the young lady. Look how they're gazing at each other – you see? Now he wants to caress her; he's caressing her now. Now he's going to ask her to marry him and in a little while he's going to be abandoning her.'

The result of this paternalism was that poor Aunt Luisita found the sudden loss of the exemplary man who was always Aunt Leonor's daddy not only distressing but also extremely complicated. With this sorrow and this complication they entered the notary's office in search of assistance. They found him to be so solicitous and efficacious that Aunt Leonor, still in mourning, married notary Palacios a year and a half later.

Her life was never again as easy as it was back then. In the sole critical moment, she had followed her mother's advice: shut your eyes and say an Ave María. In truth, many Ave Marías, because at times her immoderate husband could take as long as ten mysteries of the rosary before arriving at the series of moans and gasps culminating the circus which inevitably began when, for some reason, foreseen or not, he placed his hand on Leonor's short, delicate waist.

Aunt Leonor lacked for nothing a woman under twenty-five should want: hats, veils, French shoes, German tableware, a diamond ring, a necklace of unmatched pearls, turquoise, coral and filigree earrings. Everything, from underdrawers embroidered by Trinitarian nuns to a tiara like Princess Margaret's. She had whatever she chanced to want, including her husband's devotion, in that little by little he began to realize that life without exactly this woman would be intolerable.

From out of the affectionate circus that the notary mounted at least three times a week, first a girl then two boys materialized in Aunt Leonor's belly. And as only happens in the movies, Aunt Leonor's body inflated and deflated all three times without apparent damage. The notary would have liked to draw up a certificate bearing testimony to such a miracle, but he limited himself to merely enjoying it, helped along as he was by the polite and placid diligence which time and curiosity had bestowed upon his wife. The circus improved so much that Leonor stopped getting through it with the rosary in her hands and even began to thank him for it, falling asleep afterwards with a smile that lasted all day.

Life couldn't have been better for this family. People always spoke well of them; they were a model couple. The neighbour women could not find a better example of kindness and companionship than that offered by Mr Palacios to the lucky Leonor, and their men, when they were angriest, evoked the peaceful smile of Mrs Palacios while their wives strung together a litany of laments.

Perhaps everything would have gone on the same way if it hadn't occurred to Aunt Leonor to buy medlar fruit one Sunday. Her Sunday trips to market had become a happy, solitary rite. First she looked the whole place over, without trying to discern exactly from which fruit came which colour, mixing the tomato stands with those that sold lemons. She walked without pausing until she reached an immense woman fashioning fat blue tacos, her one hundred years showing on her face. Leonorcita picked out one filled with pot cheese from the clay tortilla plate, carefully put a bit of red sauce on it, and ate it slowly while making her purchases.

Medlars are small fruit with intensely yellow, velvet-like skin. Some are bitter and others sweet. They grow together on the branches of a tree with large, dark leaves. Many afternoons when she was a girl with braids and agile as a cat, Aunt Leonor climbed the medlar tree at her grandparents' house. There she sat to eat quickly: three bitter ones, a sweet one, seven bitter, two sweet – until the search for and mixture of flavours became a delicious game. Girls were prohibited from climbing the tree, but her cousin Sergio, a boy of precocious eyes, thin lips and a determined voice, induced her into unheard-of, secret adventures. Climbing the tree was among the easiest of them.

She saw the medlars in the market, and they seemed strange; far from the tree yet not completely apart from it, for medlars are cut still on the most delicate, full-leafed branches.

She took them home, showed them to her children, and sat the kids down to eat, meanwhile telling them stories of her grandfather's strong legs and her grandmother's snub nose. In a little while, her mouth was brimming with slippery pits and velvety peelings. Then suddenly, being ten years old came back, his avid hands, her forgotten desire for Sergio, up in the tree, winking at her.

Only then did she realize that something had been torn out of her the day they told her that cousins couldn't marry each other, because God would punish them with children that seemed like drunkards. And then she could no longer return to the days past. The afternoons of her happiness were muted from then on by this unspeakable, sudden nostalgia.

No one else would have dared to ask for more: to add – to her full tranquillity when her children were floating paper boats in the rain, and to the unhesitating affection of her generous and hardworking husband – the certainty in her entire body that the cousin who had made her perfect navel tremble was not prohibited, and that she deserved him for all reasons and forever. No one, that is, but the outrageous Leonor.

One afternoon she ran into Sergio walking down Cinco de Mayo Street. She was walking out of the church of Santo Domingo holding a child by each hand. She'd taken them to make a floral offering, as on every afternoon that month: the girl in a long dress of lace and white organdy, a little garland of straw and an enormous, impetuous veil. Like a five-year-old bride. The boy, with a girlish acolyte's costume that made him even at seven feel embarrassed.

'If you hadn't run away from our grandparents' house that Saturday, this pair would be mine,' said Sergio, kissing her.

'I live with that regret,' Aunt Leonor answered.

That response startled one of the most eligible bachelors in the city. At twenty-seven, recently returned from Spain, where it was said he had learned the best techniques for cultivating olives, Cousin Sergio was heir to a ranch in Veracruz, another in San Martín, and one more in nearby Asalan.

Aunt Leonor noticed the confusion in his eyes and in the tongue with which he wet his lips, and later she heard him answer:

'If everything were like climbing the tree again.'

Grandmother's house was on 11 Sur Street; it was huge and full of nooks and crannies. It had a basement with five doors in which Grandfather spent hours doing experiments that often soiled his face and made him forget for a while about the first-floor rooms, occupying himself instead playing billiards with friends in the salon constructed on the rooftop. Grandmother's house had a breakfast room that gave on to the garden and the ash tree, a jai-alai court that they'd always used for rollerskating, a rose-coloured front room with a grand piano and a drained aquarium, a bedroom for Grandfather and one for Grandmother; and the rooms that had once been the children's were various sitting rooms that had come to be known by the colours of their walls. Grandmother, sound of mind but palsied, had settled herself in to paint in the blue room. There they found her drawing lines with a pencil on the envelopes of the old wedding invitations she'd always liked to save. She offered them a glass of sweet wine, then fresh cheese, then stale chocolates. Everything was the same at Grandmother's house. After a while, the old woman noticed the only thing that was different:

'I haven't seen you two together in years.'

'Not since you told me that cousins who marry each other have idiot children,' Aunt Leonor answered.

Grandmother smiled, poised above the paper on which she was sketching an infinite flower, petals upon petals without respite.

'Not since you nearly killed yourself getting down from the medlar tree,' said Sergio.

'You two were good at cutting medlars. Now I can't find anyone who can do it right.'

'We're still good,' said Aunt Leonor, bending her perfect waist.

They left the blue room, just about to peel off their clothes, and went down to the garden as if drawn by a spell. They returned three hours later with peace in their bodies and three branches of medlars.

'We're out of practise,' Aunt Leonor said.

'Get it back, get it back, because time is short,' answered Grandmother, with a mouth full of medlar pits.

Aunt Jose

Aunt Jose Rivadeneira had a daughter with eyes like two moons, as big as wishes. The first time she was placed in her mother's arms, still damp and unsteady, the child opened her eyes and something in the corner of her mouth looked like a question.

'What do you want to know?' Aunt Jose asked her, pretending to understand that gesture.

Like all mothers, Aunt Jose thought there had never in the world been a creature as beautiful as her daughter. Aunt Jose was dazzled by the colour of her skin, the length of her eyelashes and the serenity of her sleep. She trembled with pride imagining what her daughter would do with the blood and chimeras that pulsed through her body.

Aunt Jose devoted herself to contemplating the girl with pride and joy for more than three weeks. Then unassailable fate caused the child to fall ill with a malady that within five hours had turned her extraordinary liveliness into a weak and distant dream that seemed to be sending her back towards death.

When all of her own curative talents failed to make the child any better,

Aunt Jose, pale with terror, took her to the hospital. There they tore her from Aunt Jose's arms and a dozen doctors and nurses fussed over the child with agitation and confusion. Aunt Jose watched her child disappear behind a door barred to her, and she let herself sink to the floor, unable to control herself or bear that pain like a steep hill.

Her husband, a prudent, sensible man (as most men pretend to be), found her there. He helped her up and scolded her for her lack of hope and good sense. Her husband had faith in medical science and spoke of it the way others speak of God. He was disturbed by the state of foolishness into which his wife had settled, unable to do anything but cry and curse fate.

They isolated the child in intensive care. A clean white place which the mothers could only enter for half an hour daily. So it filled up with prayers and pleas. All the women made the sign of the cross over their children's faces, they covered their little bodies with prayer cards and holy water, they begged God to let them live. All Aunt Jose could do was make it to the crib where her daughter lay, barely breathing, and beg: 'Don't die.' Afterwards she cried and cried without drying her eyes or moving an inch until the nurses told her to leave.

Then she'd sit down again on the benches near the door, her head in her hands, without appetite or voice, angry and surly, fervent and desperate. What could she do? Why should her daughter live? What could she ever offer her tiny body full of needles and catheters that might interest her enough to stay in this world? What could she say to convince her it would be worthwhile to make the effort, instead of die?

One morning, without knowing why, enlightened only by the ghosts in her heart, she went up to the child and began to tell her tales about her ancestors. Who they had been, which women wove their lives together with which men before she and her daughter were united at mouth and navel. What they were made of, what sort of work they had done, what sorrows and frolics the child now carried as her inheritance. Who sowed, with intrepidity and fantasies, the life it was up to her to extend.

For many days she remembered, imagined, invented. Every minute of every available hour Aunt Jose spoke ceaselessly into the ear of her daughter. Finally, at dawn one Thursday, while she was implacably telling one of these stories, the child opened her eyes and looked at her intently, as she would for the rest of her long life.

Aunt Jose's husband thanked the doctors, the doctors thanked the advances in medical science, Aunt Jose hugged her daughter and left the hospital without saying a word. Only she knew who to thank for the life of her daughter. Only she knew that no science was capable of doing as much as that element hidden in the rough and subtle discoveries of other women with big eyes.

Aunt Concha Esparza

Near the end of her life she cultivated violets. She had a bright room that she filled with flowers. She learned how to grow the most extravagant strains, and she liked to give them as gifts so that everybody had in their houses the inescapable aroma of Concha Esparza.

She died surrounded by inconsolable relatives, reposing in her brilliant blue silk robe, with painted lips and with an enormous disappointment because life didn't want to grant her more than eighty-five years.

No one knew why she hadn't tired of living; she had worked like a mule driver for almost all of her life. But those earlier generations had something that made them able to withstand more. Like all earlier things, like the cars, the watches, the lamps, the chairs, the plates and pots of yesteryear.

Concepción Esparza had, like all her sisters, thin legs, huge breasts and a hard smile, absolute disbelief in the plaster saints, and blind faith in spirits and their clownish jokes.

She was the daughter of a physician who participated in the Revolution of Tuxtepec, who was a federal deputy in 1882, and who joined the anti-reelection movement of 1908. A wise and fascinating man who filled life with his taste for music and lost causes.

However, as fate likes to even the score, Concha had more than enough father but less than enough husband. She married a man named Hiniesta whose only defect was that he was so much like his children that she had to treat him just like another one of them. He wasn't much good at earning money, and the idea that men support their families, so common in the thirties, didn't govern his existence To put food on the table, keep house and buy coverlets for the beds, to pay for the children's schooling, clothe them and take care of other such trifles, was always up to his wife, Concha. He, meanwhile, schemed up big business deals which he never pulled off. To close one of these deals, he had the bright idea of writing a cheque on insufficient funds for a sum so large that an order was given for his arrest and the police arrived looking for him at his home.

When Concha found out what it was all about, she said the first thing that popped into her mind:

'What's happened is that this man is crazy. Totally nuts, he is.'

With this line of reasoning, she accompanied him to his trial, with this line of reasoning she kept him from mounting his own defence, which might have really done him in, and with this line of reasoning she kept him from being thrown in jail. Instead of that horrible fate, with the same argument Concha Esparza arranged for her husband to be put in an insane asylum near the pyramid of Cholula. It was a tranquil place, run by friars, at the foot of the hills.

Grateful for the medical visits of Concha's father, the friars agreed that Mr Hiniesta could stay there until the incident of the cheque was forgotten. Of course, Concha had to pay for the monthly maintenance of that sane man within the impregnable walls of the asylum.

For six months she made an effort to pay for his stay. When her finances could allow no more, she decided to retrieve her husband, after first having herself declared his legal guardian.

One Sunday she went to get him in Cholula. She found him breakfasting among the friars, entertaining them with a tale about a sailor who had a mermaid tattooed on his bald spot.

'One wouldn't look bad on you, Father,' he was saying to the friar with the biggest smile.

While Mr Hiniesta was talking, he watched his wife coming down the corridor to the refectory. He kept talking and laughing for the whole time it took Aunt Concha to arrive at the table at which he and the friars were talking with that childish joy that men only seem to have when they know they're among themselves.

As if unaware of the rules of a gathering such as this, Concha Esparza walked around the table in the clickety-clacking high heels she wore on occasions she considered important. When she was in front of her husband, she greeted the group with a smile.

'And you, what are you doing here?' Mr Hiniesta asked her, more uncomfortable than surprised.

'I came to get you,' Aunt Concha told him, speaking as she did to her children when she met them at school, pretending to trade them the treasure of their freedom in exchange for a hug.

'Why?' said Hiniesta, annoyed. 'I'm safe here. It's not right for me to leave here. What's more, I'm having a good time. There's an atmosphere of gardens and peace here that does wonders for my spirit.'

'What?' asked Concha Esparza.

'What I'm telling you is that for now I'm fine right where I am. Don't worry. I have some good friends among those who are sane, and I don't get along badly with the loonies. Some of them have moments of exceptional inspiration, others are excellent speakers. The rest has done me good, because in this place even the screamers make less noise than your kids,' he said, as though he'd had nothing to do with the existence of those children.

'Hiniesta, what am I going to do with you?' Concha Esparza enquired of the empty air. Then she turned and walked towards the exit with its iron grille.

'Please, Father,' she said to the friar accompanying her. 'You explain to him that his vacations cost money, and I'm not going to pay for one day more.'

One can only guess what the father told Mr Hiniesta, but in fact that Monday morning the latch on Aunt Concha's front door made a slow sound, the same leisurely noise it used to make when her husband pushed it open.

'I came home, Mother,' Hiniesta said, with a mourner's sadness.

'That's good, Son,' answered his wife without showing any surprise. 'Mr Benítez is waiting to see you.'

'To offer me a business deal,' he said, and his voice recovered some liveliness. 'You'll see. You'll see what a deal, Concha. This time you'll see.'

'And that's the way this man was,' Aunt commented many years later. 'All his life he was like that.'

By then Aunt Concha's guesthouse had been a success, and had provided her with earnings that she used to open a restaurant, which she closed some time later to get into real estate, and which even gave her the opportunity to buy some land in Polanco* and some more in Acapulco.

When her children were grown, and after Mr Hiniesta's death, she learned how to paint the waves at 'La Quebrada,' and how to communicate with the spirit of her father. Few people have been as happy as she was then.

That is why life really infuriated her, leaving her just when she was beginning to enjoy it.

Translated by Amy Schildhouse

---

* Polanco: an expensive district in Mexico City

Fernando Ampuero

Taxi Driver, *Minus Robert De Niro*

That night the little motor driving the wipers wasn't working properly, so the windscreen was smeared with drizzle. But I could see, or imagine, what was going on. It was more or less the same old story I knew so well. The two drunks were standing in the middle of the street, oblivious to the traffic. Great hugs of affection, staggering about, with occasional clashes of heads that made them seem like two bulls about to lock horns in combat. Yet instead of fighting, these poor guys – dressed up like office workers, probably bank clerks – did nothing more than roar with laughter and gesticulate like opera singers.

And all the while I was parked by the side of the road, silently waiting. With my lights off, my hand on the ignition. And once again, I had doubts about it. It was hard to decide whether or not to go on with this dirty business.

My most recent experiences hadn't exactly been good ones. Profitable, yes, but not good by any stretch of the imagination. And that was precisely my problem. I needed to earn a lot more money. My youngest boy, Raulito, was born with one of those freak illnesses that occur once in every hundred thousand – weak neck muscles that keep him from holding his head straight, which means he constantly needs treatment and medicines. If I'd still been in the law practice, like a year ago, things wouldn't have been so bad. My job as legal assistant could be profitable. But now I was out of a job – the legal hounds in the labour division couldn't find any work, because the present government couldn't give a damn about strikes or labour stability. So since then I've been going flat out with the taxi, and doing the drunks at weekends.

Becoming a taxi driver was the obvious thing to do, because I owned my own car – an ancient Pontiac – and had nothing else to do. I worked twelve-hour shifts each day, as if it were a rented car. The other thing, the drunks that is, seemed at first just like another crazy stunt in this crazy city, and yet it gradually became a temptation. A taxi-driver friend, a black guy called Raimundo, explained it to me.

'What you do is you steal and sell drunks,' he said. 'It's heaven sent! You earn more in a night than others make in over a week. Are you up for it?'

I laughed a good while at this. I could understand stealing from a drunk, but it was the first time I'd heard that anyone could sell one.'

'Are you serious?' I asked him.

'Of course!' I'd only known Raimundo for a few months, but felt I could trust him. 'First you catch your drunk, then you clean him out, then you sell what's left. It's the best way to take full advantage, without getting your hands dirty or leaving any traces ... it's pretty unlikely that the guy will remember you a few days later anyway, but if they find a gold lighter or a smart watch on you, you could end up in the slammer. So it's better all round to sell the drunk.'

'But who d'you sell him to?'

'There's lots of joints with crackheads and others who're keen to buy. Depending on what you've got to offer, they'll give you between fifteen and eighteen soles. What they're after is the drunk's clothes, his shoes, his things, and above all, if he has money, his credit cards.'

When I realized he was serious, I got worried.

'Isn't it dangerous?' I said.

'A bit, but not very. The biggest risk you run is having to drive around a bit while you wait for the drunk to fall asleep in your taxi.'

'I can't see that.'

'I swear there's nothing more to it!'

'What happens if the guy wakes up just as you're picking his wallet?'

'Nothing! Remember, the guy's drunk and you have the perfect excuse. You can say you were looking for a card to find out his address. You could get mad and shout at him for falling asleep, making you waste your time, getting the seats dirty.'

Raimundo certainly had it all worked out. He'd been at it for a year, and apart from taking care over all the details, he was obsessed with playing safe. The very first thing you do, he said, is to check all the bulges in their clothing, because with the way things are these days, a lot of people carry a gun in their belt.

'So what d'you do then?'

'Some people just steal the gun and carry on,' he said. 'But not me. I prefer to wake the drunk up and ask him to get out. With guns you never know what might happen.'

Methodical to the point of being obsessively meticulous, Raimundo had been a government employee. He was one of thousands who took redundancy money to give up their job (as part of the cutbacks in bureaucracy) and invested their capital in a taxi. He drove a 1987 Toyota Corolla, in great condition, and he was a persuasive talker. Like a true friend, all Raimundo wanted was to give me a helping hand so I could become his associate.

It took me a good three weeks to weigh up the pros and cons of his scheme.

Throughout those weeks, aware that something had changed inside me, I plied my trade as usual. But it wasn't the same. As the days went by, I could feel I was different: I didn't say a word to my passengers, I wasn't listening to the news on the radio all the time, I didn't curse my bad luck. I was going over and over the business with the drunks in my mind. The idea was stuck in me like a splinter in a very sensitive nerve.

Then at the beginning of August, on one cold morning between Friday and Saturday, I finally decided to follow in Raimundo's footsteps, and I picked up my first drunk.

That was in Breña. I had just dropped off a customer and had turned into a wide, deserted avenue to try to find my way back to the centre, when I saw him on the corner. He looked like the perfect candidate. He was reeling all over the street, with a stupid grin on his face. As soon as he saw me, his hand shot out as if he was catching a bird in flight.

I came to a halt. The drunk stuck his head in the right-hand window.

'Evening,' I said.

'Goo' evenin',' he replied. ''M goin' to Chacarilla ... Hu ... how mush?'

'Eight soles.'

'Eight solesh!' he complained, his eyes glazed over. 'You outta your min'?'

That was a nice touch from a lunatic like him, but I was ready to put up with anything.

'It's fifty per cent extra after midnight,' I explained. 'Besides, it's a long way.'

'I'se pay you six,' he said.

'No, it's not worth it.'

'Se'en.'

'No thanks. Eight. Take it or leave it.'

The guy stared at me, screwing up his eyes. The way I had stuck to my price and refused to bargain must have created a good impression, because if I intended to rob him, I wouldn't have risked losing my victim like that. He got in.

'Head for the Primavera bridge,' he said, settling in the back seat. 'When we get there, I ... I'll tell you the way. Got any music?'

'Of course,' I said, and switched on a station playing boleros.

Five minutes later, when we had only reached Lince, the guy was flat out: sleeping the sleep of the just.

But I, goddamn it, felt as guilty as Cain. I was sweating so much the steering wheel kept slipping through my hands. I was scared we might run into a police car or a private security firm. But I took the chance and drove over towards Campo de Marte, headed down a dark street, swerved around a few times to make sure he was fast asleep, then cleaned him out. He had a ten dollar bill and two hundred and twenty-five soles in his wallet. Not exactly a fortune, but the fact is it was just what I needed.

It was an unfinished job, typical of a greenhorn. I looked for a park bench, got the drunk out of the car as gently as I could, then led him to the seat – the poor guy let himself be led like a stone blind man – and laid him down on his side so he wouldn't fall flat on his face. How long would he be safe like that? Not very long, I reckoned, because even before I drove off I could see the park bushes swaying about suspiciously.

Yet it had worked, more or less. And it had whetted my appetite to get started properly.

*

Generous and a smoothtalker, Raimundo was an excellent teacher. He devoted over an hour of his next Saturday-night shift not only to going over the basic points but also to showing me two guys sleeping blissfully stark naked in the middle of the street: 'That's how our clients end up,' he said, and then gave me a tour of several outlets for selling drunks in La Victoria.

'First rule: never take two drunks together,' he told me. 'I've heard of a lot of greedy people who are no longer with us because they thought they could stuff their pockets with both hands at once … ah, and another thing, that'll save you time: study the way people behave and get your eyes trained. Not every drunk looks as if they're about to fall over; there's also the ones holding themselves very erect so you hardly notice a thing. But you can tell by the way they walk: all of a sudden their legs give way on them. They're the ones I say are drunk on air.'

'On air?'

'Yes, on air, from the shock it gives them. They spend all night drinking in a stuffy bar, then they come out into the fresh air. They feel dizzy, but fight it, and soon you can see them up against a wall, blinking their eyes as though they were seeing double. There's a lot of them in the disco doorways in the centre of town, or outside the salsa dives. All you have to do is wait: if you drive past slowly, they always hail you.'

'But do they doze off straightaway?'

'In an instant. Of course, you have to bear in mind that you'll always come across the odd one who's so stubborn he refuses to keel over, but most of them do.'

'I put mine to sleep with boleros.'

'That's a good idea,' smiled Raimundo, glancing down at the glove compartment of his car. 'But I can recommend something better,' he pulled out a cassette: 'Chopin. Sonatas, piano music, it never fails. You can buy it in any street market.'

Clutching my Chopin and all the courage I could muster, I set out on an incongruous tour of bars, discos, provincial clubs and salsa dives, determined to succeed. In the space of two months, I picked up a record of sixteen drunks, at an average of two hundred and fifty soles each, without counting selling them on, which brought me between fifteen and twenty more a head.

As time went by, I learnt a lot of other things as well. My buyers not only took account of the value of the drunk's clothing, glasses and other personal effects, but above all how deeply he was asleep. If he were only dozing, they gave me less. If on the other hand they shook him a couple of times and he still slept like a log, they paid up without a word. Above all, they wanted to avoid any struggle, fight, or possible trouble with the law.

I also found out there were about five of us taxi drivers in on the business, and gradually got to know them all. And although we didn't all sell our merchandise at the same places, at least three others had followed Raimundo's advice and put their faith in Chopin. Once Raimundo organized it so all five of us met up in a bar and got drunk together. Afterwards we stood out in the street a good while, watching the other taxis go by. It gave me the shivers.

But don't imagine all our work was simple plain sailing. It had its good points, of course: it's a real pleasure to drive at night, the roads are clear and there's no danger of the engine overheating, but then there are always people who are just waiting to fall on you at any moment, gangs who attack taxis, if you're lucky, you can escape wielding the wrench – everyone in our group said he'd been attacked at least two or three times – and then there's the police, who are even more difficult to shake off, most of them invent some nonsense to get their bribe.

So with the drunks it's win some, lose some, but you win a lot more, and that includes a fair share of 'eye-openers' as Raimundo calls them, because as well as helping me to make ends meet (which is still the main reason for me being involved in this business) it's changed my view of things.

Nowadays it's 'an unimpeded view in the rear mirror'. The whole world passes through that tiny rectangle and takes shape as it does so. Sometimes it's a smile; at others, a threat. I see faces, dozens of faces pass by: timid young men, provincial bumpkins, loudmouths, silent types, sad old folk, unfathomable ones, women with marks of the violence they have to suffer, even despicable people who try to jump out without paying.

And I've more than one odd experience to tell of . . .

A few days ago, past midnight in Quilca, I picked up a woman who was silently watching two people fighting. She got into the front – she smelt of a mixture of perfume and drink – and gave me an address in Jesus Maria. To avoid being joined by her argumentative friends, I stepped on it. She seemed decent enough. I glanced at her silhouette out of the corner of my eye a couple of times. About thirty-five, well dressed, respectable looking, and still attractive despite being on the plump side. She stared straight in front of her for the entire journey. It was only a block before we arrived that she turned towards me: 'Stop here, will you?' she asked. 'I don't have any money, but there's something I can do for you.' She took me so much by surprise I didn't say a word. Seconds later she unzipped my flies with disturbing speed, and plunged her face into my crotch. Her mouth was so wet, her hair moved so gently . . . I couldn't control myself. I lay with my head back on the seat, panting, exhausted.

The woman got out of the car without another word, while I sat there, a strange sensation flooding my body. I wasn't thinking of the petrol or the money I had lost, or the medicines Raulito needed, or anything else in particular. I think it was more like a feeling of anxiety, a kind of painful relief, though I'm not sure if that explains it.

Another drunk I think of a lot was a fat guy who was completely out of it, and fell over every couple of steps. He stopped me, dived into the back seat muttering something about his mother's age: 'she's so old, so old' and before we'd gone ten blocks was snoring loudly. While I was searching for a dark street, I took a good look at him. He was a perfectly ordinary fellow, a bit ridiculous-looking perhaps, but with nothing special to distinguish him from any other drunk in the world. As I pulled out his wallet, which only contained about three hundred soles, I felt something fall to the floor. I switched the car light on and saw it was a photo in a plastic cover. On it was written: 'To my only son, with all my love.'

As I switched the light off, the fat guy stirred: 'What's going on? What's going on?' he protested in a feeble voice. He waved his arms about in surprise almost like a child, but before I could say a word he had fallen asleep again, so I headed for one of my usual buyers. In the journey though he woke up another three times. I looked in the rear-view and saw his head was lolling about as he kept weakly repeating: 'What's going on? What's going on?' I thought if I heard him say it one more time, my brain would explode. And when he did, I screeched to a halt, took his wallet out again, stuffed the money back in it, and gave him a couple of slaps to wake him up properly

'Where d'you live?' I shouted furiously at him.

The little plump guy looked at me, terrified.

'In Arenales avenue,' he said: '32nd street.'

I put my foot down, and ten minutes later the fat guy disappeared into a grimy three-storey building. I still don't know why he of all people managed to drive me crazy like that.

*

It wouldn't be so bad if that was all there was to it. Unfortunately, there was more: something even more unpleasant happened to me. I had been thinking about it, and was at the point where I was wondering whether to give up the whole business or not, when Raimundo suddenly appeared and pulled up in front of me. He got out of his car, slid into mine, and realized I was checking out the two drunks screeching like opera singers.

'You waiting for them to split up?'

'Yes, but I think it's going to be a while yet.'

'When they take their time like that, it means they live in different directions.'

'So?'

'So perhaps we can take one each.'

'Maybe.'

My voice must have betrayed a certain reluctance or lack of interest, because Raimundo looked at me closely and asked in a worried tone:

'Is something wrong?'

I could have smiled back at him or denied it, said there was no problem, but I was still upset. So I told him all about it.

'It's something that happened last night,' I said, keeping my possible client in sight. 'I picked up a drunk whose clothes were dirty, as if he'd fallen down or been propped up against a wall. He was one of those whose tongue gets tied when they try to speak, and to tell the truth I didn't think I'd get much out of him.'

'So it was wasted effort?'

'No, on the contrary: he had fifteen hundred soles on him.'

'Fifteen hundred!' fascinated, Raimundo almost shouted the words. 'Who was he? The sweet potato king?'

'No, he looked as if he came from here, from Lima. He was stocky, broad-shouldered, he looked a cool customer, a bit of a creep. He fell asleep in the back, and slowly slid down out of the rear-view mirror. He must have been a money changer or an electronic goods salesman to have all that money on him; I've no idea which. But he was wearing a solid gold bracelet on his right wrist, a real hefty piece.'

Raimundo bridled, suspecting I had stolen the drunk's bracelet, but I told him that wasn't what had happened.

'What did happen then?' he asked impatiently.

'I had another kind of problem, pal . . . the guy kicked it.'

'Kicked it?' Raimundo repeated, in astonishment. 'Are you trying to tell me he died?'

'Yes.'

'What? While you were going through his things . . .? Don't tell me you hit him with something!'

'No, he just died all of a sudden, I don't know why. It must have been a massive heart attack, because from the moment he fell asleep, he didn't budge an inch. And what really got me was that I hadn't realized! The coloured guys at Iquitos street, which was the closest place, were the first ones to get the shock. 'Listen, pal, this one's a stiff,' the kid who prices the merchandise told me. You know, that sick, skinny one with the needle-marks all over his arms. I thought he was trying to be smart, but when I looked round I saw the drunk lying on his side staring up at the roof, his eyes wide open and a trail of spittle dangling from his chin.'

'Holy shit!' Raimundo groaned. 'So what did you do?'

'That's what I'm so upset about . . . what I did was . . . I looked up and down the street, staying as calm as I could; I looked at it all with a smile on my face, scratching my head as if nothing unusual had happened; the coloured kid was still inside the car, working out how much the bracelet, the clothes, the shoes, the credit cards were worth, and swapping glances with two of his friends outside. 'Yes, brother, this one's cold alright,' he told me again. So, I gripped the steering wheel tight and said to him: 'then you'll have to pay death duties: another five soles. Twenty-five altogether.' The kid shrugged in astonishment, then looked angry, but I wasn't going to back down: 'Dead people don't fight or wake up,' I said straight out. 'All the easier for you.' The kid thought it over . . . looked at the bracelet again, nodded his head a couple of times, and finally put his hand in his pocket.

Tense, leaning against the car door, Raimundo looked at me amazed: 'I don't believe it,' he murmured, 'shit, I don't believe it!' Then he fell silent for a while. All of a sudden though, as if by magic, he sat up beaming and burst out laughing. He was really excited, and beat out a wild rhythm with both hands on the dashboard. 'That's great, brother, just great!' and he added: 'You were fantastic! that means you've sold your first stiff!' He burst out laughing again, and said: 'That really makes you leader of the gang!'

He didn't give me time to react.

I think I felt that deep down he was proud of me, that he sincerely admired me, even put me on a pedestal as a model to be copied.

And by the time I got round to wanting to talk to him about my doubts and worries, the opera singers caught our attention again.

'Look,' said Raimundo, who had been keeping an eye on them. The two of them had started off in opposite directions. 'The farewells are over.'

We saw the drunker of the two come to a halt under the red glow of a traffic light.

'That one's mine,' I said.

Then everything changed: we were caught up in the chase, everything came down to a single, shared objective.

Raimundo left my car and went cautiously back to his own. I mentally filed my stiff as a closed case, another lesson learned, turned my key in the ignition and started the engine. A gentle rumbling filled the air, like a domesticated peal of thunder. A few metres away, the engine of Raimundo's taxi started up exactly the same, although you could tell the engine was less powerful. Then, in unison, as if we had agreed on it, our headlights came on. The street was lit up. Blinded, one of the drunks lifted an arm across his face; the other one came lurching towards me, raising a limp hand in the air.

Translated by Nick Caistor

Senel Paz

Don't Tell Her You Love Her

Arnaldo told everyone I was going to be sleeping with a woman that night. He didn't tell them it was Vivian, of course, but really, someone must have guessed because no one at school is that stupid. So that day I waited for everyone to finish showering, and when there was no one left and there was no one to start hurrying me up, I went in and started to have a shower myself, nice and slowly. I scrubbed myself hard, pretty hard, soaped myself over and over again, and even did my fingernails. I thought perhaps she might smell me here, or there she'd touch me. I don't know, she really was going to touch me and I wanted to be nice and clean and smell good. I went over in my mind the places where, when it was my turn, I might kiss her, where I *had* to kiss her, according to Arnaldo, so that she'd *never* forget me, so that she'd never forget this first time with a man, with me, and so that, even as a little old lady, when she thought of me she could only remember me in a good light. Then Arnaldo had gone over three or four things that you *have* to do to women, and above all he explained that I should never, ever, tell her I loved her, not even at the moment of climax, because if a woman knows you love her, you see, that's when you're a goner, she gets it in for you and makes you suffer as much as she can. But that day I was singing away and everything. I scrubbed my ears, this way and that, I shampooed my hair, I scrubbed my back, I shaved carefully, I brushed my teeth and my tongue, I tell you. I was gleaming and I was so content that I smiled whenever I passed my image in the mirror and made little signs to myself as if I was Charles Chaplin or someone like that because, just think, I knew what was going to happen, and it was the first time, and it was with Vivian and, I swear to you, I was trying not to think about anything, not to jump the gun, trying to make sure I had a lot of respect for her in my mind; but you know what your mind's like, what my mind's like, I can say to my head don't think about that because it's not respectful and it says: *yeah, yeah, course I won't think about that.* But really it's all lies, that's what it's thinking about more than anything else. So, okay, I faced up to what that head of mine was thinking, but I did want to respect Vivian and I didn't want to come on to her too fast; but, my mind, I'm telling you, it was thinking about that and my penis, by itself, was getting all carried away, and so what I did was to grab hold of the wash basin and concentrate hard on a field of little flowers, a very large field, very many little flowers, and it all went away and I respected her, because when I get turned on for the thrill of it or when I shouldn't, like in the classroom, for example, I always think of little flowers and it works. But they have to be yellow. So that day, as I've mentioned, I was in the bathroom, ecstatic with that feeling I get when I think of Vivian, and with other feelings as well. I'd finished and was sparkling clean and I opened the door. What a shock, everyone was waiting for me, so quiet I hadn't heard them, in a double line which went all the way to my bed, the court that's going to awaken the king and queen. 'Ha, ha-ha, ha-haaaah, ha!' they greeted me. The sods. And straight away they started hitting me with pillows and slapping me round the neck. I tried to shut the door. 'So you were going to do the dirty deed without telling the lads, eh? they said. 'We need to spruce him up!' And they carried me naked and put me on a chair, clipping me round the head and shoving me around. 'Shall we put polish on his balls to make them shine?' 'No, no, gentlemen, not a good idea, takes too long.' 'And toothpaste under his arms?' 'Get some talcum powder!' They decided I wouldn't be smart enough in my going-out shirt – I'd kept that pretty quiet, hadn't I? – but should wear the little lilac-coloured pullover that they'd brought back for Jorge from Czechoslovakia. I'd had oysters, hadn't I? – they put something like five types of deodorant and aftershave on me, they forced me to eat a peppermint so my breath shouldn't smell. 'My breath never smells.' They checked my nails, took me over to the mirror and when they'd had enough of combing my hair they decided there wasn't a film actor who was better looking. They checked through my wallet and added the lads' contribution. They were messing around, they were friends, and envious, but it was nearly three o'clock, 'gentlemen please', it was late, and so they left me, those sods. Arnaldo once again went over how I had to act so that people there wouldn't know it was my first time, and he wished me luck, a lot of luck, and said that when I got back I must wake him up and tell him how it went, that I shouldn't tell Vivian I loved her. He told me again I shouldn't say it, because you could see that I was the sort who might fall into that trap. I still had my doubts, I can tell you, at that moment. No, right then I began to have more doubts than ever before and to get nervous. I wanted time to go backwards and for the moment not to arrive, right then. I wondered if I was doing the right thing, if I'd been right to demand this from Vivian and if asking for her to do it really meant that I loved her in the way that I did love her. But I couldn't back down now, there was no way, just imagine it. Arnaldo, what would he think? And now the others knew. Do you see, I couldn't back down? Unless I got a terrible stomach ache or the rain really started pouring hard. No way. And then suddenly I remembered the caramel custards. That's what I remembered. I never used to like sweet things, or I didn't like them very much, but here in the halls they're always serving them up and it's their soft movement, their erect shape, their colour, that flirty 'come-and-get-me' way the custards look at you, that reminds me of Vivian's breasts, you'll probably say I'm mad, her very beautiful breasts that fit in the cup of my hand, a single kiss of my mouth, and I gobble up three, four, five custards. I swap them for fish. I don't know if it was at that moment that the custards passed through my mind, or if it was later, while I was on my way to fetch her from her hostel. She came out for me dressed in black. A blonde girl dressed in black is the most beautiful thing there is. And I couldn't back out because I had a political commitment. You see. Last year I was the best young cadet but I couldn't be admitted as a full party member because I was a bit immature, they said, and I had to work. They gave me a year to work and become more mature, to read the newspapers, to learn about the international situation. And I was doing all that until along came Vivian to the class, and I've told you what happened to me. In the cadets assembly I hardly got any votes at all. I'd already jumped the gun and had sent word home that I'd been chosen as the best cadet and that this time for sure I'd be a full member. I jumped the gun and they didn't vote for me. Instead I had one hour there with them criticizing me, saying I'd lost fitness and how did I feel because the important thing was for me to be able to take criticism, to process it as the Youth Leader says, and I said yes, I could accept it, I was processing it, but you can be sure I made a good note of those who didn't vote for me. Javierito for one didn't vote for me. Then Arnaldo told me that holding something back was worse than not taking criticism and that I should realize that I wasn't keeping up with classes and that I was spending all my time holding hands with Vivian. 'And on top of that you haven't got any fighting spirit, Pedro, son, and the world needs you to pay more attention to *that*.' There was me and Arnaldo in a corner discussing, analysing things. He'd been sent to do political work with me, I realized, and I did feel sorry because he was like a brother to me, and things were going to be tough for him. I felt sorry until he said to me: 'You know what's up with you? Your problem with Vivian.' 'I haven't got any problem with Vivian, give me a break.' 'Yes you have, boy. Vivian is a very demanding woman; and your relationship has reached a point, has reached such a point of development, how can I put it, well, that you've got to sleep together. Otherwise you'll *never* be a party member.' What kind of woman did he think she was? 'Look, comrade,' he butted in, 'persuade her. You know what? Things are different these days. In the past, you'd get to thirteen or fourteen and your dad or a brother of yours would take you to a brothel and that's how you started. Not now of course, because we're under socialism and that was a social blight and it had to be eliminated. But, you know what? We've been left high and dry. They should've kept a brothel, just one, an educational one for students like us. What do you reckon?' I looked at him, not very convinced, and he continued his explanation: 'So you have to sleep with your girlfriend. *The Communist Manifesto* says that under socialism love is free.' '*The Communist Manifesto* says that? I'm going to read it.' 'Read it, read it, it says other things as well.' I thought about this for a while. The political side, I mean. And I swore to myself I would take more of an interest in the world, really, and wouldn't make any more mistakes. I didn't swear this to Che because Che isn't a saint or anything, but I started to remember him when I made the promise to myself. Of course, this wasn't what I was thinking about when I went to pick Vivian up that day. I was thinking about her and working out how I could arrange my change so it wouldn't keep jingling in my pockets as I walked. I was thinking about our conversations, I went over them in my head, those endless conversations of ours in the classroom, during the breaks. Thanks to them I know, off by heart, the names of her relatives, their birthdays, and she mine, the layout of her house, the moles we've got. We've told each other millions of times how our hostels are arranged, who sleeps in each bunk, who has a shower every day and the faults they have, if they're selfish, if they share their food, if they snore, the party members we think are all right. We've talked and talked: about the headmaster, the teachers, the school, about what we'd do if we suddenly saw Fidel. I've told her almost everything I know about what it's like to be a man, how our bodies develop, that my nipples used to hurt like mad when I was twelve or thirteen and that there's nothing worse than something hitting you in the testicles and she said the same about her breasts. Don't you talk like this with your girlfriend? *We do* and we write to each other inside the back of our exercise books, in mine anyway because she's very protective of hers. She puts covers on them, and on each cover a photograph of Che. We look at him sometimes, Che. 'Where do you suppose he is now?' she asks me. 'Somewhere on the mainland', I tell her. 'Sometimes I think something might happen to him.' 'To Che? No, girl, no. Are you crazy?' And while we talk we look at each other closely, into each other's eyes, I look at her mouth, so red, what a mouth Vivian has. And we hold each other's hands to see if they're cold or warm, to see whose are bigger and it's always mine,

to study the life and death lines. All this was pretend, you understand?
because at that time we still weren't boyfriend and girlfriend. She likes the
Beatles and Silvio Rodríquez, and I just like the Beatles, although I don't
know if it's all right for us to like the Beatles because they're American or
English. What she most likes about Silvio Rodríguez is that, although he's a
revolutionary and all that, he goes around with long hair and dirty clothes.
That's being a hippie, a rebel for fun, I protest, but she defends him and
defends him. 'Really!' I explode sometimes, 'that's just your style.' 'No, it
isn't; but it makes me angry you don't understand that what he's trying to
say is that we are what we are and that they shouldn't plan things out so
much for us.' Do you remember that awful day? I had told her we had to
talk about something very important, we had to meet at break time. I was
going to win her heart. I couldn't go on without winning her love and I
wanted to find a very original way. Arnaldo told me he'd won the heart of
a girl by playing hangman in an exercise book. He wrote, for her, *I fancy
you*, the *F* and the dashes, and she guessed it. But Vivian as soon as she saw
what it said didn't want to carry on. In a novel I read that a girl said to a
boy, showing him her palms, 'Read my destiny.' And he replied, 'Your
destiny isn't in your hands but in mine.' That was so nice, comrade, why
didn't I come up with that? But when we got to school, that morning,
everyone was lined up in the main school yard, even the second-year
students, who have lessons in the afternoon, and people were quieter than
they'd ever been in that yard, this particular morning. I sought her out and
looked at her from a distance, trying to tell her that at break time we'd talk
about that very important thing, did she remember? But she, what she
asked me with her eyes was, '*What's going on? Do you know what's going
on?*', and then I realized that something was up. The teachers were standing
under the almond trees and they knew. Some of the women teachers were
crying. The headmaster went up to the dais and looked at us all, all of us
focused on him. If you could have seen that look in the headmaster's eyes.
There was no doubt that something serious had happened, but what was
it, were they going to throw someone out? The headmaster nervously
tapped the microphone a few times, although it was working perfectly well
and he didn't need to tap it at all, but he just couldn't speak. The words
wouldn't come out and he just looked at us, until at last he blurted out,
'Che's been killed in Bolivia. We're going to the Main Square to a formal
ceremony, everyone on their best behaviour, go off to your classrooms.'
That was it. I felt Vivian throwing herself on to my shoulder and I heard
her sobbing. 'I knew it might happen one day,' she said, and we went off
towards the classroom, feeling ill, seeing Che's face everywhere, his smile,

when he says *imperialism cannot be trusted even a tiny bit*, as if we were walking under a sky of images of Che and on each leaf of the almond trees there were images of him. María joined us. 'Oh, Vivian, oh Pedrito!' she said, and we went off with our arms round each other. How sad Vivian's books were. She took the covers off and put them away in silence. Finally she said she didn't believe it, she didn't believe it at all because it just couldn't be so. And I said if only, Vivian, but think about it, you must be mad not to see it's true? Even so, we kept our little hopes up until we were in the Square, all of us in the Square, and the saddest Fidel ever said yes, that Che had been killed in Bolivia, but that we couldn't die because of something like that. We went back to the school, she and I holding hands, not because we were boyfriend and girlfriend, no, but rather to support each other. And that was the reason why my desire vanished. I didn't win her heart that week, I don't think it was the next one either, I don't remember ... And so it was the other day when she had the black dress on, as I was telling you, and we went to the cinema and when we came out of the Payret, the night was so lovely. It had rained and there were lights and colours and lots of people and it was muggy and she was walking along beside me; squeezed up against me, with her hair loose. 'Why are you going so fast? What did you think of the film? Let's talk about,' and she began to give her opinion, the social slant and I don't know what else. I couldn't hear her nor had I really seen the film and my heart was in my mouth because in the cinema, can you imagine, I was remembering how I'd been told that there are couples who can't do it the first time: she gets scared, that membrane of hers is too tough and won't break, the girl loses loads of blood and you have to call an ambulance, or he can't get it up because he's too nervous, his nerves won't let him. If my nerves do that to me I'll kill them. I told her, 'We're not going to the halls.' 'So, where are we going?' 'Somewhere.' Afer she'd agreed to come with me I didn't tell her any more details until we'd arrived. We went into a building, quickly, I spoke to a man, quickly, paid two eighty, quickly, we went up a flight of stairs, quickly, we went through doors, we went through more doors, quickly, the key wouldn't turn, it turned, we went in ... and I stood against the wall, listening to my heart pounding. The light was on and Vivian took two or three steps forward, stopped, switched her handbag over to her other hand, as only she can switch her handbag over to her other hand. The room had a high ceiling and was ugly, horrible, to tell you the truth. There was a little wardrobe, without any doors and wire hangers that were past it. On a table, where the varnish was coming off, was a bowl of water, an aluminium jug, two little glasses from the Soviet Union, toilet paper and scented soap. The yellowish light projected shapes on to the wall, where there were drawings and rude graffiti. Vivian went over to the window, which was open, and I could read right above her head, concealed a little behind her hair, and a long way off, that red sign that says *Revolution is construction* which is on some building in Havana. I read it about five times and I didn't dare speak. Through the window there was also the moon and some cloud cover passing over it. It was beautiful, I couldn't stop gazing at it and suddenly I calmed down a little. I know that really we shouldn't look at the moon and that it's being romantic and soppy, that's the bit I don't tell Arnaldo, but it looked beautiful, I swear, and Vivian turned round, slowly. What an impression she made on me. Better than ever. I close my eyes and I can see her. She was so beautiful, you know, so beautiful. I am so in love with her that I'd be ashamed if I didn't tell you. The little prickling in my heart, the things I do. She asked me in a terrible voice, 'This is a rent-a-room joint, isn't it?' I was going to answer that it wasn't, to tell her it was a poor, second-rate hotel, but I told her the truth. 'Yes.' A tiny little yes. She turned her back on me. After a while I heard her say, 'Oh, my goodness, here I am in a rent-a-room joint. That's what my Mum says: I'm bad, I can't be trusted. There she is thinking I'm ever so happy in the school and really I'm in a place like this with my boyfriend.' I started to walk towards her, I didn't know what to say to her, what to do, can you imagine, she was right, for a lad it's not the same, if I tell my Mum I'm in a rent-a-room joint with a woman she'd be thrilled. I begin to feel ill, to regret having taken her there, to see things from her point of view. Just as well I remembered what Arnaldo says, that you can't feel sorry for women because they don't even like to do that to themselves. She swung round, you know, eyes wide open. 'Didn't you have anywhere else to take me?' No, I didn't, what did I know about those places? It was the first time for me as well. It hurt that she spoke to me like that, that she didn't understand me, and I felt worse. 'If you want,' I said to her, 'if you don't like the place, we'll go and I won't get angry or anything.' And I hugged her, so that she wouldn't be alone, so that she wouldn't feel it was all her fault. Well really it was my fault, wasn't it? I hugged her to tell her yes, she *was* there, but with a man who, well, loved her very much, who was Mister Right, and so the place wasn't important She hugged me, too, and said she loved me and I stood by the open window. A bus went past making a heck of a racket. 'Must be a 27,' I thought. 'Let's not get uptight,' she said, 'it's just it's a shame we have to do it in such a horrible room.' In truth, you know, those places ought to be nicer, and not so you feel you're doing something bad. Then she turned off the light, women like the light off, and she started to undress. It was beautiful the way she took off her clothes, can you imagine, and she sat down on the side of the bed. The light coming in through the window, the moonlight, shone on her. I took off my pullover. I heard the pullover flop on to the floor and I felt happy I'd put my black trousers on, not the other pair, because the black ones zip up, and I love the sound of the zip, I felt so masculine unzipping it in front of a woman and knowing that she too had heard it, and the trousers sliding down my thighs, coming off my legs, falling to the ground, and we were both naked, without looking at each other, a little yellowish because of the light, a little red, without really knowing what to do. We were scared that at that moment the door might open and in might come the headmaster from the school, her mother, the Minister of Education, all outraged, and her Mum might shout, 'Oh, my God, Heavenly Virgin, Great Power of God, look what my daughter is doing. If her father catches her he'll kill her.' I swear. We waited and waited and no one appeared. I walked up to her, we looked at each other, we embraced as if for the first time in the world, and we dropped slowly on to the sheets. We began to undo the awkwardness, to follow our feelings, to be carried away by a breeze that was blowing, the strong sea smell. Instinct guided us and we didn't feel we were embracing tightly enough until we discovered the flowers. There were wet flowers in the whole room: they were in a padded layer over the floor and the bed, they adorned the walls, they hung down from the ceiling, they stuck up from the window sill. We stopped and listened and the little sounds of love reached our ears: a distant sea, snails, two leaves and our bodies were also there, with her skin and mine, our lips and hands and eyes and hair. We were drinking each other, so much that we saw two children running in the dawn, uphill, through a meadow of shining sunflowers. They were scaring the butterflies away. She was carrying a parasol, he a sword and a drum, both of them dressed in white and holding hands. When the rain began they threw themselves on to the sunflowers, but they didn't sink down, they remained afloat and they began to turn round and round, embracing, surrounded by butterflies; they looked into each other's eyes, and she saw that he was rising, he was raising his sword, its tip shone, with a bluish glint, and he sensed that he was killing her and they still embraced, they rolled once more amongst the flowers, their eyes closed, and they began to plunge farther and farther, pursued by all the sunflowers, and as they went down, leaving in their wake a trail of colours, they named out loud everything they could see: allspice, leaves, sand, porch, obelisk, rabbit, palms, calabash, starch, doves … and when the last word drifted away and disappeared, they were lying under a shady tree, as if they had been abandoned there by the tide, and the two of us, Vivian and myself, were dying, elsewhere, or there itself, very far or very near, and in the last moment of life we saw, or sensed, that the children were sitting up, dressed in white, and hand in hand were walking away; they passed over us, she, with the ribbon in her hand, had lost the parasol, he tapping away on the drum; she was saying something to Vivian, in a very loud voice because they were already some way off, and I couldn't understand what it was although I felt happy; he was speaking to me, happily, waving and moving farther and farther away, farther away, happier, until they vanished, they vanished . . .

Little by little we were coming round. The words came back into our heads, the air into our lungs and I moved on top of Vivian, who complained softly and smiled, no longer with the strength to keep her hands in my hair. I sat up a bit, and didn't disturb what I was feeling. I was listening to distant music, never before heard, and I sat up a bit higher, I sniffed the air, and I still felt this strange feeling, and I saw her hair flowing over the pillow, and her smile, and breasts, and eyes, open but shut, which dripped with liquid gleam, and though I remembered Arnaldo, I couldn't help it and I told her: *I love you*, I said, I embraced her body again, and a huge flock of birds launched into flight in my head, like a stampede.

Translated by Jeremy Munday

Alberto Ruy Sánchez

Voices of the Water

for Margarita

Men walk along various paths. Whoever follows and compares them will witness the emergence of strange figures. These figures are part of the secret writing that permeates everything and can be perceived in everything: on unfolding wings, on eggshells, in the motion of clouds, in snow, in crystals and petrifications, on frozen waters, on the inside and outside of rocks, plants, animals, men, in the nocturnal sparkle of the stars, on one glass surface rubbed and stuck to another, resinous surface; in the arc filings form around a magnet and in the surprising coincidences of chance. Visible in all these figures is the key to a hidden writing, its grammar, but this visibility does not mean it can be reduced to fixed forms, and it resists being turned into a lasting key. One might say that a universal solvent – the alchemists' alkahest – had been spilled over men's senses. Their desires and thoughts seem to congeal only for a moment or two. Then their premonitions surge, and a moment later everything before their eyes becomes confused once more, as it was before.

– Novalis

The rain suddenly breaks the dry calm of the afternoon. Its thousand voices pursuing and succeeding one another thoroughly drown out all conversation. They simultaenously stop a dogfight and a couple making love outdoors. The windows cry out, the rooftops cry out, the trees howl as their leaves sway, and on the ground water falls on water like one tempest trampling another.

The afternoon had turned to confused music and through it runs a woman like a beam of light rushing into a pool of water. The joy in her face not only makes her more beautiful, it makes one think that this woman isn't worried about getting wet. She runs, but not to get out of the rain;

something else calls her. She is like a narrow river that enters a wider river and crosses it almost without mingling.

She makes her way through the rain, passes through it. One might also say she looks down at it, for her hurried steps kick the reflection of the rain she sees on the ground. Now and then a few drops slide past her head, and her hunched shoulders carry them down the length of her back where, following the same course, they enter a deeper riverbed. Then she shudders once or twice, a reminder that even deep inside her it is raining.

The packet of papers she is trying to protect with her arm and hands is a bunch of letters poorly wrapped in a yellow envelope, together with other pages written in the same washed-out, nearly illegible hand. She sees his name is abandoning the paper, she can almost see it floating on the water. A small piece remains in her hands: her thumb squeezing a drop of water against the letters and the half-drowned ink seeping from either side. So too the sheets of paper were slipping from the packet, and so from her skin an impatient legion of nanny goats was emerging, hoping to feed on the words imprisoned in those letters.

And now, to clarify what wave it was that moistened her movements, I should explain that before reading the letters, she opened the door with a single turn of the key, looked at the table, and carefully poured paper over wood. In so doing, she rapidly laid down a beach where her impatient glance might finally settle. To one side, four letters written on various kinds of paper. To the other, a more plentiful packet of pages that says on the first page: voices of the water.

*

First letter. The most yellowed sheet of the paper. The most elated penmanship. Undated. At the top, his name, legible only to her.

The December afternoon when we gathered a thin caress of dark earth on the skin of our backs, just a few yards from our braided bodies the lower bank of the cemetery was beginning to be eaten away, as it was every night by the amorous advance of the waves. Five slender crosses revealing submerged graves seemed to scratch at the surface of the water, which, as the day slowly drew to a close, took on the irritated shade of reddened skin. By then the wind was similarly abusing our nakedness. Its chilly whistle hastened us to unravel arms and legs and put an end to the little candescent death to which we offered ourselves.

Before the black line of the horizon could spread itself over the whole of the sea and sky, we gazed at a white sail that was flapping violently in the distance. The shifting crew members were barely distinguishable. The sail seemed to be sinking but would escape from sight only to spring up again from its invisible hiding place, tinted by the advanced twilight. It was an image whose outline shimmered: at first a bright goose feather stuck in the belly of the tide, suddenly it was floating dragon vomit. The white blaze lasted three blinks of an eye. We thought the vessel had gone down following the movement of the night, but as we later learned, it reached – needle on cloth – the shelter of the dock.

As the cold insisted on sealing our pores, we got dressed. Abandoning the cemetery, we found ourselves surrounded by a thousand luminous specks nibbling at the night – crab eyes and fugitive phosphorus from the graves. The fragile black veil with its intermittent lights unwittingly illustrated the inconstancy of our emotions: there was something in us, too, mute and blinking, that seemed to have escaped from those graves, moving towards another life. We shivered as if the wind had lodged in our clothes and wanted to deposit its turbulence in our bones and guide our steps.

Embracing one another, we walked until we could no longer see the silhouettes of the graves. We began to wet words in a café-bar in the port. We simulated a boiling waterfall to drive off the intrusive wind and make our bodies' new riverbed our own. A burning sensation slicked our throats. We slid down the drinks – a two-mouthed skin-flask – as if our swift lubrication were fuelling a fire.

*

Second letter. Various sheets of paper of different sizes. A long stain on the first page. The writing becomes illegible towards the end. The date is written twice, one over the other.

After so many months of silence, I send you at last the long letter you were asking me for. If I began on the previous page by describing to you one of the last moments we spent together, it wasn't to celebrate any eruption of my memory, even as its infectious fluids moisten the sheets you hold in your hand like cheap perfume. I would like to tell you calmly of the chain of accidents and obsessions that, little by little, have cornered me this time. Of course, you might see all this as just a bunch of excuses and justifications for not having written to you sooner. But it is, moreover, an awkward attempt to tell you, almost in your ear and with unavoidable clumsiness, of the songs, bellowings and stampings of a strange force that dances through this kind of confinement. And if I should mention again the last afternoon we spent in the Séte cemetery, by the sea, it is only because that is where the obstinate, haughty sensation that pounds in me to this moment first began to inhabit me.

When I found myself in the knot of our bodies, gently rolling around among dry flowers and gravestones of sand, my eyes were pummelled by rage, objects, memories. I shuddered for the first time when I thought how we were, that afternoon in Séte, like something that dies and turns into something else: a parody. I know this isn't very clear, but I can't say it in just a few words because I myself still don't understand what it might mean to have the sensation of acting out a macabre mockery of all I had lived and desired up to that point.

It was as if each minute in time were not succeeding the previous one, but paralysing it. As if all things were transforming themselves, laughing at what they had been before. It was like believing that the butterfly learns to fly in order to mock the self-absorbed caterpillar, or that the foam of a wave falling on the sand is the laughter caused by the withdrawal of the previous wave. Ice wants to point out water's clumsiness and steam, its bad temper. An erect penis is the stuck-up laughter at its moment of limpness, while a flaccid penis mocks the stiff one with more expressive mimicry.

Here in Mogador, they say the world was created in bursts of laughter, that it was made by nine gods with three heads each. The nine gods were making fun of each other, as usual, when it occurred to one of them to create a strange thing that was a caricature of its victim. The insulted god responded with a new freak that quickened the hilarity of the other gods. Then one would respond by creating a consumptive cat or a bat-frog that was no longer simply the grotesque portrait of one of the gods but a mockery of the previous caricature as well – that is, of the previous creation. Suddenly the nine gods were creating strange, foul plants, dry planets, black holes in the universe, axolotls, viruses, tiny edible dogs. Successive mockeries that have given us the illusion that certain animals derive directly from others or are their lovely evolution, when everyone here knows that man is nothing but a badly made monkey with the ridiculed profile of one of the gods. This scene of the final creation ends, as they tell it, with an explosion of euphoria of which it is known only that laughter interfered with breathing and turned a few faces purple. The three heads of each of the nine gods all began to parody each other, then each of their appendages, and still later, they were laughing down to their most minuscule particles. As the world continued to grow amidst this turbulent confusion, it soon became impossible to distinguish who was imitating whom and where motion began.

Suddenly I could see the farcical kinship between all things, and on occasion, I even find my own skin harbouring altered machinery. Something has inhabited me since that night and it is never the same inhabitant. Things happen in me, deteriorating in order to take on forgettable formations. Against my will, I am exposed to the incessant passage of a watery snake with a thousand successive bodies. It shapes me from within, differently every time, and leaves without the slightest pretext, inserting itself, inserting me into any other body whatsoever, penetrating a pair of eyes or a couple of words, spreading itself over the pavement cracks, racing down lines of sight, compelling me to hold images of myself I had never suspected.

What I wanted to describe to you is this sensation of fluid in a thousand forms, of vast permeability. The passage of time – and of the world through time – as endless parody is merely the visible form of this flow, its crudest face.

If I could maintain the same mood, at least while I write, you would receive not several letters but a single, stable one in which I would calmly describe for you the small, trivial incidents which, from that afternoon in the cemetery through to this morning, have allowed me to recover what I am now sending you together with these letters.

*

Third letter. This is the penultimate series of small pages in the first packet. The paper is of two colours. Each character is round and stable like that of a manuscript copied several times over. The date is recent and indicates the passage of more than a month since the previous letter. To look at each page is to experience a state of tranquillity that allows one to think of certain landscapes and certain movements.

Only two or three unsettling dreams still make me feel as I did when I wrote what you've read up to now. I begin again, but with simpler objectives. I think those sensations are fading now. I say this because I am slightly ashamed at the elation of the previous pages.

We said goodbye that night in Séte and the next day I embarked on the Agadir, the Moroccan boat that would take me to Mogador. I was dwelling on your image as I boarded, and there in the boat it merged with what I least expected. I need not explain how the gestures of the French from the port contrasted with those of the Arab sailors. I recognized something familiar in them, yet at the same time, very distant. I don't need to explain to you how extremely comforting their gaze, their proximity, the casual manner of their labyrinthine intimacy, were to me.

Dinner was the only thing lacking that night to add to the mood I had carried in me from the cemetery on the beach, the pleasure of the tiny explosions that accompany a strange spice. The subtlest of disturbances entered through my mouth and through my mouth it would leave, finally taking the form of silence. It was dawn when we entered the Gulf of Lions. I was with several other passengers in a sailor's cabin, listening to a long tale of transactions and tongue twisters, when I had my first premonition that the phantom of the Gulf – seasickness – had leapt to my tongue. I don't remember my tongue having ever been so surprised. The contractions continued to squeeze my stomach although it no longer held even the idea of a single damp crumb. Even the memory of food had been left afloat on the choppy, open sea. Minute particles lost in the jaws of the waves that seemed to bite us. I tried to reach my place in the boat, assisted somewhat by a sailor who was also on the verge of overflowing.

As I was travelling third-class, we descended six long flights of stairs, far below the boat's waterline. Then he left, just as the smell rising from my passenger compartment hit me. We were close to eighty people in a room full of rows of semi-reclining seats. Obviously there were no windows. A blanket bearing the name of the boat was folded on each seat. It was like a movie theatre with neither screen nor emergency exit.

Nearly all the passengers there were Moroccan workers returning home after having worked a long time in France. I thought I was the only one whose tongue was horrified, but when I reached the compartment I realized that I was one of those least harmed. People were running to the only bathroom and never getting there in time. When people did make it, they found the bathroom as overflowing as they themselves were. You had to lie on the floor because the queasiness in your mouth increased when you stood up. Lying on the floor under and between the seats, it hardly mattered where you put your face. It was so difficult to stay in one place that even the pills and suppositories a doctor gave us refused to stay in our bodies. Some said it was colder than in any blizzard. The cold never relented; nothing gave off warmth, not even for an instant, and since we were right in the prow where the boat took the brunt of the waves, we absorbed the blows of the tormented sea almost directly into our bodies. Nor did the motion ever cease: each blow was the inevitable notification of the next.

Then there was the smell, the greatest cause of the delirium of food-stuffs. Furthermore, I still remember with horror the exceedingly Arab manner in which my companions sang out their troubled self-confidence without inhibition. I can remember in detail the mass of slow and excessive belches that would begin with a dry blast and end with a repeatedly fluid one. No one held back a sound; no one could have.

Several men were crying with their children in the back of the compartment. Two tattooed women were shouting out their prayers, as if wanting to conquer the insistence of the waves with the harshness of their words. Knees and forehead touching the floor, they would lift up their heads and whip them back against the floor. The people watching these women shut their eyes, but even their eyes could not remain in one position for long.

It's hard for me to go on telling you about that night. Imagine that it lasted so many hours that the moment arrived when time no longer mattered. No one could sleep, stay warm or keep from smelling or hearing the clamour of mouths mimicking the sea. We were submerged in that intestinal storm, which seemed to be shaking the sea rather than vice versa. It was an abdominal contraction that stretched frightfully into the world. It was the world stirred up by the turmoil of a few 'intestinal snakes' deposited in the most fragile corner of a boat.

Sleep did not arrive with the night that time: it was more of a generalized faint that came over us. We didn't fall asleep; we practically fell unconscious. The contractions continued. The women praying in Arabic continued hitting the floor and we could feel their blows even in our eyelids, despite our efforts to keep them closed.

Dawn didn't follow either. Day doesn't follow night in a pit. Rather, it was as if something else had begun: something like the arrival of someone you've been expecting for some time. When I opened my eyes, everyone in the compartment was calm. Who could say how many hours had passed? Everyone knew each other's most primal responses and now glances intertwined in recognition. We had all sung and were now gathering up our grains of voice scattered among the others.

In the back of the room, a circle had formed around a man. Eight or nine people were listening to him. He was moving his arms and the dance of his fingers was so eloquent it almost allowed me to guess a few details of descriptions in Arabic. Now and then the people listening to him would hesitantly utter a word and he would shake his head or nod in approval. I asked someone to explain the story to me and bit by bit I was given the rough outline of a brief sea epic. It concerned a strange boat which our narrator, Ibn Hazam, swore he had seen two years earlier on this same passage after a great storm.

This man had his listeners knitting their brows on the periphery of his tale. If I understood correctly, there was a time when the cities of the

Mediterranean expelled everyone who didn't fit the logic laid out by the streets. City dwellers would pay sailors to take these people away and throw them into the sea. On occasion, after weeks at sea, since the logic of the ocean was contrary to that of the streets, it would become difficult to distinguish between the people who had been expelled and the crew. And so, one of those boats came to hold only those whom the Arabs called 'people without corners'. The people living in the ports then began to speak of a boat they referred to as crudely as 'the ship of loons'. Ibn Hazam said he had seen the ship emerge from the horizon issuing a shrill, monotonous music. Everyone pressed him for details. I don't know if I understood what he was saying or what I preferred to understand. But certainly I inserted my own images into his. I liked the remote story of the ship.

But in less than an hour the prayers broke loose again in response to the disquieting litany of building waves. Imagine everyone's horror when they saw that what they thought was over had begun again. This time the jolting was gentler but the passengers' torment and wailing were greater. A woman and her two children tied themselves about the waist with a length of cord so as not to be separated when the boat broke up. A pallid boy came down to the compartment swearing at the top of his voice that he had seen the captain and his assistant very seasick and in tears. The two women began again to whip themselves against the floor in distress and the few men who could still articulate a few words joined them.

Also on board was a guilt-ridden missionary – Christian, of course – who wished to give a sermon relating the life of the holy Portuguese nun who, in the midst of a storm, saved the crew of a ship that was carrying thirty women to the Barbary Coast to pay a large ransom for their husbands. He told how they flung a handkerchief full of relics belonging to the holy woman into the sea and that the floating bundle was immediately surrounded by a halo of tranquil water. The halo grew and grew and by the time the bundle reached the horizon, harmony reigned over all the sea and all the sky. And suddenly the sun came out and land was sighted, as if joyfully welcoming the vessel.

The more the missionary sweetened the ending, hoping to instil optimism in the passengers and crew, the more desperate they got. Everyone was talking at the top of their lungs and it was just as well they couldn't hear him, for they might have thrown him into the water, relics and all, to see if it was true.

I lost consciousness more quickly than before, and only remember hearing people shouting insistently that we were becoming the very ship Ibn Hazam had described. I know I thought a good deal about this before my eyes gave out.

I awoke in the ship's infirmary. The sunlight, filtered and refracted through a bottle of serum knocking against the metal window frame, scratched me. I know you can't trust everything you see, but there in the distance was an orange canvas sail and a tall topmast covered with foliage. A clown with bells tangled in his hair was climbing the mast to untie a roasted chicken that hung from its branches. It was the tree of knowledge of good and evil, Ibn Hazam had said, but I saw in addition four goats perched in the tree, grazing on its leaves. The ship was crammed full of people and it was difficult to see how it remained high in the water. I wanted to go up on deck to get a better look at it with the others but it was out of my sight in an instant. The last thing I remember is the bright colour of a long plank emerging from one end of the ship, which a gluttonous monk and a singing nun supported on their legs as if it were a table. Piles of cherries rolled down the plank, crashing at last into the sea.

The ship's doctor came to calm me down. I found his assurance insulting. He said that it was all my imagination, afire from the weakness of my body, and he left the hospital cabin saying in a loud voice, accompanied by rhetorical, operatic gestures: *Oh, great sea endowed with deliria!* And he slammed the door after nearly shouting at me: *The wind is on the rise ... You must try to live!*

Eight other people on the boat had seen the ship. But the nine of us gave very different and even contradictory testimony of what we believed we had witnessed. I can understand that it must have been difficult to believe us at the time. I thought then that while we were indeed all very weak and perhaps inclined to delirium and while the ship might be a phantom, she certainly sails, if only on an imaginary sea that extends to wherever any of us who saw her might be.

Her voyage, suspect and less personal than I imagined at the time, was part of the journey and began for me the afternoon at the cemetery and which, somehow or other, ends as I send you the packet of impossible chronicles of the ship's passage and the voices issuing from it, which you should find together with these letters

*

Fourth piece of correspondence. A small sheet of paper dated a day after the previous one.

I have experienced this journey of the things and people that touch me inside as confluence, magma, confusion. When I desired you and evoked your image, a thousand phantoms emerged to inhabit this new region of invocations. The nights in the boat extended the boundaries of this region until I lost it over the horizon. Perhaps my need to travel from port to port collecting everything people would tell me about the ship was a way of touching once more that lost territory over which, directly or indirectly, you reign. Beyond that, I can explain nothing. What is certain is that in completing my collection of voices, I felt like someone who traces a circle in the air and, to close the circle, I needed you to read all of this.

Arriving at the port of Mogador – I'll tell you later of my amazement when I entered this walled city, magical and inaccessible as you are – I was surprised that so many people spoke to me of the ship. At the slightest instigation, they would start to tell me what they knew of her, and I noted everything down and later assembled each of the stories that follow. Almost everyone spoke to me of the ship's crew. It struck me as odd that they should know about their lives in such detail. But one woman explained it to me very clearly: 'Here, before seeing the boat you speak of, we hear it. The sea breeze carries a tangle of noises to the coast, by which we know that it is passing close by. Those who hear it for the first time are frightened; the others run to climb the tower of the fortress in order to hear better, or stand at the end of the dock. And when in the distance a speck appears, those with good eyesight say that the people on the boat all have their mouths wide open, that they approach shouting out the stories of their lives, of their sorrows. Everyone talks at the same time. Thus, the stories intermingle. That's why the stories that reach us are already well worn. But given that each person hears the story he or she can catch, and catches the story he or she prefers to hear, one is always more or less content when the boat passes by.'

Translated by Mark Schafer

Antonio López Ortega

from *Naturalezas menores*

In the Palm of Your Hand

Daniela was new to the gang. Her eyes, her lips and the sunken shape of her navel were also something new to us. We saw her chewing gum on the little train in the park, we saw her eating pizza in the cinema as Tarzan hollered, we saw her sunbathing at the swimming pool in a bikini we all tried to undo.

Daniela didn't speak much. She stuck to staring at us now and then and breaking into sharp laughter, a sort of ha, ha, ha. She would turn up strolling aimlessly along getting her feet wet on the grass that had just been watered. She would appear and open her big, green eyes from under the blonde hair which her shoulders could hardly support.

By some quirk of fate which I still celebrate, Daniela was in the same class as my sister. One afternoon I got home dying of thirst to find her sitting with my sister making a big map of Venezuela. The wet papier mâché, I could see, would be the Llanos plains; the cloth which she was scrunching up in her hands, the Andes. Adding other pieces in the course of the afternoon, I helped them finish the map. I sensed a sharp laugh within Daniela, a sort of ha, ha, ha.

At night, crawling on all fours from my bedroom, I whispered to my sister that I was in love with Daniela, that love was a hard scab that grew on your chest and that she had to help me.

After that confession, matters took a rather erratic turn. I know that the following week we went to the cinema, I know that my sister was sitting next to her, I know that I saw her pass by with a pizza, the melted cheese hanging between the paper plate and her teeth, I know that on screen Tarzan was in a fight to the death with a black gladiator, I know that from the back row I managed to pass the note with my declaration on it from hand to hand down to Daniela, I know that she opened it as the defeated black gladiator was tumbling into a boiling cauldron, I know that, unexpectedly, the light went out and the show had to be halted.

Amongst the swirl of faces coming out of the cinema, I searched anxiously for Daniela's. I found her in the distance, with a certain amount of embarrassment, and I could see she was smiling at me. Even now, I still wonder what kind of echo the words in that note must have made in her brain. Even now, I'm still waiting for her reply.

The Lines of Your Hand

The end-of-year photo froze Carmen's appearance for ever: angular features, copper skin, short hair, matchstick legs. Her gaze is a spear which must have unnerved the photographer, a calm ocean that brought together the disparate fragments of a life.

Two sides of her character were prominent: the quest for perfection in everything she tackled (a drawing, her handwriting in notes she took, a balsa-wood model) and ensuring that any conversation with someone close to her should always remain strictly confidential. The first side, as we would discover much later, hid a love for appearances, for form, for responses to beauty; the second, a passion for words, for secret pacts, for friendship.

At a particular moment, shortly before or after the photo, Carmen actually became, in our eyes, beautiful, angelic, unreachable. There were some who had succumbed to her charms and she, wiser than us, bridged a gap between the passion for the wild life and the calm balance of her natural gifts.

Angel's arrival at school marked the start of her loss of composure. Angel combined, in a dazzling presence, the young, barrel-chested hunk with gelled hair and shades, and the not-yet-grown man who hid in the toilets to have a smoke and claimed verses by famous poets like Rubén Darío or Neruda as his own.

Seeing him for the first time in the corridor gave her an electric shock from head to toe. From that very moment on, Carmen changed. At first, she tried to attract him with her trump cards: sweetness, a little smile, her gestures; then she debased herself with artificial female posing which was no more successful in attracting the newcomer's attention.

Defeated in the deepest part of her intimate soul, Carmen saw him parade from arm to arm building a collection of hate and misunderstandings. Something within her, flesh or pain, waited for him in the shade. She trusted that some day, after all the twists and turns, he would arrive thirstily at her shores.

She gradually turned herself into the diligent confidante, almost a traditional matchmaker. We would all tell her our hopes and troubles. Even the girls who, disillusioned, passed through Angel's hands.

Carmen put on weight every evening of her life eating pistachios in front of the TV. The latest news is that she is a resident doctor in a Maracaibo hospital attending fractures and emergencies.

Canoes

My mother used to venture out on to the bumpy main road that went all the way to the port of Bachaquero. The car would jolt along, falling religiously into the potholes full of rain and exposing the windscreen to jets of brown water which shot up out of the puddles.

Arriving at the port meant witnessing the world of what she called 'the canoes': heavy launches which docked in swarming dozens carrying in their open bellies a veritable cornucopia of everything the other lands produced: bunches of green plantains, fresh bulging fish, bowls of white cheese, pawpaw from Casigua, Andean coffee beans, whole cattle from Santa Barbara, purple-coloured jars of coco plums.

Despite the anxiety about the winding road (which day by day became more eaten away by the weeds) the journey really was worth the risk: a veritable inventory, a veritable hymn to the agriculture of the torrid region, which scintillated before our eyes like a reflection.

Finally, as slowly as the sun orbits the heavens, a troop of fat, narrow-eyed men would be brooding between the jetty and the lighters under the dictate of an unknown law: a law that said that nothing was more important than the lengthy evolution of life, nothing was more important than to let their eyes wander over all that seemed out of the ordinary to them. That is why the brute with the swollen belly, the tatty T-shirt, the protruding navel and emerald green eyes, stares at the boy who, steaming up the glass with his fear-choked breath, is still staring out of the rear window of the stationary car.

Translated by Jeremy Munday

Juan Villoro

Coyote

Hilda's friend had been on a bullet train but he spoke wonders of its slowness: they would cross the desert little by little, as the hours passed the horizon seemed to shine not through the windows but from their faces, the reddened reflections of the land where the peyote cactus grew. Pedro was thinking he was a complete idiot; unfortunately, he only became truly convinced of this after he had followed his own advice.

They changed trains on a hillside where the rails disappeared off into infinity. They entered a wooden coach with too many live birds. There was an overbearing smell of animal muck until it was replaced by another smell when someone urinated at the back. The hard seats were full of women whose youth had been assaulted by dust, with expressionless eyes that were now devoid of hope. It looked like they'd rounded up a whole generation from the desert and taken them off to some kind of extermination. A soldier was dozing on his carbine. Julieta tried to rescue something from the scene of disaster and began to talk about magic realism. Pedro wondered at what moment that stupid girl had become a good friend.

To be honest, the trip had started to seem odd from the moment Hilda introduced Alfredo. People who dress completely in black are usually either on the edge of obsession or they're shameless exhibitionists. Alfredo didn't fit into either extreme. Everything about him defied pigeon-holing: he wore a ponytail, he was a lawyer (international affairs: drug-trafficking), he took natural drugs.

He completed the group of six: Clara and Pedro, Julieta and Sergio, Hilda and Alfredo. In the evening they ate in a place where the pancakes seemed to be made of rubber. Sergio was very critical of the flour; he could speak as an expert on such matters. He let us know he wouldn't be having any peyote; after a decade on psychotropics (which included a friend throwing himself off the pyramid of Tepoztlán and four months in a hospital in San Diego) he was cured of temporary paradises:

'I'll go with you but I'm not taking anything.'

There was no one better than him to keep an eye on us. Sergio was one of those people who find a use even for things they've never seen before and who prepare exquisite casseroles with horrible-looking vegetables.

Julieta, Sergio's wife, wrote plays which, according to Pedro, were hugely successful: he'd turned his nose up at every one of her works until he found out they'd been performed over three hundred times.

Alfredo left the table for a moment (to pay the bill, with his silent way of deciding things for everyone else) and Clara leaned over to Hilda and said something in her ear, they had a good laugh.

Pedro looked at Clara, who was thrilled to be going to the valley with her best girlfriend, and he felt the intense and sad emotion of being in the presence of something good of which he wasn't a part: Clara's shining eyes didn't include him, and tasting some of that happiness was just a way of feeling hurt. A memory struck at him with its distant joy: Clara in the exuberance of the first meeting, her mind open to the future and its promises, with her life still intact.

During the weeks which seemed months, Pedro had railed against returning. Wasn't it a contradiction to repeat an initiation rite? Was there any sense in searching for the magic they'd wrecked by two years of living together? Once, in another century, they had made love on the high desert; where had the energy they'd shared gone, the naked fullness of those hours, perhaps the only ones where they had existed free of all responsibility, tied to nothing but themselves? That afternoon, in a city of countless streets, they had fought over a broken umbrella. And it wasn't even raining! What had their complaints, the tiny carriage, the broken locomotives, to do with the naked paradise of the desert? No, there were no second journeys. However, seeing Clara's smile and her little-girl's eyes entranced by the world, he realized he would return; rarely had he wanted her so much, even though at that moment nothing might have been so difficult as being with her: Clara was somewhere else, beyond herself, on the journey which, in its way, had already begun.

The idea of taking a slow train had comfortably won the day: the spiritual wanderers had deliberately decided on the most arduous route. However, after half a day of scorching heat, their choice seemed terrible. That was when Alfredo mentioned the bullet train. The look on Pedro's face reduced him to silence. Hilda bit her nails until they bled.

'Calm down, silly,' Clara told her.

In the following village Alfredo got off to buy some juice: six rubber bags with a horrible whitish water which nevertheless they all drank.

The land, sometimes yellow, almost always red, rolled past the windows. In the evening they saw a jagged ridge, the crags which marked the entrance to the valley. They moved forward so slowly it increased their torture having the destination exposed to view in the distance.

The train stopped beside a metal shack in the middle of nowhere. Two men got on board. They were carrying high-calibre rifles.

After half an hour (something which in the wide expanse of the journey was equivalent to a single instant) the two men managed to step over the bodies sitting in the corridor and sit themselves down next to their group.

Julieta had handed out the juice: the squelchy bag was getting warm between her hands. One of the men pointed to the liquid, but when he spoke it was to Sergio:

'Wouldn't you rather have some *hard stuff*, man?'

The canteen passed from mouth to mouth. A throat-searing *mescal.*

'Are you off to hunt deer?' asked Sergio.

'Anything that moves,' and he pointed to the land where nothing, absolutely nothing, moved.

The sun had worked on the faces of the hunters in a strange way, as if it had burnt them in blotches: with their cheeks burning with circulation that didn't reach the rest of their faces, and with their purple-coloured necks. They had hardly anything to say but they seemed very eager to say it; they fell over themselves to speak to Sergio about small game, they asked if they were going 'camping', shooting a glance at the women.

The mere sight of Hilda's dark glasses was enough to know they were after peyote.

'The wandering tribe of the *huicholes* don't go by train. They walk in from the coast,' an edge of aggression appeared in the hunter's voice.

Pedro wasn't the only one to see Hilda's walkman. Was there anything more ridiculous than those six spiritual tourists? They were bound to come off second best from that encounter on the train; however, as on so many improbable occasions, Julieta saved the day. She lifted her fringe with a puff of air and tried to find out about the *gambusinos.* One of the hunters took off his baseball cap and scratched his head.

'The people who wash the sand in the rivers, looking for gold,' explained Julieta.

'There aren't any rivers here,' said the man.

The dialogue continued in this absurd fashion. Julieta was putting together a scene for her next play.

The hunters were going to a canyon which was called, or they called it, 'Come out if you can.'

'Just over there,' they pointed, their hands upright, their five fingers directed at an indecipherable place.

'Have a look,' they handed them the telescopic sight from one of the rifles: very distant rocks, the air vibrating in the grooved circle.

'Are there still any deer left?'

'Hardly any.'

'Pumas?'

'You're joking!'

What animals made it worth the effort of going all the way to the canyon? A few hares, maybe a quail.

They took their leave when it began to get dark.

'Here you are, just in case.'

Pedro hadn't opened his mouth. He was so taken aback he'd been chosen for the present, he couldn't turn it down. A hunting knife, with an inscription on the blade: *I am my owner's.*

The twilight made up for their tiredness. A deep blue sky which was rounded off by a final red line.

The train halted in a hollow surrounded by the night. Alfredo recognized the stop.

There wasn't so much as a tin roof there. They felt the painful relief of being able to stretch their legs. A kerosene lamp on the locomotive waved them off.

The night was so dark the rails vanished within three yards. But they didn't turn the torches on right away: insect noises, the cry of an owl. The inert landscape, observed during the boiling-hot day, was returning to thronging life. In the distance, some sparks that could have been fireflies. There was no moon, a sky of fine, shining sand. They'd made the right choice after all; they were arriving by the best route.

They turned on the torches. Alfredo guided them to a corner where they found ashes from a fire.

'It's less windy here.'

Only then did Pedro feel the insidious air which was blowing the round shrubs.

'They're called *witches*,' explained Sergio; then he set about gathering stones and branches. He lit a tremendous bonfire which would have taken Pedro hours.

Clara suggested they pick out the constellations, knowing full well they'd only find Orion's belt. Pedro kissed her; his cool, wet tongue still tasted of the scorching *mescal.* They stretched out on the uneven ground and he thought he saw a shooting star.

'Did you see it?'

Clara had fallen asleep on his shoulder. He stroked her neck and, as he touched her soft skin, he realized he had sand on his fingers.

He woke very early, his neck as hard as a rock. The remains of the fire were giving off a pleasant woody smell. Sky light blue, still no sun.

A little after six they were drinking coffee, the only thing they would have all day. Pedro looked at the faces, happy, although they were somewhat the worse for wear from the discomforts of the journey, the harsh, icy night, the wall of nopals where they had to go to urinate and defecate. Hilda looked as if she hadn't slept for years. She had two aspirins in her hand and took them with her coffee.

'The lousy mescal,' she said.

Alfredo rolled up the blanket with his boot and threw it over his shoulder, a movement straight out of one of those cowboy ads.

Pedro thought about the hunters. What were they looking for in that upland? Alfredo seemed to read his thoughts because he spoke about caged animals on their way to foreign zoos:

'They even take roadrunners,' he brushed his hair furiously, tied his ponytail, pointed out an impressive cactus. 'The Japanese pull them out root and all and before you know what's what they're on the other side of the Pacific.'

People were suing over it, he had the papers on his desk. Who on earth was it who was suing, was it the owner of the desert, was it the impossible vigilantes of that waterless forest?

Pedro started to walk. His kiss from Clara dried immediately; a muzzy feeling on his mouth. He breathed in the clean, hot, unbearable air. Each of them had to find his own peyote, the large pale green roses which remain concealed from those who are unworthy. The idea of the pillaged desert was going round and round in his mind.

He went into an area of gum trees and huisaches; in the distance, a hill provided a landmark. 'The desert air is so pure, things appear closer.' Who'd warned him about that? He walked forwards without getting any nearer the hill. He chose a point that was nearer: a tree that appeared to have been split in two by lightning. The cacti prevented you walking in a straight line; he skirted loads of plants before reaching the dead trunk, full of red ants. He took off his palm-leaf hat, as if the tree were still casting shade. His hair was soaking. A short, though still uncertain distance away, rose the hill; its slopes were shimmering in a bluish hue. He took out his canteen, took a mouthful, spat it out

He carried on walking, and after a while he noticed the beneficial effect of the sun: to toast yourself like this, on and on and on, until you end up with no thoughts, no words in your head. A turkey vulture hanging in the sky, prickly pears like clots of blood. The hill was no more than a stretch of land that went from blue to green and to brown.

He felt more hot than tired and climbed without any enormous effort, dripping sweat. On the summit he looked at his soaking feet, his socks reminded him of tennis matches where the commentators would speak of dehydration. He lay down in a clearing where there were no spikes. His body was giving off an intense, pungent, sexual smell. For a moment he remembered a hotel room, a terribly shabby place where he had copulated with a nameless woman. The same smell of damp sheets, of lost foreign bodies, of the bed where a woman received him violently and melted in a fire that erased her face.

In what part of the desert might Clara be sweating? He didn't have the energy to carry on thinking. He sat up. The valley stretched away, blotched with shadows. An arduous immensity of sorry plants. The clouds were floating, dense, pointed, in rigid formation, almost petrified. They didn't cover the sun, they only cast oily spots on the high desert. Far off in the distance, he saw dots moving. They might be people. *Huicholes* chanting their *maracame*, perhaps. He was in the region of the five blue altars protected by the mythical deer. At night they would be celebrating the fire rite where the words are burnt. What was the sense of being there, so far away from the ceremony? Two years before, on a friend's estate, they'd delighted in peyote drinks as new initiates. After the purgatory of nausea ('a drug for Mexicans!' moaned Clara) their bodies oozed a thick, vegetable smell. Then, when they were convincing themselves that it was only pain and vomit, came several phenomenal hours: pure electricity in the brain: asterisks, spirals, pink, yellow, celestial stars. Pedro went off to urinate and gazed at the lonely village in the distance, with its fluorescent walls. The stars were liquid and the trees were throbbing. He broke off a branch with his hands and he felt that he was in possession of a very specific power. Clara was waiting for him inside and for the first time he realized he was protecting her, in a physical way, against the cold and the unending land; life was becoming close and raw, the countryside was giving off a fresh, impassioned smell, the fire was reflecting in the eyes of a girl.

Did it have anything to do with those nights of his life: the burning body between his hands in an almost forgotten port, Clara's eyes in front of the chimney? And at the same time: did it have anything to do with city life which totally wore them down with its charges, its disjointed timetables, its useless bellhops? Clara only knew one remedy for unhappiness: to go back to the valley. Now they were there, surrounded by land, their spirits rather worn down by tiredness, the sun which at times seemed to snatch away their thoughts.

The procession was moving along in the distance, followed by a curtain of dust.

Pedro turned round to look in the other direction: an almost unimaginable distance away he saw some tiny coloured spots that must have been his friends. He decided to push on; the hill would guide him, he'd go back after a few hours to continue the journey with the others. For the moment, however, he could enjoy the pathless vastness, inhabited by cacti and minerals, open to the wind, to the clouds that would never cover it all.

He went down the hill and made his way into a wood of huisaches. Suddenly he lost his bearings. Everything closing in: little birds were jumping from one nopal to another; purple, yellow prickly pear fruit. He pictured in his mind the place where the *huicholes* had been moving, he pictured in his mind a direct route, passing over the shrubs, and tried to correct his zigzagging steps. So engrossing was the task of skirting the magueys that he almost forgot the peyote; at one moment he touched the rubber bag he was carrying round his waist, an uncomfortable, burning sash.

He reached an area where the soil was becoming sandy; the cacti were opening out, forming a clearing overlooked by a large rock. A hexagonal boulder, polished by the wind. Pedro walked up to it: the rock came up to his chest. Strange not to find any ashes, crumbs, vegetable paint, signs that others had previously felt the attraction of the rock. He grazed his forearms as he climbed up. He studied the surface carefully. He knew nothing about minerals but he felt that there was a consummate ideal, an abstract perfection there. In a way, the boulder was imposing some kind of order on the scattered cacti, as if it crystallized a different, plain, inextricable logic. Nothing farther from a refuge than those pointed stones: the rock had no use at all, but in its sheer simplicity it was a fascinating symbol of the uses that it might end up fulfilling: a table, an altar, a cenotaph.

He lay down on the stone hexagon. The sun had risen high in the sky. He felt his mind hardened, almost inert. Even with his hat over his face and his eyes shut, he could see a vivid yellow film. He suddenly became frightened he might catch sunstroke: the huisaches had iridescent circles. He looked in every direction. Only then did he realize the hill had disappeared.

At what point did the land take him to that hollow? Pedro couldn't recognize the side he'd gone up to get to the top of the rock. He searched for the footprints of his trainers. Nothing. Nor did he find, in the distance, a trace of dust that bore witness to the way the wanderers had gone. His heart was pounding. He'd got lost, in the motionless drift of that raft of stone. He felt a frenetic need to descend, to plunge into any one of the flanks of greenery. He searched for a sign, anything that would reveal his route to the rock. A greyish, artificial dot restored his sanity. There was a button down there! It had come off his shirt as he'd climbed. He jumped down and picked up the circle of plastic, smooth to the touch. After hours in the desert, all he had to go on was the discovery of that item from his clothes. At least he knew which way he'd come. He walked, resolutely, towards the uneven, spiky horizon, which marked the way home.

Once again he tried to follow an imaginary straight line but he was forced to make detours. The vegetation got thicker and thicker; there must be an underground spring in the area; the tall cacti towered over him, a chaos that opened and then merged. He took a few steps to the side, bending down under the branches of the bisnaga cactus, without taking his gaze off the small cacti scattered on the ground.

He'd deviated from his route: on the way up he hadn't passed that tangle of hardened leaves. His only thought was to get out, to get to a paradise where there were fewer cacti, when he slipped and fell against a round plant, with a double line of spikes, which precisely and absurdly reminded him of the magnification of a flu virus he'd seen in a museum. The spikes stuck into his hands. Large spikes, which he was easily able to remove. He wiped the blood on his thighs. What the hell was he doing there, with a nameless plant and thinking of a vinyl virus?

He spent a good while looking for an aloe vera plant. When he finally found one, the blood had stopped. Even so, he took out the hunting knife, cut a stalk and felt the goodness of the sap on his wounds.

There came a moment when he realized he hadn't urinated all day. He found it a hard job to get even a few drops; perspiration was drying him up inside. He halted to pick some prickly pears. One of the few things he knew about the desert was that the husk was covered in invisible spikes. He split the pears open with the knife and ate greedily. Only then did he notice he was dying of thirst and hunger.

Now and again he would belch up the sweet smell of the prickly pears. The only pleasant thing in that endless solitude. The cacti encouraged him to walk in a direction that might have followed a single, imperceptible curve. The idea of travelling an infinite circle caused him to yell out, knowing that no one would hear him.

When the sun went down, he saw a hare leap up and quails run, fast animals who had escaped the heat. He saw a patch of scrub a few yards ahead and felt like stretching out on the sandy clumps; only a madman would dare upset the hours that were the true desert night, that were his burning repose.

Then he kicked a pebble, and then another; the soil became drier, a rough scrunching sound under his shoes. He managed to walk a few yards without stepping round any plants; a piece of land which in that primeval world signalled a way out. He knelt down, exhausted, with a sense of happiness that in a humbling and elemental way was connected to the nopals which were thinning out.

When he started walking again the sun was going down in the distance. A green streak appeared before his eyes. An illusion of his scorched mind, for sure. He supposed it would dissolve from one step to the next. The streak remained there. A palisade of nopals, a distinct line, a planted field, a fence. He ran to see what was on the other side: a desert identical to the one which stretched endlessly out behind him. The wall seemed to separate an image from its reflection. He sat down on a rock. He looked again at the other desert, with the resigned amazement of someone admiring a marvel that is of no use to him.

He closed his eyes. The shadow of a bird stroked his body. He cried, for a long time, surprised his body could still release liquid.

When he opened his eyes the sky was acquiring a deep hue. A watery star was shining far away.

Then he heard a shot.

Knowing that someone, nearby, was killing something, gave him unexpected, animal pleasure. He yelled or rather, he tried to yell: a hoarse roar as if his throat were full of dust.

Another shot. Then a defiant silence. He dragged himself towards the place the shooting was coming from: joy at meeting someone was beginning to be tempered by the fear of becoming their target. Perhaps he wasn't following a shot but its echo lost in the desert. Could he trust any of his senses? Even so, he carried on crawling, getting his knees and forearms scratched, scared of walking into an ambush or, even worse, getting there too late, when there would only be a trail of blood left.

Pedro found himself in a place of low shrubs, which was silent.

He sat up slowly: he made out a circle of big black birds that seemed nearby. He started walking again, upright.

He went across an extremely arid area, a sea of limestone and fossils; from time to time, a burr raised an exhausted stump. The circle of birds dissolved in a sky where it was now difficult to distinguish anything except the stars.

His situation was so absurd, any change would improve it; he was as pleased to see the shadows of some huisaches as he had been earlier to escape the maze of plants.

He made his way towards the curtain of shadows and in the darkness overlooked the stalks scattered on the ground. A nopal leaf stuck to him like a second sole. He removed it with the knife, his eyes brimming with tears.

After a while it surprised him how easy it was to walk with an injured foot; weariness was dulling his senses. He reached the spiky branches of the huisaches and didn't have time to recover his breath. On the other side, in a hollow, there were lamps, fires, intense activity. His mind turned to the *huicholes* and their fire rite; by a complex twist of fortune he had caught up with the wanderers. At that point a huge shadow worried the desert. There was a sharp screeching. Pedro discovered the crane, the taut pulleys that raised a monstrous configuration, a plant full of extremities that in the night looked like crazed tentacles. The men down there were tearing up a plant by its roots. He didn't quiver; in the chaos of that day it was a lesser disorder to confuse the *huicholes* with plant thieves. He resigned himself to going down to the spot where they were digging. Then a shot rang out. There was yelling in the camp, the cactus danced in the air, the men stamped out the fires, crazy shadows everywhere.

Pedro threw himself to the ground, on top of a mat of foul-smelling vegetation. Another shot froze him in the rotting mess. The camp was returning fire. From some recess of his mind came the expression 'crossfire', that was where he was, in the line where attackers merge with defenders. He prayed in that bank of shadow, knowing that when the shooting stopped he couldn't risk showing himself to either of the groups.

Then, when he started walking again, in a rather vague direction, he wondered if he really was moving away from the bullets or if he would get caught up in another skirmish.

He stretched out on the ground but didn't shut his eyes, his eyelids being held open by tense exhaustion; what's more he realized, with infinite sadness, that shutting his eyes was by now his only chance of getting home: he didn't want to imagine Clara's soft hands nor the fire where his friends would be talking about him; he couldn't give in to the delirium where return became a precise picture of the imagination.

He had become used to the darkness; however, rather than seeing, he *sensed* a strange presence. A warm body had entered the twilight. He turned round, very slowly, trying to dampen his astonishment, his neck almost dislocated, the blood coursing through his throat.

Nothing could have prepared him for the encounter: a three-legged coyote was looking at Pedro, its fangs squeezing into its snout out of which was coming a continuous growl, almost a purr. The animal was visibly bleeding. Pedro couldn't take his eyes off the emaciated stump, he moved his hand to take out the knife and the coyote jumped on him. Its jaws sank into his fingers; he managed to protect himself with his left hand while the right was struggling with the animal's unbearable kicking until it found a route, slid the knife in forcefully, slit open the three-legged animal. He felt his chest bathed in blood, the fangs weakened their grip. The last contact: a soft lick of the tongue on his neck.

A peculiar energy took hold of his limbs: he had survived, in close combat. He wiped the blade of the knife and tore up his shirt in order to bind his wounds. The animal was lying, huge, in a black pool. He tried to lift it but it was very heavy. He knelt down, pulled out its warm insides and felt an indescribable relief when he plunged his aching hands into that soft, wet substance. If the fight with the coyote had been a matter of seconds, with the body it was hours. Finally he managed to remove the skin. He couldn't be too sure of what would happen but he threw it over his shoulder, proudly, and walked on.

Ecstasy is of the moment; Pedro couldn't describe his feelings, he walked on, still filled with that instant, his body enthused, breathing the sharp wind, a wind made of the finest metals.

He looked up at the starry sky. Somewhere else, Clara would also be gazing at the sky they did not know.

Now and again he crashed into branches that might have had spikes on them. He was at the edge of his physical endurance. Something dug into his thigh, he removed it without stopping. At some point he noticed he was carrying the drawn knife: a senseless glint danced on the blade. He had a hard job putting it back in the sheath; he was losing control of his smallest movements. He collapsed. Before or after falling asleep he caught sight of the starry sky, like a sparkling sand dune.

He awoke with the coyote skin stuck to his back, enveloped in an acrid smell. It was getting light. A salty taste in his mouth. He heard a buzzing very near by; he sat up, surrounded by botflies. The desert was vibrating like a sparse expanse. He had a hard job focusing on the crag in the distance and maybe this deflated his happiness: he'd returned to the hill.

He reached the slope at noon. The sun was beating down straight overhead, his temples were pounding, feverishly; even so, when he got to the summit, he could see a well-defined landscape: the other valley and two columns of smoke. The camp.

He set off into the distance towards where his friends were, at what to him seemed a fast pace and which was no doubt very slow. He arrived as night was falling.

After having been lost in a land where green was the only colour that broke up the brown, he felt indescribable joy on seeing the bright T-shirts. He yelled, or rather he tried to. Dry dizziness caused Julieta to turn round and utter a real howl.

He didn't move until he heard steps approaching that displayed unprecedented urgency: Sergio, the protector, seemingly annoyed and lucid, with a look of fierce reproach, and Clara, her face white, sleepless from waiting.

Sergio stopped a few yards away, perhaps so that Clara should be the first to hug him. Pedro closed his eyes, in anticipation of the hands that would encircle him. When he opened them, Clara was still there, three very distant paces away.

'What have you been doing?' she asked, in a tone of what was now tired amazement, very similar to disgust.

Pedro swallowed some thick saliva.

'What's that crap?' Clara pointed to the skin over his shoulder.

He remembered the fight in the night and tried to broadcast his dark victory: he'd saved himself, here was his trophy! But all he did was make an unclear movement.

'Where did you get to?' Sergio moved a step nearer.

Where? Where? Where? The question bounced around in his head. Where were the others, in what corner of the world were they hallucinating this scene? Pedro fell on his knees.

'Fuck, it's disgusting! Why?' Clara's voice was becoming caustic.

'Give me the canteen,' ordered Sergio.

He got a cold dunking and drank the liquid that ran down his face, an acid aftertaste, a mixture of his blood and the animal's.

'Let's take that shitty thing off him,' suggested an obsessive voice, able to say 'shitty thing' with total calmness.

He felt they were removing a scab. The skin fell down by his knees.

'Bloody hell, it stinks!'

There was a slow silence. Clara knelt down beside him, without touching him; she looked at him from an indefinable distance.

Sergio returned after a little while, with a stick:

'Bury it, buddy,' and he slapped him on the back of the neck, the first contact since the fight with the coyote, a touch of electrifying gentleness. 'Better leave him on his own.'

They went off.

It was getting dark. He felt the animal skin he'd crossed the desert with. He smiled and a sharp pain stabbed at his cheeks, any useless gesture became a means of showing he was alive. He looked up. The sky was filling up again with unknown stars. He began to dig.

He threw the mess into a hole and patted the earth down carefully, making a soft layer with his sore hands. He put his hands behind his neck. Shortly before dropping off to sleep, he heard a groan, but by now he didn't want to open his eyes. He'd got back. He could sleep. Here. Now.

Translated by Jeremy Munday

Rodrigo Fresán

National Sovereignty

> Rataplan, plan, plan;
> Rataplan, plan, plan;
> Rataplan!
> Rataplan!
> Rataplan, rataplan, plan, rataplan
>   – Kurt Vonnegut, Jr
>   *The Sirens of Titan*

Yesterday afternoon I saw my first Gurkha. He was sitting down, kneeling in front of a small fire. How it stayed alight in the rain I don't know. He was smiling into space and cleaning his knife with the weary devotion of a mother changing her child's nappy.

I had got separated from my group almost without realizing it. The idea was to go and look for a quiet place to write a letter that wasn't going anywhere. We're writing a lot these days. We look like statues hunched over sheets of paper, with our backs to the wind, holding our pencils tightly in our fists so that the letters don't fly away. We write our letters in the certain knowledge that no one is going to read them because, as everyone knows, the post has never been what you would call efficient. So what we do is write them and read them out loud to each other. And so we turn into girlfriends and family and friends, and it takes the edge off the feeling of writing in vain. Sergeant Beaten gives us an hour every day to go and get lost and get together in this exercise of dubious worth.

But yesterday I wanted to write on my own. Because I was going to write the most useless letter of all. I was going to write to London, and I didn't want to read it out loud. Better not. There's always some madman, like that guy who never stops mending his uniform, who is going to think that I'm a traitor or something like that just because I'm writing to London. That's where my elder brother is. He works in a restaurant, and I can't help wondering what on earth my brother is doing in a restaurant in London. No great mystery in the mystery. I suppose that the idea, as ever, is to send him a long way away: my brother has what many people see as a *problematical personality.* Anyway, the point is that he is over there now. And I am here. And I was writing to him when I saw my first Gurkha.

We used to talk about them the whole time, but until now no one had actually come across one and, this is going to sound stupid, my first thought was to ask him for his autograph. But then I immediately got scared. The Gurkhas cut people's ears off, or at least that's what they say. Anyway, I stood where I was, with my hands on my head. The Gurkha came skipping over towards me. He did it without wasting a single movement, and I couldn't help being surprised when he opened his mouth and spoke to me in perfect English.

'What's up?' he said, in a Bugs Bunny voice.

I let out a long sigh while I thought that, obviously, this was all a nightmare and I was going to wake up any minute now; because the idea of a Gurkha who does Bugs Bunny impressions was even more impossible and ridiculous than this whole war put together.

But no. I opened and closed and opened my eyes and there was the candid smile of Bugs Gurkha. He asked me if I spoke English and I told him that part of my family was English.

'Really?' he said. He hadn't stopped being funny.

He took out a pack of cigarettes and offered me one. We smoked in silence.

'And how is everything going over there?' he asked after a few minutes.

I replied that I didn't know what he meant by 'over there'.

'Over there . . .' He made a vague gesture that could have included the rest of the world. 'You know.'

'I suppose it's alright,' I said, just so as not to cross him. I was carrying my rifle on my shoulder and the Gurkha, as far as I could tell, only had a knife. But I had only ever squeezed the trigger a couple of times, and the Gurkha was talking and juggling with his knife all the while as if it was an extension of his arm. I dropped my rifle and put my hands on my head again. It was all over. They were going to take me prisoner. I thought about the Rolling Stones fanatic back in the barracks, at the port. Pity he's not here, I thought.

The Gurkha blinked a few times as if he didn't understand and eventually burst unexpectedly into laughter. As if he was laughing in ideograms painted in black ink.

'You don't understand . . . you don't understand,' he said, clutching his stomach. And, when he tried to explain to me, his laughter again, and my sensation of being dreamed by someone else, by some unknown person.

'*I* am your prisoner,' he said at last, and handed me the knife, handle first.

I said no, not at all, the prisoner was me. He carried on shaking his head, moving it from side to side with the firm determination of someone who has more than once had to find the resolve to refuse his soup.

'I AM YOUR PRISONER,' he repeated, pronouncing it in capital letters and hitting his chest with the flat of his hand.

I tried to explain that this wasn't in his interest. If I took him prisoner, one of those horrific things that are always happening to me might happen to him. I told him it was no coincidence that I was wandering around the battle front on my own. Nobody wanted to have anything to do with me. That's why the best thing would be for him to take me prisoner, hand me over to his superiors, and have me locked up in a sealed room on one of the battleships. Or on the *Queen Elizabeth*. They had more than enough room. And I needed a place like that to be able to think in peace.

Finally I told him that, after all, I had surrendered first. The Geneva Convention was on my side.

'No, my friend, just because I'm a Gurkha it doesn't mean I have to be all superstitious. You can keep all that for the devotees of the goddess Khali ... Because I am your prisoner. So let's go. Which way to the barracks?'

I told him alright then; he needn't take me prisoner, but he should get out of there fast because it wasn't a good idea to be around me. I told him that I am always terribly unlucky and that I actually bring bad luck. But it was no use. 'Prisoner I am,' he explained, as if changing the order of the words could convince me.

Then he bent down to pick up the rifle and give it to me and then, of course, the rifle went off.

*

I must admit I thought those little Gurkha guys were smaller. Well, I mean, the Chinese are all small, aren't they? But this one was almost as tall as me. Maybe it's just that they stretch a bit when they're dead. They brought the little Gurkha guy in the day before yesterday. Poor sod. I know he's the enemy and all that, but dying like that, I mean really, you can keep it. With the bullet-hole right between the eyes. And who'd have thought that loser Alejo had such good aim. Or was so brave. The point is the war is over for both of them now. The Gurkha guy is underground and Alejo's in hospital and from there straight back home. And that's what it's all about, some live and others die. It's all rock 'n' roll, but I like it. Apparently the Gurkha guy threw himself on top of Alejo from behind, came crawling up like a snake and stuck the knife in his arm. They started fighting, Alejo broke away, took aim and bang! peint it blac and on to something else, man. Coming so far to die. And they displayed him all round the barracks as if it was the corpse of Brian Jones.

And here we are, in a war. Who'd have thought it? Me, in a war. And as a volunteer too. Some guys look at me as if I was mad. But I've got it all worked out. The thing is I can't tell them why I signed myself up for this. I have to play it all long live the fatherland, high up in the heavens, behind its veil of mist, all of that. Because if Beaten finds out there'll be one hell of a stink. Beaten is Sergeant Beaten. Poor fat bastard, a soldier and with a name like that. Beaten is the one who is more or less in charge of us. I say more or less because the fact of the matter is that nobody here has the faintest sodding idea what's going on. There are some days when it looks like everyone's been smoking and shit! I can't believe how much I miss a good smoke! I can get nou – tananan – I can get nou – tananan – satisfacshon, nou satisfacshon . . .

I miss smoking almost as much as I miss Susana. If it wasn't for the fact that on the last night Susana gave in, I would miss smoking more. But I must admit rosy-cheeks did herself credit. And all that stuff about her being a virgin and that's why she didn't want to. I must admit, since the outbreak of hostilities, as they say here, that seems a bit dubious to me. But it doesn't matter. I've got her under my thumb now.

When she gets my first letter from London she's going to go mad. Because this is the plan: as soon as we go out on patrol and things start hotting up, I'll go off towards one flank, pretend I'm wounded and surrender. Simple as that, man. I'll tell them in English. Meic lov not uar and now you can cart me off. Because the idea is that they'll take me prisoner to London, I wait until all this war thing is over, and that's when I go to a Stones concert and heaven, man. How could I miss this opportunity? How else was I going to get to see Mic and Keit? And I swear that after the encores I'll slip round to the back and I won't give up until I've spoken to Keit. They might even suddenly decide to give me a job and everything. I'm alright with electrics. From watching my old man. Can you imagine? Roadie for the Stones. Really cool man. That's why I went forward march and straight to the little island in distress. Really cool man. You freeze your balls off, but it's not so bad. And Beaten makes you run around a lot less than any of those bores I had on military service last year.

They're taking the Gurkha away now. I'm going to see if I can get a photo with the stiff and send it to Susana.

Misiu beibi.

You can't always get what you want; no you can't always get what you want; no, no you can't always get what you want, but if you try sometime, you might just find you get what you need.

*

By the time they discover those two bastards, I'll be famous already. I'll be a hero already. That's why I'm calm; I'm not really thinking about the thing at all. There's not much time to think either. We're here laying claim to what's legitimately ours by right, and they're not shifting us.

Our flag has never been tied to the enemy's chariot. And we are the sons of our great leaders. We must not let them down.

The problem is that not everyone thinks like I do. The problem is the human material. Most of the officers thought that all this was going to be easy, they didn't think they would send down the fleet.

Wrong.

A true warrior should always think that he's going to lose. Analyse the causes of his hypothetical defeat and then neutralize them one by one, like someone putting out candles with their fingers. Without getting burnt.

But I'm speaking for myself. Unfortunately I can't speak for the others. And the others are almost all of them. There they are playing football in the rain. They're falling over in the mud, bumping into each other, filthy as pigs, their uniforms a disgrace. The uniform isn't important for them. And they even laugh at me. They laugh at how I look after my uniform, at how I sew the buttons back on and mend the holes. For a soldier, his uniform is his skin. They can't understand that. They have no concept of heroism.

And I am going to be a hero. When they find them I will be famous already, and who is going to think about that after all I did for the beloved fatherland, for the mother country. I wonder if they've found them; but not as much as before. Every day that goes by I think less about them and more about me.

And that's as it should be. Because the day of the Great Battle is approaching. Yesterday I dreamed about the day of the Great Battle again. In actual fact to start with I was dreaming about them. I saw them in each others' arms on that filthy mattress, then the gunshots became the gunshots from the Great Battle and I saw myself running through the snow. My arm in the air leading my platoon towards the ultimate victory. That victory from which you return a new person. Because it is in the act of conquest that lies the difference between gods and mortals.

I saw myself as a god. With a uniform worthy of a god.

All my bullets found their target and the death of the enemy was something beautiful for them because it wasn't their death, because their death became part of my life and my glory. I watched them fall and I felt them die, with a father's pride because they were born to be killed by me. They had been born so far away and had reached the ends of the earth so that, in the final act of their existences, I could give their lives true meaning.

I woke up in a state of excitement and masturbated, thinking about whether they would have found them yet. Sons of bitches. They didn't even have time to get dressed. I shut the door of that shitty little flat and went from there to the barracks and from the barracks to the planes. I was sorry to throw away the revolver. It was my grandfather's.

The rain is beating against the sides of the sandbags. The pit is filling up with water. I woke several people up but they didn't pay me any attention. They're still sleeping, wet, like those fish rotting in the mud. I went to tell Sergeant Beaten. He told me to stop breaking his balls, that we'd see to it tomorrow, to go back to sleep.

I'm outside the cave, covering myself with my coat, eyes closed. I wanted to get back into my dream about the Great Battle.

I've been dreaming about the Great Battle for as long as I can remember, for about five years now. I used to dream about a different Great Battle. With different uniforms. Like in the television series and the films. My fellow soldiers had foreign names, and that did bother me a bit, even though they were better soldiers than the ones here. But I think the change is good for me. I'm the best; yesterday a colonel inspected us and put me forward as an example. My uniform is impeccable. It's better than when they gave it to me.

I've got a needle and thread.

I've got the best aim in the whole platoon.

Yesterday I broke all the bottles.

Ten bottles.

Ten bullets.

Mustn't waste ammunition.

Like with those two. I should think they must be stinking out the whole building by now. No, they must have found them. But they won't link me to any of that. They won't even think of me. I was very careful too. Everything shiny clean. No blood.

Just like my uniform for the Great Battle.

I dream about the Great Battle again but it's not the same. This Great Battle has flaws. I am asleep but I know straight away that it's a dream. There are things wrong. That guy who killed the Gurkha is there and the other one too. The one who wouldn't stop talking about the Rolling Stones, the one that Beaten had tied to a stake because they caught him stealing chocolate. He spent the whole night singing, screaming. In English. When we untied him the next morning he didn't recognize anyone, his teeth were chattering and he wouldn't stop calling me Keith. His feet were purple. They say they had to amputate them. Not as far as I know. Anyway, that's how they used to punish thieves. We didn't see him again. That's why this version of the Great Battle annoyed me a bit: the thief was running along beside me and wouldn't stop singing in English. I yelled at him to shut up and then suddenly I was telling Inés and Pedro to shut up, that it was no use saying they were sorry.

I'm sorry, Inés was saying, the little whore, naked.

Go easy ... Pedro was smiling at me. It took him a while to realize that go easy and a little smile weren't going to be enough. Then he tried giving me explanations. He told me that it had been her who had called to tell him that they were sending me off to fight and that she didn't feel too good and why didn't she come round for a coffee. I swear it was her idea, he said.

Inés started swearing at him like she was crazy. And me sitting there, with the revolver in my hand, moving my head up and down, left and right, rubbing it against the wall. I love doing that. I've got short, spiky hair. It's a nice feeling, and them yelling and yelling and blaming each other.

Then Beaten wakes me up with a kick. He's finding it hard to walk. He's having trouble keeping his balance and he's looking at me like you would look at someone important, at history itself.

We're winning, Beaten tells me.

Vengeance is mine, saith the Lord.

Translated by Norman Thomas di Giovanni

Pablo Soler Frost

Clamour

A Castilian king confined his court, with its knights and prelates, scribes, and prisoners – Moors and Christians – behind high walls on a horrible mountain. He was a man of letters and studied both stars and stones. He also knew scars, wounds, and tears, for though he was a king he was still a man. And before his throne, the properties of plants and trees were discussed; and he and others under his aegis sought the spiritual treasures scattered here and there by Providence. Like Alexander the Great, he had architects in his service, and like Milinda he argued as a philosopher and not as a king. In his name, manuscripts were copied and great deeds sung by minstrels. He himself did not disdain taking up the pen, unlike others who would disdain taking up the sword. In his name, gardeners sought traces of the Divine Presence in labyrinths of topiary art, while others used a game of chess, which once a year was played with real elephants, horses, and footmen.

He was a good king, not wise enough for his barons and too wise for his alchemists. He had his good days, but he also had bad ones, some as sharp as a lance, others dull and barren, like the plains of Spain. Much of his anguish came from not being able to divine the plans of the Lord, and the rest came from having to suffer the people of his age, the violent men and cruel women he sought to guide as a good shepherd leads his lambs. His subjects, however, were worse than a pack of wolves from France.

But the principal cause for his incurable melancholy was the fact that he was a mere mortal unable to attain all the knowledge that lay deep within the nine circles of Hell, the nine heavens, and the nine planets. And although he prayed, he could not put those yearnings away from himself.

Outside, of course, all was the clamour of war and charge of horsemen. Even on his throne, he could hear the screams, the coarse jabber of the lancers, the violent thud of falling horses and men: the blood and sweat in the courtyard. Men hunted each other down and murdered each other as if the only begotten Son of God had never come to this world, as if His Precious Blood had not been spilled for all of us. When he was weary, the king thought his subjects were merely the enemies of God, clinging to the walls of their vanity, hoping to defeat or ignore the embrace of His Love.

This king was also unique in that he befriended Moors and Jews, especially those who could recount interesting journeys, speak to him of Theophrastus, or procure some ancient text for him. One night, the king was entertaining two such travellers, when he suddenly said:

'If I had been present in the days of the Creation, I would have given God advice on certain things.' The visitors, men from beyond the Guadalupe River, were horrified at the blasphemy expressed by this Christian monarch. The king's confessor, who usually encouraged his disquisitions, was also shocked at what his lord had said and told him his soul was in great danger.

Then the king began to see everything in sombre hues: the flowers were imperfect, the court pages ugly, letters on the page crooked. At the same time, fear attacked him and vehemently grew in his soul. Demons began speaking to him, praising him for his knowledge and mocking him for his ignorance. He had thought an evil thought, a thought full of pride and ingratitude towards the Creator.

There were nights when he could sleep a little, but on waking up, he thought the same thing again, even before feeling his mouth was dry, even before praying. 'A wise king would be able to give Him good advice.' Sometimes, even during a banquet, he would wander through mental corridors, meditating about what he might have said to God, if he could struggle with Him, as Jacob had struggled. He wished God would strike him down, as He had Saul, and grant him a vision. So many bad things had been unleashed on a world that seemed abandoned by the angels. And from those evils sprang others, complicated and bloody.

His books, his codices, his observatory interested him no longer. Only questions, such as: Why are there so many Moors, so many villains? Were they in fact really necessary? And the way men were formed and the composition of things: Were they not, perhaps, too ephemeral, too imperfect, all given to their vices and failings? Many things left much to be desired: the sea was salt water instead of fresh; it didn't rain milk but water, and there were years when it didn't rain at all. And in the meanwhile, time consumed everything. Sometimes it bounded ahead, sometimes it moved like a land snail leaving its moist and decayed trail over the leaves. Now, old envies and rivalries infested his kingdom with wars. He saw much of what was his being destroyed without being able to stop it now that he was overwhelmed by his thoughts.

But why had it pleased God that there be so many pestiferous animals infesting the land? Perhaps on the fourth and fifth days of Creation there was a need to make so many animals of so many kinds and of so fearsome a nature and grant them claws and instinct and cunning. Perhaps there wasn't enough suffering so it was necessary that maggots proliferate in wounds, that flies swarm around the stumps after arms and legs had been severed, that dogs and horses be plagued with fleas and ticks. And if ants and bees were examples of how the republics and monarchies of men should be, why was it necessary there be ferocious war, why should the heresy of the Arabs exist, why should there be defeats, and dust, and losses?

And he tried to console and distract himself in his idle moments, but everything repelled him. And he came to fear a spell had been put upon him, like the Lady of Marañón, who saw serpents and lizards in her dreams. They had to lock her away. He even thought of locking himself away, but he could not leave his kingdom to his false sons and courtiers. In the chapel, on his knees and sometimes prostrate on the floor, he prayed, but he could not stop thinking and questioning God, who gave no sign of listening to him. Why had God made him so powerful and yet so weak, so filled with love and so lacking of love?

Suddenly, he found Faith. It happened one day when he was next to a beautiful and cold mountain spring. He was sitting on a stone that amused him because it resembled his own throne. He ate some bread and drank some wine: The wine was poisoned. For two hours, he groaned on the ground, fearing the demons were leading him through a dark corridor. But he had been acclimatized by his doctors to potions and venoms, had spent years ingesting them. So the poison, instead of killing him, cured him.

As soon as he was able, he knelt in prayer. He made his confession and bathed. The clamour that had shaken him had now passed, and he entered the throne room relieved. All quarrels were now resolved, and the din in his soul quieted. That night, under the dark stars, he felt in truth that he understood the divine plan even if he could explain it to no one, and he rested, free at last of temptation.

Translated by Alfred Mac Adam

Author Biographies

FERNANDO AMPUERO was born in Lima in 1949. He studied in the Theatre Club and the Catholic University in Lima. His first book, *Paren el mundo que acá me bajo* (1972), appeared later under the name *Deliremos juntos* (1975). His novel *Caramelo verde* was a big success in 1992. Ampuero has published volumes of short stories, chronicles and poetry. *Cuentos escogidos* (1998) is his latest book.

INÉS ARREDONDO was born in Mexico in 1928. She is the author of three collections of stories: *La señal* (1965), *Río subterráneo* (1979) and *Los espejos* (1988). She died in 1989.

JOSÉ BALZA was born in Venezuela in 1939. He is the author of many works including *Marzo anterior* (1965), *Percusión* (1982) and *Media noche en video 1/5* (1988). His stories are in *La mujer de espaldas* (1990).

JORGE LUIS BORGES was born in Buenos Aires in 1899. His first 'ficciones' are from the 1940s. *Ficciones* and *El Aleph* are his best-known books. His poetry was collected in *Obra poética* (1923–1964). Borges died in Geneva in 1986.

JULIO CORTÁZAR was born in Brussels in 1914 to Argentine parents who moved back to their native country when he was four years old. The author of many collections of short stories, among others, *Bestiario*, *Final del juego*, *Las armas secretas* and *Octaedro*, he also published a playful and innovative novel, *Rayuela*, in 1963. He died in 1984.

JOSÉ DONOSO was born in Santiago, Chile, in 1924. After studying at Princeton University, he became a professor at the Catholic University of Chile and later in the writers' workshop at the University of Iowa. He collected his short stories in *Cuentos* (1971). He has also written a variety of novels including *Coronación* (1958) and *El obsceno pájaro de la noche* (1970). He died in 1996.

ALFREDO BRYCE ECHENIQUE was born in Peru in 1939. He has published three collections of stories: *Huerto cerrado* (1968), *La felicidad ja ja* (1972) and *Magdalena peruana y otros cuentos* (1986). Among his novels are *Un mundo para Julius* (1970), *La vida exagerada de Martín Romaña* (1981) and *La amigdalitis de Tarzán* (1999).

RODRIGO FRESÁN was born in Argentina in 1963. His first work of fiction, *Historia argentina* (1991), appeared on bestseller lists for six months. He is also the author of *Vidas de santos* (1993), *Trabajos manuales* (1994), and *Esperanto* (1995).

PABLO SOLER FROST was born in Mexico in 1965. He has published two novels and two short-story collections, one of them being *El sitio de Bagdad y otras aventuras del doctor Green* (1995).

SALVADOR GARMENDIA was born in Venezuela in 1928. He is the author of a number of short-story collections on the antiheroism of urban daily life as well as of novels on the process of writing, *El único lugar posible* among them.

FILISBERTO HERNÁNDEZ was born in Uruguay in 1902. Besides being an accomplished writer, he was also a composer and pianist. He paid for the publication of his first four books of short stories and later found a publisher for three short-story collections. He died in 1964.

RODOLFO HINOSTROZA was born in Peru in 1941. He is a well-known poet and writer, the author of *Consejero del lobo* and *Contra natura*, poems, and *Fata Morgana*, a novel.

MARIO LEVRERO was born in Uruguay in 1949. He is the imaginative author of *La ciudad* (1970), *Caza de conejos* (1982) and *Espacios libres* (1987). He has recently begun writing detective fiction.

CLARICE LISPECTOR was born in the Ukraine in 1925, where her parents had stopped on their way to the New World; the family arrived in Brazil two months later. Lispector's first novel, *Perto do Coração Salvagem*, appeared in 1944. Her first collection of short stories can be found in *Family Ties* (1960). She died in 1977.

LUIS LOAYZA was born in Lima in 1934. A novelist, essayist, and translator, he is the author of the narratives *El avaro y otros textos* (1974) and *Otra tardes* (1985). He wrote the novel *Una piel de serpiente*, which was published in 1964. He resides in Geneva, where he is a translator for the United Nations.

GABRIEL GARCÍA MÁRQUEZ was born in Colombia in 1928. He has lived most of his life in Mexico and Europe. He worked as staff reporter and film critic for the Colombian newspaper *El Espectador*. *One Hundred Years of Solitude* was first translated into English in 1970. He won the Nobel Prize in 1982.

ANGELES MASTRETTA was born in Mexico in 1949. She wrote *Arráncame la vida* (1985), a novel which was a great success in her native country and has been translated into many languages. Her other books are *Mujeres de ojos grandes* and *Mal de amores*.

Juan Carlos Onetti was born in Uruguay in 1909. He was forced to live in exile in Madrid in 1975. He published many works, including *El pozo* (1939) and his most famous novel, *La vida breve* (1950). He died in 1994.

Antonio López Ortega was born in Venezuela in 1957. He was a founding member of the innovative magazine *La gaveta ilustrada* and studied Hispanic Literature in the University of Sorbonne in Paris. He published a volume of narrative prose, *Cartas de relación* (1982), and a collection of eleven 'ministories', *Naturalezas menoves* (1991).

José Emilio Pacheco was born in Mexico in 1939. He is a poet and also writes narratives and literary history. He has published two volumes of work: *El viento distante* (1963) and *El principio del placer* (1972). He has also written two novels, *Morirás lejos* (1967) and *Las batallas en el desierto* (1981).

Senel Paz was born in Cuba in 1950. He won the David prize in 1979 for his short stories in *El niño aquel* (1980). His novel *Fresa y chocolate* (1994) was the basis for the 1995 film *Strawberries and Chocolate*, directed by Tomás Gutiérrez Alea, which was an international success.

Virgilio Piñera was born in Havana in 1912. He studied literature and philosophy at the University of Havana. In 1950 he moved to Argentina and published his first short stories and novels. He returned to Cuba in 1957. There he worked on *Revolución* until 1961 when he was arrested for 'political and moral crimes'. He was soon freed and attracted a following of young writers who admired his independence. His best stories are in *Cuentos fríos*. He died in 1979.

Nélida Piñón was born in Rio de Janeiro in 1937 to a family of Spanish origin. She has won many awards for her writing including the Neustadt Prize in 1988. She has written more than ten books of short stories and novels, among them *A casa da Paizao* (1972), which won the Mario de Andrade Prize as the best work of fiction in 1973.

Sergio Pitol was born in Mexico in 1933. He is one of the most influential figures in new Mexican writing. Pitol is the author of a number of novels and short-story collections as well as translations from English and Polish. Among his best works are *El tañido de una flauta* (1972), *Juegos florales* (1982), *El desfile de amor* (1984), *Domar a la divina garza* (1988) and *La vida conyugal* (1991). The story included here is from his collection *Vals de Mefisto* (1984).

Maria Luisa Puga was born in Mexico in 1944. She is the author of *Las posibilidades del odio* (1978), *Accidentes* (1981), and *Intentos* (1987).

SERGIO RAMÍREZ was born in Nicaragua in 1942. He was vice-president of his country during the Sandinista government. He has published many works, among them *Castigo divino* (1987) and *Cuentos completos* (1997). 'The Center-fielder' is in *Charles Atlas también muere* (1976).

JULIO RAMÓN RIBEYRO was born in Peru in 1929 and lived in Paris most of his life. He is fundamentally an author of short stories, although he has also published novels, dramas, and essays. His stories can be found in a series of three volumes entitled *La palabra del mudo* (1973). He died in 1994, shortly after his return to Peru.

ANTONIO BENÍTEZ ROJO was born in Havana in 1931. He is the former director of the Center for Caribbean Studies at Casa de las Américas in Cuba. He left his native country in 1980 and is currently a professor of Romance languages at Amherst College. He has won numerous awards for his writing, including a 1985–86 Pushcart Prize for his story 'Heaven and Earth'.

JOÃO GUIMARÃES ROSA was born in Brazil in 1908. He received his degree as a medical doctor in 1930 and also became a diplomat in 1934. He published a collection of short stories in *Sagarana* (1934) and many other works including a major novel, *Grande Sertão: Veredas* (1956). He died in 1967.

ALEJANDRO ROSSI was born in Florence in 1932. After studying philosophy in Germany and England, he became a Mexican national. He founded the Latin American philosophy magazine *Crítica*. He is the author of *Manual del distraido* and *La fábula de las regiones*, among other books of short stories and creative essays.

JUAN RULFO was born in Mexico in 1917. He is the author of two influential books, *El llano en llamas* (1953), short stories, and the novel *Pedro Páramo* (1955). He died in 1986.

LUIS RAFAEL SÁNCHEZ was born in Puerto Rico in 1939. He studied in the universities of Puerto Rico, New York and Madrid. A dramatist and novelist who was named Berlin's visiting author in 1985 and won a Guggenheim Fellowship in 1979, he is a professor at the City University of New York. His works include *La importancia de llamarse Daniel Santos* (1988) and *En cuerpo de camisa* (1966). His best-known work is the novel *La guaracha del Macho Camacho* (1977).

ALBERTO RUY SÁNCHEZ was born in Mexico in 1951. He is a fiction writer, essayist and editor. He has published *Los nombres del aire* (1987), *Los demonios de la lengua* (1987) and other books of fiction, as well as essays on Gide and contemporary literature. He is the editor of *Artes de México*.

MOACYR SCLIAR was born in Brazil in 1937. He is the author of a number of short-story collections, among them *O carnaval dos animais* and also a novel, *O exército de um homem só*. He has won many awards including the Prize of the Americas in 1989. Scliar currently practises medicine in Pôrto Alegre.

ANTONIO SKÁRMETA was born in Chile in 1940. He is author of many narratives, including *El entusiasmo* (1967), *Desnudo en el tejado* (1969), *Tiro libre* (1973), and *Ardiente paciencia* (1983). He has lived in Berlin since 1975 and is a professor in the Academy of Film.

LUISA VALENZUELA was born in Argentina in 1938. She lived in New York for many years before returning to Buenos Aires. She is the author of *Hay que sonreir* (1966), *Los heréticos* (1967), *El gato eficaz* (1972), *Aquí pasan cosas raras* (1976), *Como en la guerra* (1977), and *Donde viven las águilas* (1983).

POLICARPO VARÓN was born in Colombia in 1941. He describes violent images of resistance and dehumanization in his two books, *El festín* (1973) and *El falso sueño* (1979).

JUAN VILLORO was born in Mexico City in 1956. He was the editor of 'La Jornada Semanal' in Mexico City. He is the author of *El disparo de Argón* (1991) and the book of short stories *Música para diseñar* (1991).

HERNÁN LARA ZAVALA was born in Mexico in 1946. He has published two books of short stories, *De Zitilchén* (1981) and *El mismo cielo* (1987, Latin American Coimo Award for published work), an essay, *Las novelas en el Quijote* (1988), a novel, *Charras* (1990), and a book of essays, *Contra el ángel* (1990).

Copyright Acknowledgements

Every effort has been made by the publishers to contact the copyright holders of the material published in this book, but any omissions will be restituted at the earliest opportunity.

JORGE LUIS BORGES. 'The Aleph' from *The Aleph and Other Stories*. Copyright © 1949 Maria Kodoma Agency. First published by Jonathan Cape 1969. English translation © 1969 Thomas di Giovanni and the author.

FILISIBERTO HERNÁNDEZ. 'The Balcony' copyright © 1976 Calicanto. English translation copyright © 1993 Luis Harss.*

JOÃO GUIMARÃES ROSA. 'The Third Bank of the River' from *Modern Brazilian Short Stories*. Copyright © 1967 University of California Press. English translation copyright © 1967 William L. Grossman.

VIRGILIO PIÑERA. 'The One Who Came to Save Me' copyright © 1967 Marsilio. English translation copyright © 1998 Mark Schafer.

JUAN CARLOS ONETTI. 'Hell Most Feared' translated by Daniel Balderston, from *Goodbyes and Stories*. Copyright © 1990 University of Texas Press. English translation copyright © 1990 University of Texas Press.

JUAN RULFO. 'Luvina' from *Burning Plain and Other Stories*. Copyright © 1953 University of Texas Press, translation copyright © 1967, renewed 1996 University of Texas Press.

JULIO CORTÁZAR. 'Blow up' copyright © 1964 Sudamericana, Buenos Aires. Translated by Paul Blackburn, English translation copyright © 1967 Random House Inc New York.*

CLARICE LISPECTOR. 'Love' translated by Giovanni Pontiero, taken from *Family Ties*. Copyright © 1960 Clarice Lispector. English translation copyright © 1972 University of Texas Press.

JOSÉ DONOSO. 'Ana María' copyright © 1980 Seix Barral. Translated by Jeremy Munday, English translation copyright © 1998 Macmillan Publishers Ltd.*

GABRIEL GARCÍA MÁRQUEZ. 'The Handsomest Drowned Man in the World'